DIFFERENTIATION OF SELF

Bowen theory views the family as an emotional unit. The family is a natural system that has evolved, like all living systems. The elegance and unity of the concept of differentiation of self, and of Bowen theory in its entirety, is that they describe the basis of individual functioning in relation to others within the emotional systems of family, occupation, community, and larger society.

This volume consists of essays elucidating and applying differentiation of self, the central concept of Bowen family systems theory and therapy. The purpose of the volume is fourfold:

- to describe the historical evolution of differentiation of self;
- to analyze the complex dimension of this concept as the integrating cornerstone of Bowen theory;
- to present applications of the concept for both the therapist/coach and in clinical practice; and
- to examine the problems and possibilities of researching differentiation of self.

The largest part of this volume is the presentation of in-depth case studies of clients or therapists in their efforts to differentiate or define self. This provides an understanding of the *what* and *how* that go into the differentiation of self. Contributed to by professionals who have studied, applied, and taught Bowen theory in their own lives, practices, educational settings, and training settings, this volume is a must-have for any therapist/coach working within a systems perspective.

Peter Titelman, PhD, maintains a private practice in clinical psychology, specializing in Bowen family systems therapy, consultation, and professional education in Northampton, Massachusetts. He is one of the founders of the New England Seminar, in Worcester, Massachusetts, and the founder of the Northampton Seminar on Bowen Theory and its applications.

"This collection, including Dr. Titelman's comprehensive and insightful review, shows the depth and breadth of differentiation of self as an emotional process with deep origins in the history of life, and as a scientific concept and variable. There is likely little in the way of human emotional life and functioning that is not mediated by differentiation of self, and these papers reflect work long in progress in which the impact of differentiation is observed in physiology, psychology, behavior and relationships in the context of emotional systems."

—Laura Havstad, PhD, Executive Director,
Programs in Bowen Theory, Sebastopol, California

"Titelman is to be admired for his long-term study of Bowen's concepts and methods of differentiation. This book, the latest of his texts, is an anthology of the work of Bowen's students and Titelman's colleagues as they attempt to ford the stream of life's stresses and emotional processes."

—Philip J. Guerin Jr., MD; Author, Family Therapy:
Theory and Practice; *Co-author,* Working with Relationship Triangles:
The One-Two-Three of Psychotherapy; *Co-editor,* The Evaluation and
Treatment of Marital Conflict: A Four-Stage Approach

"This volume on Differentiation is the latest of Peter Titelman's multiple volumes on Bowen Theory. Dr. Titelman has chosen many of the well-known writers on the topic. This text offers a comprehensive view of the theory from the clinical and research parameters. Readers will be exposed to an in-depth view of Differentiation and Bowen Theory."

—Paulina McCullough, MSW, ACSW, Executive Director Emeritus,
Western Pennsylvania Family Center

"Titelman's team comprehensively describes various views of Bowen family systems theory. Readers will find the chapters fascinating and instructive. This book is for serious students who want to learn about differentiation."

—Edward W. Beal, MD, The Bowen Center for the Study of Family;
Clinical Professor, Department of Psychiatry, Georgetown University
School of Medicine; Co-author, Adult Children of Divorce

"This collection of papers about differentiation of self is a rich exploration of the utility and complexity of this theoretical construct. Dr. Bowen, in his final professional interview, spoke of the common misunderstandings about this concept as people are prone to treat it clumsily rather than seriously. He entreated some to take over the effort to understand it and to do the best they can with it. The writers of this collection have risen to this entreaty through their own research, personal observations and connection with the sciences. Bowen's original research and writing is honored while at the same time each writer has made the theory his or her own. The diversity of applications speaks to the far reaching relevance of what goes into differentiation of self. Through this volume, the world will have better access to this theory for understanding human functioning within the full spectrum of relationship contexts, from the family to the larger society."

—*Jenny Brown, MSW, PhD candidate UNSW, Director of the Family Systems Institute, Sydney, Australia; Author,* Growing Yourself Up: How to Bring Your Best to All of Life's Relationships

"This is a book well worth reading for anyone who knows Bowen Theory and for all those who want to understand more about the underlying processes that Bowen described."

—*Ann D. Bunting, PhD, Founder, Vermont Center for Family Studies*

"Titelman's books are the appetizer to the main course, which is Dr. Bowen's own writings. I have no doubt that this book on 'differentiation of self' will be the same. Titelman has brought together many of the 'heavy hitters' in this volume, who know well and write well about the theory and practice of this seminal idea. It is a welcome addition to this field of study."

—*James B. Smith, MS, Director, Western Pennsylvania Family Center*

"*Differentiation of Self* assembles a stellar array of essays, by some of the top Bowen theory practitioners, illuminating a key concept of systems thinking. The book will be valuable for therapists, clergy, and other leaders who have found family systems theory to provide a reliable compass for navigating the challenges of family, congregational, and organizational life in these increasingly anxious times. It is essential reading for all who want to deepen their understanding of the concept of differentiation, as a foundation for staying on course in the ongoing effort to be true to self, while honoring others."

—*Rev. Richard Blackburn Executive Director, Lombard Mennonite Peace Center*

BOWEN FAMILY SYSTEMS THEORY
TITLES OF RELATED INTEREST

DIFFERENTIATION OF SELF

Bowen Family Systems Theory Perspectives

Edited by
Peter Titelman

Routledge
Taylor & Francis Group

NEW YORK AND LONDON

First published 2014
by Routledge
711 Third Avenue, New York, NY 10017

and by Routledge
27 Church Road, Hove, East Sussex BN3 2FA

Routledge is an imprint of the Taylor & Francis Group, an informa business

© 2014 Taylor & Francis

Library of Congress Cataloging-in-Publication Data
A catalog record for this book has been requested

ISBN: 978-0-415-52204-5 (hbk)
ISBN: 978-0-415-52205-2 (pbk)
ISBN: 978-0-203-12162-7 (ebk)

Typeset in Bembo
by Apex CoVantage, LLC

Printed and bound in the United States of America by Publishers Graphics, LLC on sustainably sourced paper.

Dedicated to all those who provided formal or informal coaching over the past forty plus years of my efforts to work on differentiating a self in my family, profession, and society: Paulina McCullough, MSW, Thomas F. Fogarty, MD, James B. Smith, MS, Michael E. Kerr, MD, and Katharine Gratwick Baker, PhD.

CONTENTS

CONTENTS

FOREWORD

Since 1987, Peter Titelman has engaged key concepts of Bowen theory, developed by Murray Bowen, MD, by carefully assembling and editing volumes that offer various aspects and applications of the theory from a highly knowledgeable group of authors. In *The Therapist's Own Family: Toward the Differentiation of Self* (1987), *Clinical Applications of Bowen Family Systems Theory* (1998), *Emotional Cutoff: Bowen Family Systems Theory Perspectives* (2003), and *Triangles: Bowen Family Systems Theory Perspectives* (2008), Bowen theory has gained from the depth and breadth of the authors' contributions.

Differentiation of self, the subject of Dr. Titelman's latest compendium, is the cornerstone of Bowen theory through which all the other seven concepts of the theory interface. Titelman explains in his introductory chapter that Bowen conceptualized the family as an emotional unit, a distinctly different view than would have been suggested from Bowen's psychoanalytic training. As his thinking evolved over time, Bowen theorized that competing forces for individuality, a thoughtful self-directed direction toward autonomy, and togetherness, based on the desire to belong and the need for approval of the group, reside in each individual. The balance of these forces varies in families, so that some act as a calmer interactive relationship system, able to collaborate on solving life's challenges, while others are flooded with reactivity and symptoms. Bowen believed that an individual could work toward changing that balance in self and in turn the balance in the family may change. He described the process of differentiation as the effort to remain neutral and in contact with important others at periods of high emotion. He thought that this effort to manage self based on principles, rather than emotion, could change a life course and have a positive effect on the rest of the family.

Titelman has a talent for pulling together contributors who add a multi-faceted approach to the concepts he is illustrating. These authors amplify the dimensions of the concept of differentiation in a variety of theoretical applications, their own lives, their clinical work, and their research. One of the ideas that Bowen espoused was that the therapist or other professionals who worked from the theoretic framework of Bowen theory could best understand differentiation by seeking to apply the concept to their own functioning in their families. Almost kinesthetic in nature, differentiation of self can be described in words, but only really understood in practice. The application of differentiation as a concept for change relates to the efforts an individual makes to be more thoughtful, more mature, and more autonomous in his or her family and life.

In the course of my own study of Bowen theory over time, I have had a few clear glimpses of how the effort toward differentiation has impacted the course of my life and the lives of my children. These include the capacity to define clear positions with my children, even when I do not know the outcome, the ability to hear my partner's criticism without rushing to defend myself, the effort to think about a decision and to see reactivity as a part of my thinking, the move to more personal relationships in my family, and the effort to manage my chronic helpfulness. These sometimes modest, often challenging, efforts in the work toward differentiation have made a difference in my life course and that of my family.

Bowen theory is not published widely and is not well understood. Titelman has engaged many of the leaders of the theory who are represented in this book, and has made an effort to change that. Their writing captures not only the theory, but the substance of working to live in a different way, less encumbered by reactions of others, fear of disapproval, or distancing from important relationships. It is a valuable addition to the knowledge available in the world about the importance of differentiation and the way it can help families and organizations face the dilemmas of life. Dr. Titelman has made a significant contribution to putting Bowen's concept of differentiation into the world.

Anne McKnight, EdD
Director
Bowen Center for the Study of the Family
Washington, DC

PREFACE

Bowen theory views the family as an emotional unit. The family is a natural system that has evolved, like all living systems. The elegance and utility of the concept of differentiation of self, and of Bowen theory in its entirety, is that they describe the basis of individual functioning in relation to others within the emotional systems of family, occupation, community, and the larger society in which he or she is embedded.

Bowen described the process of differentiation of self as being similar to the way cells differentiate in embryology and biology. Differentiation provides a design for understanding the development of each individual in the family but primarily in relation to parents, and secondarily in relation to all other significant relationships within the nuclear and extended families. To a lesser extent differentiation also provides a design for an individual's relation to significant members within his or her nonfamily emotional systems.

According to Bowen theory the family is an instinctual, emotionally propelled system that is reflected in the interaction between two variables: the level of differentiation of self—the degree of integration of self—and the degree of chronic anxiety.

Differentiation of self is the capacity to separate thoughtful, goal-directed response from reactive response. Bowen's continuum of differentiation of self describes individuals according to their ability to differentiate between emotional and intellectual functioning.

Each of the seven additional concepts that make up Bowen theory—emotional triangles, the nuclear family emotional system, the family projection process, sibling position, the multigenerational transmission process, emotional cutoff, and emotional process in society—is expressed differently depending upon an individual's level of differentiation of self, and how that is integrated with his or her level of chronic anxiety.

Differentiation of self also affects the way the emotional forces of togetherness and individuality are expressed and balanced or unbalanced. A full understanding of this concept requires observing how individuals, couples, and the multigenerational family express the variation in the balance between individuality and togetherness through the patterns and intensity that go into managing anxiety and reactivity in the nuclear family emotional process. It is also necessary to observe and assess the degree and intensity of the family projection process, the flexibility/inflexibility in the way individuals function in their sibling positions, the ascending/descending levels of differentiation over multiple generations, and the presence/absence and intensity of emotional cutoffs in the nuclear and extended families. Differentiated/undifferentiated functioning is present in the relationships between individuals in the nuclear family and extended family, in relationships involving emotional process in work systems, and in small and large societal systems.

This volume consists of essays elucidating and applying differentiation of self, the central concept of Bowen family systems theory and therapy. The purpose of this volume is fourfold: 1) to describe historical evolution of the concept of differentiation of self; 2) to describe the complex dimension of the concept of differentiation of self as the integrating cornerstone of Bowen theory; 3) to describe applications of the concept of differentiation of self for both the therapist/coach and in clinical practice; and 4) to examine the problems and possibilities of researching differentiation of self.

Many of Bowen's seminal concepts, such as triangles, emotional cutoff, and the family diagram, have been appropriated into common usage by family therapists of many persuasions. Nevertheless, differentiation of self, the foundation concept of Bowen's theory, has remained the most significant and, at the same time, the most complex and misunderstood of the eight major concepts in the theory. The largest part of this volume is the presentation of in-depth case studies of clients or therapists in their efforts to differentiate or define self. This will provide a better understanding of the *what* and *how* that goes into the differentiation of self effort both on the part of the differentiating-one in a family and on the part of that individual's therapist/coach.

As I have written in the past, meaningfully grasping any of the major concepts in Bowen theory involves understanding the interrelationships among all of them. I refer the reader who is not familiar with Bowen theory to the original writings of Bowen (1978) and the expositions of Bowen theory by Kerr and Bowen (1988) and Papero (1990). Other suggested readings include this editor's edited volumes: *The Therapist's Own Family: Toward the Differentiation of Self* (1987), *Clinical Applications of Bowen Family Systems Theory* (1998), *Emotional Cutoff: Bowen Family Systems Theory Perspectives* (2003), and *Triangles: Bowen Family Systems Theory Perspectives* (2008).

All but three of the contributors included in this volume have had direct professional contact with Murray Bowen. The majority of the contributors have studied, applied, and taught Bowen theory in their own lives and in practices and educational and training settings for a quarter of a century or more. Each contributor has his or her own way of digesting and communicating the concept of differentiation of self as a teacher or therapist/coach, and in this case as contributors to this volume. Each has worked at defining self in his or her own family, in clinical work, and in teaching Bowen theory.

The book is divided into four parts:

Part I. Theoretical Perspectives on the Concept of Differentiation of Self provides a theoretical context for understanding the concept of differentiation of self and its application. It also links the presence of differentiation in other natural systems to the human family.

In Chapter 1, Peter Titelman presents a historical and conceptual overview of the concept of differentiation of self, and its application. It consists of three foci: the historical evolution of the concept of differentiation of self; the concept of differentiation of self in the context of Bowen theory; and the application of differentiation of self.

In Chapter 2, Daniel V. Papero discusses three salient areas related to Bowen's theoretical formulation of the ability of the individual to separate the emotional and intellectual systems. The first area addresses what Bowen actually proposes about the emotional and intellectual systems and the challenge of differentiation of self for the individual. The second reviews relevant findings from research in neuroscience that provide empirical support for Bowen's viewpoint. The third presents findings that point to grey or still to be resolved issues regarding the integration of emotion and cognition.

In Chapter 3, Robert J. Noone discusses how individual differences in differentiation of self emerge and are transmitted from multigenerational emotional process. He also discusses recent developments in neuroscience, including epigenetics, that shed light on how family interactions can have such profound effect on cognitive, emotional, and physiological functioning. He includes a discussion of epigenetics and the environmental regulation of the genome.

In Chapter 4, Leann S. Howard explores the ancient roots of differentiation. She cites evidence of primitive indicators of differentiation in ancient species such as harvester ants and Indian paper wasps. These observations are presented along with other interesting data that fit well with Bowen's thinking about the human emotional system and differentiation.

In Chapter 5, Stephanie J. Ferrera describes how understanding altruism and empathy in the animal world deepens our understanding of these aspects of human behavior. The chapter begins with an exploration of the biological roots of these behaviors, drawing from the fields of evolutionary biology, primatology, and neuroscience. This is followed by some important principles that characterize a helping relationship, be it clinical or personal.

Part II. Differentiation of Self in the Therapist's Own Family includes four chapters that describe the therapist's own efforts to define or differentiate self.

In Chapter 6, Peter Titelman describes how differentiation of self includes defining self in family, profession, and society. He describes specific efforts regarding important family themes and nodal events in his family of origin and extended family. Second, he describes an effort to define a self in a significant professional relationship. Third, the chapter describes an effort to define a self in the context of two large societal issues.

In Chapter 7, Phillip Klever presents how he applied the concept of differentiation of self in his own family of origin relationships over a 10-year period. There were several foci in his efforts: 1) being more of a self in his primary triangle and developing a one-to-one relationship with each parent; 2) learning to be more defined in two of his key interlocking triangles involving his brother and parents; 3) developing relationships with his siblings and extended family members to learn more of the facts and alternative perspectives on the family; and 4) examining his goals and standards for self, and reducing his patterns of accommodation, pleasing, and passivity.

In Chapter 8, Anthony J. Wilgus describes one person's differentiating efforts over the course of 30 years with particular focus upon two remarriages. This overview includes the individual's attempts to become more of a self both in the family of origin and in the nuclear family. Embedded in this chronicle is the contention that this long-term effort ultimately contributed to a calmer, more thoughtful, and ultimately, more stable remarriage.

In Chapter 9, James C. Maloni describes a period of four decades since he was first introduced to Bowen theory and the concept of differentiation of self. His foci are defining self in his marriage, divorce, and remarriage. His efforts include working on the maternal line of his extended family through contacts with his mother. In addition, he discusses his efforts to define self in his professional life through his research on emotional process in society.

Part III. Differentiation of Self in Clinical Practice contains four chapters in which the focus is on individual clients who work to increase their functioning through their efforts in defining or differentiating themselves. The choice of examples of individuals working on differentiation of self over long periods of time was made in order that the reader can better understand what a substantial task is involved in this process. In most clinical practices based on Bowen theory there will be variation in the length of treatment reflecting client motivation.

In Chapter 10, Katharine Gratwick Baker describes a long-term coaching relationship between a client and a coach as each of them works toward a higher level of differentiation of self. The reciprocity between coach and client requires that they both work on self in the context of an examination of the client's emotional functioning over time. The effectiveness of long-term coaching is discussed.

In Chapter 11, Priscilla J. Friesen provides a case study that illustrates how family consultation and neurofeedback are combined for the purpose of differentiating a self. It provides an example of addressing chronic anxiety from the top down, as has been the traditional Bowen theory consultation model of differentiation of self; and from the bottom up, using neurofeedback to provide information at the level of the central nervous system about the nature of chronic anxiety. A combination of Bowen theory and neurofeedback provides a synergy potentiating the process of differentiation of self.

In Chapter 12, Ann V. Nicholson focuses on one individual's effort to define a self in her nuclear and extended family. Monthly or bimonthly clinical sessions were the norm for the earlier years with less frequent contact over subsequent years. The chapter focuses on the individual's effort, the therapy or coaching process, and the therapist's functioning, including her own effort to be a more responsible self in relation to her clients. This chapter is a detailed review of the process of defining a self over a long period of time.

In Chapter 13, Patricia Hanes Meyer focuses on a family in which there was multigenerational dysfunction. She describes the work of differentiation of self on the part of a client whose adopted son began showing significant emotional difficulties in late childhood. The chapter concludes with a summary of the impact on a family with chronic symptoms when a family member can act as a solid self, a thoughtful, defined, calm presence in the midst of intense reactivity.

Part IV. Researching Differentiation of Self presents three chapters. The first chapter focuses on the issues and difficulties of doing research on the concept of differentiation of self. The second chapter is research that employs a single case study utilizing the methodology of biofeedback and neurofeedback instruments. The third chapter provides an example of research using a scale of differentiation.

In Chapter 14, Randall T. Frost describes some of the challenges of conducting research on Bowen's concept of differentiation by better defining the nature of the problems to be solved in order for research design to reflect the operation of families as living systems. To be valid, the approach and method of research must be shaped by Bowen family systems theory, and not based on reductionistic, cause–and–effect social science theory and methodology. He describes the possibilities of assessing variation in the ability of a family to adapt to stress within a Bowen theory framework.

In Chapter 15, Victoria A. Harrison uses F1000 biofeedback and neurofeedback instruments to obtain simultaneous measures of nervous system activity, muscle tension, and brain waves for family members who participate in therapy based in Bowen theory. She also describes a research protocol designed to study physiological indicators of fusion and differentiation of self within the family. This clinical case study reports patterns of physiological reactivity in family members that indicate differences in degrees of emotional fusion and in differentiation of self associated with relationship patterns, levels of anxiety, and symptoms experienced by each individual.

In Chapter 16, Elizabeth A. Skowron and colleagues review existing published research on differentiation of self that employs the Differentiation of Self Inventory (DSI), created by the authors grounded in Bowen family systems theory. The authors summarize what we know, and do not yet know, about the role of differentiation of self in health and relationship functioning, including psychotherapy.

Materials drawn from clinical cases presented in this book have been modified to protect the confidentiality of the individuals discussed and their families.

Though each contributor presents the concept of differentiation of self from his or her own perspective on Bowen theory, it is my belief that the volume as a whole provides a view that is consonant with Bowen's original conception.

References

Bowen, M. (1978). *Family therapy in clinical practice.* New York: Jason Aronson.

Kerr, M. E. & Bowen, M. (1988). *Family evaluation: An approach based on Bowen theory.* New York: W. W. Norton.

Papero, D. (1990). *Bowen family systems theory.* Boston: Allyn and Bacon.

Titelman, P. (Ed.). (1987). *The therapist's own family: Toward the differentiation of self.* New York: Jason Aronson.

Titelman, P. (Ed.). (1998). *Clinical applications of Bowen family systems theory.* Binghamton, NY: The Haworth Press.

Titelman, P. (Ed.). (2003). *Emotional Cutoff: Bowen family systems theory perspectives.* Binghamton, NY: The Haworth Press.

Titelman, P. (Ed.). (2008). *Triangles: Bowen family systems theory perspectives.* New York: The Haworth Press, Taylor & Francis.

ACKNOWLEDGMENTS

I appreciate all the contributors for the thinking and effort that went into each of their chapters. As in each of the five books I have edited on Bowen theory and its applications, I have learned much from them, and over the years many have contributed to more than one of my edited books. They are colleagues and friends.

Stephanie Ferrera, LCSW, Randy Frost, MDiv, and Catherine Rakow, LCSW, generously gave thoughtful comments and editorial suggestions regarding my introductory chapter, "The Concept of Differentiation of Self in Bowen Theory."

I want to acknowledge Elizabeth Utschig for her excellent and creative graphic design work, for reading the manuscript, and for editing the massive details of the entire book.

I appreciate Ed Miller's editorial work on my chapter, "Defining a Self in Family, Profession, and Society."

Thanks go to Charlie White for directing me to Fred Coppersmith, the developmental editor at Routledge, and to Fred for encouraging me to submit my book proposal to Routledge.

Grateful appreciation goes to my editor at Routledge, Marta Moldvai, who has been not only supportive on the long journey of producing this volume, but also for her interest in Bowen theory and my work.

Most of all, I want to thank my wife, Katharine Gratwick Baker, who has been my partner in the creation of this book, and three previous ones, through her editing, ideas, contribution of a chapter, and the emotional and intellectual presence she provided during the long saga of bringing this volume to fruition.

ABOUT THE EDITOR

Peter Titelman, PhD, maintains a private practice in clinical psychology, specializing in Bowen family systems therapy, consultation, and professional education in Northampton, Massachusetts. Dr. Titelman has been leading a consultation group on the professional's own family for 35 years as founder and faculty of the Northampton Seminar on Bowen theory and its Applications. He is also a founding member of the New England Seminar on Bowen Theory in Worcester, Massachusetts. He is the editor of *The Therapist's Own Family: Toward the Differentiation of Self; Clinical Applications of Bowen Family Systems Theory; Emotional Cutoff: Bowen Family Systems Theory Perspectives; and Triangles: Bowen Family Systems Theory Perspectives.* Dr. Titelman was on the faculty of Leadership in Ministry in Newton, Massachusetts. He was a co-founder and clinical director of the Family Living Consultants of the Pioneer Valley in Northampton, Massachusetts. Dr. Titelman has taught and supervised graduate students as an adjunct faculty member at Antioch New England Graduate School, Keene, New Hampshire; Massachusetts School of Professional Psychology, Newton, Massachusetts; St. Joseph's College, West Hartford, Connecticut; and Smith College of Social Work, Northampton, Massachusetts. He has given presentations and training events nationally and internationally, including teaching Bowen family systems theory at the Society of Family Consultants and Psychotherapists in Moscow, Russia, and he presented a seminar at An-Najah University in the West Bank of Palestine. Dr. Titelman has presented papers at the following centers in the Bowen theory network: Bowen Center for the Study of the Family, Washington, DC; Center for Family Consultation, Evanston, Illinois; New England Seminar on Bowen Theory, Worcester, Massachusetts; Princeton Family Center for Education, Princeton, New Jersey; the Vermont Family Center, Burlington, Vermont; and the Western Pennsylvania Family Center, Pittsburgh, Pennsylvania. His current research interests, in addition to the concept and process of differentiation of self, include the concept of emotional process in society, specifically the Israeli–Palestinian conflict from a Bowen theory perspective.

CONTRIBUTORS

Katharine Gratwick Baker, PhD, LICSW
Private Practice
Northampton, MA

Elizabeth A. Cipriano-Essel, PhD
Postdoctoral Researcher
Human Development and Family Studies World Campus Instructor
Penn State University
Penn State, PA

John J. Van Epps, MEd
Doctoral Candidate in Counselor Education,
Counseling Psychology, and Rehabilitation Services
Penn State University
Penn State, PA

Stephanie J. Ferrera, MSW
Faculty, Center for Family Consultation
Evanston, IL
Private Practice
Oak Park, IL

Priscilla J. Friesen, LICSW
Founder, The Learning Space
Faculty, Bowen Center for the Study of the Family
Washington, DC

Randall T. Frost, MDiv
Director of Training and Research, Living systems
Private Practice
North Vancouver, British Columbia
Canada

Victoria A. Harrison, MA
Director, Center for the Study of Natural Systems
Faculty, Bowen Center for the Study of the Family
Private Practice
Houston, TX

Leann S. Howard, MSW, MA
Private Practice
Shawnee Mission and Kansas City, KS

Phillip Klever, LCSW, LMFT
Private Practice
Kansas City, MO

James C. Maloni, PhD
Faculty, Western Pennsylvania Center
Pittsburgh, PA
Retired from Private Practice
Pittsburgh, PA

Patricia Hanes Meyer, LCSW
Private Practice
Herndon, VA

Ann V. Nicholson, RN, MS, CS
Chair, New England Seminar on Bowen Theory
Worcester, MA
Private Practice
Boston, MA

Robert J. Noone, PhD
Co-founder, Center for Family Consultation
Private Practice
Evanston, IL

Daniel V. Papero, PhD, MSSW
Faculty, Bowen Center for the Study of the Family
Private Practice and Organizational Consultant
Washington, DC

CONTRIBUTORS

Elizabeth A. Skowron, PhD
Associate Professor of Counseling Psychology
Director, Graduate Specialization on Preventive Science
University of Oregon
Eugene, OR

Anthony J. Wilgus, ACSW
Associate Professor of Social Work
University of Findlay
Findlay, OH

I

THEORETICAL PERSPECTIVES ON THE CONCEPT OF DIFFERENTIATION OF SELF

1

THE CONCEPT OF DIFFERENTIATION OF SELF IN BOWEN THEORY

Peter Titelman

This introductory chapter is an overview of the concept of differentiation of self, the cornerstone of Bowen theory. It will be placed in the context of Bowen theory as a whole. Bowen theory views the family as an emotional unit that has evolved, like all living systems. The elegance and utility of the concept of differentiation, and of Bowen theory in its entirety, are that they describe the basis of individual functioning in relation to others within the emotional systems of the family, occupation, community, and larger society.

Differentiation of self is the cornerstone concept of Bowen family systems theory. It describes the broad variation in human functioning and relationships. This chapter proposes to answer three questions: how did Murray Bowen develop the concept of differentiation of self? What are the components of the concept? And how is the concept applied in clinical practice and for therapists or coaches? The chapter is divided into the following four parts: 1) the historical evolution of Bowen's concept of differentiation of self, 2) the concept of differentiation of self in the context of Bowen theory, 3) differentiation of self and the other seven concepts, and 4) the application of differentiation of self.

The Historical Evolution of Bowen's Concept of Differentiation of Self

How did Bowen come to formulate the concept of differentiation of self? His ideas about the concept emerged from the interplay between his family experience, his education, the professional and societal contexts in which he lived, and their impact on his theory development, research, and clinical practice.

Bowen's Life Experience from Childhood through Middle Adulthood (1913–1946)

Murray Bowen was the oldest sibling and a natural leader in his family of origin. He was followed by two brothers and two sisters. Bowen's father owned and ran a funeral home in Waverly, Tennessee. At one point his father not only owned the funeral home but also a small department store, and was the mayor of Waverly. Bowen lived there until he went to college. In the town, his family knew everyone. They were highly respected and highly involved in that community.

Bowen grew up on the family farm steeped in contact with the natural world of animals and other forms of nature. This experience undoubtedly played a part in his later interest in natural systems. And his involvement with the family funeral home put him in touch with death as a natural part of the human life cycle.

As a young man Bowen was drawn more to science than the arts. He chose to go to medical school at the University of Tennessee in Memphis. He applied for a residency in surgery after finishing medical school and was accepted. History, however, intervened and he spent five years in the army as a medical doctor both on bases in the United States and overseas in Europe during World War II. He rose from lieutenant to major. His experience in treating traumatic war neuroses led to his changing his focus from surgery to psychiatry. It is likely that he observed variation in the way soldiers recovered from war traumas, and this experience may have played a part in development of the idea of a continuum of human functioning or levels of differentiation of self.

The Menninger Foundation Years: The Beginning of Bowen's Transition From Psychoanalytic Theory Toward a Natural Systems Theory (1946–1954)

After the war Bowen applied to the Menninger Foundation in Topeka, Kansas, for his psychiatric residency and was accepted in 1946. Psychoanalytic theory was the dominant psychiatric theory after World War II, and Bowen studied it at Menninger. He wrote that:

> The basic formula was to learn all there was to know about psychoanalytic theory, as much as was possible to know about the theory that governed professional disciplines, and to use clinical practice for the clues that might connect Freudian theory to the accepted scientific disciplines.
>
> (1978, p. 348)

Bowen was deeply involved in psychoanalytic theory, but he began to question its viability because of its lack of scientific grounding.

Bowen was on the library committee at the Menninger Foundation for many years. Through his library studies he began to develop the seeds of a theory of human behavior that would be grounded on a natural science foundation and on his careful readings in the following disciplines: psychiatry, psychoanalysis, psychology, medicine, sociology, anthropology, ethology, physiology, biology, philosophy, social work, religion, mathematics, physics, botany, chemistry, evolution, systems theory, astronomy, paleontology, and others (1978, p. 359).

He had many questions that were not adequately accounted for in psychoanalytic theory. The following are some examples: maternal deprivation did not necessarily lead to mental illness; schizophrenogenic parents who had one schizophrenic offspring often had other children who appeared normal; and, while some individuals suffered severely from single emotional traumas, this ". . . appeared logical in specific cases, but did not explain the large number of people who suffered trauma without developing symptoms" (1978, p. 353). He wrote:

> There were assumptions that emotional illness was the product of a process of forces of socialization even though the same basic emotional illness was present in all cultures. Most of the assumptions considered emotional illness as specific to humans, then there is evidence that a similar process was also present in lower forms of life. These and many other questions led me to extensive reading in evolution, biology, and the natural sciences as part of a search for clues that could lead to a broader theoretical frame of reference. My hunch was that emotional illness comes from the part of man he shares with the lower forms of life.
>
> (1978, p. 353)

The discrepancies that Bowen perceived in psychoanalytic theory and his openness to science, specifically evolutionary theory and a natural systems theory of living organisms, led him to (eventually) fashion a ". . . natural systems theory, designed to fit with the principles of evolution and the human as an evolutionary being" (Bowen, 1978, p. 360).

It may be that the earliest seeds of the concepts of psychological symbiosis and emotional fusion, differentiation of self, the multigenerational transmission process, the emotional system, the feeling system, and the intellectual system began to percolate in Bowen's head before he had even begun his research on schizophrenia and the family. They may have been rooted in his contact with nature growing up and from readings in the area of the natural sciences.

As early as 1951 Bowen wrote: "I had fooled around with patients and parents in Topeka in 1951" (Boyd, 2007, p. 204). When Bowen presented his ideas about the family system to the Menninger staff, he was criticized and told to seek more psychoanalysis for himself (Sykes-Wylie, 1991, p. 28). He then began to realize that he would have to seek a different work setting in order to develop his newly emerging natural systems assumptions and family systems concepts. The next stop on his odyssey was the National Institute of Mental Health, in Bethesda, Maryland, in 1954.

The National Institute of Mental Health Years: Research on Schizophrenia and the Family, From a Dyadic Model to the Family as an Emotional Unit (1954–1959)

Bowen came to NIMH, in Bethesda, Maryland, where he directed a study of schizophrenia and the family on an inpatient unit. The research started with the hospitalization of one mother-daughter pair in November 1954, and increased to three mother-daughter pairs during the next year. The *initial hypothesis* of the study—with its dyadic focus—was that a symbiotic attachment, both positive and negative, between mother and offspring was the basis of schizophrenia. A mutual overdependency—a psychological symbiosis—between mother and daughter was the essential ingredient in the emergence of the offspring's schizophrenia. This hypothesis was generated from the theoretical and clinical milieu at the Menninger Foundation, and the concept of the "schizophrenogenic mother" that practitioners such as Frieda Fromm-Reichman (1950) were espousing. The mother-offspring symbiosis was seen by Bowen to be a process of undifferentiation in the dyad.

One year into the research project, in December 1955, the first father was added to the mother-daughter pairs. Bowen and his research colleagues began to see the role of the father as the outsider in the father-mother-offspring triadic configuration. This led to Bowen's eventual refinement of the concept of the emotional triangle.[1] He, and his research associates, modified their initial hypothesis: "From seeing schizophrenia as a process between mother and patient to an orientation of seeing schizophrenia as a manifestation of a distraught family" (Rakow, 2004, p. 10). In 1957 Bowen wrote:

> It was more than a state of two people *responding* and *reacting* to each other in a specific way but more a state of two people *living and acting and being for each other*. There was a striking lack of definiteness in the boundary of the problem as well as lack of ego boundaries in the symbiotic pairs. The relationship was more than two people with a problem involving chiefly each other; it appeared to be more a dependent fragment of a larger family problem.
>
> (1978, p. 10)

The shift, from the dyadic focus to the triad to the entire family in 1955, was the beginning of Bowen's conception of the family as an emotional system or unit. This became part of the foundation of Bowen's concept of the undifferentiated family ego mass—later renamed the nuclear family system—the emotional oneness or emotional stuck-togetherness of the nuclear family in which there was a schizophrenic offspring.

The undifferentiated-ego-mass was, according to Bowen, a term that mixed the languages of biology (undifferentiated), psychoanalytic (ego), and physics (mass). Just as he had used the term "triad" for a number of years before switching to the term "emotional triangle" in order to communicate to the outside research world, the psychoanalytic community, Bowen made a similar switch when he used the term "undifferentiated-ego-mass," and then changed it to the "nuclear family emotional system." In 1965 he wrote:

> I have used the term "undifferentiated family ego mass" to refer to the family emotional oneness. The term has certain inaccuracies but it aptly describes the over-all family dynamics, and no other term has been effective in communicating the concept to others. I conceive of a fused cluster of egos of individual family members with a common ego boundary. Some egos are more completely fused into the mass than others. Certain egos are intensely involved in the family mass during emotional stress and are relatively detached at other times.
>
> (1978, pp. 122–123)

In a seminal paper published in 1966, "The Use of Family Theory in Clinical Practice," Bowen wrote: "The term *family undifferentiated ego mass* has been more utilitarian than accurate. Precisely defined, the four words do not belong together, but the term has been most effective of all in communicating the concept so that others might 'hear'" (1978, p. 160). It was not until 1971 that the concept that describes the emotional family oneness was renamed *the nuclear family emotional system* (1978, p. 203).

During the research years at NIMH Bowen wrote that he began to think about terms for his understanding the concept of differentiation of self in biological terms: "The term 'differentiation' was similar to the differentiation of cells in embryology and biology. The terms 'fusion' and 'cutoff' describe the way cells agglutinate and the way they separate to start new colonies of cells" (1978, p. 362). He saw similar patterns occurring in close family relationships.

It is clear that Bowen had an incipient view of the family regarding the emotional system, differentiation of self, the family projection process, and multigenerational transmission process, rooted in the evolutionary biological perspective of the human phenomenon. His earliest reference to the incipient concepts of *differentiation of self* and the *family projection* process occurs in 1957, in his first published paper, "Treatment of Family Groups with a Schizophrenic Member":

> Considerable effort goes into helping the individual define his own 'self' and to differentiate self from others. A common observation is a kind of family projection process in which the family weakness is projected to the patient who resists ineffectively and then accepts it.
>
> (1978, p. 12)

In 1985, Bowen outlined the evolution of his thinking in a letter to a colleague:

> It is factual that I had "been thinking extended family for years before the start of the formal research in July 1954; that I had developed my own method of family therapy during the summer of 1955 (I had never heard about it before); that my already worked out plan for family therapy was operationalized in November 1955 when my first full family was admitted." . . . After the NIMH research began in 1954 I developed the FAMILY DIAGRAM. That was essential. Every principle developed in research was tried on my own nuclear and extended family after 1954. . . . I had an active family therapy practice after December 1955. The framework of my basic theoretical concepts was developed in the 1956–57 period of NIMH. Extended family ideas were in everything I did. I moved from NIMH to [Georgetown University Medical Center] in July 1959. Extended family ideas were in everything I did.
>
> (Boyd, 2007, pp. 204–205)

Colleagues at the National Institute of Mental Health Whose Research and Theoretical Ideas Were Congruent With Bowen's

Bowen hired Lewis Hill, a psychiatrist, to be a consultant to the research project in 1955. He wrote:

> The investigation of the three-generation idea began in 1955 with the statement of our consultant, Dr. Lewis Hill, that it requires three generations for schizophrenia to develop. This was an extension of the thinking in his book, *Psychotherapeutic Interventions in Schizophrenia* (1955). Dr. Hill died in February 1958 while this paper was being written, but I believe the three-generation idea as expressed here is a fairly accurate representation of his thinking.
>
> (1978, p. 69)

In a 1958 paper Bowen came to regard schizophrenia as a process that requires three generations to develop:

> To summarize this three-generation idea, the grandparents were relatively mature but their combined immaturities were acquired by one child who was more attached to the mother. When this child married a spouse with an equal degree of immaturity, and when the same process repeated itself in the third generation, it resulted in one child (the patient) with a high degree of immaturity, while the other siblings are much more mature. We have not worked with

families with complicated family histories involving the death of a
parent, divorces, remarriages, or multiple neuroses and psychoses in
the same sibling group.

(1978, p. 51)

This provides an early clue to Bowen's eventual concept of the *multigen-erational transmission process*, and differentiation of self as a multigenerational, natural systems process that he described as taking at least three generations. Years later he spoke of this process taking more than three generations, perhaps as many as six, seven, or more.

In Bowen's first article on the NIMH research, "Treatment of Groups with a Schizophrenic Member," written in collaboration with Dysinger, Brody, and Basmania, and published in 1957, he cites Hill (1955), who spoke of ". . . symbiotic marriages among the fathers and mothers of schizophrenic patients" (Bowen, 1978, p. 4). Bowen related Hill's idea to the range of symbiotic attachments between mother and child, and wrote: "This would include the large group in which the child disrupts the tie to mother only to duplicate it in marriage or other relationships throughout life" (1978, p. 4).

Two important natural systems scientists and colleagues of Bowen with whom he exchanged many ideas and had long-term friendships were Paul MacLean, a neurologist, Chief of the National Institute of Mental Health Laboratory of Brain Evolution and Behavior, and John Calhoun, a researcher at NIMH studying population, environmental design, social consciousness, mental health, and human evolution.

Personal discussions and contact with the research of MacLean and Cal-houn supported Bowen's belief in the evolutionary perspective that guided his natural systems theory of human functioning, with a focus on the family as an emotional unit. Bowen was looking for a way to utilize evolutionary theory, with its instinctual emotional base for human behavior, to replace such subjective psychoanalytic terms and concepts as the *id*, *ego*, and *superego*, and Freud's systems of the *unconscious*, *preconscious*, and *conscious*. Bowen wanted to account for the instinctual base that drives human behavior, but he wanted his theory and terminology to be founded on concepts that were rooted in natural science.

He found that MacLean's (1990) concept of the triune brain, the inte-gration of three brains in one, offered a significant step in understanding the relationship between human emotion and thinking. MacLean described two evolutionary older brains, the R-complex, or the reptilian brain, and the limbic system as the seat of emotion and automatic behavior. The third and newest brain he described as the neo-mammalian brain, or the neocortex, that has neural mechanisms for verbal communication.

Although MacLean's description of the triune brain does not correspond with more recent scientific findings regarding the correspondence between functions, interrelationships, and anatomical structures, and it may never be possible to establish the specific one-to-one correspondence between them, it is clear that MacLean's concepts and neurological formulations show obvious parallels to Bowen's concepts of the emotional, feeling, and intellectual systems.

Papero describes how MacLean's work on the R-complex and limbic system paralleled Bowen's definition of the emotional system:

> It suggests that much of human behavior may be automatic and outside of human awareness, let alone control. More importantly, it fits the development of the human family into evolution and places the human brain alongside all of its evolutionary forebears. Such a view of the family is rooted in biology and points in the same direction as Bowen theory, which assumes the basic commonality of all living things.
>
> (Papero, 1990, p. 9)

Calhoun studied the impact of stress on functioning of rat and mice populations. He found that overpopulation in experimental mice universes led to a breakdown of individual and group functioning that appeared to have similarities with Bowen's observations that overpopulation and environmental conflict could lead to chronic anxiety and societal regression in humans. Calhoun found that when mouse population density increased significantly, the less stable strain of mice became dysfunctional. However, the more stable strain functioned with calmer interactions under the same conditions. Bowen may have seen Calhoun's research as a parallel to his concept of the variation in differentiation of self in the human species.

Department of Psychiatry at Georgetown University Medical Center (1959–1975)

When Bowen's grant ended at NIMH in July 1959, the development of his theory continued as he moved his research base to the department of psychiatry at Georgetown University Medical Center in Washington, DC. He became a half-time faculty member there as a clinical professor and Director of Family Programs. Bowen's six original theoretical concepts became clearer in the years between 1960 and 1966. In the latter year he integrated them into a theory he named *Family Systems Theory and Therapy*. It was first presented in a paper, "The Use of Family Theory in Clinical Practice," published in October 1966 (1978, pp. 147–181). It was based on reflection on the NIMH research and on his outpatient psychotherapy practice with psychotic and less disturbed families that began in 1955. The concept of differentiation of self as a continuum became clearer to Bowen through this work.

In addition to training psychiatric residents in family systems theory and therapy at the Georgetown Medical Center, Bowen founded a postgraduate family therapy training program for mental health professionals in 1969. His psychiatric residents initiated a symposium on family systems theory and therapy in 1965, and it became a national symposium, celebrating its fiftieth anniversary in 2013. (There had been two symposiums per year in the beginning.)

Bowen continued to extend and complete his family systems theory. Bowen added his final concept of *emotional process in society*, in 1972, and the *emotional cutoff* concept in 1975, the last concept added to his theory. At that time the theory was enlarged to consist of eight interlocking major concepts.

In 1974, Bowen changed the name of his family systems theory and therapy—to distinguish it from communications theory and general systems theory—to Bowen family systems theory and therapy, or more succinctly the *Bowen theory*.

Founder and Director of the Georgetown Family Center (1975–1990)

Bowen founded the Georgetown Family Center, a nonprofit organization, in 1975, and directed it until his death in 1990. The center was established to offer postgraduate training for psychiatrists and other mental health practitioners in family systems theory and therapy and family systems research, and also provided a low-fee outpatient clinic. The symposiums on family systems theory and psychotherapy were continued, and additional postgraduate training events for psychiatrists, psychologists, social workers, psychiatric nurses, other mental health professionals, clergy, and nonprofessionals were offered and are still taking place.

In 1976 the eight major concepts that make up Bowen theory were described together for the first time in Bowen's chapter, "Theory in the Practice of Psychotherapy" published in Guerin's (1976) edited book, *Family Therapy: Theory and Practice.* Two years later the selection of Bowen's (1978) most important papers, *Family Therapy in Clinical Practice,* was published as a book. Bowen went on to write "An Odyssey toward Science," a long epilogue to Michael Kerr's *Family Evaluation* (Kerr and Bowen, 1988). In his final testament, Bowen summarized the history and evolution of his effort to move toward creating a bridge between his family systems theory and the current knowledge in the natural sciences.

In 2000 the name of the Georgetown Family Center was changed to the Bowen Center for the Study of the Family, and it continues to provide training and education on Bowen family systems theory and research to mental health providers, a low-fee outpatient clinic, research on Bowen theory, and other projects. Bowen's archives are located in the National Library of Medicine in Bethesda, Maryland (www.murraybowenarchives.org).

Bowen's Efforts to Differentiate a Self in His Family, Profession, and Work Systems (1954–1990)

In his extensive correspondence with colleagues and in his writing, Bowen often described how he broadly applied his concept of differentiation of self in his own life. In a letter to a colleague on January 22, 1985, Bowen summarized his effort to define himself in his family and his professional life. He wrote: "Every principle developed in the [NIMH] research was tried on my own nuclear and extended family after 1954" (Boyd, 2007, p. 2005). In another letter Bowen wrote to a colleague, on April 5, 1977, summarizing his own efforts to differentiate and define a self in all spheres of his life:

I have spent my professional life on defining and practicing 'differentiation of self' which is usually misheard as emotional distancing. For me 'differentiation' involves the ability to remain an emotionally contained entity while in the middle of emotional chaos while relating actively to every person in the field. I have spent decades working towards differentiating my own self from my wife and children and from my [family] of origin, and from the emotional conglomerates in which I work, and from the families I see clinically. It was a great period in my life when I was able to walk through the emotional chaos in my clinical work without getting depressed when the clinical situation became depressed, nor elated when the situation became elated, and when I could operate effectively without the clinical situation getting into my personal functioning. I achieved a fair level of that in the clinical arena before I was able to do it in my own family. The greatest period of my life came with the definition of the triangle concept, which contained the key to differentiation in my [family] of origin, later presented in the "anonymous" paper at EPPI [Eastern Pennsylvania Psychiatric Institute] in March 1967. That contained the 1–2–3 step by step formula for accomplishing the mission whenever I wished to get outside the emotional system. . . . Insofar as I am able to practice operational differentiation with my wife and children, and with my extended families, and with the people I see clinically, then I am a free agent in the field, able to relate everywhere without the emotionality in any field interfering with my functioning. I could even handle it if my own family mixed it up emotionally with the families in my practice. If this happens, I simply "detriangle" the situation. In the earlier years my "patients" were real interested in what went on in my family and my family had kind of an interest in what went on in my clinical work—transference phenomenon. After I got beyond transference, my clinical families do not have fantasies about personal things in my [own family] and my own family is never occupied with what goes on in my practice, other than very broad general things. I have been able to work professionally and most profitably with a wide circle of personal friends and relatives. There is no way this can trip me up emotionally or professionally . . . My wife and I have our own personal life, fairly well differentiated from each other, far better than anything in our early married years. I can relate to her as a person, and she to me as a person, without either of us having to 'triangle' in my clinical relationships or her social-friendship relationships. (These outside relationships are simply not a part of our lives together.)

(Boyd, 2007, pp. 180–181)

Bowen's Effort to Differentiate a Self in His Family (1954–1966)

During the early years of defining himself in his marriage, nuclear family, and family of origin, from 1954 to 1966, Bowen's most extensive efforts were directed at having one-to-one relationships in the primary triangle with his two parents. In this work he tried to apply the new concept of the *emotional triangle* and the effort to achieve *person-to-person relationships.*

Bowen's ending his own psychoanalysis in 1960 may have been related to his increasing focus on defining a self in his own family, over a period of six years. In the same time period he was beginning to consolidate his natural systems based family systems theory and therapy.

After studying a few clinical families going back over many generations, Bowen (1978) decided that this work was too time consuming, so he would study his own family instead. He began gathering genealogical information in 1954 and he continued to do so through the middle 1970s:

My goal was to get factual information in order to understand the emotional forces in each nuclear family, and I went back as many generations as it was possible to go. Until this time I had no special interest in family history or genealogy. In less than ten years, working a few hours a week, I have acquired family tree knowledge of twenty-four families of origin, including detailed knowledge about one that traced back 300 years, another 250 years, and several that were traced backed 150 to 200 years.

(Kerr and Bowen, 1988, pp. 491–492)

Bowen described what he learned from the study of his multigenerational family as follows: ". . . there are no angels or devils in one's family; each member of the family has strengths and weaknesses, each doing the best he or she could in the course of life" (Kerr and Bowen, 1988, p. 492).

During this period (1954–1966) Bowen tried, with modest success and some failure, to be less emotionally fused, less reactive, and more objective

13

in the undifferentiated mass of his family of origin. He worked to detriangle himself in the primary triangle with the following strategies: 1) having open discussions about problems; 2) leaving his wife at home while visiting or taking her and his children with him when visiting the family of origin, but breaking the visits up with a short vacation before returning to spend another short visit with the family of origin; 3) visiting the family of origin alone but combining it with a break, going to a professional meeting, and then returning to visit the family (none of these efforts were really successful as he tried to stay objective and nonreactive to the emotional fusion in his family of origin); and finally, 4) defining a self by writing letters and making telephone calls to his family of origin; often their response was to speak on behalf of the whole family, rather than for themselves.

Bowen sought to communicate directly with as many members of the extended family as possible. The return on this effort was equivalent to a "long-term dividend," as it modified his image within his entire family. Another project was Bowen's effort to *define a person-to-person relationship* with each of his parents and as many people as possible in his extended family. The effort with each parent was more extensive. It began with writing individual letters to each parent. He reports that this method did not accomplish a basic change in the pattern of his mother being the dominant communicator with him and his father being less communicative. Telephone contacts did not change this, as Bowen's mother would take over the conversation from his father. This continued the reciprocal process of some level of emotional overinvolvement of his mother and underinvolvement with his father (1978, ff. 492–502).

Bowen believed that having time with each parent alone is essential for establishing a one-to-one relationship, but that private communication with one parent does not modify the triangle of self and parents. He did report that when each of his parents was hospitalized, at different times, these visits provided opportunities where he made more progress in his person-to-person relationships with each parent. The father spoke of fears of death and other personal topics with Bowen during his hospitalization without the mother being present. When Bowen's mother had elective surgery, Bowen had the opportunity to speak with her individually in the hospital, and with his father alone in the evening at home. At these times Bowen found that past history was a valuable subject for personal communication. As he had been working on multigenerational family history, his ears were open to hearing all that each parent could remember about themselves and family members. A year or two later the next opportunity for developing a one-to-one relationship with his mother involved a trip he took with her to explore a segment of her family: churches, cemeteries where they were buried, houses they had built, and other things of personal interest. It covered the period from

14

1720–1850, when that part of the family moved west (1978, ff. 492–502). He described that trip as ". . . a solid week of intense person-to-person contact with very little talking about others" (1978, p. 502).

Bowen's effort to define himself in relationships with each parent consisted of developing person-to-person relationships and efforts to detriangle himself in the primary triangle. Before 1966 Bowen believed he could differentiate a self from his family of origin by differentiating himself from his parents without having to deal with all ". . . the other triangles in which my parents were embedded" (p. 502). Although he wrote earlier that he had the notion about *interlocking triangles,* this author has not found a written reference prior to 1966 (Bowen, 1978).

After he completed his seminal paper in August 1966, while traveling with his nuclear family to visit his family of origin, he awoke from a dream with a new awareness of how interlocking triangles operate.

Bowen's Breakthrough Experience: The Application of the Concept of Interlocking Emotional Triangles

Bowen's frustration in working on his relationship with his parents—using his understanding of the person-to-person relationship and detriangling in the primary triangle of parents and offspring—led to his further development of his idea of interlocking triangles. The frustration stemmed from the fact that he was unable to have an entire visit with his parents or his entire family of origin without becoming fused into the emotional system. After a visit where key family members were absent, he devised the following plan for his next trip home scheduled for February 1967:

> The months went into a precise plan worked out on paper. Letters were written and rewritten to touch on vital points. Private letters went to one person in each important triangle. The goal was to cause the triangle to come to me, rather than me pursuing absent triangles. Not even my own nuclear family knew the plan. The key triangle knew the time of my arrival. *My arrival on February 11, 1967, was a hallmark in the history of the family.* Every important triangle in the family met in one living room. For some 12 years, I had been making regular trips home, with a little progress on each trip. I expected February 1967 to be a little better. By the time this new meeting was 30 minutes old, *I knew that I was totally successful on the first try.* I was inwardly exhilarated, not because it had been helpful to me, or my family, but simply because *I finally knew one way through the impenetrable thicket which is the family emotional system.*
>
> (Kerr and Bowen, 1988, pp. 379–380)

Given the constraints of this chapter, the reader should seek out Bowen's chapter "On the Differentiation of Self" (1978, pp. 467–528). A version of it was initially presented to a group of distinguished family theorists, researchers, and therapists at the Eastern Pennsylvania Family Institute in Philadelphia in March 1967, just a month after Bowen's "breakthrough experience." It had involved finding a way to get outside of the emotional oneness of the *family emotional unit* while being able to actively relate to it. The chapter was initially published in 1972, anonymously at the publisher's request because of the personal nature of the family material (Bowen, 1972). The chapter provides the theoretical gains in understanding the importance and use of the concept of the interlocking triangle. It describes Bowen's application of a strategy that used new understanding in his effort to define himself in his family. In addition, the reader may find the chapter "Bowen's Effort to Differentiate a Self: Detriangling from Triangles and Interlocking Triangles" (Titelman, 2008, pp. 109–128) useful in providing a context for Bowen's effort.

Bowen wrote about how his experience in dealing with the emotional oneness in the Menninger Foundation emotional system taught him a great deal about emotional fusion in the workplace. He found it to be kind of a "control" experience for the same phenomenon in his family: "Finally after I mastered the experience with my own family that is reported here, I returned to the old work system for a long visit and was able to relate intimately to those important to the system without a single episode of 'fusion'" (1978, p. 486).

Bowen's Efforts to Define a Self in the "Family of Family Therapists"

In addition to his efforts to define himself in relation to his family, Bowen made efforts to define himself in relation to his professional colleagues. This section describes, through two letters to colleagues, two of Bowen's many efforts to define himself in relation to the "family of family therapists." He used quotation marks around the idea of the family of family therapists or the work system because, while these emotional systems have similarities to the family, they are not the equivalent.

A presentation to the "family of family therapists" took place at Eastern Pennsylvania Family Institute in March 1967. It was an opportunity for Bowen to find a way to present his theory that could be "heard" more effectively than in previous presentations. He described his effort in relation to the prominent family therapists who were his colleagues as follows:

> For some years I have been aware of the "undifferentiated family ego mass" that exists among the prominent family therapists. The same emotional system exists in the 'family' of family therapists that

operates in the 'sick' families they describe at meetings. In a conference room, talking about relationship patterns in 'sick' families,
therapists do the same thing to each other that members of 'sick'
families do. They even do the same things to each other while talking about what they do to each other.

(1978, p. 468)

Bowen's strategy was to send the discussants a formal paper and then
describe the breakthrough experience with his family by bringing all the
interlocking triangles in his family of origin together while staying out of the
family emotional oneness:

Most of the conference participants reacted as positively to the presentation as my family did. There were those who reacted emotionally to the extent that they considered the presentation as my family
did. There were those who reacted emotionally to the extent that
they considered the presentation to be selfish and hostile and hurtful,
but even they were mostly positive in reserving an over-all opinion.

(1978, p. 520)

Another opportunity for Bowen to define himself in "the family of family
therapists" took place at the Double-Bind Conference in 1977 in New York.
He described it in a letter to a colleague:

I had two main goals, similar to my goals when I did the paper about
my own family in 1967. People have read my papers about "staying
out of the emotional system" but no one has really understood it.
First I was going to try to stay outside the emotional system in the
demonstration interview. . . . It was a near perfect interview, from my
point of view. I did not get "snookered" a single time, and this was
a family with schizophrenia, which is far more difficult than other
families. The deadly serious family got more loose and casual as the
interview progressed . . . my second goal was to stay outside of the
emotional system of the people on stage. I had been rehearsing this
in my head for days. The peak of that came in the room, the night
before the meeting, when I paced back and forth for about two hours,
drinking coffee and thinking up detriangling "one liners" to use during the meeting. I had a great time chuckling to myself as I tried
to prepare casual sounding "one liner comments" for every anticipated situation. . . . It was not possible to use more than a few of the
stockpile of comments. I did better than okay in keeping myself out
of the impossible polarized situations. Within myself I was delighted
with success as I would define success. It was worth all the time and
preparation . . . most people were able to "hear" better this time than

ever before but few had really grasped what I had been trying to do. . . . People who have considered me "cold and distant" were thrown off by my personal letter to the family the day after . . .

(Boyd, 2007, p. 175)

Defining a Self in Relation to Staff, Patients, and the Patients' Parents as Director of the NIMH Research Project on Schizophrenia and the Family (1954–1959)

Bowen developed a new approach to understanding schizophrenia using his research design of hospitalizing families with a schizophrenic offspring to do long-term observation, study, and treatment. It was a radical effort to go beyond the individual, "cause and effect" thinking for understanding emotional illness. Developing and implementing a systems model involved defining self in the profession of psychiatry. His effort emerged from using a different paradigm. It included getting rid of diagnostic language in favor of terms that described how individuals related to the family and how the family as a whole functioned as an emotional unit. This was a courageous effort in the face of the medical model that existed at that time, and still does today.

Bowen's ability to allow the parents to maintain their functions as parents with the hospitalized schizophrenic offspring and additional hospitalized offspring, was as challenging as was his effort to be neutral in the face of the regressive and helpless behavior of the family members. At the same time Bowen's capacity to elicit and respond to the mature—or more differentiated—functioning of the hospitalized family members illustrated his own differentiated functioning and ability to not over manage or control the families. Rather, he was able to be a neutral, observing presence, while lending a hand to his patients. He showed the same qualities of differentiated leadership in the manner in which he related to his staff. They found it very difficult to stay out of the patient families' emotional fields, with all the family triangles and highly charged emotional processes that occurred within and between the inpatient families.

Under Bowen's direction the rules for the inpatient unit were based on the concept of differentiation of self. One step was to create an "open society." For example, the families were permitted to see their own records, and they were invited to all staff meetings. This rule helped to break down the secrecy within families and between patients and staff that mirrored the patients' family secrets (Kerr and Bowen, 1988, p. 363).

The staff worked hard at creating a neutral language, using descriptive terminology rather than diagnostic labels to characterize patients and their families. Bowen (1988) wrote:

The nursing and research staffs worked hard at developing neutral language that did not categorize anyone. That was the most difficult task of all. It continued over the years. The staff reached a point at which they had to think before they spoke. When they forgot to think, the old categorizing terms emerged. Finally, the staff developed a different language. It was cumbersome to use simple descriptive words to replace diagnostic labels, but the staff thought in a different way.

(Kerr and Bowen, p. 363)

Bowen's Efforts to Practice Principles of Differentiation of Self in His Administrative and Leadership Functions (1954–1990)

Bowen observed that the emotional process in social and work systems is identical to those found in the relationship patterns in families. The difference is that generally the emotional process in family patterns is more intense than those found in the work system, with some exceptions. The work system is similar to the family, but it is not the family.

He (1978) realized that he was overresponsible for his staff and underresponsible in other areas of his functioning:

> My effort went into clarification of my responsibility as head of the research, and functioning responsibly there, without assuming responsibility for others. Very quickly I learned that if there was an emotional issue in the organization, I was playing a part in it, and if I could modify the part I was playing, the others would do the same. This principle has been used through the years in my own family, in my clinical work, and in my administrative functioning. Any time one key member of an organization can be responsibly responsible for self, the problem in the organization will resolve.

(1978, p. 463)

The Concept of Differentiation of Self in the Context of Bowen Theory

This part of the chapter is divided into the following sections: 1) the approach underlying Bowen theory is drawn from natural systems theory; 2) the family as a system: an emerging paradigm; 3) an outline of the conceptual framework of Bowen theory; and 4) the concept of differentiation of self; and the dimensions of differentiation of self.

The Approach Underlying Bowen Theory Is Drawn From Natural Systems Theory

Research or theory development is always preceded by the researcher's *approach*. Giorgi wrote: "By approach is meant the fundamental viewpoint

19

toward man and the world that the scientist brings, or adopts, with respect to his work as a scientist, whether this viewpoint is made explicit or remains implicit" (1970, p. 126).

Bowen's approach to understanding the human family stemmed from a natural systems viewpoint, evolutionary theory, and Darwin's theory of emotions and variation within species.

Earlier in this chapter it was noted that Bowen sought a natural systems foundation for his family systems theory when he realized that psychoanalytic theory lacked that foundation. Bowen believed that emotional function and dysfunction have an instinctual base that humans share with other species, particularly mammals. He believed that man was descended from earlier and simpler forms of life and that the human was connected to all living beings. He wrote:

> The following are some of the basic notions about the nature of man that guided the selection of the various concepts of this systems theory. Man is conceived as the most complex form of life that evolved from the lower forms intimately connected with all living things. The most important difference between man and the lower forms is his cerebral cortex and his ability to think and reason. Intellectual functioning is regarded distinctly differently from emotional functioning, which man shares with the older forms. Emotional functioning includes the automatic forces that govern protoplasmic life. It includes the force that biology defines as instinct, reproduction, the automatic activity controlled by the nervous system, subjective emotional and feeling states, and the forces that govern relationship systems. There are varying degrees of overlap between emotional and intellectual function. In broad terms, the emotional system governs the 'dance of life' in all living things. It is deep in the phylogenetic past and is much older than the intellectual system. A "feeling" is considered the derivative of a deeper emotional state.
>
> (1978, pp. 305–306)

Bowen believed that Darwin's theory of the variation within species was applicable to the functioning of human individuals. He believed that a multigenerational emotional transmission process determines the levels of differentiation of individuals and families over the period of multiple generations. In this process he assumed that individuals marry spouses at the same level of differentiation and in turn they produce children, for the most part, with the same, slightly higher, or slightly lower levels of differentiation. In an interview in 1976, Bowen said: "At this period of time I can do no more than to say that the levels of differentiation are transmitted from generation to generation in a genetic-like pattern which has nothing to do with genetics as genetics is currently defined" (1978, p. 410). (See Chapters 2 and 3 in regard to how the research on epigenetics connects with Bowen's thinking on the multigenerational transmission process.)

When Bowen began developing his family systems theory he made a decision to choose terms, when possible, that would be congruent with biology. He wrote:

> It was a decision . . . to use simple descriptive words when possible, to make biological comparisons when appropriate. The term 'differentiation' was similar to the differentiation of cell in embryology and biology. The terms 'fusion' and 'cutoff' describe the ways cells agglutinate and the way they separate to start new colonies of cells.
>
> (Kerr and Bowen, 1988, p. 362)

The Family as a System: An Emerging Paradigm

Bowen was one of several investigators who initiated the *family therapy movement* in the late 1940s and 1950s. Lidz (1957), Ackerman (1956), Bateson (1956), Wynne (1958), Jackson (1956), and Whitaker (1967) all perceived and conceived of the family as a unit or system. Bowen described this movement as follows:

> As the focus shifted from the individual to the family, each [investigator] was confronted with the dilemma of describing and conceptualizing the family relationship system. Individual theory did not have a conceptual model for a relationship system. Each investigator was 'on his own' in conceptualizing his observations. There were terms for the distortion and rigidity, the reciprocal functioning, and the "interlocking," "binding," "stuck togetherness" of the system. . . . Lidz et al. (1957) used the concept, "schism and skew," and Wynne and his co-workers (1958) used the concept, "pseudomutuality." Ackerman, one of the earliest workers (1958) in the field, presented a conceptual model in his 1956 paper, "Interlocking Pathology in Family Relationships.". . . Jackson and his co-workers (Bateson et al. 1956) used a different model with the concept of the "double bind."
>
> (1978, p. 150)

Bowen's theoretical description of the *family as a system* took place in 1955 during the beginning of a paradigm[2] shift from an individual to a family focus as the unit of psychotherapy, theory, and research in a small nationwide group of psychotherapists and researchers. Bowen and other family therapists initially used the phrase "the family is the unit of treatment," and the shorthand phrase became, "the family as a unit," in the context of clinical practice. This paradigm shift began to emerge from "the family movement" during the middle of the 1950s.

Bowen used the phrase *the family is a system* to describe his *natural systems* theoretical version of the new *paradigm*. His most general definition of the *family system* was as follows: "The family is a system in that a change in part of the system is followed by compensatory change in other parts of the system" (Bowen, 1978 pp. 154–155). He thought of the family as ". . . a combination of 'emotional' and 'relationship' systems." The term "emotional" refers to the force that motivates the system and "relationship" refers to the way it is expressed (1978, p. 158).

The components of Bowen's foundational paradigm of Bowen theory, "the family as a system," are the following:

1) The family is *a multigenerational emotional system* that consists of the individuals in the family, the nuclear family, and the extended family. It includes all living members of the family, usually involving three generations, and sometimes more;

2) The family is driven, or motivated by, the *emotional system*, the forces of togetherness and individuality. These instincts are expressed through emotional process in the relationship system;

3) Family emotional process is the emotional activity or reactivity that occurs between two or more individuals in the family. Bowen described *emotional process* as: ". . . The emotional responsiveness by which one family member responds automatically to the emotional state of another. . . . It operates during periods of conflict and periods of calm harmony" (1978, p. 66);

4) The family system is held together, like an emotional magnet. The term *emotional fusion* in Bowen theory describes the behavioral expression of the emotional stuck-togetherness, or emotional oneness, that is found in all parts of the multigenerational emotional family;

5) The *family system* includes *the interlocking, reciprocal functioning in the relationship system:* change in one person in the family, or one segment in the family, brings about compensatory change in other(s) or other parts of the family;

6) *Overadequate-inadequate reciprocity*, which later was renamed *underfunctioning-overfunctioning reciprocity*, is the borrowing and lending of self in the reciprocal functioning between two family members. When this occurs, both selves are compromised, at least to some degree;

7) Function is a biological term that Bowen uses to describe the behavior of an individual, a part of the family system, or the family as a whole. *Functioning position* refers neutrally to the position an individual occupies in the family system in relation to the reciprocally determined positions of the other family members.

The family as a multigenerational emotional system is a theoretical description in which Bowen delineated his specific version of the emerging paradigm shift from an individual focus to a focus on the family as a system, from the perspective of his natural systems approach. It undergirds Bowen theory: the postulates, differentiation of self, the cornerstone concept, the other seven interlocking concepts, the components of those concepts, and the variables(s) that constitute the theory.

An Outline of the Conceptual Framework of Bowen Family Systems Theory

Bowen family systems theory is grounded in *a natural systems approach* that rests upon facts drawn from evolutionary biology in conjunction with Bowen's own participant-observation research at NIMH and in his clinical, private practice. Bowen observed the family system with an open mind. He formulated his hypotheses and observed the families in action. This led to new theoretical formulations that in turn evolved into new hypotheses. His model was a circular one: observe the human family inductively, then reflect on the observations, and then deductively formulate hypotheses based on new theoretical understandings of how the family and its individual family members function. This research process continued until Bowen formulated the concepts that interlocked, and eventually constituted his family systems theory.

The cornerstone concept of Bowen theory is differentiation of self and there are seven other major concepts—triangles, nuclear family emotional system, family projection process, multigenerational transmission process, emotional cutoff, and sibling position. The concepts are interlocking and describe the functioning of the multigenerational family emotional system. The eighth major concept, emotional process in society, provides a description of how Bowen theory concepts interlock with and can be utilized to understand emotional process in human social systems that are larger than the family.

The eight foundational concepts, including the concept of differentiation of self, contain foundational postulates, components, and variables. The postulates, or as Bowen describes them, assumptions, are 1) the forces, or instincts, of togetherness and individuality, 2) the emotional system, 3) the feeling system, and 4) the intellectual system. They are the biological and neurological systems that Bowen assumed underlay differentiation of self and the other foundational concepts. Bowen viewed MacLean's (1990) triune brain model as quite consonant with his views of the emotional, feeling, and intellectual systems. Current natural systems research has supported what were Bowen's original assumptions of the relationship between emotion, feeling, and intellect.

Examples of components that are part of one or more of the eight concepts are: 1) emotional process, 2) emotional reactivity, 3) reciprocal functioning in the relationship system, and 4) under- or overfunctioning in one, or more, relationships in family and nonfamily systems. An important component of the concept of differentiation is the *self*. It has two dimensions, *solid self* and *pseudo-self*. *Differentiation of self* also has two levels: basic and functional.

The variables in Bowen theory specific to differentiation of self are the levels of 1) chronic anxiety, 2) stress, and 3) adaptiveness.

The Concept of Differentiation of Self

Differentiation of self is an automatic, natural process. Defining a self is an intentional process in the human species. Bowen (1972) describes the natural process of differentiation in humans as follows:

> The term "differentiation of self" was chosen as one that most accurately describes this long-term process in which the child slowly disengages from the original fusion with his mother and moves toward his own emotional autonomy. . . . [It] deals with the degree to which a person becomes emotionally "differentiated" from the parent. In a broad sense the infant separation is slow and complicated, and at best incomplete. Originally, it has to do more with factors in the mother and her ability to permit the child to grow away from her, than with factors in the infant.
>
> (1972, p. 74)

The original biological symbiosis between the mother and the fetus *in utero* and the earliest months of infancy becomes a psychological symbiosis that includes the child. The psychological fusion within the family is expressed both within both the individual and the family unit. The outcome of the process of differentiation leads to the formation of basic self that remains relatively stable by the time an individual leaves his or her parental home and attempts to start a life of his or her own. Since no one ever achieves complete differentiation, there is always a degree of undifferentiation.

Both the natural process of differentiation of self and the intentional process of defining a self refer to an individual's capacity, or lack of capacity, to separate instinctually driven emotional reactivity from thoughtful, goal-directed activity. The instinctual forces of individuality and togetherness are the substrata of differentiation of self. Both forces originate in the emotional system. However, relationship and balance between the togetherness and individuality forces are integrated in the intellectual system. Differentiation of self resides along a continuum from lower to higher functioning. The integration is an automatic, natural process, but it can be modified by an individual's intentional effort to raise his or her level of differentiation of self.

Bowen wrote: "The core of my theory had to do with the degree to which people are able to distinguish between the *feeling* process and the *intellectual* process" (1978, p. 355). The essence of the continuum of differentiation/undifferentiation is the degree of emotional stuck-togetherness, emotional oneness, or emotional fusion of the members of a family. Bowen originally described this as *the family undifferentiated family ego mass*, and later as the nuclear family emotional system.

The continuum of differentiation takes place in the emotional fields of the multigenerational emotional family system. Bowen defined the *emotional field* as: "The emotional process in any area being considered at the moment" (1978, p. 161). For the *individual* in the family, level of differentiation is described by his/her ability to distinguish the difference between the feeling process and the intellectual process. In the emotional field of *the nuclear family* differentiation/undifferentiation is expressed by the degree of emotional fusion—emotional oneness—between family members in the nuclear family and in the nuclear family as a whole. In the emotional field of the individual who has separated from his/her *family of origin,* differentiation of self is the degree of unresolved attachment—the emotional fusion—between an individual and his/her parents. Differentiation of self in the emotional field of *the extended family*—the entire network of living relatives, usually contained in the three-generational family system that includes grandparents, parents, and children—is manifested by the emotional fusion or oneness in any one or all segments of the extended family.

Differentiation of self can be described as the variation in an individual's capacity to be an individual while functioning as part of a group (Kerr, 1988, footnote, p. 63). Also, differentiation can be described as the variation in one's ability to act for oneself without being selfish while being able to act for others without being selfless.

The Dimensions of Differentiation of Self

Bowen postulated that there are two instinctual forces underlying differentiation of self: *togetherness and individuality.* Bowen described them as residing in the emotional system. Although there is no scientific proof that these instinctual forces exist, Bowen theorists and clinicians have documented empirically—through clinical and nonclinical observation—the behaviors that clearly express these phenomena.

The instinct for *togetherness* propels an individual to be connected, dependent, and an indistinct part of a couple, family, or nonfamily group. The instinct for *individuality* propels the individual to be a separate, independent, and distinct entity, following his/her own directives. Differentiation of self, natural or modified by an individual's intentional efforts, is the balancing of these two instincts in the intellectual system. The more emotion dominates the balance of the two instincts, the lower an individual's level of differentiation of self. The more intellect dominates the balance of the two instincts, the higher an individual's level of differentiation of self.

The Emotional, Feeling, and Intellectual Systems

From Bowen's perspective, man's *emotional system* emerges from man's protoplasmic being:

> I believe that the laws that govern man's emotional functioning are as orderly as those that govern other natural systems. . . . There are emotional mechanisms as automatic as a reflex and that occur as predictably as the force that causes the sunflower to turn its face toward the sun.
>
> (1978, p. 158)

He also wrote that

> Emotional functioning includes automatic forces that govern protoplasmic life. It includes the forces that biology defines as instinct, reproduction, the automatic activity controlled by the nervous system, subjective emotional and feeling states, and the forces that govern relationships systems. There are varying degrees of overlap between emotional and intellectual functioning. In broad terms, the emotional system governs the 'dance of life' in all living things.
>
> (1978, pp. 304–305)

Bowen postulated that the *feeling* system is a link between the emotional and intellectual systems. It represents certain emotional states that are accessible to conscious awareness (1978, p. 356). He describes the *intellectual system* as:

> A function of the cerebral cortex which appeared last in man's evolutionary development, and is the main difference between man and the lower forms of life. The cerebral cortex involves the ability to think, reason, and reflect, and enables man to govern his life, in certain areas, according to logic, intellect, and reason.
>
> (1978, p. 356)

Bowen wisely described the emotional, feeling, and intellectual systems as brain functions without designating specific locations in the brain (1978, p. 372). Scientific research has clarified the specificity of their locations, to some degree, and how they neuronally interlock to some degree. Over time Bowen theorists, drawing on the work of biologists, neuroscientists, and other natural systems scientists, have shown that their findings are broadly congruent with Bowen's conception of the emotional system, feeling system, and intellectual system (see Chapter 2).

What Constitutes the Self in the Concept of Differentiation of Self?

From a Bowen theory perspective, there can be no *self* without the *other.* Self is not defined outside of relationships with others. One cannot define a self in a solipsistic vacuum. Self is always formed in relationships in the family, and to some degree with nonfamily members who become important to self.

Self involves an awareness of the continuity of sameness, of who one is as an individual over time. The continuity and solidity of self vary based on the level of differentiation of the individual. Bowen wrote:

> I would consider "differentiation of self" to be equivalent to "iden-
> tity" or "individuality," provided one does not confuse identity
> with the psychoanalytic concept of "identification.". . . A person
> with a high level of "differentiation of self," or "identity," or "indi-
> viduality," is one who can be emotionally close to others without
> emotional fusions or loss of self, or loss of identity, because he has
> attained a higher level of differentiation of self.
>
> (1978, p. 109)

The self evolves slowly as an individual moves from the symbiotic *in utero* attachment to the mother: through birth, into the extra-uterine world of other humans who preceded him or her. Initially the world of others exists mostly as the world of one's family, but as time goes on it grows to include the world of nonfamily others.

Bowen wrote that the self is constituted by a number of components, but he left out how they were integrated, believing that research in the natural sciences would provide a clearer picture:

> The "self" is composed of constitutional, physical, physiological,
> biological, genetic, and cellular reactivity factors, as they move in
> unison with psychological factors. On a simple level, it is composed
> of the confluence of more fixed personality factors as they move in
> unison with rapidly moving psychological states. Each factor influ-
> ences the other and is influenced by others.
>
> (1978, p. 342)

His description of self always included the idea that what a person did was more important than what he or she said. Self, in Bowen theory, is a description of the actions, reactions, and interactions of the individual in relation primarily to his or her family of origin, nuclear family, and extended family, and secondarily by the actions, reactions, and interactions between an individual and nonfamily members and societal entities in which he or she participates.

The Self Consists of Two Interlocking Systems: The Solid Self and the Pseudo-Self

Solid self and pseudo-self represent two separate modes of functioning that run along a continuum, with pseudo-self at the lower end of differentiated functioning and solid self at the higher end of differentiated functioning. The balance of pseudo-self and solid self depends upon which of the two is more prominent. If the pseudo-self is dominant, this correlates with lower levels of differentiation of self. And, conversely, if the solid self is more dominant than the pseudo-self, this correlates with higher levels of differentiation.

The solid self, for the most part, is stable but adaptive to the pressures of reality. The pseudo-self is constantly responding, overadapting, and fusing with the other's anxiety and wishes, among other explicit or implicit demands.

The solid self is made up of defined beliefs, convictions, and life principles that are not given up in the face of pressure from the other. Bowen wrote: "Each belief and principle is consistent with the others and [solid] self will take responsible action on the principles even in situations of high anxiety" (1978, p. 406). The solid self is expressed through taking I-positions. This is where an individual stands against the pressure of the family (or nonfamily members) to bend to the forces of togetherness, and to adapt to the other(s)' views or behaviors in which the self does not believe.

The solid self is very consistent and changes are very slow and hard won. Working on differentiation of self has the potential to raise, to some degree, solid self. One of the great difficulties in assessing the basic level of differentiation of self is that it is formed over multiple generations (at least three or more), so that the functioning of the preceding generation, the present generation, and the next generation must be, hypothetically, taken into account in the assessment of an individual.

The pseudo-self is a "pretend" self. It is both acquired by and can be changed by emotional pressure from others. Bowen described the pseudo-self in the following way: "It is made up of random and discrepant beliefs and principles, acquired because they were required, it is the right thing to believe or to do, or to enhance self image in the social amalgam" (1978, p. 406). Bowen (1978) described it as either going along with or fighting the social environment. It ". . . pretends to be in harmony with all kinds of discrepant groups, beliefs, and social institutions. . . . [O]ne can pretend to be more important or less, stronger or weaker, or more or less attractive than is realistic or consistent" (p. 406).

Bowen notes that the level of solid self is much lower than the level of pseudo-self. This is the case because the former can acknowledge the inconsistency of his or her beliefs, whereas the latter's "pretend self" is unaware of the discrepancies in his or her beliefs. He wrote: "From experience with this concept, the level of solid self is much lower, and the level of pseudo self is much higher in all of us than any of us can easily accept" (p. 407).

Anxiety and Differentiation of Self

Differentiation of self, or the integration of self, and chronic anxiety are the two most important variables in Bowen theory. Differentiation is both the cornerstone concept in Bowen theory and a variable. It is a variable in the continuum of differentiation of self, and it also interlocks with all of the other concepts in Bowen theory. The level of differentiation and the level of anxiety are always significant factors in assessing each of the concepts in Bowen theory.

Anxiety in Bowen theory is defined as a response to real or imagined threats. Acute anxiety is the individual's psychological and/or physiological response to real threat. It usually is time limited. Chronic anxiety is a response to perceived or imagined threat that is usually unlimited in time. In short, chronic anxiety is acute anxiety that doesn't go away. According to Kerr:

> Chronic anxiety often strains or exceeds people's ability to adapt to it. Acute anxiety is fed by fear of what is; chronic anxiety is fed by fear of what might be. . . . [W]hile specific events or issues are usually the principal generators of acute anxiety, the principal generators of chronic anxiety are people's reactions to a disturbance in the balance of a relationship system.
>
> (Kerr and Bowen, 1978, p. 113)

On the continuum of differentiation, higher levels of chronic anxiety are associated with lower basic levels of differentiation of self. Lower levels of chronic anxiety are associated with higher basic levels of differentiation of self. Acute anxiety is associated with functional levels of differentiation. When levels of acute anxiety are high, functional differentiation is lower. Conversely, when levels of acute anxiety are lower, functional differentiation rises.

Emotional Reactivity and Differentiation of Self

Emotional reactivity is the behavioral and physiological expression of anxiety, acute or chronic, in response to another individual. It initially occurs in the family relationship system, and then later in other nonfamily relationships. Reactivity in one triggers reactivity in the other. Chronic reactivity, in the context of chronic anxiety, leads to a disturbance in the balance of a relationship system.

The intensity of emotional reactivity, like that of chronic anxiety, is also linked to the level of differentiation. The lower the level of differentiation, the more frequent the episodes of emotional reactivity, and they are more frequently at higher levels of intensity. At higher levels of differentiation of self, there are less frequent episodes of reactivity and the levels of emotional reactivity are less intense.

For humans, engaging with others—or "bumping into one another"—is part of the activity or "give and take of life." For example, members of a couple frequently have differences that get expressed through reciprocal emotional reactivity. The expression of reactivity takes the form of varied internal, physiological disruptions, and varied external, behavioral and psychological expressions. When reactivity is overly intense, or overly submerged, then the flexibility and balance of the relationship system is disturbed.

Blaming self or blaming the other is a form of emotional reactivity. It involves cause and effect thinking that leads to an individual taking too little responsibility for self, or taking too much responsibility for another individual. Reactivity can be expressed in many ways: through attacking, denying, distancing, cutting off, and triangling, among other behavioral expressions. Facial or vocal responses can be expressions of reactivity and in turn can trigger reciprocal reactivity in others.

The difference between an *active* and a *reactive* response to another is important. Relationships between individuals, families, and larger systems consist of self-regulated active responses, automatic unregulated overactive responses, and underactive responses. An active response involves self-regulation, neither attacking, distancing, nor involving oneself in the projection process to the other(s). The latter are higher levels of differentiated responses. Under- and overreactions to the other(s) refer to less self-regulated activity. They are both forms of reactivity and are frequently a part of lower levels of differentiated responses.

Bowen described emotional reactiveness, his earlier term for what he later described as emotional reactivity, as an "... *emotional reflex* which is accurate and which makes it a little more synonymous with biology" (1978, p. 422). By that he meant that the emotional reflex consists of automatic responses to all sensory modalities, but the majority of emotionally reactive reflexes are visual and auditory. For example, a husband comes home from work with an angry "look" on his face. His spouse's anxiety rises and is expressed in the rise of the tone of her verbal response. Her reactive response can lead to a reactive response from the husband and that can escalate into conflict or distance between them. Bowen wrote: "Systems therapy directed at helping spouses discover the reflexes can give each a bit of control over the automatic emotional reactiveness" (1978, p. 422).

30

Like all human interaction, activity and reactivity are varied and are expressed differently depending on where individuals lie along the continuum of differentiation of self, as well as the presence of acute and chronic anxiety.

Stress, Anxiety, Reactivity, Adaptiveness, and Differentiation of Self

Stress is another variable in Bowen theory. It is a source of external pressure that can generate anxiety and emotional reactivity in individuals and families. Stressors include many life events, such as the birth of a child, a child leaving home, the loss of a job, the death of a family member, among other nodal experiences.

Adaptiveness is a term drawn from evolutionary biology. The evolutionary biologist Dobzhansky defines *adaptation* as ". . . the evolutionary process whereby an organism becomes better able to live in its habitat or habitats" (Dobzhansky and Hecht, 1968, pp. 1–34). A high level of chronic anxiety and or emotional reactivity in response to a low level of stress is consistent with a low level of adaptiveness. A low level of chronic anxiety or emotional reactivity in response to a high level of stress is consistent with a high level of adaptiveness. Kerr wrote that "[t]he levels of adaptiveness parallel the levels of differentiation of self" (Kerr and Bowen, 1988, p. 321). When chronic anxiety increases, the adaptiveness of the family decreases and vice versa; when chronic anxiety decreases, the adaptiveness of the family increases. Adaptiveness is the capacity of the individual and the family to regulate their anxiety and emotional reactivity in order to maintain the emotional equilibrium in the family.

Basic and Functional Levels of Differentiation of Self

Basic levels of differentiation remain fairly constant over a lifetime. However, through fortuitous interactions with special individuals within and outside of the family or through working on differentiating a self under the direction of a Bowen-trained coach, an individual's basic level of differentiation of self can increase over time. Bowen noted:

> It is not possible ever to make more than minor changes in one's basic level of self; but from clinical practice I can say it is possible to make slow changes, and each small change results in a new world of a different life. As I see it now, the critical stage is passed when the individual can begin to know the difference between emotional functioning and intellectual functioning, and when he has developed ways for using the knowledge for solving future problems in a lifelong effort of his own.
>
> (1978, p. 371)

One of the quandaries in conceptualizing and assessing the basic level of human functioning involves the discrepancy between the basic and functional levels of individual functioning. This discrepancy is the outcome of humans having both a solid self and a pseudo-self, as was described in a previous section. When an individual is "borrowing" and "lending" self in his or her relationships with spouse, children, parents, or extended family, and significant nonfamily members—through the process of emotional fusion or undifferentiation—he or she will present as having a higher or lower level of functional differentiation in comparison to his or her basic level of differentiation.

It is more difficult to make an accurate assessment of differentiation of self for individuals with lower levels, because the pseudo-selves of those individuals involve more fusion—"borrowing," "lending," and "sharing of self"—within the nuclear family emotional system. Bowen wrote:

> The degree of pseudo self varies so much it is not possible to make a valid estimate of solid self except from estimating the life patterns over long periods of time. . . . With all the variables it is possible to do a reasonably accurate estimate of the degree of differentiation of self from the fusion patterns in past generations and from the overall course of a life in the present. Estimates of scale levels provide important clues for family therapy and for predicting, within broad limits, the future adaptive patterns of family members.
>
> (1978, p. 306)

Bowen believed that an accurate estimate of an individual's level of differentiation would take a long period of time or even an entire life to determine (1978, p. 402).

Bowen described how he came to assess a basic level of differentiation of self: "Clinically, I make estimates from the average functional level of self as it operates through periods of stress and calm. The real test of the stability of the differentiation comes when the person is again subjected to chronic severe stress" (1978, p. 371).

In short, in pragmatic terms, functional differentiation becomes basic differentiation when it is stable over a long period of an individual's life, or over an entire lifetime. Basic differentiation is functional differentiation that doesn't go away.

Differentiation of Self Describes a Continuum of Human Functioning

Bowen wanted to illustrate that all humans function along one continuum, at least in the dimension that he believed was the single most significant variable, differentiation of self. He wanted to describe the universality of human functioning on the part of individuals in the context of their most significant family and nonfamily relationships on a continuum that portrays human functioning from its lowest to the highest levels. He was most interested in describing the characteristics of the human functioning on a continuum. He also did not want to create a reductionist scale on which individual functioning would be pegged to an exact number. With these ideas in mind, he developed what he called a differentiation of self scale.

Bowen wrote:

> The schematic framework and the use of the term scale resulted in hundreds of letters requesting copies of "the scale." Most who wrote had not grasped the concept or the variables that govern the functional levels of differentiation. The letters slowed down my effort to develop a more definite scale that could be used clinically. The theoretical concept is most important. It eliminates the barriers between schizophrenia, neurosis, and normal; it also transcends categories such as genius, social class, and cultural-ethnic differences. It applies to human forms of life. . . . Knowledge of the concept permits the easy development of all kinds of research instruments . . . but to attempt to use the scale without knowledge of the concept can result in chaos.
>
> (1978, p. 364)

He was unhappy about the way many people heard his idea about the scale of differentiation of self:

> I was merely trying to communicate that people are defineably different from each other in the way they handle the mix between emotional and cognitive functioning, and that that difference was on a continuum from its most intense to its less intense form.
>
> (1978, p. 402)

One hundred on the scale was equal to a hypothetically complete level of differentiation of self or emotional maturity, or a complete self. Zero on the scale was equivalent to complete undifferentiation of self. Of course all people function from low to high. No one is either a total *no self* or a total *complete self.* In 1966, Bowen wrote that he had never seen anyone in his clinical work whose level of differentiation was in the 75 to 100 range on the scale, and he hardly knew anyone in his social or professional relationships who was in that range (1978, p. 164). In the later years of his career, he came to believe that almost no one was in the highest quartile of differentiation of self and that the human population has very few individuals whose level of differentiation of self exceeds 60. The few highest functioning individuals fall in the 65 to 70 range and most people are below 50 on the scale (1978, p. 442). Again, this was a descriptive number used to indicate that very high emotional maturity does not easily or frequently present itself in the human parade. Early in Bowen's career he believed the distribution of differentiation of self would be more even along the scale. Later his experience led him to believe that 90 percent of the population is found in the lower half of the scale and 10 percent in the third segment (1978, p. 405).

While no one has a level of differentiation of 0 or 100, the scale as a continuum includes hypothetical levels for descriptive purposes. In retrospect, it might have been heard better and been more accurate if Bowen had chosen to call it *the* continuum of differentiation of self rather than the scale of differentiation of self, since he was seeking to describe the variation in the level of differentiation between people, rather than creating a numerical scale that would measure exact levels of differentiation of self. In the future it may be possible that Bowen researchers can further clarify and define the differences between functional and basic differentiation (see Chapter 15), utilizing methodologies that include longitudinal studies (studies of three or more generations and the members of the nuclear families of multiple generations) and observation of families *in situ*. Naturally observing and describing differentiation of self will only lead to clarity and accuracy if the researcher has a solid, theoretical understanding of what differentiation of self is.

Another problem for researching differentiation of self, as well as the other concepts in Bowen theory, is its complexity. The theory focuses on the actions, reactions, and interactions between individuals and within entire families, but the complexity of the phenomena cannot be accounted for without drawing upon a person's self-report, which includes his or her subjective experience, including observations, perceptions, and reactions, among other modalities that can never be completely objective. All species can be somewhat deceptive as part of their effort to survive, and human verbal communication cannot be dismissed in researching the human's efforts, deceptions, beliefs, values, and I-positions, among the range of human behavior and experience. However, reducing human behavior to a narrow and reductionist methodological approach leads to the incipient view that *measurement precedes existence*. That is too limited an approach to do justice to the complexity of the human's integration of emotion and intellect.

Bowen theory emphasizes that the goal of increasing one's level of objectivity and reducing subjectivity will lead one to be more neutral and thoughtful about one's self and others. And yet, Bowen realized that understanding and studying human functioning would include both *the facts of functioning* and *functional facts*. The facts of functioning include one's age, marital status, education, occupation, and health status, among other objective facts. Bowen formulated a way to deal with subjectivity that he described using the term "functioning facts":

> Efforts have been made to discover formulas for converting subjective observations into objective and measureable facts. For example,

when applied to dreams, the formula says, "That man dreams is a scientific fact, but what he dreams is not necessarily a fact." The same formula can be applied to a whole range of subjective concepts, such as, "That man feels (or thinks or talks) is a scientific fact, but what he feels (or thinks or says) is not necessarily a fact." The entire spectrum of subjective states, even the intensity of love, [and] hate, can similarly be stated as functional facts.

(1978, pp. 261–262)

It is important to understand that the continuum of differentiation does not indicate the presence or diagnoses of emotional illness or psychopathology. There are people who are on the low end of the scale who keep in emotional equilibrium without being emotionally dysfunctional, and vice versa. There are those who are at the higher end of the scale of differentiation who develop severe symptoms under stressful conditions. However, since those who are at the low level of differentiation are prone to become anxious when stressed, they are more prone to develop symptoms, and when they do, the symptoms are more likely to become chronic. People higher on the scale are quicker to regain emotional equilibrium when the stress passes.

Profiles of the Continuum of Differentiation of Self

In 1976, 10 years after Bowen had first presented the scale of differentiation of self, he realized that the scale was not developed enough to discriminate between specific measureable levels of differentiation of self. In addition, feedback from mental health professionals indicated they hoped to use the scale as a measurement tool. Therefore, Bowen chose to describe the difference between levels of differentiation of self on a continuum by presenting the differences between various lifestyles exhibited by *profiles*, rather than by an actual scale. Although the scale had been meant to describe the continuum of differentiation of self, it gave a false impression to concretistic thinkers that it was a measurement instrument. They often had an inadequate understanding of the underlying theoretical concept of differentiation of self and the other interlocking concepts of Bowen theory (1978, pp. 161–165, 364–373).

Bowen's further clinical, professional, and social experience led him to the conclusion that he should not include a profile for the uppermost range that was previously designated to be from 75 to 100. The latter profile had not been understood, as Bowen meant it to be a hypothetical description of a range of what might evolve for man with possible future evolutionary change.

The following are summaries of the three profiles of levels of differentiation of self: 1) low levels of differentiation, 2) moderate levels of differentiation of self, and 3) moderate to good differentiation of self.

Profile of Low Levels of Differentiation

This level was previously presented as ranging from 0 to 25 in the differentiation of self scale. Of course even the individuals at the lowest level of differentiation of self have a minimal amount of differentiation. Individuals at this level live in a world dominated by feeling. They are not able to distinguish feeling from fact. They cannot differentiate between the feeling system and the intellectual system. At this level people are so relationship focused, seeking approval, love, and harmony, that they have no energy to direct toward their own life goals. Their time is spent struggling to keep their relationships in balance in order to maintain some equilibrium and keep anxiety down. Their life energy goes toward getting comfortable. People at this level grow up appended to their parents and have little emotional separateness from their parents. This pattern continues when they form other relationships that allow them to borrow strength to function. If individuals in this group amass an adequate system of attachments, they may function throughout life without symptoms. If they can gain sufficient comfort by borrowing strength from those attachments, they are content. Many of them suffer from severe psychological, physical, and social symptoms, and high chronic anxiety, and they are unable to find, or maintain, relationships from which they can borrow self. They are often chronically symptomatic (Bowen, 1978, pp. 366–367).

Profile of Moderate Levels of Differentiation of Self

This level was previously presented as ranging from 25 to 50 on the scale of differentiation of self. At this level there is some evidence of differentiation between the emotional and intellectual systems, although most of the self presents as pseudo-self. The life orientations are more flexible than those of the lower levels of differentiation, although their lives are directed by the emotional system. In this range of functioning there is more flexibility expressed by the interplay of emotionality and intellect. Functioning can resemble higher levels of functioning when acute anxiety is low. And, conversely, when acute anxiety is high, functioning can resemble lower levels of differentiation. At the latter times, there is a higher presence of emotional fusion in relationships; much life energy goes into seeking approval, loving, and seeking love from others. Considerable energy goes into what others think and into getting the approval of friends, rather than putting energy into achieving personal goals. At this level of differentiation the sense of identity and self-esteem depends on others. Bowen describes their pseudo-selves as consisting of the following:

> . . . discrepant principles, beliefs, philosophies, and ideologies that are used in pretend postures to blend with different relationship systems. . . . Lacking a solid self-conviction about the world's knowledge, they use

pseudo-self statements such as, "the rule says . . ." or "Science has proved . . ." taking information out of context to make their points. They may have enough free-functioning intellect to have mastered academic knowledge and impersonal things; they use the knowledge in the relationship system. However, intellect about personal matters is lacking, and their personal lives are in chaos.

(1978, p. 368)

The pseudo-self at the moderate level of differentiation of self may either conform to or rebel against a particular philosophy, religion, or set of principles. He or she may become a disciple or a rebel. Bowen wrote: "A conviction can be so fused with feeling that it becomes a 'cause'" (1978, p. 163).

He also wrote: "It is relationship-oriented energy that goes back and forth on the same points, the issue on each side being determined by the position of the other; neither is capable of a position not determined by the other" (1978, p. 368).

People who function in the moderate range of differentiation express intense feelings. Their focus on relationships makes them sensitive to the expression of the feelings of the others. They are constantly seeking the ideal relationship. They seek emotional closeness and open communication of feelings with others.

Bowen described those in the moderate range and below as living in *a feeling* world. And those at the extreme lowest end of the continuum of differentiation can be too distressed to express or experience feelings. The important decisions in life are based on what feels right. Success in the arena of business, or occupation, is determined by the approval of supervisors and other members of the relationship system.

Bowen is clear that levels on the continuum cannot be correlated with clinical categories. The most severe emotional disorders are usually found at the lowest end, but less severe disorders, such as transient psychotic episodes and delinquency problems, occur in the lower end of the moderate range of differentiation of self (1978, pp. 367–369).

Profile of Moderate to Good Levels of Differentiation of Self

This level was previously presented as ranging from 50 to 75 on the scale of differentiation. At this level people are capable of separating the emotional and intellectual systems to the extent that the two systems can function in balance with each other. The intellectual system is not dominated by the emotional system when anxiety increases, as is the case in people below 50. Above 50, the intellectual system is developed enough to make a few decisions on its own: "The intellect learns that it requires a bit of discipline to overrule the emotional system, but in the long-term it is worth the effort" (Bowen, 1978, p. 369).

The difference between people in the lower part of this group in comparison to those in the higher part of this group is that they understand there is a better way of functioning, but their intellect is less solidly formed. They usually end up following the life courses of those below 50.

People who are in the upper part of the 50 to 75 group have more solid self. They are less controlled by the emotional-feeling world. In Bowen's words:

> They can participate fully in emotional events knowing that they can extricate themselves with logical reasoning when the need arises. There may be periods of laxness in which they may permit the automatic pilot of the emotional system to have full control, but when trouble develops they can take over, calm the anxiety, and avoid a life crisis.
>
> (1978, pp. 369–370)

The following are characteristics of the lifestyle of people who are higher in the moderate- to high-level group as compared with those in the lower segment of that group. They are:

- Clearer about the differences between emotion and intellect;
- Better able to state their own convictions and beliefs calmly, without attacking the beliefs of others, and without defending their own;
- Better able to accurately assess themselves in relation to others without overvaluing or undervaluing themselves;
- Able to have marriages that are a functioning partnership; spouses can express a range of emotional intimacy without the loss of self to the other;
- Can allow their children to grow up and develop autonomous selves without trying to create their children as copies of themselves;
- Are more responsible individuals: they don't blame others for their failures, or credit others for their successes;
- Better able to function with others, or alone, based on what the situation requires;
- Better equipped to live orderly lives, cope successfully with a broader range of life situations, and are freer from the full range of human problems (Bowen, 1978, pp. 369–370).

Differentiation of Self and the Other Seven Concepts

Central to Bowen theory is the idea that differentiation of self exists along a continuum from low to high. The same kind of variation takes place in the other seven concepts in Bowen theory: triangles, the nuclear family emotional systems, the family projection process, emotional cutoff, the multigenerational transmission, sibling position, and emotional process in society.

The variation in individual human functioning and in the family as a whole is expressed in all the concepts and is affected by the levels of anxiety and differentiation of self in all family members. If the family has higher levels of basic differentiation and lower levels of chronic anxiety, the interlocking functioning in those concepts will be more flexible and have less vulnerability to psychological, physical, and social symptoms. Conversely, if the family has lower levels of basic differentiation and higher levels of chronic anxiety, the expression of the seven concepts will be more inflexible and the family will be more vulnerable to psychological, physical, and social symptoms.

Triangles and Differentiation of Self

The emotional triangle is the smallest stable unit in the multigenerational family emotional system and in all emotional systems (social, work, and societal). A two-person system is stable as long as anxiety is low, but when anxiety rises, one member of the dyad automatically brings in a vulnerable third person and the dyad becomes a triangle. This is a reciprocal process involving all three members of the triangle. More than one individual can occupy a position in a triangle. For example, both parents can share one position, with their son occupying the second position, and his wife occupying the third position. The emotional process in the family is always changing through constantly shifting triangular patterns. In triangles, two individuals occupy the close inside positions, and the third occupies the distant outside position. When the family relationship system is highly anxious, the outside position is preferred, and when anxiety is low, the inside positions are preferred. An emotional triangle will be more or less intense and function differently at varying levels of differentiation of self.

In more highly differentiated families the triangles are less fixed and the patterns are less rigid. At lower levels of differentiation, in conjunction with higher levels of anxiety, triangles will be more rigid and fixed, without the flexibility to change, leading to greater levels of dysfunction. For example, in a primary triangle of mother, father, and child, the mother may spoil her child, the father may be overly strict, and there may be some conflict between the parents regarding how to parent their child. But if their levels of basic differentiation of self are higher, and acute and chronic anxiety in their family system are lower, there is more flexibility, and it is less likely that dysfunction or symptoms will emerge. However, if symptoms and problematic triangles emerge, it is more likely that they can be modified, through either a natural or an intentional process.

The Nuclear Family Emotional System and Differentiation of Self

The nuclear family emotional system describes the patterns of the relationship system transmitted through the reciprocal, interlocking emotional process between the members of the family unit or system. This concept describes the way differentiation and undifferentiation are expressed in the nuclear family, in other words the degree, intensity, and form that express how the family members emotionally fuse together as a conglomerate—their emotional oneness or emotional stuck-togetherness. The nuclear family consists of the emotional nucleus of the family and all those attached to it. The nucleus of the family is that individual or reproductive pair—usually one parent or both—who is the central guiding or directing figure around which the children orbit. However, there are modified nuclear families that functionally include stepparents, adoptive parents, grandparents, and occasionally other important caretakers who may make up the household over a significant period of time.

Automatic patterns that absorb and express the anxiety and undifferentiation in the nuclear family are the following: 1) marital conflict, distance, pursuit, and/or distance and pursuit; 2) underfunctioning and overfunctioning between the spouses whereby one spouse may end up carrying more of the family anxiety than the other, manifesting in psychological, physical, or social symptoms—the overfunctioner may gradually become overwhelmed and also develop symptoms; 3) impairment of one or more children who may receive the brunt of the anxiety that originates in the parental couple's relationship or that stems from issues originating in one or both parents. Most families have a combination of all three automatic and reciprocally recycling patterns, and when these patterns coexist, symptoms are less intense.

Nuclear families with low to moderate levels of differentiation and high chronic anxiety usually have higher levels of conflict and/or distance, less balanced partnerships, and higher levels of over- and underfunctioning reciprocity leading to higher levels of dysfunction in one spouse (psychiatric, physical, or social), and more impairment in a child through the projection of parental anxiety onto the child. Nuclear families with moderate to good levels of differentiation have fewer dysfunctional patterns.

The Family Projection Process and Differentiation of Self

The family projection process is a specific form of the triangle that takes place between the mother, father, and child, and exists to some degree in all families. The parents' chronic level of anxiety and undifferentiation is transmitted to one child—or in very low differentiated families to more than one—by one, or both, parents directing over- or underpositive or negative feelings to the triangled recipient. The projection process between parent and child involves the transfer of the parent's anxiety to the latter, and in so doing the child that receives the intensive negative or positive focus automatically takes on and lives out the parental anxiety. In this process the child "helps" his or her mother, or father, by taking on the anxiety while the parent's anxiety is reduced. The family projection process binds the anxiety of the parent(s) and often binds the anxiety of the entire family. The triangled child in the nuclear family develops a lower level of basic differentiation than his or her siblings, and in turn he or she has a higher degree of unresolved attachment to the parents as he or she moves into adulthood. The process usually begins with anxiety in the mother. When the child responds to the mother's anxiety, she misperceives it as a problem in the child. Bowen wrote: "Thus, a situation that begins *as a feeling in the mother, becomes a reality in the child*" (1978, p. 59). The father provides a supportive role to the process. He is sensitive to the mother's anxiety, and he "helps" by going along with her and supporting her anxious mothering.

The family projection process occurs in all families to some extent. However, it occurs at higher levels of impairment to the children in families with low to moderate levels of differentiation and high chronic anxiety. There is significantly less impairment to the recipient of the family projection process in families at moderate to good levels of differentiation and low chronic anxiety.

Emotional Cutoff and Differentiation of Self

The concept of emotional cutoff deals with the way individuals separate themselves from their families of origin in order to start their adult lives in the present generation. The automatic pattern for this process is internal emotional distancing or a combination of emotional distancing and geographic distancing between the generations of children and parents. Similar to the automatic patterns of emotional fusion that bind anxiety and undifferentiation in the nuclear family emotional system, a cutoff between an offspring and parent(s) is always an expression of unresolved attachment between child and parent(s). The degree of cutoff between a child, or a child who is chronologically grown up, and his or her parent(s) is the degree of a residue of emotional fusion between the child and one or both parents. This form of unresolved fusion is usually embedded in the primary parent-child triangle.

The continuum of emotional cutoff is intertwined with the continuum of differentiation. At moderate to higher levels of differentiation, the process can be described in terms of an individual *growing away* from his or her family of origin, leading to the development of an autonomous self. At moderate levels of differentiation, the process can be described in terms of an individual *tearing away* from the family of origin based on the presence of more pseudo-self and less solid self. At lower levels of differentiation the process can be described as an *intense or complete degree of cutting off.*

Growing away takes place at the more highly differentiated end of the continuum. Minimal distancing and withdrawal can occur. The individual maintains relatively open communication and relatively direct one-to-one relationships with his or her parents.

Tearing away, characterized by a moderate level of differentiation with his or her parents, involves distancing behavior that leans more in the direction of cutoff than those whose higher level of differentiation places them in the growing away range. These individuals have relationships with their parents that are characterized by the absence of direct communication. The relationships are often closed and distant. The distance may be internal, involving severe emotional withdrawal.

Intense or complete cutoff is characteristic of lower levels of differentiation of self. The rebellious youth who runs away and the young adult, or adolescent, who stays or returns home but withdraws or collapses internally are emotionally cut off from their parents. Both have an intense amount of unresolved attachment to their parents. Emotional cutoff is always a two-way process insofar as the parent(s) and child are both a part of it and the unresolved attachment out of which it emerges.

Like all of the concepts in Bowen theory, the process of emotional cutoff is a multigenerational one. It involves, for example, fusion between parents followed by distance and cutoff, leading to fusion between one parent and a vulnerable child. That process can move down through multiple generations, and the variation among siblings leads to further variation in multiple branches of a family. In each generation there is variation in level of differentiation determined by triangling and projection processes.

The Multigenerational Transmission Process and Differentiation of Self

The concept of the multigenerational transmission process describes how the level of differentiation increases or decreases for individuals in all families over multiple generations. This emotional process includes the automatic patterns that bind chronic anxiety in the fused emotional process of the nuclear family, the presence and intensity of the family projection process, the presence and intensity of emotional cutoff, and the regression and progression of the emotional process in society. The most potent automatic processes in the transmission of levels of differentiation of self over the generations are triangles and interlocking triangles.

The multigenerational transmission process assumes that all members of every nuclear family, in each generation, have relatively equal levels of differentiation. However, the child who receives the greatest amount of the family projection process—the *most triangled child* in the family—ends up with a somewhat lower level of differentiation than that of the parents. Conversely, the child who receives a lesser amount of the projection process ends up with the same or a slightly higher level of differentiation of self than his or her parents. The variation in differentiation between the siblings is small in each generation, but it is meaningful. Over many generations this process leads one or more individuals to have extremely low levels of differentiation, often characterized by chronic psychological, physical, or social symptoms. It also leads to individuals who function at relatively higher levels of differentiation, often with fewer and milder symptoms. Other family branches fall at points in between.

David Berenson interviewed Bowen in 1976 and the following is a schematic outline, in chronological order, in which Bowen answered the following question: *Why are some people more differentiated than others?*

- Your differentiation level is determined by the differentiation level of your parents at the time you were born;
- Your sex and how that fitted into the family plan or configuration;
- Your sibling position;
- The normality or lack of it in your genetic composition;
- The emotional climate in each of your parents and in their marriage before and after your birth;
- The quality of the relationship each of your parents had with their parental families;
- The number of reality problems in your parents' lives in the period before your birth and the years after your birth;
- Your parents' ability to cope with the emotional and reality problems of their time, and other details that apply to the broad configuration;
- The level of differentiation in each of your parents as determined by the very same order of factors in the situation into which they were born and grew up;
- The levels of differentiation in each grandparent as determined by the same factors in their families of origin, and on back through the generations.

(Bowen, 1978, p. 409)

Bowen believed that the biological, genetic, and emotional programming that goes into reproduction and birth is a stable process. However, it is influenced, to some degree, by both positive and negative unexpected and fortuitous circumstances over the process before birth, during infancy, and in early childhood. This process is modified to some degree by positive or negative experiences during childhood and adolescence. The basic level of differentiation is finally established about the time the young adult establishes self separately from his family of origin (1978, p. 410). The basic level of differentiation of self is transmitted through multiple generations as a process that is relatively stable.

In the final question of the interview, Berenson asked: *"What does this have to do with genetics?"* Bowen answered as follows: "At this period of time, I can do no more than say that the levels of differentiation are transmitted from generation to generation in a genetic-like pattern which has nothing to do with genetics as genetics is currently defined" (Bowen, 1978, p. 410; see Chapters 2 and 3 for further clarification of the multigenerational transmission of differentiation of self that draws on more recent natural science research and theory).

Sibling Position and Differentiation of Self

The concept of sibling position in Bowen theory was adapted in 1961 from the research of Walter Toman (1969). Toman provided personality profiles of the oldest, youngest, and middle siblings as well as the typical or expected characteristics of the functioning positions of siblings, with the caveat *all things being equal*. Toman described 10 basic profiles of the various interlocks between the three sibling positions. The concept of sibling position also addresses the way these positions relate and are determined by their interaction with their parents and with siblings who hold other reciprocal positions. It also addresses the way spouses and parents interact, based on their birth positions.

Toman's research addressed the complementarity of the functioning of sibling position and the variety of complementarity in the relationships of marriage partners. Stereotypically, individuals are drawn to others who duplicate the patterns of their sibling relationships. For example, males who have female siblings are usually comfortable in relationships with females as adults and vice versa. And males who do not have female siblings may be more uncomfortable in close relationships with females in adult relationships and vice versa.

Bowen incorporated Toman's descriptions of sibling position into his theory but with the caveat that the functioning of sibling positions will vary depending on the level of differentiation and the intensity of the projection process in any particular family. For example, if the projection process is focused on an oldest son or daughter, he or she will usually have a lower level of differentiation than the other siblings and may function more like a dependent or rebellious youngest. If his or her level of differentiation is moderate or low, he or she may function as an autocrat rather than as a responsible oldest with leadership expectations and potential.

Emotional Process in Society and Differentiation of Self

The concept of emotional process in society refers to an overarching arena in which the other seven concepts in Bowen theory, including differentiation, in conjunction with the concept of anxiety, can be applied to social units larger than the family. However, emotional process in society is more than an arena for emotional process writ large. It is a natural extension of Bowen's family systems theory, which includes the individual, the couple, the nuclear family, extended families. It includes larger social systems in society—the tribe, state, nation, country, and world as part of the interlocking emotional process in which the human is embedded.

In 1972 Bowen was invited to present a formal paper for a conference given by the Environmental Protection Agency. He was drawn to the subject of emotional process in society because he wanted to understand the way chronic anxiety had an impact on differentiation of self at the societal level.

Bowen used his observations about juvenile delinquency to link emotional functioning in the family to that of the larger society. He described parent and delinquent adolescent triangles that interlocked with societal institutions such as schools, police, and other community agencies. These institutions and the parents vacillated between overpermissiveness and overstrictness in their reactiveness and general helplessness with regard to the management of young people's behavior. The lack of structure and lack of consistent discipline in responding to delinquent youth, as well as the overt disrespect expressed by juveniles for their elders, appeared to Bowen to be evidence of emotional regression in American society over a period of 20 years (from about 1950 to 1970). Bowen drew on this period to suggest a significant drop in the level of differentiation in the population of the United States.

An example that illustrates this pattern of societal regression starts with anxious parents who are overly permissive with their children, who do not provide sufficient structure with regard to school attendance and completion of homework. The school blames the parents and anxiously expels the students who are out of control, rebellious, or delinquent. They are then referred to an anxious Department of Social Services, which may vacillate in the way they deal with them. The parents are too anxious to support an adequate balance of rights and responsibilities in their expectations for their children and neither do the larger societal systems.

In extending the application of chronic anxiety to the concept of differentiation in larger social units, Bowen described the following stressors as being significant and possibly causal in generating societal crises and societal regression: the depletion of natural resources, overpopulation, and the closing of frontiers (see 1978, Chapters 13 and 18).

The Application of Differentiation of Self

Defining a self, or differentiating a self, is an intentional process through which a motivated individual, most often working with a Bowen-trained coach or consultant, works to increase his or her functional level of differentiation, and possibly to increase basic differentiation.[3] Defining a self involves understanding one's position in relation to all significant others in the systems in which one participates and making thoughtful, planned efforts to clarify one's responsible functioning in every significant emotional system of which one is a part. The differentiating or defining-one works to modify self through being present and accounted for—in other words being a responsible participant in all important relationships—and being an individual and a contributing member of the team, especially around significant issues and nodal events in the family, work, and society, in an effort to increase his or her functional level of differentiation, and possibly raise his or her basic level of differentiation of self, even if it is by a small increment.

Bowen's Clinical Approach

Bowen's phrase the *"theoretical-therapeutic* system" was a shorthand expression for how he integrated his observational research, theory, and therapy. The evolution of his therapy and coaching was based on observation, developing a hypothesis, and then applying it clinically. The approach was circular: observation of how individuals and families function, followed by deductive thinking, followed by a clinical hypothesis, followed by objective observation and analysis, followed by a modification of the inadequate hypothesis, and then a formulation of a new principle, clinical intervention or format, or all three.

In a previous section on Bowen's theoretical approach, his basic evolutionary biological view of the human and his family was described. However, although evolutionary biology accounts for the *emotional process* in a human family, Bowen (1981) stated that the *relationship system* accounts for the content. Through Bowen's observations and reflections on client behaviors, expression of feelings, and thinking over many years of clinical practice, and his experience with his own family, he developed a theory and strategies for treating clients. The overall goal is to assist in modifying their life issues through the process of lowering chronic anxiety and raising differentiation of self. Bowen theory relies on observing and describing what individuals and families do and report. The theoretical-therapeutic system uses the descriptive language of everyday life.

From the time Bowen began his research on schizophrenia and the family at NIMH, his basic goals, whether working with the mother and offspring, the nuclear family, the couple, the multifamily groups, or individuals, were to lower anxiety and increase the differentiation of self of motivated individuals and the family as a whole. When anxiety could be reduced, then an increase in the functional level of differentiation, and sometimes in the basic level of differentiation, can take place. Bowen wrote:

> . . . we speak of increasing the level of differentiation. Most of the time this refers to the functional levels of differentiation. If we can control the anxiety, and the reactiveness to anxiety, the functional level will improve. Beyond that I believe it is possible, over a long period of time, to increase the basic level to some degree. Systems therapy cannot remake that which nature created, but through learning how the organism operates, controlling anxiety and learning to

better adapt to the fortunes and misfortunes of life, it can give nature a better chance.

(1978, p. 410)

Kerr has said that increasing differentiation is ". . . a way of thinking that is translated into a way of being . . . thinking differently precedes acting differently" (2009, n.p.). Bowen family systems theory does not view the human predicament in terms of pathology versus health or in terms of discrete, differential medical model diagnosis. The clinical approach of Bowen theory is focused on facilitating the effort the family member makes to deal with emotional process within self and in relation to one's family in the face of anxiety-provoking life situations and nodal events in the present and the future. This focus on emotional process is in stark contrast to a focus on specific symptoms. From the Bowen theory perspective, reducing anxiety predictably leads to the reduction of symptoms. And in turn it leads to the opportunity to work toward becoming a more solid and mature self, more defined and less fused in the family and more present and accounted for in the family.

Bowen family systems therapy is not defined by the number of family members in the therapy room. Family therapy takes place when the thinking process is directed toward the family as an emotional system or unit. From the perspective of Bowen's theoretical-therapeutic system, Bowen family systems therapy is based on the way the therapist or coach *thinks* about the family as a unit, whether the effort is with multiple family members, the two members of the couple, or only an individual family member.

Bowen sought to replace the terms "therapy" and "therapist" and began to use the terms supervisor, consultant, and coach. The terms therapy and therapist can be used interchangeably with coaching and coach.[4]

In Bowen's theoretical-therapeutic system the effort goes into minimizing the transference rather than maximizing it, as was the case in psychoanalytic and other relationship-based psychotherapies. His view was that often the intense transference relationship between the individually oriented therapist and patient created a triangle in which the family of the patient was in the outside position, and the therapist and patient were in the close, inside position of the emotional triangle. From a Bowen theory perspective, therapy that focuses and evokes transference can often increase distance or cutoff between the patient and his or her family. This can solidify the unresolved attachment between the patient and the family, resulting in distant-fusion between the client, his or her parents, and other family members.

The Bowen-trained therapist or coach seeks to adopt a *research* attitude in order to stay out of an overinvolvement in the intensity of the transference with the client. Using the theoretical-therapeutic system of Bowen theory, the therapist or coach draws from his or her experience and knowledge gained from dealing with triangles in his or her own family, in order to keep the work between the client and his or her family.

Understanding the concept of triangles provides a blueprint for reading automatic emotional reactivity in a clinical setting. This allows the coach to control his or her own participation in the emotional process. The effort is to keep the clients relating to their families, *in situ*, working on differentiating a self in his or her own family. This allows the therapist/coach to detriangle from the client(s) and other family members. Bowen stated that the key to staying out of the transference was to understand and apply the process of detriangling.

If the differentiating-one(s) are working actively on the issues within their own family, then transference, positive or negative, will usually not be a problem in their relationship with the therapist or coach. And, on the other side of the coin, if the therapist's or coach's focus is on the client's efforts to seek and improve person-to-person relationships with his or her parents and other significant family members, in the process of defining a responsible self, then positive or negative transference toward the client will usually not be a significant issue.

Bowen's theoretical-therapeutic system differs from other individual and family therapies in preferring to work with the higher functioning individual(s) in the family rather than with the lower functioning individual(s). The Bowen-trained coach or therapist prefers to work with the top of the system—the parents or the most motivated individual—rather than the family member who is the identified patient carrying symptoms or the child who is not a free agent. Bowen also sought to find the leader of the family who would most likely be able to take the first steps toward becoming the differentiating-one in the family. Bowen learned that working with the higher functioning, more motivated leader of the family brings about changes faster than working with the followers and lower functioning individuals. When the former begins to define his or her position, the mature side of other family members begins to emerge and they too begin to define themselves more clearly. Working with the lower functioning individuals in the family takes much longer to bring about change, and may be counterproductive if it intensifies focus on a lower functioning member.

Evolution of Clinical Formats in Bowen Family Systems Theory[5]

In 1954–1955, during Bowen's 1954–1959 NIMH research project on schizophrenia, the initial clinical format was individual therapy for the schizophrenic patient and the mother. The effort was to loosen up the psychological symbiosis between mother and daughter. In 1955 with Bowen's second hypothesis, the family as an emotional unit, the second format was family systems therapy. First it included the parents and the schizophrenic offspring. Shortly thereafter the sibling of the schizophrenic offspring was included in the therapy with the nuclear family; the third format was a combination of the nuclear family format and multiple family group consisting of all the families and staff in a group setting. After transitioning from NIMH to an outpatient setting in 1960, Bowen's fourth format involved the parental couple without the identified patient. This format followed Bowen's development of the concept of the emotional triangle. In this format, the triangled offspring is replaced by the therapist. His or her effort is to avoid becoming triangled. If he got caught in the triangle, he worked to extract himself from the emotional process between the couple, while still maintaining contact with both members of the couple. In 1965 Bowen's fifth format was multiple-family therapy. He began seeing couples in a group, focusing on the relationships within each couple while the other couples observed. This format avoided group process as each couple worked with Bowen separately while the other two couples listened to the therapeutic work. In this way, each couple had the opportunity to learn about family functioning from the other couples' dilemmas and how they were working on them. Also, in the mid-1960s Bowen began coaching individuals in their efforts to differentiate a self in the family, as preparation for having a spouse join the therapy. In 1967 Bowen's sixth format involved coaching individuals. This major transition occurred after he made an important breakthrough in his own differentiation effort in his family of origin in 1967 that same year (Bowen, 1978, pp. 467–528). In these individual coaching sessions the primary focus shifted from the emotional process in the nuclear family and in the marriage to a focus on the family of origin. Bowen considered the last format to be one of his most important contributions to clinical practice.

The two basic formats that Bowen continued for the long term were working with the couple together and coaching individuals. Eventually, in the late 1970s, working with couples, he sometimes split the therapy session, working with one spouse for half an hour while the other listened quietly, and then reversing the process. In this way he could shift the focus to each partner's efforts to work on his or her own differentiation, with the benefit of one spouse learning about the other's efforts.

The Functions of the Therapist or Coach:
Principles and Strategies

Training to be a Bowen therapist/coach involves working on one's own differentiation of self in one's own family; mastering Bowen theory and therapy and internalizing it rather than mimicking it; learning natural systems thinking; and applying it not only in one's own family and the clinical realm, but also in professional relationships and in the larger society in which one lives.

The central goal of the therapist is to support the differentiation of self of his or her client, whether it is an individual, members of a couple, or a larger configuration of family members. It is necessary to lower anxiety for an individual to be able to work on differentiating or defining self in his or her family. Anxiety can be reduced in many ways including: physical exercise, breathing exercises, meditating, playing or listening to music, yoga, and biofeedback or neurofeedback, among other physical, spiritual, or social activities. Primarily, anxiety can be reduced by contact with the coach's calmness and broader perspectives. When anxiety is reduced, symptom reduction automatically takes place. When anxiety is lowered, the motivated individual can begin to separate his or her emotional reactivity from more thoughtful, reflective responses. This enhances the opportunity to learn about the emotional processes in oneself and in one's relationships in the family. At this point the process of increasing functional differentiation can move forward. And, with enough motivation and perseverance, the basic level of differentiation may increase a certain amount.

The principles of functioning for the therapist or the coach seeing a couple are: 1) defining and clarifying the relationship between spouses; 2) seeking to be neutral and objective; 3) detriangling or remaining outside the emotional system of the client's family; 4) taking I-positions; and 5) learning and teaching about how family systems operate.

Defining and Clarifying the Relationship Between Spouses

The application chapters in this volume focus on coaching individuals in the differentiation of self. When coaching or doing therapy with couples working on differentiation of self, defining and clarifying the relationship between the spouses is the starting point for the work.[6] The therapist or coach creates a clinical structure so that both spouses can think about their feelings, rather than expressing them emotionally and therefore creating more reactivity between the two. The latter would enhance emotional fusion expressed in conflict or distancing. The principal method that allows the two spouses or partners to clarify their relationship is to have each of them speak directly to the therapist in a relatively factual and calm voice. The therapeutic principle is to focus on process rather than content and to keep emotional tension low. Typically the therapist or coach elicits a comment from one spouse and then, avoiding the possibility of triangling, the therapist or coach asks the other spouse to respond with his or her thought about the original spouse's comments. When either spouse's responses are minimal, the therapist or coach asks a series of questions to draw out a clearer view of that spouse's thinking.

The process of evoking the couple's thoughts and ideas rather than feelings sets the stage for differentiation of self; they begin to achieve an awareness of self and the other and of their differences that was not previously possible. By doing this ". . . a line of demarcation begins developing between the spouses and they clarify the beliefs and principles that differ one from the other" (Bowen, 1978, p. 225).

Seeking to Be Neutral and Objective

In Bowen's theoretical-therapeutic system, *neutrality* is an attitude that sets the ground for the coach, and the client who is the differentiating-one, to be objective and able to stay outside of the emotional system by detriangling. Neutrality is a principle, but in practice it is an attitude or a way of thinking and speaking. It is the ability to apply systems thinking to the situation at hand. Neutrality involves being able to see the views of each member of the family, whether present or not, without taking sides. The therapist or coach must "think systems" instead of thinking in terms of "cause and effect." This requires the neutral third party to not be polarized on one side of an issue or to be overly connected with one individual rather than another in the family emotional system. A Bowen-trained therapist or coach often uses the phrase "thinking systems," which refers to the ability to move from linear, "cause and effect" thinking to perceiving the interdependence of the family emotional system. An example of this capacity is moving beyond blaming self or others as the cause of a problem and seeing emotional reactivity as the source of difficulties in family relationships.

Bowen developed the strategy of making every family he saw in clinical practice *a research project*. Taking a research stance enhanced his objectivity and neutrality. Understanding and learning about each family was more important than interpreting or taking the "expert fixer" position. Bowen believed that the therapist or coach should have unending Bowen theory-based questions for the family and that the family had to provide their own answers. Each question leads to further questions. It might be said that Bowen's approach to therapy was a Socratic one: questions leading to answers from the family leading to more questions, leading to more hypotheses and observations and answers. It is a circular process that evolves into a partnership between therapist or coach-researcher and the differentiating-one, in a process of discovery for which the differentiating-one is ultimately responsible.

The therapist or coach relies on questions rather than statements or interpretations in order to stimulate family member(s) to use their intellect to rein in emotional reactivity directed at other family and nonfamily members in the service of becoming a more defined self. The following are the kinds of questions a Bowen-trained therapist or coach might ask: "How do you go about getting out of a helpless position?" "Do praise and criticism get in your way?" "It seems like you can't live with your wife, and you can't live without her. How do you understand that contradiction?" "How did you arrive at your goals for yourself?" "How close do you come to reaching the goals you set for yourself?" "What would it take to . . . ?" "What keeps people doing something that doesn't work?" "What would it take to shift that pattern of behavior?" "What are the benefits and costs of appeasing your mother, father, sibling, child, boss . . . ?" "What is the parallel between your paternal grandparents' relationship, and your parents' relationship, and how did it get transferred into the relationship between you and your spouse?"

Systems questioning includes asking the differentiating-one how each member in the family would see a particular issue that is being examined. This allows the differentiating-one to move beyond his or her own subjectivity to see the perspectives of the spouse, children, parents, grandparents, and extended family members. The research perspective and systems questioning enhance the differentiating-one's ability to see both his or her part and the part of others in the family emotional system. They make it more possible to see the "big picture," to increase "systems thinking," and to reduce self-blaming or blaming the other by falling into "cause and effect" thinking. They increase the possibility of obtaining a higher level of functioning.

Detriangling: Seeking to Keep Self Outside the Family Emotional System

The central principle and process of Bowen's theoretical-therapeutic system for the therapist or coach, and for the client who is the differentiating-one(s), is to learn to be on the outside of the emotional stuck-togetherness or oneness of the family through the process of detriangling. Detriangling involves disrupting the stuck homeostasis of an inflexible or rigidly fused and closed family emotional system that is blocking the differentiation process.

The following are two descriptions of the basic principle and process of detriangling from Bowen's (1978) writings:

> . . . the emotional problem between two people will resolve automatically if they can remain in contact with a third person who can remain free of the emotional field between them, while actively relating to each.
>
> (p. 251)

> When there is finally one who can control his emotional responsiveness and not take sides with either of the other two, and stay constantly in contact with the other two, the emotional intensity within the twosome will decrease and both will move to a higher level of differentiation. Unless the triangled person can remain in emotional contact, the twosome will triangle in someone else.
>
> (p. 480)

Bowen became less focused on technique in the 1980s. He expressed concern that there was too much focus on technique rather than on the knowledge of Bowen theory, natural systems theory, and the effort for the therapist or coach to define or differentiate a self in his or her own family. He continued to believe that understanding triangles and detriangling provides the blueprint for modifying a family member's position in the family emotional process.

Strategies that Bowen and other Bowen-trained therapists have used to facilitate detriangling include the use of humor, seriousness, reversal, and putting the other together with the other while putting self outside.

The Use of Humor, Seriousness, and Reversal

The use of humor and reversal are two strategies that can de-intensify an emotionally loaded situation in a family. The *reversal or paradoxical* statement focuses on the opposite side of an issue. The comment neutralizes a polarizing position or statement that is held by one or more family members. These strategies are only effective when the therapist or coach is able to communicate from a neutral perspective and without anger or sarcasm, and they help the coach to detriangle from the family. Bowen sought to find the right balance between humor and seriousness that would communicate to the family that he was not taking their dilemmas too seriously or too lightly (1978, p. 25). He wrote:

> If the family goes too serious, I have an appropriate humorous remark to defuse the seriousness. If the family starts to kid or joke, I have an appropriate serious remark to restore neutrality. An example was a wife going into detail about her critical, nagging, bossy mother. The husband was indicating his agreement. If the therapist got them to believe he also agreed, he would be in the emotional process with them. His comment, "I thought you appreciated your mother's devotion to you," was enough to change the seriousness to a chuckle and defuse the emotional tension.
>
> (1978, p. 313)

A casual comment or reversal is an effective way of defusing or decompressing an emotionally intense situation, helping the therapist or coach maintain a neutral position and offering a clear message to the family that he or she is not overinvolved. If the therapist or coach becomes emotionally overinvolved with the family, the reversal is heard as an expression of sarcasm or hostility, and the effort fails (Bowen, 1978, pp. 251, 313, 315). For example, if the coach says to the husband, who is reacting emotionally to a controlling wife who runs the show, "What keeps you from appreciating how much your wife does for you," the comment may be heard either as hostile or sarcastic if the timing or tone of the reversal is not neutrally expressed by the therapist/coach.

Putting the Other Together With the Other and Putting Oneself Outside

This is a detriangling strategy that Bowen used in his effort to be outside of the emotional oneness of his own family, clinical families, and his professional family. This strategy is utilized in the service of working to be differentiated from the togetherness of the *herd*. The strategy consisted of "taking every person you meet and bringing in a third person. . . . You can get out of the fusion by putting the other together with the other" (Bowen, 1979, videotape). Bowen put each person together with the other in order to detriangle himself. He spent more time getting people to not take his side, rather than seeking alliances.

Bowen gave the following example of "putting the other together with another and putting self outside." His mother would share negative "stories" about his father in letters she wrote to Bowen. He responded in the following manner:

> In the next mail I wrote to my father that his wife had just told me this story about him, and I wondered why she told me instead of telling him. He shared the letter with her, and she fussed about not being able to trust me. Several letters such as this, plus similar exchanges when I was with both parents had been reasonably effective at detriangling me from them. During that period, mother made comments about my reading too much between the lines, and I made comments about her writing too much between the lines.
>
> (1978, p. 506)

Demonstrating Differentiation by Taking I-Positions

The therapist or coach defines him or herself in relation to the families he or she is working with by taking I-positions during the course of therapy/ coaching. From the onset of therapy he or she defines the Bowen theoretical-therapeutic system and how it differs from other theoretical approaches. The I-position is the action manifestation of the underlying force of individuality that counterbalances the force of togetherness. The latter is manifested by We-positions.

Bowen described the I-position in the following way:

> The "I position" defines principle and action in terms of, "This is what I think, or believe" and, "This is what I will do or not do," without impinging one's own values or beliefs on others. It is the "responsible I" which assumes responsibility for one's own happiness and comfort, and it avoids thinking that tends to blame and hold others responsible for one's own unhappiness or failures. The "responsible I" avoids the "irresponsible I" which makes demands on others with, "I want, or I deserve, or this is my right, or my privilege." A reasonably differentiated person is capable of genuine concern for others without expecting something in return, but the togetherness forces treat differentiation as selfish and hostile.
>
> (1978, p. 495)

When the therapist or coach defines his or her own beliefs and principles in the course of therapy or coaching, clients will begin to take I-positions, defining themselves in relation to each other (Bowen, 1978, p. 230). Bowen described the process of differentiation of self in a family as an interlocking process.

> When one member of a family can calmly state his own convictions and beliefs, and take action on his convictions without criticism of the beliefs of others, and without becoming involved in emotional debate, then other family members will start the same process of becoming more sure of self and more accepting of others.
>
> (1978, p. 252)

Learning How Family Emotional Systems Function

The therapist or coach functions as researcher and does not provide answers for the family. He or she has unending questions to ask the family member(s). Bowen proposed to the motivated family member(s) the task of becoming a *research-observer(s)* of his or her own family. A major part of the therapy session is spent on the report of the differentiating-one(s) on the effort(s) to see oneself as he or she functions in the context of the family emotional system. Bowen wrote: "A goal of this therapy is to help the other make a research project out of life" (1978, p. 179). Responsibility for change and the choices to change rest with the family.

Bowen family systems therapy or coaching provides an opportunity for the differentiating-one to incorporate Bowen systems thinking that can guide his or her effort to modify and define self in the family emotional system, and potentially initiate change in the family.

In collaboration with the differentiating-one's providing his or her knowledge and family research, the coach creates a three, or more, generation family diagram.[7] Over time this becomes a fuller map of *who* the family members are in the nuclear family, family of origin, and the extended family; *where* they are geographically located in the past and present; *what* their education and occupation are, as well as psychological, physical, and social problems, birth order, marital/separation/divorce status, and birth and death status; *when* the above events occurred; and *how* the differentiating-one(s) and the other family members fulfill their functioning positions in the family emotional system. Differentiating a self involves understanding one's position in the nuclear family, the family of origin, the extended family, and the functioning positions of all family members that are alive. It includes doing research on and contacting all living family members in person. It involves researching the family members who have died, how they fit into the differentiating-one's multigenerational family, and specifically how this knowledge can inform him or her about how the living family is functioning, and its impact on him or her and his or her impact on the members of the living family.

When anxiety is high in a family, teaching is expressed through I-positions, and the therapist or coach may use parables or displacement material. These consist of stories that describe how other families operate and make efforts to modify similar life situations. When anxiety is low in a family, teaching directly about how family emotional systems operate can be useful. At this point teaching can be directly didactic. Teaching directly, when anxiety is low, is a major part of Bowen family systems therapy or coaching. The initial sessions are devoted to teaching the motivated family member about emotional functioning in family systems, encouraging visits back home to check the accuracy of his or her formulations, doing a multigenerational family history, and defining self in relation to the family in a variety of settings, using different modalities such as letter writing, visits, and phone calls to make one-to-one contact with family members, particularly the differentiating-one's parents. When the therapy or coaching has made sufficient progress and the level of differentiation is rising, the differentiating-one(s) may decide to attend conferences and training sessions on Bowen theory.

Defining a Self in One's Family of Origin and the Extended Family

Bowen's evolution in his theoretical-therapeutic formats led to his focus on coaching motivated individuals in their efforts to define a self in their family of origin and extended family. In his own family he moved from focusing on the primary triangle with his parents and himself to the interlocking triangles within his family of origin. The breakthrough came from his seeing that it is not possible to differentiate a self in any single triangle without a method or strategy for dealing with interlocking triangles.

The Differentiating-One: Principles and Strategies

The functions, principles, and strategies of the client or the differentiating-one, and the therapist or coach are similar and overlap. The coaching that Bowen trainees receive may be individual or in a group setting. The coaching of individual clients followed Bowen's own efforts to apply his understanding of interlocking triangles to his efforts to define himself in his family of origin and extended family (1978, pp. 529–543). He first applied this format with psychiatric residents in 1967. He then began applying it with many of his clients. He found the results to be better than when the focus was on the interdependence in the marriage. Bowen's overall conclusion was as follows:

Families in which the focus is on the differentiation of self in the families of origin automatically make as much or more progress in working out the relationship system with spouses and children as families seen in formal family therapy in which there is a principal focus on the interdependence in the marriage.

(1978, p. 545)

He also continued successfully to focus on both the family of origin effort and the marital relationship with some couples. He believed that:

. . . the extended family approach required far more skill, more continuing work on himself, and more attention to detail than does more conventional therapy. On the other hand, the extended family approach requires less direct time with the family. The frequency of appointments with the extended family approach is determined by the amount of work the family member is able to do between appointments. Some can keep the effort alive and productive as often as once a month. Some have been seen as infrequently as once or twice a year. The over-all results with very infrequent appointments have not been very rewarding. People tend to let the efforts lapse and to make some kind of a visit with their families just before the appointments. Over-all, for a motivated person, half a dozen one-hour appointments a year are more productive than weekly formal family therapy appointments, which focus on the relationship between spouses.

(1978, pp. 546–547)

Many Bowen trainees have found that defining one's self is a lifelong process, often continuing over several decades. The total number of sessions and their frequency is much lower than for many other forms of individual or family therapy. Bowen family systems therapy is best described as a coaching process and with very little transference present; it does not promote dependency on the coach.

Defining a Self in the Family of Origin and the Extended Family: Principles and Strategies

The processes and strategies of the differentiating- or motivated-one are: 1) developing person-to-person relationships; 2) becoming a better observer of self and one's family and controlling one's emotional reactivity; 3) adopting a research attitude and researching one's multigenerational family history; and 4) detriangling from emotional situations through formulating, planning, and taking I-positions in significant emotional triangles. These principles and strategies overlap with those of the coaches or therapists in their efforts to define themselves in relation to their own families.

Developing Person-to-Person Relationships

In person-to-person relationships two people can relate personally to each other about each other, without triangling, talking about others, and without talking about impersonal "things." There are very few people who can maintain a person-to-person relationship for more than a few minutes before their anxiety increases and is expressed in silences, talking about trivial things, or talking about others.

Bowen (1978) often suggested that if one could get a person-to-person relationship with every living member in his or her extended family, this process would help him or her to "grow up" more than anything else he or she could accomplish in life. A lesser goal might be to suggest that people achieve a person-to-person relationship with each parent. However, this is no easy matter. This endeavor will bring out the emotional problems that his or her parents had in their own relationships and the problems they had had in their own families of origin. This is where it can be useful to have a coach who has had experience in work on defining him or herself in his or her own family. Without the help of the coach, an individual can make emotionally based critical decisions that can lead to months of useless dead ends. A coach can help the differentiating-one avoid errors that lead to togetherness and away from differentiation of self. The following are examples of such errors: 1) visiting one's parents with one's nuclear family. It's more effective to go alone to visit one's family instead of going with others. 2) Writing to both parents, in one letter, addressed to "Dear Mom and Dad" is not an effective way to break up the fused amalgam of the parental couple. It is better to write letters to each parent individually in order to avoid conglomerating the parents into the fusion of emotional oneness that impedes personal, one-to-one relationships with each parent as a separate individual.

Becoming a Better Observer and Controlling One's Own Emotional Reactivity

Becoming a better observer and controlling one's own emotional reactivity are interlocking processes. When one becomes a more objective observer in learning more about one's family, emotional reactivity is reduced and this in turn helps one become a better observer. It is a circular process but one that creates a relationship system that is more open, direct, and personal. In Bowen's words:

> One never becomes completely objective and no one ever gets the process to the point of not reacting emotionally to family situations.

A little progress on this helps the trainee begin to get a little "outside" the family emotional system, and this in turn helps the trainee to a different view of the human phenomenon. It enables the observer to get "beyond blaming" and "beyond anger" to a level of objectivity that is far more than an intellectual exercise. It is fairly easy for most people to intellectually accept the notion that no one is to blame in family situations, but the idea remains intellectual until it is possible to know it emotionally in one's own family. The family gains [when] one member is able to relate more freely without taking sides and becoming entangled in the family emotional system.

(1978, p. 541)

Adopting a Research Attitude and Researching One's Multigenerational Family History

Adopting a research attitude and making one's family a research project involves learning how the nuclear family operates in terms of conflict, distance, dysfunction in one spouse, and the family projection process. The same goes for the family of origin, and extended family as far back as the differentiating-one, the researcher, can find the data. Research on triangles in current and past generations, and working toward knowing dead family members can be accomplished by gathering factual information, separating what is known from what is unknown, testing hypotheses, evaluating actions taken, and raising questions for future research. Undertaking this research is an important part of differentiation of self.

Detriangling Self From Emotional Situations

The effort that goes into bringing about personal relationships, learning about the family through observation, and controlling one's own emotional reactiveness can create a more open relationship system. It can recapitulate the family emotional system as it was before the individual left home. In Bowen's words:

> Now it is possible to see the triangles in which one grew up, and to be different in relation to them. The process of detriangling is essentially the same as has been described in doing family therapy with two spouses. . . . The overall goal is to be constantly in contact with an emotional issue involving two other people and self, without taking sides, without counterattacking or defending self, and to always have a neutral response.

(1978, p. 542)

One part of the process of defining oneself is to be more objective and less reactive than one's other family members during discussion of an emotional issue. *The key action in the process of defining one's self is only possible through detriangling in the presence of an emotional issue around which one can relate with two significant family members.* The motivated- or differentiating-one is coached, whenever possible, to go home when there is a significant, nodal event in the family that is likely to bring up serious emotional issues, including a serious illness, a death, holidays, and reunions. These events often generate a level of anxiety that can enhance the opportunity to relate to the family. When a family is very calm, there are few issues around which to relate. The differentiating-one may need to introduce small emotional issues from the past or present, but not use emotional confrontation. The biggest error many people make in working with their family of origin or extended family is to address issues through confrontation, since it generates resistance and a hardening of positions and polarization within the family triangles. Detriangling is more effective in opening up relationships.

Having developed a reasonably good person-to-person relationship inside a single triangle with an issue, and/or in the interlocking triangles, the differentiating-one formulates a detriangling plan, which he or she will seek to implement. Implementation of a detriangling plan involves being able to control one's reactivity, being knowledgeable about the relationship history in one's family, the others' part in the issue or problem, one's own part in that situation, and being objective about the facts that make up the issue or stress in the triangle at hand. For example, there are strategies for dealing with the primary triangle with one's parents when the differentiating-one is living in a different city. If she is closer to her mother and more distant from her father, she may want to be able to develop a deeper relationship with her father, but she finds that telephoning always leads to the mother monopolizing the phone conversation. The client may be coached to find out when and where she could call the father when the mother is not at home. She might find out when the father may be reached outside of the home or by cell phone. The differentiating-one may also choose to write individual, rather than joint letters to each parent as a way of breaking up the parental amalgam in order to get to know each parent as a separate individual.

Planned trips to see one's parents need to take into consideration the amount of time that is designated to spend with them individually and together. If emotional reactivity is high on either the part of one or the other parent or self, a shorter, structured trip will be more successful. If the issue is serious, it should be dealt with individually, and then taken up when the differentiating-one has a good sense of how the other two in the triangle, and the relevant interlocking triangles, will respond to the issue. In this way reactivity from one or both of the others is less likely and one can be more objective about the issues.

The following are some additional guidelines for relating to the family of origin and extended family in the service of differentiation of self:

- Work toward a person-to-person relationship with each person in the family of origin and extended family;
- Recognize that the primary triangle is the most significant relationship in the family; the parents are often an emotionally fused amalgam, with one being the spokesperson;
- When the differentiating-one is "locked into" the parental triangle, sometimes the block can be productively approached through a sibling. This is some sometimes called "detriangling through the backdoor triangle";
- Do not spend too much time differentiating from siblings; it is more useful to go back to the extended family, relating to family members in the parents' generation or, if available, people in the generation before the parents;
- When one or both parents are dead, other living family members can be used to reconstruct an effective family emotional system for differentiating a self;
- Go home frequently and when anxiety is high; the goal is to get as much individual time with each member as possible; it can, however, be difficult getting individuals alone when one is working against family fusion;
- Take responsibility for self in the family system;
- Do the work for self; do not seek to change the family; accept responsibility for self and for being a responsible family member;
- Avoid confrontation; confrontation communicates that the confronter is trying to square the ledger; the expression of negative feelings to counter togetherness usually only leads to short-term if any gains;
- Get information from cousins and other more distant family members; at times, contact with cousins can be more fruitful than contact with the nuclear family; "societies of cousins" can provide a magical connection; if the whole family is dead, go back to friends of your dead family;
- Use approaches specific to explosive and peace/agree families: with peace/agree families one has to stir up a "tempest in a teapot," and in an explosive family, one has to work double-time to find peaceful resolutions (Bowen, 1980).

Summary

This chapter has been a review of the concept of differentiation of self in Bowen family systems theory. It has covered the historical evolution of the concept, the concept itself, and the relationship between the concept of differentiation of self and the other seven concepts that make up the theory. It also described the application to the therapist's/coach's personal effort to be a more solid self and the focus on differentiation of self in clinical practice.

NOTES

1 For a more complete description of Bowen's movement from psychoanalytic to systems theory, from the individual, to the dyad, to the triangle, see Titelman (2008, pp. 3–16).

2 According to Hacking, Thomas Kuhn, in *Scientific Revolutions,* described the term paradigm as being "constituted by various kinds of commitment and practices, among which he emphasizes symbolic generalizations, models and exemplars" (2012, p. xxiv).

3 Bowen (1978, p. 535) wrote that *defining a self* is essentially synonymous with *differentiating a self.* These terms are used interchangeably in this chapter, but differentiating a self is used as the more generic term and defining a self is used to describe the action positions the differentiating-one takes in relation to his or her effort to modify or affirm where he or she stands and or differs on a significant issue, theme, ritual, or nodal event involving parents, important family member(s), or the whole family.

4 The term *therapist* is used more frequently in referring to work with more than one family member in the consultation. The term *coach* is more frequently used in reference to the consultation process with a single member of the family. The term *family therapist* refers to the overall process of Bowen family systems therapy. It describes the therapist's management of self: maintaining an attitude of neutrality and working to stay detriangled, taking I-positions. It also involves teaching one or more family members how the family operates as an emotional system. The term *coaching* refers to the therapist's activity of developing an action plan with an individual family member that involves encouraging the client to observe the functioning of self and other members of the family system, and then coaching the differentiating-one in his or her detriangling efforts and other aspects of differentiating a self. The family member implements this effort outside the coach's consultation office, in direct contact with members of his or her family. Bowen believed that the term *coach* "is best in conveying the connotation of an active expert coaching both individual players and the team to the best of their abilities" (1978, p. 310).

5 For a fuller description of clinical application of Bowen family systems theory, see Bowen's *Family Therapy in Clinical Practice* (1978) and Titelman's *Clinical Application of Bowen Family Systems Theory* (1998).

6 See Bowen (1978, pp. 223–254 and pp. 313–315) for more detail on the therapist's function of defining and clarifying the relationship between spouses in the format of seeing the couple.

7 See Appendix I, A Key for the Family Diagram and Emotional Process Symbols. Bowen coined the term *family diagram* in 1954 when he was the director of his research project on schizophrenia and the family at the NIMH. The term *family genogram* was coined by Phillip Guerin, a student of Murray Bowen and the director of the Center for Family Learning in Rye, New York. Monica McGoldrick (1986) popularized the term *genogram* in her writings. Bowen did not like the term *genogram* because of its association with the term *gene.* He believed that family patterns and processes revealed were based on the transmission of emotional patterns rather than genetic patterns.

REFERENCES

Ackerman, N. W. (1956). Interlocking pathology in family relationships. In S. Rado and G. Daniels (Eds.), *Changing concepts of psychoanalytic medicine* (pp. 135–150). New York: Grune and Stratton.

Ackerman, N. W. (1958). *The psychodynamics of family life*. New York: Basic Books.

Bateson, G., Jackson, D. D., Haley, J. & Weakland, J. (1956). Toward a theory of schizophrenia. *Behavioral Science, 1*, 251–164.

Bowen, M. (1972). Toward the differentiation of self in one's family of origin. In *Georgetown Family Symposia: A collection of selected papers* (Vol. 1, 1971–1972). Washington, DC: Georgetown University Family Center.

Bowen, M. (1976). Family theory in the practice of psychotherapy. In P. Guerin (Ed.), *Family therapy: Theory and practice* (pp. 335–348). New York: Gardner Press.

Bowen, M. (1978). *Family therapy in clinical practice*. New York: Jason Aronson.

Bowen, M. (1979). "Triangles and differentiation." Videotape. Western Pennsylvania Family Center, Pittsburgh, PA. (Producer).

Bowen, M. (1980). "Defining a self in one's family of origin—Part II." Videotape. Georgetown Family Center, Washington, DC. (Producer).

Bowen, M. (1981). "A Day with Murray Bowen, MD." Lecture sponsored by Family Living Consultants of the Pioneer Valley, Northampton, MA, November 4, 1981.

Boyd, C. (Ed.). (2007). *Commitment to principles: The letters of Murray Bowen, MD*. Unpublished manuscript.

Dobzhansky, T. & Hecht, M. K. (1968). On some fundamental concepts of evolutionary biology. In *Evolutionary biology* (Vol. 2, 1st ed., pp. 1–34). New York: Appleton-Century-Crofts.

Fromm-Reichman, F. (1950). *Principles of intensive psychotherapy*. Chicago: University of Chicago Press.

Giorgi, A. (1970). *Psychology as a human science: A phenomenologically based approach*. New York: Harper and Row.

Guerin, P. (1976). *Family therapy: Theory and practice* (pp. 335–348). New York: Gardner Press.

Hacking, I. (2012). Introductory essay. In T. S. Kuhn, *The structure of scientific revolutions* (pp. vii–xxxvii). Chicago: University of Chicago Press.

Hill, L. B. (1955). *Psychotherapeutic intervention in schizophrenia*. Chicago: University of Chicago Press.

Jackson, D. D. & Bateson, G. (1956). Toward a theory of schizophrenia. *Behavioral Science, 1*, 251–254.

Kerr, M. E. (2009, May 11). *Differentiation of self*. Webcast conference.

Kerr, M. E. & Bowen, M. (1988). *Family evaluation: An approach based on Bowen theory*. New York: W. W. Norton.

Lidz, T., Cornelison, A. & Terry, D. (1957). The interfamilial environment of schizophrenic patients; II marital schism and marital skew. *American Journal of Psychiatry, 114*, 241–248.

McGoldrick, M. (1986). *Genograms in family assessment*. New York: W. W. Norton.

MacLean, P. D. (1990). *The triune brain in evolution: Role in paleocerebral functions*. New York: Plenum Press.

Papero, D. V. (1990). *Bowen family systems theory*. Boston: Allyn and Bacon.

Rakow, C. (2004, March). Contributions to Bowen family systems theory from the NIMH project. In *The importance of research for family theory and therapy* (pp. 1–16). Conference sponsored by the North Shore Counseling Centre, Vancouver, Canada.

Sykes-Wylie, M. (1991). Family therapy's neglected prophet. *The Family Therapy Networker*, March/April, 25–37, 77.

Titelman, P. (Ed.). (1998). *Clinical applications of Bowen family systems theory perspectives.* Binghamton, NY: The Haworth Press.

Titelman, P. (Ed.). (2008). *Triangles: Bowen family systems theory perspectives.* Binghamton, NY: The Haworth Press.

Toman, W. (1969). *Family constellation* (2nd ed.). New York: Springer.

Whitaker, C. A. (1967). The growing edge in techniques of family therapy. In J. Haley and L. Hoffman (Eds.), *Techniques of family therapy* (pp. 260–265). New York: Basic Books.

Wynne, L., Ryckoff, I. & Hirsch, S. H. (1958). Pseudo-mutuality in schizophrenia. *Psychiatry Interpersonal & Biological Processes, 21,* 205–220.

2

EMOTION AND INTELLECT IN
BOWEN THEORY

Daniel V. Papero

This chapter will discuss three salient areas related to Bowen's theoretical formulation of the ability of the individual to distinguish between the emotional and intellectual systems, an essential component of differentiation of self. The first area will address what Bowen actually proposes about the emotional and intellectual systems and the challenge of differentiation of systems for the individual. The second will review relevant findings from research in neuroscience that provide empirical support for Bowen's viewpoint. The third will review findings that point to grey or still-to-be-resolved issues regarding the integration of emotion and cognition.

What Bowen Proposes

The Scale of Differentiation

The concept of the scale of differentiation of self lies at the heart of Bowen theory. The theory proposes a range or continuum of an individual's variation around a specific variable, the ability of the individual to distinguish between intellectual process and the feeling process (Bowen, 1978, p. 355). The concept rests on research observations of families with a schizophrenic family member initially and subsequently observed in all families. Bowen describes the research observation in the following manner:

> Early in the research, we found that the parents of schizophrenic people who appear on the surface to function well, have difficulty distinguishing between the subjective feeling process and the more objective thinking process. This is most marked in a close personal relationship.
> (Bowen, 1978, p. 355)

Bowen often used somewhat different terms to convey this idea, substituting for "thinking" the term *intellectual system* and for "feeling" the term *emotional system*. Bowen views the intellectual system as comprising the functions of the brain that produce logic, reasoning, and analysis, and the emotional system as comprising the functions of the brain that govern the automatic, generally non-conscious activities of the organism from the functioning of individual cells to the instinctive responses of the complete organism to environmental challenge and opportunity.

The ultimate value of the ability to distinguish between thinking and feeling systems (or intellectual and emotional systems) lies in the person's ability to integrate these systems effectively. Both play important roles in the behavior of the individual. The feeling system provides motivational energy and sets up judgments or biases based on previous experiences that assist (under favorable conditions) the person's effective decision-making. The thinking system provides a more objective process of collecting factual information and applying the processes of logic and reason to an analysis of a situation requiring a decision. When integrated well, both systems operate as critical components of decision-making processes.

Bowen notes, however, that when the ability to distinguish between thinking and feeling, and ultimately to utilize both effectively in decision-making, has not developed fully, the person displays a tendency to decide and behave on the basis of feeling or emotion predominantly (Bowen, 1978, p. 162ff). Such a person is thought to have a lower level of basic differentiation of self than a person whose development of both systems has been more robust and complete. The latter is thought to have a higher level of differentiation of self. When deciding and behaving under the influence of the dominant emotional system, the person is described as "emotionally reactive." Bowen also notes that anxiety exerts an erosive effect on the ability to distinguish between thinking and feeling. Consequently, depending upon the degree or intensity of anxiety, a person with a higher level of differentiation can also lose the ability to effectively utilize the thinking system, resulting in decision-making and behavior that reflect predominantly the influence of the feeling system. The person becomes emotionally reactive.

The Forces for Togetherness and Individuality

Bowen's observation that people's ability to distinguish between the two systems (thinking and feeling) declined in close personal relationships requires further discussion. He proposes that the individual experiences the tug between two powerful composite forces. The togetherness forces stem from the human need for connection and closeness to other people. The human desire for closeness, harmony, approval, love, and to be an accepted member of the group (family, community, etc.) reflects the influence of the togetherness forces. The individuality force, on the other hand, reflects the innate desire (Bowen uses the term *drive*) of the person to live a productive and relatively autonomous life, free from the dictates or pressures of the group (Bowen, 1978, p. 277ff). The forces are built into the individual, instinctive and in that sense emotional.

Each person in a family develops a balance between these two sets of forces that exert significant influence on the individual's ability to utilize thinking and feeling cooperatively and effectively. For example, this is reflected in the degree to which one feels the pressure to accommodate to the wishes and dictates, among other pressures, of others versus the degree to which one feels the pressure to pursue one's own self-determined objectives. The family develops a balance between the forces as well that constitutes a norm for the group and serves as an expectation for individual behavior (how much individual difference the other family members will tolerate).

Anxiety places an erosive pressure on the person's ability to utilize the thinking system effectively. In close personal relationships, anxiety transfers rapidly between participants. The effect is twofold. On the one hand, with the transfer of anxiety, the person's ability to utilize the balanced relationship between emotion and intellect is challenged. On the other hand, the anxious relationship partner(s) will place a greater demand for togetherness (or, said differently, will tolerate less individuality) on the person.

Emotion in Bowen Theory: Understanding Bowen Theory's Use of the Term Emotional System

As used in Bowen theory, the term *emotional system*, and by inference *emotion*, possesses broad boundaries. Bowen suggests, for example, that the term can be applied to plants as well as to animals and to single-celled forms like bacteria. In these areas the term refers to the force or energy that both produces and results from the interaction between discrete living entities and between a living thing and its environment.

Bowen notes that a number of definitions of emotion exist and does not supply one of his own. Instead he describes the domain of the emotional system as follows.

> Operationally I regard the emotional system as something deep that is in contact with cellular and somatic processes, and a feeling system as bridge that is in contact with parts of the emotional system on one side and with the intellectual system on the other.
>
> (Bowen, 1978, pp. 158–159)

In this usage, the term *emotional system* clearly refers to a property or characteristic of the individual organism. But the term also applies to the processes of interaction between and among individuals in a relationship system, for example the emotional system of the family.

The role of the emotional system in the direction of the individual becomes evident in behavior, particularly in terms of behavior expressed in relationship to others:

> For the purposes of this theoretical-therapeutic system, I think of the family as a combination of 'emotional' and 'relationship' systems. The term *emotional* refers to the force that motivates the system and *relationship* to the ways it is expressed. Under relationship would be subsumed communication, interaction, and other relationship modalities.
>
> (Bowen, 1978, p. 158)

In the years that have elapsed since Bowen formulated his notion of the emotional system, scientists have proposed new definitions of emotion. Each definition differs to some degree from the others, but common themes emerge. Nesse refers to emotions as "specialized modes of operation shaped by natural selection" that facilitate the organism's capacity to adapt to both threats and opportunities in the environment (Nesse, 1990, p. 268). Panksepp points to emotions as "psychoneural processes" that influence the strength and patterning of behavior in the interactive process between animals and between the individual and objects in the environment (Panksepp, 2004, p. 48). Both definitions convey the notion of inherited responses that facilitate adaptation to challenging environmental situations, and each would fit nicely into Bowen theory's understanding of emotion and its function.

Intellect in Bowen Theory: Understanding Bowen's Use of the Term Intellectual System

Bowen explained what he meant by the term *intellectual system* in the following manner.

> The *intellectual system* is a function of the cerebral cortex which appeared last in man's evolutionary development, and is the main difference between man and the lower forms of life. The cerebral cortex involves the ability to think, reason, and reflect, and enables man to govern his life, in certain areas, according to logic, intellect, and reason.
>
> (Bowen, 1978, p. 356)

All of the functions Bowen notes above rest upon processes in the brain generally referred to as *cognitive* or *cognition*. LeDoux (1994) uses the term to refer to "a group of related but diverse information-processing functions, including sensory processing, perception, imagery, attention, memory reasoning, and problem-solving" (p. 216). Many researchers would add decision-making to this list of functions. The cognitive processes are thought to heavily involve various sections of the frontal lobes of the brain in order to carry out these functions. In essence Bowen's concept of differentiation of self can be understood as referring to the degrees of integration between cognitive and emotional systems and the individual's ability to use cognitive processes to become aware of the distinction between emotional and intellectual processes in self and, when appropriate, to regulate the emotional reactivity to serve a cognitively determined goal.

Bowen Theory and Science

Intellect-Emotion and Science

In the five decades since Bowen formulated his theory, research on the structures and functions of the human brain and nervous system has progressed rapidly. This broad area of research, referred to generally as neuroscience, includes the work of many disciplines from neurochemistry to experimental psychology.

The Bowen theory generally follows the assumption that a set of basic emotions exists, and this corresponds to a viewpoint that has persisted at least since the time of Darwin.[1] The idea of a set of basic emotions posits that each emotion relies on a neural program that is hardwired at birth and is homologous with the circuitry in other mammals (Panksepp, 2004). The output of the activation of such a basic emotion circuit is an automatic process of hormonal, muscular, and autonomic effects. The operation or unfolding of a basic emotion circuit can be influenced experientially.[2] Some researchers have searched for distinctive physiology or signature for each discrete emotion, but the identification of physiological signature has proved elusive (Barrett, Ochsner, and Gross, 2007, p. 178).[3]

In addition, the idea of basic emotion posits the existence of a control system that can operate to modify the emotion that has been generated. Generally that control system is thought to be the cognitive system. For example, one of the principal elements in the developing regulation of emotion by the infant is the ability to focus attention, a cognitive process. That ability to utilize attentional control reflects the development of the cognitive system in the infant and emerges fairly early in development (Bell and Wolfe, 2007). Attentional control serves a similar function for the self-regulation of adults.

The concept of dual systems of cognition (with intellectual activity—the ability to reason, analyze, create, and perform sequences or steps, and to solve problems—depending heavily on cognitive systems) and emotion found in current discussions of brain functioning fits closely with Bowen's conceptions of the interplay between emotion and intellect in human functioning.

Researchers for decades have viewed emotions as originating in the areas of the brain referred to as the limbic area or limbic association cortex, areas below the neocortex including the amygdala, the hippocampus, the hypothalamus, the basal ganglia, and related structures.[4] Hence, emotions are believed able to exert "bottom-up" regulatory control of the brain. In contrast, the centers of cognition are generally thought to lie in the frontal lobes, the top of the brain from an anatomical viewpoint, and correspondingly cognitive control of the brain is referred to as "top-down."

Although Bowen theory does not specifically address the processes of development, its concept of multigenerational transmission that results in individual variation in degree of differentiation of self clearly implies processes affecting individual development. Pechtel and Pizzagalli (2011) outline five principles of brain development in humans: 1) human brain development is nonlinear; 2) higher order association cortices develop only after lower-order sensorimotor cortices have matured in structure and function; 3) ontogeny recapitulates phylogeny (last to mature are the most recent from an evolutionary point of view); 4) brain development is guided by genes but shaped by environment; and 5) trajectories of brain development differ for males and females. Because of this uneven developmental process, shifts in context, events, and processes occurring at different times in development can affect different brain regions and their functional coordination and can result in varying capabilities and behavior among individuals.

Intellect, Emotion, and the Developmental Process of Differentiation of Self

The effect of these principles, taken as a whole, provides a foundation for understanding the great range of variation in brain development among individuals, ultimately expressed in brain functioning and in behavior. The development of the interplay and coordination between emotional and cognitive systems are particularly relevant to the concept of differentiation of self. Principles 1, 2, and 4 form a framework for a general understanding of how variation in the development and coordination of these systems might occur. Various differences in environmental influences at any given point in the development trajectory can result in outcome variation in terms of the interplay between cognition and emotion.

Because the development of the cognitive control processes in the human brain occurs later in development than those underlying emotional response, blockages or interruptions to that developmental process can result in decreased cognitive capacity and a decreased capacity to exert cognitive control processes over emotion. This potential variation in cognitive ability among individuals may provide a partial explanation for Bowen's observation of individual differences referred to as differentiation of self.

That such developmental disruption can occur has been well documented in the situation of children exposed to early life stress (ELS). Smaller intercranial volume, reduced hemispheric integration, and a smaller corpus callosum as well as reduced hippocampal volume have been associated with ELS (Pechtel and Pizzagalli, 2011, p. 58). Additionally differences in language, memory/learning, and attention have been noted between children experiencing ELS and those who did not.

Bowen's initial formulation of the processes involved in the transfer of differentiation of self focused on the intensity of the relationship between the mother and her offspring, a process he called a symbiosis (Bowen, 1978, p. 4). The intensity of attachment rather than the type of attachment was thought to be the active process leading to a blocked developmental course for differentiation of self. The formation of the symbiosis should not be seen as something the mother does to the child for which she should be blamed. Rather the symbiosis is the natural state of the relationship during pregnancy and at birth and resolves slowly over the period of development as mother and child separate from one another. A vast number of factors help to intensify the naturally occurring bonding between mother and infant and to work against its resolution across developmental time. Cross-generational factors (the developmental conditions the mother faced and how her mother parented, conditions faced by the family in earlier generations, the context of development, and other factors) and current factors (difficulty of pregnancy, congenital conditions including illness, the state of the family during pregnancy and birth, among others) all combine to influence the intensity of the attachment.

From this perspective, Bowen theorists view maternal neglect and abuse, often cited in research on the adverse effects of the early developmental environment, as reflecting an intense attachment with a negative emotional valence. Rather than the absence of attachment or the particular type of attachment seen in neglect and abuse, Bowen theory focuses on the intensity of the attachment and the extreme discomfort for each party that results in neglect or abuse. To use a metaphor to describe the process, the parent and child seem allergic to one another.

Bowen observed that variation in differentiation of self among siblings could occur in the absence of any indication of adverse life experience with no evidence of parental neglect or abuse. Again he proposed that the active ingredient was the intensity of attachment, this time without the intense negative emotion. He posited that the anxiety in the parent, generally the mother, when focused on the child, could block the child's developmental course toward differentiation of self. Instead of neglect or abuse, an overinvolvement of the parent, often with a positive emotional tone but with underlying anxiety in the parent, could also block the child's progression towards differentiation of self.

Thus, Bowen's concept of differentiation of self posits a naturally occurring developmental process resulting in variation among individuals, not only variation related to early trauma or ELS. Nevertheless, research on the potential effects of ELS does underscore a basic assumption of the Bowen theory, that the effects of the developmental process can result in differing degrees of integration of emotional and cognitive functions in humans resulting in differing degrees of ability to use cognitive processes to regulate emotional functioning.

The Family Emotional Unit and the Context of Development

From his earliest work at the National Institute of Mental Health, Bowen came to realize that the family operated or functioned as an emotional unit. Emotion provided the energy that fueled relationships. In the family, certain relationship patterns emerged when the family became more anxious or tense. He incorporated these predictable patterns into the concept of nuclear family emotional process. Conflict between people, distance, a process of what he called reciprocal over- and underfunctioning, and the focus of the parents on a particular child comprise the patterns included in this concept. In addition he observed that two-person units or systems become inherently unstable when exposed to the pressure of prolonged and/or increasing tension. Under these conditions the twosome expanded by drawing in a third, creating a relationship process among three that he referred to as triangling. Bowen considered this observation important enough to be formalized as one of the eight concepts of his theory, the triangle.

In essence, Bowen proposed that the family emotional unit played a major role in regulating the behaviors of individual members of the family unit. The family could be considered an emotional system or field that could carry a degree of tension that varied in response to relationship interaction within the family and in response to external conditions created in the broader society in which the family was embedded. The family tension could shift frequently and rapidly or be more inherent and persistent. In addition the family emotional unit could carry a valence or tone of pleasure or discomfort. This tone could be easily changeable or more doggedly consistent and chronic to some degree linked to the level and chronicity of tension in the family system.

Furthermore, Bowen's research led him to conclude that elements of the family process were transmitted cross-generationally, passed from parents to offspring with modest variation among siblings. Such small variation among siblings could produce quite varied behavior and degrees of functioning and form the basis for the next generation's variation in degree of differentiation of self.

Essentially this concept proposes that the family—parents and siblings primarily, extended family additionally—forms a major if not the principal context of individual development. That context results in the shaping of the individual along many dimensions, including the interplay between the intellect (cognition) and emotion.

In light of the processes that link general emotional responsiveness in the infant to specific stimuli, the context of individual development assumes great importance. The earliest forms of the regulation of that responsiveness also emerge in this context. Bowen theorists propose that family forms the initial and most enduring context for the person across the lengthy period of development. The relationships of the family, particularly to the caregiver(s), shape the responses of the infant, establishing reciprocally the reactive processes between parent and child. These earliest interactions rapidly expand to include siblings and other family members of the immediate nuclear and extended families. The broader social environment (school, friendship, and organizational networks) comes later and builds upon the frameworks of reactivity and self-regulation already developed in the context of the family.

Boyce and Ellis (2005) and Ellis and Boyce (2008) have proposed a new theoretical perspective on the role of context in development particularly of the stress response in humans,[5] highlighting the idea of ". . . adaptive phenotypic plasticity, the capacity of a single genotype to support a range of phenotypes in response to particular ecological conditions that recurrently influenced fitness during a species' evolutionary history" (Ellis and Boyce, 2008, p. 183).[6] Focusing on the connection between early life experience and stress reactivity, the authors argue that intense stress reactivity may form ". . . an enhanced, neurobiologically mediated sensitivity to context, or *biological sensitivity to context* (BSC)" (Ellis and Boyce, 2008, p. 183).

Observing that children with a highly reactive stress response express a high incidence of symptomatology when raised in adverse environments but very low rates when raised with much support and in low-stress conditions, Boyce and Ellis point out the obvious—high-stress reactivity is disadvantageous under some environmental conditions or contexts and advantageous under others. They point out that although many studies show an association between early life adversity and high-stress reactivity, highly protective environments also produce children with high-stress reactivity.[7]

This latter point appears relevant to Bowen's observation that an intense, positively valenced, but anxious fusion between parent and child can lead to a low level of differentiation and functioning difficulties as well as the effects of adversity. Bowen theory proposes that low levels of differentiation of self can also spring from family environments that show no apparent adversity. The theory focuses on the intensity of the attachment between child and caregiver and the degree to which a caregiver directs an anxious focus to the child—worrying about, attempting to protect, and so forth. The effort to protect the child from environmental threats, whether real or imagined by the caregiver, provides a link to the work of Ellis and Boyce, who demonstrate that a highly protective environment can produce high-reactive children. So long as the environment remains supportive, high reactivity conveys advantages to the individual, but in adverse environments the reverse is the case. Boyce and Ellis also note that low-reactive children seem much less responsive to the environment. Bowen often observed that not all children raised in adverse environments display problems in functioning. This inherent trait possessed by some could be an important element of what Bowen referred to as the basic level of differentiation.

The increasing literature from animal research and human research also suggests that children can be buffered to some degree from the adverse effects of the developmental environment through the availability of supportive relationships and structures as well as environmental enrichment of different sorts. Boyce and Ellis conclude that constitutional factors interact with environmental factors continuously in a process that influences gene expression resulting in phenotypic variation alongside the associative learning effects long described in developmental psychology.

The broad field of epigenetics, generally defined as the study of heritable changes in the functioning of genes that occur without changes in the DNA of the organism, has exploded in the past decade and may provide insight with regard to the molecular mechanisms involved in individual variation. In the broadest sense, epigenetic research explores the effects of the environment on the expression of genomic material. The neuroscientist Michael J. Meaney of McGill University succinctly describes the approach in the following quotation: "This approach envisions development as an active process of adaptation that occurs as a function of the continuous dialogue between the genome and its environment" (Meaney, 2010, p. 42). The processes involved in epigenetic modification of an organism are complex but increasingly well understood. They include a series of changes that occur in the transcription of genes into proteins. In essence genes are turned on or silenced in the process of adaptation to environmental conditions.[8]

Although discoveries from research on epigenetics cannot be used to support or prove the Bowen theory, they do indicate that the environment of development, particularly the relationships that surround the individual during development, can and do influence the individual phenotype. This sort of cross-generational transmission that is not hereditary in the strict genetic sense shapes systems within the individual that are thought to be related to the complex interplay of emotion and intellect within the individual. In that sense, therefore, epigenetic mechanisms can provide a partial explanation of how individual variation in the interplay of emotion and intellect can arise in a human family context, that is how variation in the degree of differentiation of self can be shaped.

Bowen proposed, however, that important developmental effects (anxiety, difficulty in self-regulation, symbiotic attachment) can arise from too much mothering or caregiving without any form of abuse or neglect involved. He incorporated his observations on this process in the concept of the family projection process. Aside from Fairbank's and McGuire's (1988) report of the effects of protective mothering, little research attention has addressed this set of observations until recently, when Boyce and Ellis (see previous) proposed the idea of biological sensitivity to context.

Two studies provide examples of the effects of early adversity that does not fall into the category of abuse. In a sample of children drawn from the Catholic school system of Montreal, Canada, Lupien et al. reported that children with a low socioeconomic status (SES) showed significantly higher levels of salivary cortisol (an indicator of elevated stress) compared with children with moderate SES (Lupien, Kind, Meaney, and McEwen, 2000). Furthermore this group found that the children's cortisol levels significantly related to their mother's depressive symptomatology.[9] In another sort of study, Flinn reported that children living in stable family environments displayed significantly lower cortisol levels than children living in unstable environments (Flinn, 1999).

Bowen's discovery of the family emotional unit or system, creating an emotional field that regulates to a significant degree the behavior of individual members, establishes the family unit as the initial environment for development to which the infant must adapt across developmental time. The interaction between the child and the family field, primarily the parents initially but including siblings and others, allows for the possibility of epigenetic modification of the genome of both infant and family members, potentially leading to variation in degree of differentiation of self.

As noted previously, the Bowen theory proposes anxiety as a variable that significantly influences the functioning of the individual and of the family unit. The theory posits that a condition called *chronic anxiety* can develop. Bowen described chronic anxiety in the following way: "When anxiety increases and remains chronic for a certain period, the organism develops tension, either within itself or in the relationship, and the tension results in symptoms or dysfunction or sickness" (Bowen, 1978, pp. 361–362).

Bowen's use of the term *tension* provides a bridge to the active field of stress research. Among the consequences of the activation of the stress are muscle tension, vigilance, and rapid and intense behavioral reactivity. The person often describes him- or herself as tense. One can infer, therefore, that chronic stress is a component of chronic anxiety. The linkage between stress, particularly chronic, and health outcomes has received much attention. Sterling and Eyer (1988) introduced the term *allostasis* to indicate the processes by which the body responds to daily challenges and maintains homeostasis. The concept of allostatic load proposed by Bruce McEwen refers to the wear and tear that results from either too much stress or from inefficient management of allostasis, such as not turning off the response when it is no longer needed (McEwen, 2007, p. 880). Shonkoff et al. describe allostatic load and its effects in the following way.

> . . . under circumstance of challenge, activation of stress management systems in the brain results in a highly integrated repertoire of responses involving secretion of stress hormones, increases in heart rate and blood pressure, protective mobilization of nutrients, redirection of blood perfusion to the brain, and induction of vigilance and fear. These neurobiological responses are essential and generally protective, but when activated persistently under circumstances of chronic or overwhelming adversity, they can become pathogenic.
>
> (Shonkoff, Boyce, and McEwen, 2009, p. 2253)

Conditions of chronic stress during an individual's developmental period (including prenatally) have been linked to a host of effects, including influences on cognitive and emotional development. The link between early life stress and subsequent symptomatology in adult life has been well established. Shonkoff et al. (2009, p. 2253) propose two pathways: 1) accumulating damage to systems over time, and 2) biological embedding of adversities during sensitive developmental time. They suggest that biological embedding occurs as evolved mechanisms monitor the environment of development from the prenatal period onward, adjusting set points within important brain circuits. Although these authors highlight the role of adversity in creating these two pathways, the overall point that environmental conditions during development can have long-term effects on the individual seems most relevant to Bowen's idea of the development of differentiation of self and the multigenerational transmission of this important set of characteristics and abilities.

The effects of anxiety and stress on a person are well understood. Sensitivities to environmental stimuli intensify, cognition initially sharpens and becomes narrowly focused on the perceived threat, and behavior becomes more automatic and stereotypic, less nuanced and flexible. Bowen's proposal that anxiety can become chronic suggests that chronically anxious people display these characteristics more continuously than do less chronically anxious people, and that they reflect this condition in the physiological being.

Allostatic overload in animal models results in morphological changes in areas of the prefrontal cortex and the amygdala, potentially compromising executive functions and memory and resulting in increased levels of anxiety and aggression (McEwen, 2007, p. 881). Stress reactivity affects memory and learning. LeDoux and Phelps (2008) point out that moderate levels of stress hormones assist the establishment of declarative memory for events, but high levels of stress hormones can impair the creation of such memories. They go on to propose that during periods of intense stress the formation of conscious memories is impaired but the formation of non-conscious memories is enhanced. The effects of the stress hormone cortisol on specific regions of the hippocampus have been well documented and are thought to play a major part in such memory conditions (McEwen and Sapolsky, 1995).

The amygdala has also received much attention from researchers. Under conditions of acute and chronic stress, the amygdala can become hyperaroused, resulting behaviorally in heightened vigilance and reactivity. The connections between the amygdala and the prefrontal cortex also undergo morphological change, losing essential neurons and dendrites (Roozendaal, McEwen, and Chattarji, 2009). The combination of an aroused amygdala and an underactivated prefrontal cortex can provide one of the mechanisms by which emotion can override intellect and can also provide a pathway developmentally that can allow an individual to emerge from the developmental period with a lower level of basic differentiation of self.

Discussion

As with almost any aspect of research, no study or even group of studies can be considered fully explanatory or proof of a theoretical viewpoint. The study of cognition and emotion crosses over many disciplines with much active discussion and many differing viewpoints. For starters, no generally accepted definition of emotion exists, nor can one find similarly an accepted definition of cognition. The study of the interplay between the two processes (emotion and cognition) faces daunting conceptual and methodological challenges.[10]

Bowen theory's concept of the multigenerational transmission process and its direct relationship to the development of a degree of differentiation of self provides one area for further research. Although current research suggests epigenetic processes that may influence the development of differentiation of self in a child, the precise mechanisms of the process remain unclear. How specifically does it work? Bell and Wolfe (2007) point out that the processes of the development between cognition and emotion with respect to self-regulation can be complex. Processes of cognitive and emotional development can become increasingly reciprocal over developmental time, suggesting that the two systems function as a whole at least some if not all of the time, each exerting regulatory influence on the other. Bell and Wolfe posit a parental influence, at least in their schematic of the process, without specifying the particulars of that influence. What is the role of family emotional process in that development?

Even more challenging is the question of the actual process of interaction between cognition and emotion. As Panksepp (2004, p. 47) points out, "cognition and emotion are completely blended in mature psychological experience. . . ." Nevertheless he argues that cognition and affect represent two different, interactive aspects of brain organization. Affective (emotional) variables clearly can effect cognitive processes (specifically interpretation, judgment, decision-making, and reasoning). A view is emerging that cognitive and emotional functions are always interactive, with each able to influence the other. The effect of anxiety on cognitive processes has been most studied. Do other emotions besides anxiety/fear have similar effects on cognitive processes? The answer appears to be yes, but much remains to be explored. For example, studies on sadness report a somewhat different influence on cognitive processes. Sadness does not seem associated with an interpretive bias but does result in more careful and systematic processing of information. From their review of the research on cognition and emotion, Blanchette and Richards (2010) propose that emotion interacts and influences four types of processes that are component mechanisms of cognition:

1) Basic attentional effects;
2) Priming of concepts and knowledge structures;

3) Computational capacity;
4) Reflective processes.

Each of these can be considered an aspect of the intellectual system as Bowen uses the term, and the extent of emotional involvement in them on a non-conscious level highlights the interdependence of the two systems.

That emotion can influence intellect is not, however, the question. Bowen theory suggests that the intellectual processes can be utilized to observe and ultimately regulate emotional processes. More precisely Bowen theorists propose that a person can become aware of emotional processes, not just embody them, and can use that awareness to regulate and/or reduce their influence on cognitive processes and ultimately behavior. But which aspects of cognitive process remain automatic (outside awareness), and can those aspects be brought into awareness?

Studies of emotion regulation begin to address the question of how cognitive processes can regulate emotion. Of particular interest to students of Bowen theory, they suggest that the area of goal-oriented or directed emotion regulation has relevance to the intellectual regulation of emotion. Goals influence the processes of attention, of the knowledge processes of the brain applied to the interpretation stimuli and emotional responses, and even of bodily expressions of emotion. Another area of interest has been called person-oriented emotion regulation.

Particularly vexing to a Bowen theorist is the assertion that emotion regulation can be context sensitive. It sounds very much like Bowen's idea of pseudo-self, a blending of the person into the relationship context, deriving guidance from that context and avoiding thinking for self, which would disturb the relationship context. Under such conditions it would seem that the cognitive processes serve the emotionally based processes of fitting in, of being like the group, and so on. Can this be an example of the set of conditions in which the intellectual system serves the goals of the emotional system, in contrast to the intellectual system monitoring and correcting the emotional directions that lead one away from the thoughtful and principled position of the solid self into the pseudo-self?

These and many other questions emerge from this complicated and fascinating world of research on the interaction of emotion and cognition. So far Bowen's formulation of the interplay between emotion and intellect that forms the basis of differentiation of self appears to be generally consistent with the emerging knowledge from these broad areas of neuroscience. This consistency should be reassuring to clinicians who base their clinical approaches to families on the Bowen theory. That consistency, however, should not lead to complacency. Bowen pressed his students to think—and keep on thinking— and to base their ideas on solid factual evidence. That remains a worthy goal as the amount and complexity of research increases exponentially.

NOTES

1 Various researchers have created somewhat different lists of emotions considered basic. This is clearly a lively and developing area of research. Ortony and Turner (1990) present a comparison of various proposals. Panksepp's work (2004) provides another excellent description of basic emotions. The editions of the *Handbook of Emotions* (most recent 3rd edition, 2010) also provide information. Other lines of thought about the nature of emotion exist separately from that of basic emotion, for example, frameworks utilizing the concept of cognitive appraisal (Lazarus, 1991) and constraint satisfaction (Barrett, Ochsner, and Gross, 2007). These frameworks will not be discussed in this chapter.

2 The term *epigenetically,* if used metaphorically, could take the place of *experientially,* but for this chapter the term *epigenetic* will be reserved for specific changes in structure and function of a gene without changes in the genetic sequence.

3 Öhman (2008), however, proposes such a distinction between fear and anxiety.

4 The term *limbic* has developed over the last century and a half to refer to areas that encircle the diencephalon and lie underneath the telencephalon. Broca (1878) often receives credit for the first use of the term in the 19th century and for the distinction between limbic functions he referred to as an animal brain and the remainder of telencephalon he called the intellectual brain. James Papez (1937) in the 20th century pointed to the role of this part of the brain in emotional functions, and Paul MacLean (1952) coined the term *limbic system* to refer to this area of the brain and its functions. Despite criticism of MacLean's term as imprecise and of little use (LeDoux and Phelps, 2008), the term continues to be used broadly to refer to those subcortical structures deeply involved in the production of emotion.

5 Excellent discussions of the stress response can be found in *The End of Stress as We Know It* (McEwen, 2002) and *Why Zebras Don't Get Ulcers* (Sapolsky, 2004). In general the term *stress response* refers to the activation of the locus ceruleus-norepinephrine system, an element of the autonomic nervous system, and the hypothalamic-pituitary-adrenal system, a hormonal response system, in the presence of perceived challenge or threat to the organism. Activation of these systems leads to body-wide changes in a multitude of physiological systems and in behavior.

6 The term *genotype* refers to the complete set of genes or genetic material present in a cell or an organism. The term *phenotype* refers to the particular characteristics of a specific individual reflecting which of the genes that form the genome have been activated and which have not.

7 For a more specific review of some of these processes, see Champagne and Curley (2009).

8 For a more specific review of some of these processes, see Frances A. Champagne and James P. Curley (2009).

9 A. L. Papero (2005) provides an excellent review of the findings relevant to the effects of maternal depression, SES, and child development.

10 See Mauss and Robinson (2009) and Koole (2010) for examples of these challenges.

REFERENCES

Bowen, M. (1978). *Family therapy in clinical practice.* New York: Jason Aronson.

Boyce, W. T. & Ellis, B. J. (2005). Biological sensitivity to context: I. An evolutionary-developmental theory of the origins and function of stress reactivity. *Development and Psychopathology, 17,* 271–301.

Barrett, L. R., Ochsner, K. N. & Gross, J. J. (2007). On the automaticity of emotion. In J. A. Bargh (Ed.), *Social psychology and the unconscious: The automaticity of higher mental processes* (pp. 173–217). New York and Hove: Psychology Press.

Bell, M. A. & Wolfe, C. D. (2007). The cognitive neuroscience of early socioemotional development. In C. A. Brownell and C. B. Kopp (Eds.), *Socioemotional development in the toddler years* (pp. 345–369). New York: Guilford Press.

Blanchette, I. & Richards, A. (2010). The influence of affect on higher level cognition: A review of research on interpretation, judgement, decision making and reasoning. *Cognition and Emotion, 24*(4), 561–595.

Broca, P. (1878). Anatomie comparée des circonvolutions cérébrales: le grand lobe limbique. *Rev. Anthropol., 1*, 385–498.

Champagne, F. A. & Curley, J. P. (2009). Epigenetic mechanisms mediating long-term effects of maternal care on development. *Neuroscience and Biobehavioral Reviews, 33*, 593–600.

Ellis, B. J. & Boyce, W. T. (2008). Biological sensitivity to context. *Current Directions in Psychological Science, 17*, 183–187.

Fairbanks, L. A. & McGuire, M. T. (1988). Long-term effects of early mothering behavior on responsiveness to the environment in vervet monkeys. *Developmental Psychobiology, 21*, 711–724.

Flinn, M. V. (1999). Family environment, stress, and health during childhood. In C. Panter-Brick and C. M. Worthman (Eds.), *Hormones, health, and behavior: A socio-ecological and lifespan perspective* (pp. 105–130). Cambridge, UK: Cambridge University Press.

Koole, Sander A. (2010). The psychology of emotion regulation: An integrative review. In Jan De Houwer and Dirk Hermans (Eds.), *Cognition and emotion: Reviews of current research and theories* (pp. 128–167). Hove and New York: Psychology Press.

Lazarus, R. S. (1991). *Emotion and adaptation*. London: Oxford University Press.

LeDoux, J. E. (1994). Cognitive-emotional interactions in the brain. In P. Ekman and R. J. Davidson (Eds.), *The nature of emotion: Fundamental questions* (pp. 216–223). New York and Oxford: Oxford University Press.

LeDoux, J. E. & Phelps, E. A. (2008). Emotional networks in the brain. In M. Lewis, J. M. Haviland-Jones, and L. F. Barrett (Eds.), *Handbook of emotions* (pp. 159–179). New York: Guilford Press.

Lupien, S. J., King, S., Meaney, M. J. & McEwen, B. S. (2000). Stress hormone levels correlate with mother's socioeconomic status and depressive state. *Biological Psychiatry, 48*, 976–980.

Mauss, I. B. & Robinson, M. D. (2009). Measures of emotion: A review. *Cognition and Emotion, 23*, 209–237. Reprinted in 2010 in J. De Houwer and D. Hermans (Eds.), Cognition and emotion: Reviews of current research and theories (pp. 99–127). New York: Taylor and Francis.

MacLean P. D. (1952). Some psychiatric implications of physiological studies on frontotemporal portion of limbic system (visceral brain). *Electroencephalography and Clinical Neurophysiology, 4*, 407–418.

McEwen, B. S. & Sapolsky, R. M. (1995). Stress and cognitive function. *Current Opinion in Neurobiology, 5*, 205–216.

McEwen, B. S. & Lasley, E. N. (2002). *The end of stress as we know it.* Washington, DC: Joseph Henry Press.

McEwen, B. S. (2007). Physiology and neurobiology of stress and adaptation: Central role of the brain. *Physiological Reviews, 87*, 873–904.

Meaney, M. J. (2010). Epigenetics and the biological definition of Gene × Environment interactions. *Child Development, 81*, 41–79.

Nesse, R. M. (1990). Evolutionary explanations of emotions. *Human Nature, 1*, 261–289.

Öhman, A. (2008). Fear and anxiety: Overlaps and dissociations. In M. Lewis, J. Haviland-Jones, and L. F. Barrett (Eds.), *Handbook of Emotions* (pp. 709–729). New York and London: Guilford Press.

Ortony, A. & Turner, T. T. (1990). What's basic about basic emotions? *Psychological Review, 97*, 315–331.

Panksepp, J. (2004). *Affective neuroscience: The foundations of human and animal emotions.* New York: Oxford University Press.

Papero, A. L. (2005). Is early, high-quality daycare an asset for the children of low-income, depressed mothers? *Developmental Review, 25*(2), 181–211.

Papez, J. W. (1937). A proposed mechanism of emotion. *Archives of Neurology & Psychiatry, 38*(4), 725–743.

Pechtel, P. & Pizzagalli, D. A. (2011). Effects of early life stress on cognitive and affective function: An integrated review of human literature. *Psychopharmacology 214*, 55–70.

Roozendaal, B., McEwen, B. S. & Chattarji, S. (2009). Stress, memory and the amygdala. *Nature Reviews/Neuroscience, 10*, 423–433.

Sapolsky, R. S. (2004). *Why zebras don't get ulcers: A guide to stress and related diseases.* New York: W. H. Freeman.

Shonkoff, J. P., Boyce, W. T. & McEwen, B. S. (2009). Neuroscience, molecular biology, and the childhood roots of health disparities: Building a new framework for health promotion and disease prevention. *Journal of the American Medical Association, 301*(21), 2252–2259.

Sterling, P. & Eyer, J. (1988). Allostasis: A new paradigm to explain arousal pathology. In S. Fisher & J. Reason (Eds.), *Handbook of life stress, cognition, and health* (pp. 629–649). New York: Wiley.

3

DIFFERENTIATION OF SELF AS A MULTIGENERATIONAL PROCESS

Robert J. Noone

Most human traditions have known that the influence of ancestors continues from the past into the present and that the lives of those in the present will be a part of the lives in future generations. For the most part such traditions saw this past influence as having a benevolent or malevolent impact and it appears to have been, in part, a way of transmitting beliefs, values, and history in a given culture.

Charles Darwin's observations led to a radically different view of the unfolding of life on planet Earth. The influence of past generations extended from a few to millions, from our direct human forbearers to our earliest microbial ancestors.

While more modest in scope, Murray Bowen's observations of the human family also led to a radically different view of the influence previous generations have on the lives and behavior of those in the present. His observations were not about the evolution of human behavior, but they led to a new understanding of how our lives are shaped by processes occurring over multiple generations, processes generating differences in the basic adaptiveness of individuals.

The concept of the multigenerational family emotional process was a result of Bowen's family research and is one of eight concepts in the natural systems theory of the family he developed (Bowen, 1978a). Each concept describes an area of family functioning and exists in the context of the other concepts. Central to the theory is the concept of differentiation of self, a concept describing the basic adaptiveness[1] of individuals, which is seen as developing over the course of an individual's development and over multiple generations.

This chapter will discuss the concept of the multigenerational emotional process and the development of individual differences in differentiation of self. Recent developments in neuroscience that shed light on how family interactions can have such a profound effect on cognitive, emotional, and physiological functioning will also be discussed.

Early Research and the Mother/Child Symbiosis

More than a decade before Murray Bowen presented his formal theory of the family, he began a remarkable research study at the National Institute of

Mental Health. This project permitted him and his staff to observe families over the course of months and years while they lived on a research unit. The study took place from 1954 to 1959 and was the outgrowth of his previous work at Menninger's in Topeka, Kansas. The study resulted in a range of discoveries and led to the development of a formal systems theory of the family.

The observation that an individual's level of differentiation of self is a result of a developmental process occurring over generations can be seen as beginning with the original hypotheses Bowen brought to the study at NIMH. After a decade of pursuing his interest in the development of a science of human behavior through the study of psychoanalysis, the natural sciences, and the clinical population he saw at Menninger's, Bowen began his research at NIMH with the assumption that the mother/child symbiosis was a central mammalian characteristic vital to survival. He also brought to the study the hypothesis that this symbiosis could impede the movement of an offspring toward autonomy.

In the effort to use language that would facilitate the effort to move toward science, Bowen used terms consistent with biology. And it was in this context that he used the term *symbiosis*. He stated:

> The major concepts of the theory I had been working on came from biology. I would have dropped the concept of symbiosis because it has such specific meanings in psychiatry. Then I went back to biology and saw that it is a very specific term in that field, as is "instinct."
> (1978b, p. 105)

The study lasted five years and consisted of 14 families with a severely psychotic adolescent or adult child. Seven families lived in an inpatient unit from a range of six months to three years and 7 families were studied on an outpatient basis. He began with mother/child dyads, but within the first six months of the study he came to believe that the intensity of the relationship involved more than just the dyad. And so the fathers and some siblings in families became participants living on the unit. As he stated in a 1957 paper: "The relationship was more than two people with a problem involving chiefly each other; it appeared to be a more dependent fragment of a larger family group" (Bowen, 1978a, p. 10).

This resulted in the observation that the families functioned as units. In a sense the symbiotic regulation of behavior observed in the mother/child relationship was observed to exist in varying degrees among the members of the unit. As Bowen later described it:

> As the research was supplemented by clinical work with outpatient families, new and unanticipated discoveries could be made. The mother-patient relationship was more intense than hypothesized and it was not a circumscribed entity confined to the mother-and-patient

relationship. Instead it was a fragment of a larger family emotional system in which fathers were as intimately involved as the mothers, which was fluid and shifting, and which could extend itself to involve the entire central family unit, and even nonrelatives.

(1978a, pp. 104–105)

Two further observations made early on were that the siblings in a family were not equally involved in the emotional intensity and that the emotional intensity appeared to be a product of multiple generations. In other words, the level of emotional dependence or autonomy attained by the offspring in a family was not independent of the level attained in the previous generation.

A major question for Bowen was how to account for differences among siblings in which one moves into adulthood in an apparently orderly fashion and manages quite well, while a sibling does not quite make it as an adult. Some would posit that the differences are genotypic, while others attribute them to differences in the maternal care each received.

When Bowen expanded his observational lens to include the fathers, he observed how differently the interactions, what he later came to call the parental triangle, were in relation to each sibling. In his study of families with a member with schizophrenia, his observations led him to question whether such a significant impairment could occur in the course of just one generation. He could see that the parents functioned at a better level than their adult child with schizophrenia, but only to a degree. He observed the remarkable interdependence existing in the parent-child triangle. He described it as a "three-legged stool" with a level of emotional dependence that overshadowed the autonomy among the members of the threesome. The other siblings in the family were found to have attained more emotional autonomy than their sibling with schizophrenia.

The study of less impaired families led Bowen to observe that such interdependence existed in all families, but in varying degrees. Bowen stated that originally the idea that schizophrenia represented a multigenerational process was suggested by Lewis Hill (1955). Between 1959 and 1962 a detailed multigenerational study of several families with sufficient historical data was undertaken, including one with detailed information going back over 300 years. During this period he also began a multigenerational study of his own family, stating: "I decided that my own family would provide as much detail as any and would be more accessible" (Bowen, 1978a, p. xv).

The study of families with schizophrenia, of families functioning at a higher level, and of the multigenerational histories of a small number of families resulted in the observation that each family in each generation appeared to generate individual differences in the degree to which their children move toward maturity or emotional autonomy. The refinement of the concepts of differentiation of self, the nuclear family emotional process, and the family projection process shed light on how this variation occurred and the myriad ways in which it is manifested.

The Concept of Differentiation of Self

Since differentiation of self is presented at length in other chapters, only two elements of the concept will be briefly discussed here. The first is related to the shift in thinking from categorical thinking to what might be called continuum thinking. This represented a major shift in thinking about behavior and illness in psychiatry. It can, however, be seen as consistent with Bowen's evolutionary perspective. The evolutionary biologist Ernst Mayr described this perspective in Darwin's shift from what he termed "essentialistic thinking" to "population thinking" (Mayr, 1991).

Essentialism described objects and living forms as having basic essences from which individuals represented deviations. It was central in Western thought prior to Darwin's theory of evolution. Darwin's observations led him to see all life-forms not as having basic essences but as simply varying. It was his ability to see each individual as unique and as representing a variation in a larger population that allowed him to see each generation producing variations. All forms of life reproduce almost exactly but with some variation. This was captured in his concept of "descent with modification." In a sense he came to see that classifications don't exist in nature, but are a product of the human mind.

Similarly Bowen saw individuals and families as varying in adaptiveness and sought to develop a continuum along which all human behavior could be placed. He developed the concept of differentiation of self to define how individuals differ in their basic adaptiveness. This represented a significant shift in thinking about human behavior.

The scale or continuum of differentiation of self represents a conceptual framework along which individuals and families can be observed to vary, from the lowest possible level of adaptiveness to a potentially highest. Bowen based this continuum on two principal observations. One is that individuals appear to vary in the degree to which they emotionally separate over the course of development from their families.

An infant begins life in a state of complete dependency, requiring a caretaker for nutrition, warmth, and touch. The mother-infant interactions involve a host of physiological processes that stimulate growth. These processes involve both mother and child as the infant stimulates the mother's physiology in what Porges (2011, p. 281) describes as a symbiotic regulation. Over the course of development, from the earliest days on, the infant moves toward autonomy and the capacity for self-regulation. Bowen believed that there is a basic life force to move toward autonomy. He also observed that the symbiotic relationship necessary to support growth and development could also constrain this movement toward independence.

The human by nature is a social creature and dependent on the social environment. No one becomes entirely emotionally autonomous. But over the course of development individuals can be observed to vary in the degree to which they move toward the capacity to self-regulate. This holds true for the caretakers as well. In the intense emotional attachments of the family, individuals depend on one another for their sense of well-being and remain highly sensitized to each other. The intensity of the relationships can be more positive or negative, but the level of involvement is determined by the intensity of the relationships. The intensity of ongoing involvement also determines the level of sensitivity the family members have toward one another. Over the course of development this results in variation in the degree to which the functioning of individuals is regulated by others or by self.

A second observation that Bowen included in the concept of differentiation of self, and the scale along which individual differences in basic adaptiveness could be placed, is the degree to which what he termed the intellectual system is differentiated from the feeling and emotional systems. As Bowen (1978a) writes:

> It defines all people, from the lowest to the highest possible level of human functioning, according to a single common denominator. This has to do with the way the human handles the intermix between emotional and intellectual functioning. At the highest level are those with most "differentiation" between emotional and intellectual functioning.

> (p. 424)

Entailed in this process is the degree to which an individual's behavior is determined by an automatic responsiveness to the social environment or the degree to which one can utilize the intellectual system to have some choice in responding to the environment and in directing one's life course. He saw this manifested in the individuality-togetherness balance in which higher level individuals can maintain individuality even with constant pressure from the group, while lower level individuals lose it in relationships.

The concept of differentiation of self is seen as entailing genetic, epigenetic, physiological, psychological, and relationship variables that interact both over the course of development and over multiple generations. It involves a number of dimensions and requires the observation of an individual and family's functioning over a significant period of time. It also requires the assessment of the environmental challenges and opportunities an individual and family have been faced with and how they responded to them.

Once individuals could be seen to vary in this manner, Bowen could observe that over the course of several generations families could be seen to generate branches leading to higher levels of adaptiveness as well as branches leading to lower levels. This process was seen as nonrandom and based in family interactional patterns repeated over the generations.

Multigenerational Emotional Process

By the end of the research study in 1959, Bowen had observed consistent family patterns in both the families with schizophrenia and in better functioning families. "It was the comparison of the intense patterns in schizophrenia with the less intense patterns in others that eventually became the basis for the theory" (Bowen, 1978a, p. xiv). The more detailed multigenerational study occurred between 1959 and 1962.

Throughout the research Bowen sought to be consistent with science in the use of the terms *hypothesis, concept,* and *theory.* "During the five years to 1965 the six interlocking concepts of Family Systems Theory were developed in detail. Then came the problem of conceptualizing the concepts as parts of a unified theory and presenting it in writing" (Bowen, 1978a, p. xv). In 1966 the formal theory was published. The concepts of emotional cutoff and societal emotional process were added later to the theory.

An understanding of the concept of the multigenerational emotional process necessarily entails seeing it in the context of the other interlocking concepts in the total theory. The observation of this process required Bowen's observation of the nuclear family emotional patterns and variation in the process of differentiation of self among siblings. It also required the observation that individuals mate with others who are at similar levels of differentiation. In each generation, then, a baseline is formed from which the children remain at levels similar to the parents or vary to some degree.

The principal nuclear family patterns consist of the four adaptive mechanisms (distance, conflict, reciprocal functioning, involvement of a child) the family utilizes to manage the emotional intensity or fusion. One of the mechanisms was seen by Bowen to be sufficiently important to be defined as a separate concept, the family projection process, which describes the automatic manner in which one child is more involved in the intensity of the nuclear family. This child absorbs more of the parental anxiety and undifferentiation and emerges with a lower level of differentiation of self than the parents. This process was most easily observed in the families with schizophrenia in which emotional intensity was most exaggerated.

In an early paper, Bowen (1978a) described this process observed in the research families:

> According to our present thinking, the child becomes the "important other" to the mother. Through the child, the mother is able to attain a more stable emotional equilibrium than had otherwise been possible for her. The "tiny helplessness" of the infant permits her to function securely in the overadequate position. The emotional

stabilization of the mother then enables the father to have a less anxious relationship with the mother.

(p. 63)

He goes on to describe the reciprocal nature of the process:

I believe the child is automatically protecting his own interests by doing the things that will insure a less anxious and more predictable mother. However, once the child enters into this "being (helpless) for the mother" and the mother enters into the opposite "being (strong) for the child," they are both in a functional bind of "being for each other." When the child's self is devoted to "being for the mother," he loses the capacity of "being for himself."

(p. 63)

The child who remains most involved has a stabilizing effect on the family unit. Neither parent wants this to happen. It is automatic and generally occurs outside the awareness of those involved. The other siblings in the family are then a bit freer to "be for self" and to have a greater capacity to devote energy toward moving forward in their own lives. The child who remains most outside of the family emotional intensity may emerge from the family with a level of differentiation of self that is slightly higher than that of the parents, while the others will likely have levels similar to the parents.

Since individuals are seen as selecting a mating partner who has a similar level of differentiation of self, the variations among the siblings in this characteristic establish new baselines for the nuclear families in the next generation. When followed over a number of generations, families can be seen as generating a significant range of individuals on the scale of differentiation of self. Each nuclear family can be seen as a source point for branches that lead to branches in the family with higher levels of functioning, with lower levels, and those that remain about the same. If the concept of the multigenerational emotional process is accurate, it accounts for the full range of human functioning from the most resilient of individuals and families to those who are least adaptive. For illustrative purposes, the multigenerational process that leads to a wider range of adaptiveness over the generations is depicted in Figure 3.1.

In the first family in this illustration the parents are shown as having levels of 35 on the scale of differentiation of self. This is based on the observation that individuals select a mate with a similar level of differentiation. Over the course of development their daughter is depicted as attaining a similar level as her parents. She in turn selects a husband also at 35 on the scale. Their level of undifferentiation is seen as primarily contained in the marital unit with little projection to one of their children. Their oldest daughter emerged with a level higher (40) than her parents, while her two younger brothers attained

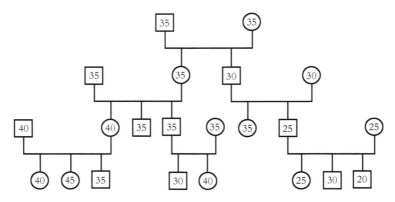

Figure 3.1 The Multigenerational Transmission of Individual Differences in Level of Differentiation of Self

levels similar to their parents. In the next generation the range of variation of basic levels of differentiation is shown to widen from 30 to 45.

As the child most involved in the parental undifferentiation, the son of the original family is depicted as emerging with a lower level (30) than that of his parents. He marries a woman at a similar level and their son also attains a level lower than theirs. The next generation is shown to have levels that are similar, higher, and lower than the parents.

In this illustration of four generations, the descendants of the original pair are shown as exhibiting a wide range of basic levels of differentiation of self, from a high of 45 to a lower level of 20. The life courses of the great-grandchildren would be predicted to vary based on their levels of differentiation, with the lives of those at the highest and lowest levels varying most significantly.

Every infant arriving on the planet, then, can be seen as taking his or her place in a functional position that has been generations in the making. While obviously genetics are involved, this is seen primarily as a phenotypic process based on family interactions and the slings and arrows of fortune. Each concept in the total theory plays some part in the overall multigenerational process. The process can be predictably observed in all families when sufficient information is available (Kerr and Bowen, 1988, p. 221). It is a probabilistic concept that takes into account a number of variables influencing the course and speed with which variation in levels of differentiation of self takes place. The following are some of the principal variables.

Differentiation of Self

The single most influential variable determining one's basic level of differentiation is the level of one's parents. As mentioned, parents are seen as having similar levels of differentiation with each other, and their children can be observed to vary only slightly in degree. The process of differentiation is one that occurs over the course of development, and the shaping of a particular level occurs in the context of the interactions of the emotionally important people one lives with. The variation among siblings is shaped by the emotional intensity of the parental triangle in which they grow and develop. The basic level of differentiation of self is not to be mistaken for the functional level, which can vary more significantly (Kerr and Bowen, 1988).

Nuclear Family Process

In each family the emotional intensity will be expressed in one or more of the adaptive patterns described by Bowen (1978a). These include emotional distance, conflict, and reciprocal functioning in the marriage along with involvement of a child in the marital fusion or undifferentiation. When most of the emotional intensity is managed by involving a child, that child will emerge with a lower level of differentiation than if the intensity had been primarily contained in the marriage. The siblings who are less involved in the parental fusion will emerge with levels about the same as the parents. At times a child will emerge at a higher level.

Family Projection Process

Bowen saw the nuclear family process of involving a child in the parental undifferentiation to be of sufficient importance that he defined it as a separate concept. It describes the way in which undifferentiation is transmitted into the next generation. The process occurs within the parental triangle, principally initiated by the mother, but supported by the father. Each individual plays an active part in the process, which can provide a stabilizing influence for the family unit. Father can anxiously respond to mother's anxiety by joining the focus on a child. The child in turn, Bowen wrote, "responds anxiously to mother, which she misperceives as a problem in the child. The anxious parental effort goes into sympathetic, solicitous, overprotective energy, which is directed more by mother's anxiety than the reality needs of the child" (Bowen, 1978a, p. 381). The level of anxiety in the family unit is then more contained in this triangle with the other siblings being less involved.

Emotional Cutoff

This concept refers to how the generations separate in order to move into the future. On reaching adulthood each child and the parents have the task of managing the level of emotional dependence they still retain. Bowen (1978a) described this as the level of unresolved emotional attachment. Some form of geographic or internal distancing will be used to adapt to this transition. The greater the level of emotional dependence or undifferentiation, the more distance needed. The individuals who as parents are able to maintain more viable contact with their family of origin will have lesser degrees of emotional intensity in the nuclear families in the next generation. The more isolated a nuclear family is from the larger extended family, the more intense will be the nuclear family interactions during stressful periods. When the family projection process is utilized to regulate the emotional intensity in the family, the involved child will be more vulnerable and less adaptive. Viable contact with the families of origin, then, can serve as a buffer in slowing down the multigenerational process to lower levels of differentiation in the next generation.

Social Context and Alloparental Care

Related to emotional cutoff, but extending beyond the family, is the extent to which the mother–child relationship is isolated or involved in a broader social network. When mothers have little access to others who might provide social support or occasionally assist with childcare, the emotional intensity of the mother–child relationship is likely to be greater and the process of separating over the course of development will be more difficult (Flinn and England, 1997; Flinn and Leone, 2007).

Sex and Birth Order

The position one is born into in a family will have some influence on how much of the emotional intensity one will experience during development. In some families the first-born receives the greatest amount of parental anxiety, while in others it may be the youngest. In some families it will be a male or female who is seen as the most vulnerable or problematic. Patterns that existed in the parents' families of origin will greatly influence which child will be most involved in the family emotional process and which will be freer to "be for self."

Family Emotional Climate During the Prenatal and Early Postnatal Periods

The level of stress a family is experiencing during a pregnancy and early development may increase the focus on a child. A loss of a family member or other significant stressors may heighten the level of reactivity in a family for a period of time. The impact on a child will depend on how the parents manage the stress and the adaptive mechanisms they use during this period. Children born during more fortunate periods may be less caught up in family intensity. A number of studies have demonstrated how significant stress during a pregnancy may influence the development of the neuroendocrine stress response systems of offspring (Champagne and Meaney, 2006; Noone, 2001; Yehuda, Mulherin Engel, Brand, Marcus, and Berkowitz, 2005).

The continued focus on a child, however, is not seen as due to the development of a less adaptive stress response system in the prenatal or early postnatal period alone. The evidence suggests that such shaping of these systems can be later modified in a favorable environment (Francis, Diorio, Plotsky, and Meaney, 2002). The family projection process involves the sustained interactional patterns between the mother and child along with the others in the family unit. It involves the perceptual and emotional responsiveness of family members to a particular child, which serves to regulate the emotional intensity in the family unit. The focus on the selected child becomes more heightened during stressful periods and decreases during periods of calm.

Biological Factors in the Multigenerational Emotional Process

The observation of a multigenerational family over five or six generations will predictably show trends toward greater and lesser adaptiveness and a wider overall range of adaptiveness than existed in the original nuclear family. The assessment of the adaptiveness of family members will include their social, emotional, and physical health in the context of their environment. One of the questions raised about this observation is to what extent genes are determining the adaptiveness of the individuals and families in the succeeding generations. How can family interactions have such a profound effect on the biology of individuals?

Bowen certainly included genes in conceptualizing what constitutes a "self" and in the multigenerational process. But there appeared to be more at play and the family patterns did not seem to fit with a strictly genetic process. In discussing the multigenerational development of schizophrenia, Bowen (1978b) once stated that it represented "a genetic type pattern that is influenced by emotional forces" (p. 107).

In the period since Bowen's formulation of the multigenerational emotional process there has been a revolution in the understanding of not only how genes are involved in both the development and functioning of individuals, but how integrated and reciprocally influential the nervous, endocrine, and immune systems are. Prior to 1970 the expression of the genetic code was seen as largely unidirectional with the information in DNA being transcribed to RNA that then was translated into proteins resulting in the phenotype. Since then, the interplay among DNA, RNA, proteins, chromatin, and other intra- and extracellular molecular signals involved in the regulation and expression of the genetic coding regions has been discovered (Shapiro, 2011). Genes themselves are now more clearly seen as part of a larger interactional process.

Similarly, it had been known for a long time that there are three primary regulatory systems in the body: the nervous, the immune, and the endocrine systems. The effort to understand how these systems work at the molecular level has revealed how highly integrated and mutually influential they are. Thinking of mind and body as separate has given way to a new understanding of how mind affects the immune and endocrine system and vice versa.

Over the past several decades significant knowledge has been gained about the mammalian neuroendocrine stress response system and the influence parental care has on its development. Much of the research has focused on the limbic-hypothalamic-pituitary-adrenal (L-HPA) system and the release of "stress hormones" into the bloodstream, which help to regulate the mind-body's response to challenge. The stress response is designed to release and channel energy to allow individuals to adapt to changing conditions and threats. This mobilization entails cognitive, emotional, physiological, and behavioral response systems mediated in part by the release of the catecholamines (epinephrine and norepinephrine) and the stress hormones corticotropin releasing hormone (CRH) and cortisol. The "stress hormones" help to coordinate a system-wide response, involving the brain, cardiovascular, immune, digestive, and reproductive systems, in order to respond to the challenge or threat at hand. This automatic response is vital to survival. The short-term elevation of cortisol in the bloodstream results in behavioral and physiological responses that are adaptive, but chronic elevations can lead to impairment in one or more of these systems (Lupien and McEwen, 1997; McEwen, 1995, 1998). Prolonged heightened L-HPA responses to stress have been found to be associated with autoimmune and cardiovascular illnesses as well as anxiety, depressive, and addictive disorders (Heim and Nemeroff, 2001; McEwen, 1998).

While genes are a part of the variability found in the stress reactivity of individuals, the parent-offspring relationship has significant and enduring effects on the physiological stress response systems and how individuals respond to stress throughout their lives. Experimental animal studies have demonstrated that subjecting one generation to uncontrollable stress results in observable behavioral and physiological changes in their offspring into adulthood.

The parental influence on the development of an offspring's physical and behavioral responsiveness to stress begins even prior to birth. Glover and O'Connor (2002), for example, reported in an epidemiological study that a strong relationship existed between maternal anxiety during the third trimester and behavioral and emotional problems in those children at age four. In a study of mothers who had been exposed to the World Trade Center collapse while pregnant, Yehuda et al. (2005) found that both the mothers who developed post-traumatic stress disorder (PTSD) and their infants at age one year had reduced cortisol levels compared with the mothers who did not develop PTSD and their infants. Reduced cortisol levels had previously been found among individuals with PTSD. Since the stress response systems are vital in adapting to life challenges, the heightened or diminished functioning of the L–HPA system can be maladaptive (McEwen and Lasley, 2002).

Champagne and Meaney (2006) found that stressing rats in the last week of gestation resulted in a decrease in oxytocin receptor levels in the mothers, influencing maternal care in a manner that increases stress reactivity of the offspring. It is important to note that cross-fostering and adoption studies have demonstrated that some of the effects of prenatal stressing can be moderated during postnatal development (Maccari et al., 1995; Weinstock, 1997).

The study of the early postnatal period has also demonstrated that the parent–offspring relationship can have a lifelong influence on regulating an offspring's responsiveness to stress. In both human and nonhuman studies, the disruption of the maternal–offspring relationship as well as overprotective, restrictive maternal behavior has been found to be associated with long-term cognitive, physiological, and behavioral effects on offspring (Essex et al., 2002; Fairbanks, 1989; Francis and Meaney, 2002; Suomi, 2002).

The influence of the early parental relationship on an offspring's later responsiveness to stress appears to be shaped by the actual "programming" of the neuroendocrine stress response system. Investigators have demonstrated that variation in particular maternal behaviors among rodents (licking and grooming, arched-backed nursing), results in stable individual differences in the neural systems that mediate fearfulness in their offspring which persist into adulthood (Francis et al., 1999). More specifically, higher or lower levels of these maternal behaviors influence gene expression of the stress hormone, CRH, in the hypothalamus and amygdala, which are involved in activating the HPA stress response system. These maternal behaviors also influence gene expression for glucocorticoid receptors in the hippocampus, which is instrumental in down-regulating the HPA stress response. Maternal behaviors, then, can shape individual differences among offspring in their reactivity to stress. Through the use of elaborate cross-fostering methods, these results were found to be influenced by the nursing mothers and not the biological mothers (Francis et al., 1999).

This work specifically is related to the expression of glucocorticoid receptors on neural cells of the hippocampus, the activation or silencing of which influences the functioning of the HPA response to stress. Epigenetic markers have been discovered that modify the expression or silencing of a gene without changing its nucleotide sequence. And this modification of the genome, resulting from parent–offspring interactions, continues into adulthood and can be transmitted nongenomically into the next generation (Meany and Szyf, 2005).

Knowledge developing in the field of epigenetics is adding to the knowledge about gene-environment interactions, and the discovery that parent-child interactions can result in the epigenetic regulation of stress reactivity is a remarkable development. As Zhang and Meaney (2010) state in reviewing this development: "These studies define a biological basis for the interplay between environmental signals and the genome in the regulation of individual differences in behavior, cognition, and physiology" (p. 439).

This does not suggest that the family multigenerational process is an epigenetic one. In the biological sense, *epigenetics* refers to changes in the activity of the genome, but does not involve a change in the nucleotide sequence. And so while epigenetics may play a part in the multigenerational emotional process, the process clearly involves a wider range of biological as well as psychological processes. The physiological stress response systems are central to the adaptiveness of individuals, but also only one component of a broader integrated system. When viewed through the lens of the family emotional unit, the behavior and biology of individuals can be seen as fitting into a dynamic whole, each influencing and being influenced by the others.

The shift from a view of the individual to the symbiotic regulation between mother and child to the larger family unit requires a shift to a systems perspective. The concept of the multigenerational emotional process is far from being established as a fact. But the development of knowledge in the sciences appears to be moving in the direction of establishing the mechanisms through which the family relationship system can be seen as a self-regulating system influencing and being influenced by the functioning of its members.

The concept of differentiation of self includes genetic, epigenetic, physiological, psychological, and relationship variables that interact both over the course of development and over multiple generations. A multigenerational view of development provides a broader framework for the study of human behavior and allows for the inclusion of considerably more variables in understanding individual differences in adaptiveness.

NOTE

1 The term *adaptiveness* is related to the broader concept of differentiation of self. It refers to how well an individual responds to life challenges. It is reflective of an individual's level of chronic anxiety, which can increase or decrease based on the stressors in one's life. Michael Kerr (1992) defines adaptiveness as "the ability to adjust to real or anticipated changes in one's life, particularly in important relationships, without a prolonged escalation of anxiety that impairs the physical, mental, or social functioning of oneself or others" (p. 101).

REFERENCES

Bowen, M. (1978a). *Family therapy in clinical practice.* New York: Jason Aronson.
Bowen, M. (1978b). Schizophrenia as a multi-generational phenomenon. In M. M. Berger (Ed.), *Beyond the double bind.* New York: Brunner/Mazel.
Champagne, F. & Meaney M. J. (2006). Stress during gestation alters postpartum maternal care and the development of the offspring in a rodent model. *Biological Psychiatry, 59,* 1227–1235.

Essex, M., Klein, M., Cho, E. & Kalin, N. (2002). Maternal stress beginning in infancy may sensitize children to later stress exposure: Effects on cortisol and behavior. *Society of Biological Psychiatry, 52,* 776–784.

Fairbanks, L. (1989). Early experience and cross-generational continuity of mother-infant contact in vervet monkeys. *Developmental Psychobiology, 22,* 669–681.

Flinn, M. & England, B. (1997). Social economics of childhood glucocorticoid stress response and health. *American Journal of Physical Anthropology, 102,* 33–53.

Flinn, M. V. & Leone, D. V. (2007). Alloparental care and the ontogeny of glucocorticoid stress response among stepchildren. In G. Bentley and R. Mace (Eds.), *Alloparental care in human societies* (pp. 212–231). Oxford: Berghahn Books.

Francis, D. D., Diorio, J., Liu, D. & Meaney, M. J. (1999). Nongenomic transmission across generations of maternal behavior and stress responses in the rat. *Science, 286,* 1155–1158.

Francis, D., Diorio, J., Plotsky, P. & Meaney, M. (2002). Environmental enrichment reverses the effects of maternal separation on stress reactivity. *Journal of Neuroscience, 22,* 7840–7843.

Francis, D. D. & Meaney, M. J. (2002). Maternal care and the development of stress responses. In J. Cacioppo et al. (Eds.), *Foundations in social neuroscience* (pp. 763–773). Cambridge, MA: MIT Press.

Glover, V. & O'Connor, T. (2002). Effects of antenatal stress and anxiety: Implications for development and psychiatry. *British Journal of Psychiatry, 180,* 389–391.

Heim, C. & Nemeroff, C. (2001). The role of childhood trauma in the neurobiology of mood and anxiety disorders: Preclinical and clinical studies. *Society of Biological Psychiatry, 49,* 1023–1039.

Hill, L. B. (1955). *Psychotherapeutic intervention in schizophrenia.* Chicago: University of Chicago Press.

Kerr, M. E. (1992). Physical illness and the family emotional system: Psoriasis as a model. *Behavioral Medicine, 18,* 101–113.

Kerr, M. E. & Bowen, M. (1988). *Family evaluation.* New York: W. W. Norton.

Lupien, S. & McEwen, B. S. (1997). The acute effects of costicorticoids on cognition: Integration of animal and human model studies. *Brain Research Reviews, 24,* 1–27.

Maccari, S., Piazza, P., Kabbaj, M., Barbazanges, A., Simon, H. & Le Moal, M. (1995). Adoption reverses the long-term impairment in glucocorticoid feedback induced by prenatal stress. *Journal of Neuroscience, 15,* 110–115.

Mayr, E. (1991). *One long argument.* Cambridge, MA: Harvard University Press.

McEwen, B. S. (1995). Stressful experience, brain, and emotions: Developmental, genetic, and hormonal influences. In M. S. Gazzaniga (Ed.), *The cognitive neurosciences* (pp. 1117–1135). Cambridge, MA: MIT Press.

McEwen, B. S. (1998). Protective and damaging effects of stress mediators. *New England Journal of Medicine, 338,* 171–179.

McEwen, B. S. & Lasley, E. N. (2002). *The end of stress as we know it.* Washington, DC: Joseph Henry Press.

Meaney, M. J. & Szyf, M. (2005). Maternal effects as a model for environmentally-dependent chromatin plasticity. *Trends in Neuroscience, 28,* 456–463.

Noone, R. (2001). The family as a source of nongenomic heritable variation. *Family Systems, 6*(1), 47–66.

Porges, S. W. (2011). *The polyvagal theory.* New York: W. W. Norton.

Shapiro, J. A. (2011). *Evolution: A view from the 21st century.* Upper Saddle River, NJ: FT Press.

Suomi, S. (2002). Attachment in rhesus monkeys. In J. Cacioppo et al. (Eds.), *Foundations in social neuroscience* (pp. 775–795). Cambridge, MA: MIT Press.

Weinstock, M. (1997). Does prenatal stress impair coping and regulation of hypothalamic-pituitary-adrenal axis? *Neuroscience Biobehavioral Review, 21*, 1–10.

Yehuda, R., Mulherin Engel, S., Brand, S., Marcus, S. & Berkowitz, G. (2005). Transgenerational effects of posttraumatic stress disorder in babies of mothers exposed to the World Trade Center attacks during pregnancy. *Journal of Clinical Endocrinology & Metabolism, 90*, 4115–4118.

Zhang, T. Y. & Meaney, M. J. (2010). Epigenetics and the environmental regulation of the genome and its function. *Annual Review of Psychology, 61*, 439–466.

4

ANCIENT ROOTS OF DIFFERENTIATION OF SELF

Leann S. Howard

Research in the natural sciences can be comprehended in a new way when viewed through the lens of Bowen theory, which supersedes the compart-mentalization of knowledge about humans and other forms of life. As an example, the study of the complex systems processes of harvester ants, when compared to processes in the human family, shows primitive indicators of differentiation and provides support for the idea that the same natural forces of individuality and togetherness govern both species. This is one example of how Bowen theory makes a potential contribution to a more comprehensive lens for understanding the process of evolution.

What Research Shows Us

Over the past 40 years researchers have worked to establish general properties of complex systems. Richard Lewontin, the evolutionary biologist, has written of the hope of scientists that "complex systems have special laws that originate in the multiplicity of interactions among many parts, laws of complexity itself" (Lewontin, 2000, p. 113). Establishing principles of behavior that apply to the unit itself has been the focus of scientists studying ants, bees, fish, and even cells that form tissues (Couzin, 2007; Greene and Gordon, 2007; Seeley, 2010).

At the same time, Bowen family systems theorists have been studying the unit of the human family. Establishing contact across disciplines is a neces-sary step in finding general principles that apply to the functioning of units in nature (Bourne, 2011). Bowen theory calls these units emotional systems. Emotion is the link between the behavior of human beings and the behavior of other animals. The field of neuroscience has exploded in the past 40 years as well. The study of the brain is a study of complex processes of compo-nent parts that produce the behavior of the whole unit. Antonio Damasio, a professor of neuroscience, psychology, and neurology, has made the multidis-ciplinary leap through his study of cognitive neuroscience. In his most recent work Damasio states about humans:

> Amazingly, self-concerned life regulation always coexists with the machinery of automated life regulation that any conscious creature

inherited from its evolutionary past. We moved from simple regulation, focused on the survival of the organism, to progressively more deliberated regulation, based on a mind equipped with identity and personhood and now seeking not mere survival but certain ranges of well-being.

(Damasio, 2010, pp. 58–59)

It [author uses *it* to refer to self and self consciousness] requires us to consider early living organisms first, and then gradually move across evolutionary history toward current organisms. It requires us to note incremental modification of nervous systems and link them to the incremental emergence of, respectively, behavior, mind, and self.

(Damasio, 2010, pp. 14–15)

Recent considerations of the evolutionary process appear to be consistent with the work of Damasio. Massimo Piattelli-Palmarini, a professor of cognitive neuroscience at the University of Arizona, accepts that evolution is a fact, but challenges the view that natural selection is the mechanism by which evolution occurs. Instead, he proposes selection forces operating on many levels that include "genes, chromosome, whole genomes, whole epigenomes, cells, developing tissues, kin groups, societies, and communities, and, of course, organisms" (Fodor and Piattelli-Palmarini, 2011, p. 57). A review article in *Science* follows a similar theme by proposing a move from a simple cause–effect model of evolution, natural selection, to a system model based on reciprocity that is the "tracing of causal influences through systems" (Laland et al., 2011, p. 1516). Michael Meaney, in a review article for the journal *Child Development,* discusses the interdependence of gene and environment in individual differences in "inherited" stress-reactivity across generations through maternal care (Meaney, 2010). Maternal effects are being studied in a range of species, from insect societies to the human. A professor of biology at Stanford University, Deborah M. Gordon, states clearly the complex systems processes of living systems:

Physiological, social, and ecological processes all operate simultaneously and none is more important or fundamental than another. Linking levels of organization is central to any study of social behavior. For humans and social animals, an individual's behavior is always embedded in a social world.

(1999, p. 96)

The Family as an Emotional Unit

Prior to the work of Murray Bowen and the work of other early pioneers in the field of family therapy, the most prominent model used for understanding human behavior was the theory defined by Sigmund Freud in the late 1800s. The psychoanalytic model places the heart of emotional difficulties within the individual resulting from unconscious conflicts that are seen to be a result of childhood experiences.

Bowen's work was unique among early pioneers in the field. Bowen was an internationally renowned psychiatrist who first studied the human family as a unit and eventually founded the Georgetown Family Center, committed to expanding his theory and disseminating the ideas based on his work (Bowen, 1978; Butler, 2011). He not only moved from an individual model to a systems perspective on the human, but he also fundamentally defined the human family as an emotional unit, an "organism."

Viewing the family as an organism can be understood by thinking of reciprocity between members of a family system: the functioning of one member of a system is established in reciprocal interaction with other members of the unit. The unit of the family is a co-created system of interaction processes.

Bowen's work began as observational research on families with an off-spring exhibiting the severe symptoms of psychosis. He observed the intense impact that family members have on one another, particularly a mother and her symptomatic offspring. He later defined the triangle as the fundamental unit of the family, in which the interdependent system of parents and psy-chotic offspring function like a tripod with no individual capable of taking a position separate from the others. He hypothesized that the symbiotic process of attachment was an exaggeration of processes found in older forms of life.

Bowen continued his field research with families exhibiting milder symp-toms as well as those families that were symptom free. He observed the same patterns in all families. Families differed in overall adaptiveness by the inten-sity of the process rather than by the process itself. Symptoms were seen to be an outcome of the functioning of the unit as a whole rather than existing under the skin of one individual.

Bowen defined the universal process in families as follows: family mem-bers attach to one another by varying degrees of intensity based on the context at the time a couple marries, conditions in the family at the time of the addition of each child, and relationships each parent has to his or her original family. Bowen theorists have identified the balance of comfortable contact and distance between members as crucial to optimal functioning of the unit: rising tensions within the unit may lead to disruption in the contact and distance balance.

If repeated patterns of conflict and distance arise, a couple may settle into a pattern of distance. As human beings are social mammals, isolation from an important other is highly anxiety-provoking. In addition, stability of the unit is compromised. To fix this, the couple may attempt to stabilize the unit and their own relationship through a process of incorporating one or more offspring into the marriage. This process is not ordinarily perceived by the parents, but it does work automatically to stabilize the relationship system. This occurs as a mother turns to one or more of her children to fill the connection not available in the marriage. The father may turn to another child or to his work for his primary investment. The unit is then stabilized. However, the child or children serving the stabilizing function will have difficulty functioning on his, her or their. In the most interdependent units, an offspring may fail to leave home, marry, or reproduce. Focusing on the difficulties in the offspring misses the underlying process and solidifies the problem in the child (Kerr, 2007).

The Bowen theory is not a proven theory. It is a systems model that is currently being studied through longitudinal research projects focused on interdependent, reciprocal processes within multigenerational family units (Eichholz, 2005; Flinn, 1999; Flinn and England, 1995; Noone, 2008).

Harvester Ants and What They Tell Us

The fieldwork research of Deborah M. Gordon is based on more than 25 years of direct study of 300 colonies of harvester ants (*Pogonomyrmix barabatus*) in southeastern Arizona. Gordon likely has observed ants longer than any other biologist. In many journal articles and two books, Gordon has outlined a detailed natural history of harvester ants (Gordon, 1999, 2010). The queen lives for up to 20 or more years and reproduces all of the workers, who do not reproduce and live only 1 year. The queen is not in charge of the process, however. She functions only as one of the interacting parts of the colony. Gordon's study of harvester ants is a systems perspective on their functioning. Fundamental patterns among ants are the outcome of simple processes of contact and distance mediated by antennal touch, or near touch, and chemical exchange. The simple interactions form interaction networks. Gordon describes the process as follows:

> Interactions with other ants determine what an ant does, and what the ant does modifies its environment, including its interactions, and this in turn modifies its subsequent interactions and the whole process runs itself. This is true of all living systems.
>
> (Gordon, 2010, p. 11)

What is fascinating about Gordon's work for purposes of this discussion is that ant colonies vary in the degree of sensitivity or reactivity of ants to one another and to the changing conditions (Gordon, 2010, pp. 64, 133). The study of foraging is particularly instructive. Each inactive ant responds to a successful ant returning to the nest with a seed by beginning to forage.

When returning foragers are removed from near the nest, some colonies slow foraging in response. However, not every colony responds in the same way (Gordon, 2010, pp. 134–135). Some colonies continue to forage with little response at all, while other colonies respond with greater sensitivity and the shutdown of foraging. The recovery of ants once foragers are returned to the nest also varies. Some individual ants become more productive in foraging activity than others. Ants also vary in the degree to which there is a propensity to forage absent the contact from patrollers, which are ants that signal the start of the foraging process. Gordon seeks to understand how variation in close regulation of foraging may be tied to variation in successful functioning and reproduction within different environments (Gordon, 2010, Chapter 6; Gordon, Holmes, and Nacu, 2008).

Life Forces Affect Behavior

Within the physical universe fundamental forces have been identified: the strong force, the electromagnetic force, the weak force, and gravity. Nothing in the physical universe makes sense outside of the interactions of individual particles as defined by these forces. Bowen identified life forces in which nothing in relationship systems makes sense outside of the interactions of individuals as defined by these forces (Kerr and Bowen, 1988). In contrast to forces in the physical sciences, life forces are not proven.

Individual organisms appear to be drawn together by a force. Harvester ant colonies live in units in the soil. Schools of fish travel together. Human families exist as interacting multigenerational units (Kerr and Bowen, 1988). The fundamental observation of Bowen was that individual members of the family unit are fundamentally regulated by relationships. Humans function in relationship reciprocity and are highly sensitized to changes in the balance of the system. Bowen called this force the togetherness force, or fusion. Early work by Theodore Schneirla (1971) on army ants seemed to come to a similar conclusion similar to Bowen's. That is, colony behavior did not arise from the individuals, but from behavioral processes themselves.

Bowen observed a counterbalancing force for individuality. Organisms, when forced together, will automatically separate to a level of distance common to the species (Kerr, 1997). Ants on the foraging trail will at times turn to avoid contact with other ants. Herds, colonies, flocks hang together but also observe distance between one another within the unit. Bowen identified this counterbalancing force as individuality or differentiation. Bowen also observed that there is variation in the balance of the two life forces (individuality/togetherness). Some systems appear to have a fairly evenly balanced level of togetherness and individuality while others appear more oriented toward togetherness. Adult family members in well-balanced systems maintain regular contact with one another that is personal while also living their own individual lives. In systems not as well balanced, members may have difficulty functioning outside of one another's physical presence, or may avoid contact altogether. The distance in this case reflects a reaction to too much togetherness or fusion.

Differentiation in the Human

Differentiation in the human concerns the capacity of an individual to be productive and goal oriented. The term refers to the degree to which an individual establishes emotional autonomy. Differentiation can be observed as the capacity to focus on one's own functioning while in the presence of other members of the group and during times of increased stress. This capacity is referred to as self regulation: the capacity to be an individual while relating to the unit (Kerr, 2010). A less differentiated individual, an individual more governed by the togetherness force, can be observed to react more strenuously to other members of the unit during times of stress. This individual is more regulated by the unit and functions as less of an individual within the unit. A fundamental assumption based on Bowen theory is that families more balanced toward togetherness are vulnerable to stress-driven disruptions in homeostatic functioning (Kerr, 2011).

The emotional state of individuals appears to be linked to the functioning of the unit and the unit regulates the functioning of individuals including epigenetic changes leading to the emergence of symptoms that are physical, emotional, or social. Michael Kerr has described a Unidisease model in which manifestations of mind/body's exaggerated efforts to restore homeostasis may lead to regression. Physical symptoms in one family member are reflective of a disturbance in relationships (Kerr, 2011).

Are Humans Like Ants?

Raghavendra Gadagkar, evolutionary biologist at the Indian Institute of Science, has been studying the primitively eusocial wasp *Ropalidia marginata* for 30 years. He has a rare perspective on the study of insect societies and what this can contribute to the study of humans.

> Biologists can do much more; they can offer us insights from a whole range of animal societies with millions of years of evolutionary history. And those of us who study insect societies can hope to harness wisdom from an altogether different subkingdom of animal life. I certainly do not think we should imitate insect societies blindly, but I do think that they can hold a mirror to us and offer us a means to reflect on our own society and learn more about ourselves.
>
> (Gadagkar, 2009, p. 1407)

The mirror Gadagkar refers to appears to be a cloudy one. Richard Lewontin cautions scientists to distinguish the mirror from the factual reality.

> It is not possible to do the work of science without using a language that is filled with metaphors. Virtually the entire body of modern

science is an attempt to explain phenomena that cannot be experienced directly by human beings, by reference to forces and processes that we cannot perceive directly because they are too small, like molecules, or too vast, like the entire known universe. . . . While we cannot dispense with metaphors in thinking about nature, there is a great risk of confusing the metaphor with the thing of real interest. . . . What is at the center of interest is the set of mechanisms that are common to all individuals and preferably to all species.

(2000, pp. 3, 9–10)

It is important to tread carefully into the metaphor of ant behavior and human behavior. The most obvious difficulty in making the comparison is that a harvester ant colony is a single organism with many parts. That is because ant colonies make new colonies. Individual ants do not (Gordon, personal communication, 2010). When considering the human family as an "organism," it is important to understand what specifically is meant.

Organism in this sense refers to a functional relationship between members of the unit. The relationship system is a highly interdependent unit in which reciprocal relationship processes significantly impact variation in lifetime adjustment to changing contexts. Not every member of a family unit is impacted in the same way. The functioning position one holds within the unit accounts for variation in lifetime adaptativeness of members. For example, the child upon whom a mother's functioning is most dependent will have considerable difficulty pursuing life goals or in some cases leaving home, marrying, and reproducing. While the unit does not generate reproduction, it does have tremendous impact on whether, in fact, certain members do reproduce. A second challenge in making a comparison between the two systems concerns the topic of stress-reactivity. Insect societies probably do not experience stress (Gordon, personal communication, 2010). Humans, however, are highly susceptible to the stress response and to having stress color perception and behavior (Noone, 2008). The relationship system of the family is the greatest source for regulating calm and anxiety within the human (Rauseo, 1995). Ants transfer information about what an ant is to do. Human families transfer stress along with information about how one is to function.

Does Differentiation Have Ancient, Biological Roots?

Gordon describes evolution of the ant colony as follows: "We know that developmental and environmental processes trigger the expression and the inhibition of genes and that somehow all of these processes lead to the traits we see in organisms" (2010, p. 131).

According to Gordon, "We know little about the processes that regulate the inheritance of behavioral responses to changing conditions"

(2010, p. 132). However, researchers such as John Calhoun speculate that universal processes underlie all living systems. He wrote: "Though each species manifests species-specific reactions, I shall view all species as subject to a universal set of processes" (1967, p. 24). Michael Kerr also wrote: "If the similarities between human beings and ants are more than analogous, the implication is that universal processes underlie these similarities" (1997, p. 4).

Regulatory processes are of fundamental significance in the functioning of all natural systems, from societies to cells. Variation in regulatory functions in harvester ant colonies may provide beginning evidence for early biological roots of variation in differentiation that appear to be present in the human.

Regulatory processes are present across many areas of harvester ant colony functioning. The ants regulate interaction rate and regulate workers moving into different tasks according to moment-to-moment shifts in the current context. Harvester ants also establish patterns of behavior that regulate the transfer of substances such as seeds, and the providing of food to larvae (Gordon, 2010, p. 48). Ants regulate foraging, including the initiation of it, and the continuation of it, as well as the slowing down and end to it each day.

These regulatory functions vary between ant colonies and appear to be connected to colony success. Gordon's work will ultimately spell out the details of factors connected to more and less successful functioning. One current area of speculation is that harvester ants that regulate foraging more closely to moment-to-moment shifts in the environment are more successful than those that do not. Another area of speculation is that, under certain circumstances, it may be important for ants to continue foraging no matter what (Gordon, 2010, p. 136).

Harvester ants appear to be heavily regulated by the togetherness force. The togetherness force can be seen in tight coordination of an ant colony and the cooperation among members of the unit in gathering food, caring for young, cleaning the nest, and defending against intruders. Individuality, while less developed in harvester ants, can be seen in the tendency of some ants to be more active and productive than others (Gordon, 2010, p. 137). It can also be observed in the tendency of ants to continue the task performed on the previous day (Gordon, 2010, p. 61). That is, the ants tend to go their own way unless intervening processes arise.

It is interesting to view the variation in regulatory function of these ants alongside regulatory functions in the human family. Families vary in the degree to which members of the unit are sensitive to one another and to changing conditions of life. Families vary in the degree to which the functioning of members is regulated by the unit itself and the degree to which individual members appear to be more self regulating while still relating to the unit. The details of the system in harvester ants are not yet complete. However, variation in regulatory function does appear to be fundamental in variation in harvester ant success.

Both natural systems are engaged in regulation of reactivity within the unit and in response to an ever-shifting environment. Some human families appear to function more like the ants, that is, regulating and being regulated by the processes of the unit itself. An example of the similarity is the tripod of parents and psychotic offspring. If the symptomatic offspring is removed from the family unit and placed in a psychiatric hospital, that offspring may begin to function more "normally" absent the presence of the atmosphere (emotional field) of the family unit. This is consistent with Damasio's view that the automatic processes remain a part of the human process. It is also consistent with the Bowen theory: some human families function in ways more consistent with more ancient natural systems.

Other families appear to utilize the more recently evolved prefrontal cortex that is capable of overcoming instinctive processes. Within the human this is still a work in progress as fear, if sustained, leads to feeling-driven actions that override thoughtful action and replace carefully considered action with automatic response (McEwen and Lasley, 2002; Panksepp, 1998, p. 42).

How Does Bowen Theory Inform the Study of Natural Systems?

The work of science is the effort to keep the theory used for the study of nature separate from nature itself. If the theory and nature are kept separate, it is possible through time to establish a model that more closely tracks how nature operates.

Psychoanalytic theory was an important beginning effort to establish a science of human behavior. The theory, which is a lens for understanding the individual, has to be revised as new data are emerging about the interrelationship between the functioning of the individual and the unit. The revised view has major implications for comprehending symptoms arising within members of a family system.

The discovery of DNA and the evolutionary synthesis established the view that random genetic mutations lead to different phenotypes upon which natural selection can act. Data arising from the study of epigenetic processes establish the fact that genes are far more plastic than once thought. The studies of Michael Meaney offer important new data about how a relationship process impacts biological functioning. The lens of Bowen theory extends the process to an understanding of the relationship system in which the mother is imbedded. An important part of the new perspective is that the mother's physiology is impacted by her own position in a relationship system that in turn impacts the physiology of her offspring. The implication of this view is that relationship processes within the emotional unit of the family influence the biology of its members.

Gordon's study of harvester ants also connects the study of the functioning of a harvester ant colony through the interaction of genes, environment, and behavior processes. While her work does not yet demonstrate the specificity of gene/environment effects found in maternal effects in the human, it does point in that direction. The Bowen theory also contributes to an understanding of the variation in functioning between insect societies and human families through the identification of the balance of life forces governing the level of interdependence of a living unit.

The theory of evolution by natural selection is one of the most important advances in the study of nature. It is the foundation upon which all biological sciences are based. New thinking regarding evolutionary process moves from the individual model based on natural selection to a systems model. The focus on reciprocity between organism, environment, and behavior processes takes into account systems processes that influence evolutionary trajectories. This perspective also includes cultural evolution based on social learning and teaching that impacts biological evolution (Laland et al., 2011).

Bowen theory's concept of multigenerational transmission process addresses the transmission of behavior across generations based on emotional programming. Emotional programming concerns the ongoing interactions of parents, grandparents, siblings, and other relatives on each child over the span of many years of development. A balance of forces for individuality and togetherness drives differences in the interaction process intensity. When a child becomes a focus of parental anxiety, the child's well-being comes to be more dependent on the attention and approval of others. This, in turn, impacts the growing child's ability to function independently beyond the family unit. All families exhibit lines of the family unit that move toward greater individuality (differentiation) and other family lines that move toward greater togetherness (fusion).

Emotional programming has not been studied in harvester ants. However, research findings based on epigenetic process, reciprocal interaction, and behavior are consistent with the concept of emotional programming. Studies may find that ant colonies resemble their parent colonies. If this is the case, emotional programming may be a useful way of accounting for varying degrees of reactivity between colonies as well as varying degrees of capacity for life regulation. Multigenerational transmission process goes beyond current thinking in the biological sciences regarding how relationship system processes program future generations.

Conclusion

In the Epilogue to *Family Evaluation* Murray Bowen wrote:

> Science will continue to expand knowledge for the millennium ahead. If knowledge about the human ever becomes an accepted science, it can share new knowledge with the accepted sciences and proceed into the future with the other sciences.
>
> (Kerr and Bowen, 1988, p. 360)

In the 25 years since he wrote those words, knowledge of the human family and knowledge across a range of disciplines has brought the study of the human's natural system closer to the study of other natural systems. Scientists and Bowen theorists have identified common processes of contact-distance, reciprocity, and regulatory mechanisms. Primitive indicators of differentiation appear in harvester ants as precursors to differentiation of self in human beings. Identifying common forces and processes between two species separated by 100 million years is an example of the potential contribution of Bowen theory to a more comprehensive view of the evolutionary process.

Acknowledgments

Many hours of study and dialogue with a range of individuals have been important in the development of my own thinking regarding ancient roots of differentiation. I am particularly grateful to Deborah M. Gordon, whose work has contributed enormously to the field of biology as well as to my own thinking. This is not to convey that Deborah M. Gordon or any other scientist whose work is cited would agree with my views, based on Bowen theory, expressed in this chapter.

REFERENCES

Bourne, G. M. (Ed.). (2011). Various points people miss: A training session by Dr. Murray Bowen at the Minnesota Institute of Family Dynamics. In O. Bregman and C. White (Eds.), *Bringing systems thinking to life* (pp. 31–60). New York: Taylor and Francis.

Bowen, M. (1978). *Family therapy in clinical practice.* New York: Jason Aronson.

Butler, J. (2011). Bowen's NIMH family study project and the origins of family psychotherapy. *Family Systems, 8*(2), 135–143.

Calhoun J. B. (1967). Ecological factors in the development of behavior anomalies. In J. Zubin and H. F. Hunt (Eds.), *Comparative psychopathology, animal and human* (pp. 1–31). The proceedings of the fifty-fifth annual meeting of the American Psychopathological Association, held in New York City, February, 1965. New York: Grune and Stratton.

Couzin, I. D. (2007). Collective minds. *Nature, 455,* 715.

Damasio, A. (2010). *Self comes to mind.* New York: Random House.

Eichholz, Alice. (2005). Quantifying multigenerational emotional process. Paper presented at the *42nd Symposium on Family Theory and Family Psychotherapy.* Bowen Center for the Study of the Family. Arlington, VA.

Flinn, M. (1999). Family environment, stress, and health during childhood. In C. Panter-Brick and C. Worthman (Eds.), *Hormones, health, and behavior* (pp. 105–138). Cambridge: Cambridge University Press.

Flinn, M. V. & England, B. G. (1995). Childhood stress and family environment. *Current Anthropology, 36,* 854–866.

Fodor, J. & Piattelli-Palmarini, M. (2011). *What Darwin got wrong.* New York: Farrar, Straus, and Giroux.

Gadagkar, R. (2009). Interrogating an insect society. *Center for Ecological Sciences and Centre for Contemporary Studies, Indian Institute of Scientific Research, 106*(26), 10407–10414.

Gordon, D. (1999). *Ants at work*. New York: Free Press, Simon and Schuster.

Gordon, D. (2010). *Ant encounters: Interaction networks and colony behavior*. Princeton, NJ: Princeton University Press.

Gordon, D. M., Holmes, S. & Nacu, S. (2008). The short-term regulation of foraging in harvester ants. *Behavioral Ecology, 19*, 217–222.

Greene, M. J. & Gordon, D . (2007). Interaction rate informs harvester ant task decision. *Behavioral Ecology, 10*, 1093.

Kerr, M. E. (1997). From the editor. *Family Systems: A Journal of Natural Systems Thinking in Psychiatry and the Sciences, 4*(1), 2–4.

Kerr, M. E. (2007). Why do siblings often turn out very differently? In A. Fogel, B. J. King, and S. G. Shankar (Eds.), *Human development in the twenty-first century: Visionary ideas from systems scientists* (pp. 200–215). Cambridge: Cambridge University Press.

Kerr, M. E. (2010). Are individuality and differentiation synonymous? Paper presented at the *47th Symposium on Family Theory and Family Psychotherapy*. Bowen Center for the Study of the Family. Arlington, VA.

Kerr, M. E. (2011). *Systems theory of individuality*. Video conference series. Bowen Center for the Study of the Family. Washington, DC.

Kerr, M. E. & Bowen, M. (1988). *Family therapy in clinical practice*. New York: Jason Aronson.

Laland, K. N., Sterelny K., Odling-Smee, J., Hoppit, W. & Uller, T. (2011). Cause and effect in biology revisited: Is Mayr's proximate-ultimate dichotomy still useful? *Science, 334*, 1512–1516.

Lewontin, R. (2000). *The triple helix*. Cambridge, MA: Harvard University Press.

McEwen, B. & Lasley, E. N. (2002). *The end of stress as we know it*. Washington, DC: Joseph Henry Press.

Meaney, M. (2010). Epigenetics and the biological definition of Gene × Environment interactions. *Child Development, 81*(1), 41–79.

Noone, B. (2008). The multigenerational transmission process and the neurobiology of and stress reactivity. *Family Systems, 8*(1), 21–31.

Panksepp, J. (1998). *Affective neuroscience: The foundations of human and animal emotions*. New York: Oxford University Press.

Rauseo, L. (1995). Relationships as primary regulators of physiology. *Family Systems, 2*(2), 101–115.

Seeley, T. D. (2010). *Honeybee democracy*. Princeton, NJ: Princeton University Press.

5

THE EVOLUTION OF HELPING

From Altruism, to Empathy, to Differentiation of Self

Stephanie J. Ferrera

To be full enough to give, and to give from one's fullness: what deeper urge is there?

These words, from novelist J. M. Coetzee (1990, p. 17), capture the deep emotional roots of altruism and empathy.

Long before humans arrived on the scene, as early as the evolution of mammals and birds, animals had developed the capacity to recognize distress in others and to respond to the needs or pain of the other. Darwin (1871/1981) saw sympathy and sacrifice for others as part of the "social instinct" that the human has in common with many other animals.

This chapter begins with an exploration of altruism and empathy in the animal world as a foundation for understanding these aspects of human behavior. Moving to the human level, we consider how the evolution of the more complex brain and more complex societies have made the development and expression of altruism and empathy more complex for humans. Bowen theory views altruism and empathy as part of the emotional process in families and societies. Knowledge of the emotional system, and knowledge of one's own emotional functioning, are valuable guides for defining principles that, like a beacon in a storm, can help one find thoughtful and responsible ways to respond in the midst of the emotional intensity of helping relationships. The author applies Bowen theory to real life with a set of principles that she developed to guide her responses to a serious illness in her own family.

Altruism

Robert Trivers defines an altruistic act as "one that confers a benefit on someone at a cost to the other" (1985, p. 41). He contrasts this with three other kinds of social interaction: selfish, in which one gains at the expense of the other; cooperative, in which both parties gain; and spiteful, in which both parties lose. Evolutionary theorists measure costs and benefits in terms of reproductive success, defined as an individual's total number of offspring surviving to a given age. The abundance of altruistic behavior seen in nature presents a puzzle, since biologists would expect natural selection to favor selfish behavior in pursuit of reproductive success.

Life, however, is not nearly that simple. Reproduction, as Trivers (1985, p. vii) noted, is a "social event," embedded in intricately interdependent relationships. Thus, the most effective avenues for reproductive success are the social avenues: helping, supporting, and cooperating with others. Biologists have explored these avenues and identified four categories of altruistic behavior: 1) Individuals will sacrifice their own interests in the pursuit of mating opportunities (sexual selection); 2) individuals will sacrifice for the benefit of offspring and close kin (kin selection); 3) individuals will engage in give-and-take exchanges for mutual benefit (reciprocal altruism); 4) individuals will sacrifice to protect the interests of their tribe or group, especially when the group is under threat (group selection).

Sexual Selection

Much of the altruism seen in nature is in the pursuit of mating and reproduction. Individuals will sacrifice a great deal for the opportunity to mate. For the male in some species of insect, mating calls for the ultimate sacrifice: He dies after copulation and may then be eaten by the female.

Intrigued by phenomena such as the peacock's tail, the deer's antlers, and male birds' plumage, traits that make their owners more conspicuous to predators and less able to flee, Darwin proposed that traits that appear detrimental to survival serve a different function: to help members of one sex compete with one another for mates. In *The Descent of Man and Selection in Relation to Sex* (1871/1981), he developed the concept of sexual selection. A century later, in his paper "Parental Investment and Sexual Selection" (1972), Robert Trivers extended the concept of sexual selection to explain why members of one sex, typically males, compete so energetically for access to the other. Parental investment is the key. Trivers defined parental investment (PI) as anything a parent does to promote the survival of an offspring. In most mammals, mother's PI significantly exceeds father's, a fact that has powerful ramifications on male-female differences in reproductive roles and strategies. Stated simply by Matt Ridley: "Males invest less and seek quantities of mates, while females invest more and seek quality of mates" (1993, p. 133).

In humans and some other species, the father's parental investment comes close to equaling that of the mother. With this, choosing mates becomes more a two-way street; the question of what males seek from females is almost as important as what females seek from males, or, in human terms, men will be expected to look for the same altruistic qualities in women as women look for in men.

Kin Selection

Kin selection is the altruism closely related individuals show one another in order to perpetuate the genes they have in common. Based on study of the highly integrated social systems of bees, wasps, and ants, William Hamilton wrote "The Evolution of Social Behavior" (1964), one of the most influential and frequently cited papers in the field of evolutionary biology. He demonstrated mathematically that the degree of altruistic behavior individuals show one another is closely correlated with the degree of genetic kinship between them. The greater the number of genes in common, the more individuals will sacrifice for one another. With kin selection, the concept of fitness is broadened to become *inclusive fitness*. Fitness is measured not only by an individual's own reproductive success, but also by the effects that individual has on the reproductive success of relatives. Examples can be found, not only in highly social species of insects but in many other species, in which a high percentage of colony or group members do not reproduce but function to support the reproductive success of the colony or group.

Reciprocal Altruism

Kin selection offers an explanation of altruistic behavior between related individuals, but much of the altruism in nature, and certainly in human relations, is between individuals who are only distantly related or not related. In another of the seminal papers in evolutionary biology, "The Evolution of Reciprocal Altruism" (1971), Trivers proposed a different kind of altruism and a pathway other than genetic relatedness through which high levels of social cohesiveness may be achieved. Whereas altruism between kin is largely a one-way street, reciprocal altruism is the two-way trading of helpful acts. Often the benefit to the receiver is greater than the cost to the giver. Give-and-take is established, with both sides enjoying a net gain. There are abundant examples of such mutually beneficial relationships in nature, and humans are masters at creating such partnerships.

For reciprocal altruism to evolve, individuals must have frequent contact, and the degree of mutual dependence that comes from living in small, stable groups as well as the cognitive skills to recognize others as individuals, to remember past transactions, and to keep an accounting of costs and benefits is required. Trivers saw reciprocal systems as unstable and vulnerable to being exploited by cheaters, and proposed that a complex psychological system evolved alongside reciprocal altruism to counteract this danger. Friendship, a sense of fairness, gratitude, sympathy, guilt, reparative altruism, trust, and suspicion are emotional responses that enable us to regulate our own altruistic and cheating tendencies and detect such tendencies in others. Yet a clever pretender can mimic these emotions and use them to his or her own advantage. Such is the complexity of reciprocal altruism.

Group Selection

The question of group selection, whether or not individuals are likely to sacrifice their own interests for the good of the group, and under what conditions, and to what extent, has been debated for decades among evolutionary biologists and social scientists. In his writings on the social instinct, Darwin took a position in support of group selection; he argued that when two tribes came into competition, the tribe that had more members "ready to give aid to each other and to sacrifice themselves for the common good, would be victorious over most other tribes, and this would be natural selection" (1871/1981, p. 166).

Edward O. Wilson refers to the phenomenon of individual sacrifice for group interests as "a primal rule of social life throughout the animal kingdom." He points out that individual advantage is bound up with group advantage, so that "loss of personal advantage by submission to the needs of the group is more than offset by gain in personal advantage due to the resulting success of the group" (1998, p. 245).

Laurie Lassiter (2011) finds support for group selection in her study of microbial species. She looked to bacteria and cellular slime molds to gain a deeper understanding of the way social systems in nature organize to promote their survival and reproduction. She describes in detail the "automatic programmed altruism" in which some cells in a colony suffer cell death while functioning in ways that promote the survival and reproduction of the colony. She speculates that the emotional system that Bowen saw in the human family might have its origins in these simpler social species:

> All life is stressed by paucity of food, energy, or space and by other environmental threats. When individuals behave so as to enhance their group's survival, does the larger emotional system survive and reproduce more predictably than do related but isolated individuals? Was the emotional system Bowen describes in human families present in early life forms?
>
> (Lassiter, 2011, p. 89)

Thinking Biologically About Altruism

Biologists use the concepts and language of selection to explain how characteristics evolve and are preserved in evolution. Traits and behaviors will be "selected for" when they are useful or "adaptive" for an organism in its pursuit of survival and reproductive success within its particular environment. It is proposed here that altruistic acts are part of the behavioral repertoires that have evolved at four levels of selection: sexual selection, kin selection, reciprocal altruism, and group selection. Correspondingly, it is proposed that altruistic behavior is adaptive in four distinctive ways: it helps individuals to attract and keep mates; it extends the individual's reproductive success, or inclusive fitness, by supporting offspring and close kin; it enlarges an individual's net benefits through reciprocal exchange; and it enhances an individual's status and security by contributing to the success of the group, or under conditions of scarcity or threat, survival and reproduction of some members is sacrificed for survival and reproductive success of the group.

To put it bluntly, we help others to help ourselves. Biologists have noted that in most cases altruism yields a return benefit to the actor. Stated by Trivers

> Models that attempt to explain altruistic behavior in terms of natural selection are models designed to take the altruism out of altruism. . . . Under certain conditions natural selection favors these altruistic behaviors because in the long run they benefit the organism performing them.
>
> (1971, p. 35)

Two further clarifications are needed to understand the way evolutionary biologists think about altruism. First, costs and benefits are measured in terms of what is profitable *to our genes*. Biologically speaking, it is accurate to say: we help others in order to help *our genes*. Many behaviors that are costly to the individual are profitable to that individual's genes, as Richard Dawkins famously explained in *The Selfish Gene* (1976). A costly sacrifice (think of the male praying mantis in mating) may yield high benefits as measured by the number of offspring produced and genes transmitted. In contrast, "genetic altruism," as defined by Bobbi S. Low (2000) is behavior that incurs a net genetic cost, benefiting reproductive competitors *at a reproductive cost to the doer.* Low offers these examples: giving your life for strangers under conditions in which no help comes back to your relatives, or giving costly help to nonrelatives without reciprocation. Such behaviors "cannot evolve through ordinary natural selection and are always vulnerable to competition from genetically selfish behaviors" (Low, 2000, p. 148). Pure unselfish altruism is found in human subjectivity and idealism, but rarely in nature. Ernst Mayr concurs: "Altruism toward strangers is a behavior not supported by natural selection," and goes on to make this important point: "We are not born with a feeling of altruism toward outsiders, *but acquire it through cultural learning*" (Mayr, 2001, p. 259; emphasis added).

Second, it is behaviors and consequences that count, not intentions or motives. The relevant question, states Dawkins, is "whether the *effect* of an act is to lower or raise the survival prospects of the presumed altruist and the survival prospects of the presumed beneficiary" (Mayr, 2001, p. 5; italics in original). It is the real effect of the act in terms of survival prospects that defines it as altruistic or not. The subjective dimensions of motives and intentions are not relevant in evolutionary analysis. Frans de Waal clarifies:

"Evolutionary explanations are built around the principle that all that natural selection can work with are the effects of behavior—not the motivation behind it" (2008, p. 280).

It is a rather challenging discipline to think with scientific objectivity about a subject endowed with as much emotion and subjectivity as the subject of altruism in human behavior. Altruism is at the center of much of the thinking on morality, often equated with virtue: "It is more blessed to give than to receive." Unselfishness is praised; selfishness chastised. In the literature of social psychology, altruism is considered "pro-social," selfishness "antisocial" (Trivers, 2002). Important social rewards come with being a "giver," and being recognized as a generous contributor to one's community. Darwin saw the "sense of glory" as an impetus to sacrifice. Beyond all of this, there is that "good feeling deep down," when one has relieved distress, brought comfort, and seen signs that a fellow creature has been helped. Said more poetically by Coetzee: "To give from one's fullness: what deeper urge is there?"

While, from an evolutionary perspective, proliferation of one's genes is understood as the underlying and ultimate force driving altruistic behavior, it is far removed from the conscious mind, which is otherwise occupied with the immediate necessities of life, concerns about taking care of oneself and others. De Waal states: "The return-benefits of altruistic behavior typically remain beyond the animal's cognitive horizon, occur so distantly in time that the organism is unlikely to connect them with the original act" (2008, p. 281). He argues that something more than an ultimate genetic payoff is needed to explain the spontaneous responsiveness to the needs of others that is seen in nature and in human social life. That "something more" leads us to shift from focusing on the *ultimate* cause, *why* a behavior evolved over thousands of generations, to focusing on the *proximate* cause, the immediate situation that triggers behavior and the role of neural and psychological processes.

This brings us to our next subject: the evolution of empathy.

Empathy

> In designing for the first time a creature that shows a concern for the suffering of other living things, nature seems to have attempted a 180-degree turnabout from what had been a reptile-eat-reptile and dog-eat-dog world.
>
> (MacLean, 1978, p. 339)

Empathy is a rapid and complex response to the distress of another individual. Over and above altruism, the capacity for empathy evolved in mammals and birds, most probably in conjunction with the early forms of parental care and family life and with the emergence of the limbic system and the prefrontal cortex in the brain.

Paul MacLean's Concept of Mammalian Behavioral Innovation

Neuroscientist Paul MacLean placed the origin of the family as a biological institution 180 million years ago with the appearance of the earliest mammals in Late Triassic times. He identified a "behavioral triad" that set mammals apart:

> In the evolution from reptiles to mammals three distinctive behavioral innovations were the development of 1) nursing in conjunction with maternal care, 2) audiovocal communication for maintaining maternal-offspring contact, and 3) playful behavior.
>
> (1982, p. 1)

With these mammalian innovations came the phenomenon of emotional attachment. De Waal notes:

> The evolution of attachment came with something the planet had never seen before: a feeling brain. The limbic system was added to the brain, allowing emotions such as affection and pleasure. This paved the way for family life, friendships, and other caring relationships.
>
> (2009, p. 68)

The three innovations identified by MacLean all have importance in the evolution of empathy. Consider first, nursing in conjunction with maternal care. When the female evolved the ability to produce what anthropologist Sarah Blaffer Hrdy calls "this biological white gold" (1999, p. 140), the period of intimacy between mothers and infants was necessarily prolonged, tied to the availability of mother's milk. Hrdy suggests that this prolonged intimacy was a significant step in the evolution of social relationships and eventually new parts of the brain, and new attributes, especially intelligence linked to empathy.

Second, consider the separation call. MacLean states: "Audiovocal communication becomes of the utmost importance in mammals for maintaining maternal-offspring contact. Separation of the offspring from the mother is calamitous" (1985, p. 415). He sees the separation cry as representing the earliest and most basic mammalian vocalization. He describes six different classes of vocalizations: peeps, chucks, twitters, errs or purrs, cackles, and noisy calls or screams. The types and intensities of calls signal the conditions under which they occur, ranging from mild distress, play, feeding, or competition to alarm and serious distress when being attacked (MacLean, 1990). The attunement of parent and offspring to one another's signals is a key step in the evolution of empathy.

Finally, consider the third innovation: play. Play behavior is often interpreted as a way for juveniles to imitate and learn adult behavior, or to discharge excess energy. MacLean's view is that play may have originally served to promote harmony in the group, and later, affiliation among group members. De Waal observes that laughter is infectious: "Human laughter is a loud display . . . that often signals mutual liking and well-being" (2009, p. 47). It is in "our primate sensitivity to others," he suggests, that empathy starts.

Frans de Waal's Russian Doll Model of Empathy

> Empathy is part of a heritage as ancient as the mammalian line. . . .
> The capacity arose long ago with motor mimicry and emotional con-
> tagion, after which evolution added layer after layer, until our ances-
> tors not only felt what others felt, but understood what others might
> want or need. The full capacity seems put together like a Russian doll.
> (2009, p. 208)

With this model, de Waal (2008, 2009) delineates three levels of empa-thy: 1) "emotional contagion" between individuals as they are affected by one another's emotional states; 2) "sympathetic concern" arising from an appraisal of the other's situation and emotions and expressed by comforting and consoling the other; and 3) "empathic perspective taking" in which one recognizes the other and the other's perspective as separate from oneself.

The innermost core of empathy is emotional contagion: emotional state-matching; automatic adoption of another's emotional state; being in sync. A flock of birds takes off all at once because one is startled; one infant in a nursery cries, and soon all are crying; an expression of fear by one individual evokes a fear response in others. There need not be any understanding of what triggered the initial response for the spreading of fear to occur. This automatic and spontaneous response is essential to survival, as when it leads a frightened individual to hide or flee, or a mother, distressed by her offspring's distress, to give reassurance to both of them through nurturing.

"Sympathetic concern" is de Waal's term for the next evolutionary step in empathy. A cognitive capacity is involved as emotional contagion is combined with appraisal of the other's situation and cause of the distress. Consolation is a manifestation of this level of empathy. Common in humans and apes, but rare in monkeys, are the gestures and signals offered to a distressed comrade, for example a bystander comforting the loser after a fight.

De Waal names the third level of empathy "empathic perspective taking." This calls for higher-level cognition. An individual not only feels the distress of another, but also understands the other's specific situation and need *separate from one's own*. Based on cognitively putting oneself in the other's place, one is capable of providing "targeted help," care that is fine-tuned to another's situa-tion. Among many examples, de Waal describes the mother ape who hears her youngster's whimper, sees that he is caught in a tree, sways her own tree toward the one her youngster is trapped in, and drapes her body between the trees to provide a bridge. "Tree bridging," he reports, is "a daily occurrence in orang-utans with mothers regularly anticipating their offspring's needs" (2008, p. 285).

De Waal makes a point that will catch the attention of anyone famil-iar with Bowen theory. He notes that the third level of empathy, empathic perspective-taking, rests on the ability to distinguish self and other as separate:

> For an individual to move beyond being sensitive to others toward an explicit other-orientation requires a shift in perspective. The emotional state induced in oneself by the other now needs to be attributed to the other instead of the self. A heightened self-identity allows a subject to relate to the object's emotional state without los-ing sight of the actual source of this state.
>
> (2008, p. 285)

Using a nautical analogy, de Waal calls the sense of self the "anchor" that holds one steady amidst waves of emotion: "In order to show genuine inter-est in someone else, offering help when required, one needs to keep one's own boat steady" (2009, p. 124).

De Waal's conceptualization of empathy as a three-stage evolutionary process resonates with the foundational concepts of Bowen theory: the emotional system and differentiation of self. Empathy originates with "emo-tional contagion," a purely emotional response, moves toward more cognitive involvement in the development of the capacity for "sympathetic concern" or "cognitive empathy," and culminates in the capacity to separate self from other cognitively in responding to distress. The "shift in perspective" de Waal is describing here is the essence of Bowen's concept of differentiation of self. The ability of one person to relate to another with empathy and compassion while also recognizing the other as separate and different from self, and the corresponding ability of one to respond to the *reality-based* need of the other rather than the projection of one's own needs to the other, are qualities of people at higher levels on the scale of differentiation. The importance of this "shift in perspective" will be explored next.

Differentiation of Self

A discussion of differentiation of self is best addressed by first looking at the context in which Bowen developed this concept: the view of the family as an emotional system.

Seeing the family as an emotional unit represents a radical departure from the prevailing view in the social sciences that sees the family as a collection of separate and largely autonomous individuals. Bowen states: "With families living together, I could see a completely different world" (1982, p. 2). That world revealed the profound degree to which the family emotional system governs and regulates the development and behavior of its members. "Systems thinking" never separates the functioning of the individual from the functioning of the family, or from other important social units, and therein lies a way of understanding human behavior that is not possible when the focus is primarily on the individual.

The difference between conceptualizing the family as a collection of separate, interacting individuals and conceptualizing the family as an emotional system makes a critical difference in the way social behavior is understood. The difference in regard to altruistic behavior is important.

When seen as one member of a collection of individuals, the individual is considered relatively autonomous and is expected to function primarily for self-interest. Individuals do this in social ways, as discussed earlier, sacrificing for mating opportunities, for the benefit of close relatives, for reciprocating partners, and for the benefit of their groups. From this perspective, such sacrifice and cooperation, while it may be subjectively motivated by social ideals, ultimately is expected to bring some return benefit, directly or indirectly, to the altruist.

From the perspective of the emotional system, the context for understanding the individual expands to include the larger family with the level of adaptability and the relationship patterns it has acquired across the generations. As part of this unit, the individual functions within the emotional climate of the family, responding to the varying levels of stress and anxiety, adapting to the pressure for togetherness. From this perspective, altruism is part of the emotional sensitivity and responsiveness among family members. On an automatic, emotional level, the sacrifices individuals make as they fit into the family may compromise their own functioning and well-being, with the only "return benefit" being the comfort of belonging.

Alongside seeing the family as an emotional unit or system, Bowen developed the concept of differentiation of self. He observed that within the family, with all of its emotional fusions and pressures for belonging or togetherness, there was also a striving by each member to develop an autonomous "self." From within the collective "we," individuals, to varying degrees, define a separate "I." The "force for individuality," like the "force for togetherness," is universal, but there is wide variation among individuals and among families in the way the two forces are balanced. Variation is the key word here. Observing the differences among family members, and between one family and another, in the levels of differentiation achieved, Bowen described variation in emotional functioning on a continuum or scale of differentiation.

Family Emotional Process in Helping Relationships

Like other mammals and primates, humans are deeply responsive to the needs and distress of others. However, empathy is by no means the only response.

Empathy is part of a mix of emotions that may include fear that the needs of others will tax one's resources or encroach upon one's freedom, anger at others for having the problems they have, or feeling overwhelmed at the seeming magnitude of the problem. In fact, all of the emotional responses that Trivers (1971) identified as intrinsic to reciprocal altruism—friendship, a sense of fairness, gratitude, sympathy, guilt, trust, and suspicion—come into play as people engage in giving and receiving help.

Because human needs and distress trigger anxiety, it is not surprising that emotional process often becomes intense in helping relationships. Anxiety, defined as emotional reactivity to a real or perceived threat, may easily overcome thinking as people address needs. Driven by anxiety, our reactions to a problem can create a bigger problem than the original problem.

Anxiety plays out in predictable relationship patterns that Bowen called "anxiety-binding mechanisms." One common pattern is distancing, a natural and universal tendency to avoid anxiety by avoiding the person or situation that triggers anxiety. An opposite response is over-involvement, the anxious tendency to try to fix the problem, often without an adequate understanding of the nature of the problem. This response easily slips into "reciprocal functioning," a pattern in which one partner takes a dominant position, the other an adaptive position. This may provide a measure of calm for all involved, but at the expense of the one who takes the adaptive or compromised posture, as Bowen notes:

> The one who functions for long periods in the adaptive position gradually loses the ability to function and make decisions for self. At that point, it requires no more than a moderate increase in stress to trigger the adaptive one into dysfunction, which can be physical illness, emotional illness, or social illness, such as drinking, acting out, and irresponsible behavior.
>
> (1978, p. 378)

Another pattern, and the one that Bowen saw as the key pathway to symptom development, is the family projection process. The essence of projection is the shift of anxiety from one person or group to another. The person in need is a ready object for the anxiety of others. Bowen astutely observed that parents and other family members often experience relief of their own anxiety as they focus attention on a child. The concept of the family projection process explains how a child, or any family member who becomes the focus of an intense family spotlight, becomes vulnerable to increased and prolonged anxiety. Thus does the family emotional process lead to impairment of those in the focus position.

The family projection process is driven by the mechanism of the triangle and interlocking triangles. Bowen observed that when the tension between two people reached a level of discomfort for either side, the more uncomfortable person would "triangle in" a third person. This creates a three-person system in which two are comfortably close and the third is a less comfortable outsider. The emotional forces within the triangle shift and change as each person seeks the most comfortable position. With added stress, the emotional process moves to involve more people, creating a series of interlocking triangles.

Laurie Lassiter proposes that the triangle is one of the ways in which an emotional system regulates its members, not only in humans but in other social species. She describes the triangle as a two-against-one process that, especially during times of real or perceived threat, will predictably encompass more individuals into a many-against-one set of interlocking triangles. In this way, the emotional unit exerts pressure on certain members to function for the survival and reproductive success of the system, at the expense of their individual interests. Lassiter states: "The triangle, as a two-or-more-against-one process is the bottom line of emotional pressure" (2008, p. 64). While an individual may be able to stand her ground with one person, she faces a different level of challenge against the concerted problem-focus of a whole family or group. Dr. Bowen often noted that, unchecked, emotional intensity would "do someone in." The one who is "done in" participates unknowingly in the process, not necessarily because she has more real problems than others, but because she is more vulnerable than others to absorbing the total family anxiety. Kathleen Kerr describes the projection process as automatic, out-of-awareness, and involving the entire family:

> The aim of the process is to dissipate anxiety in the system as a whole, not to decrease functioning in the person who is the object of the focus. This is a side effect of the process. With the best of intentions a family can "do in" its own and be deeply troubled by the end product of its own processes.
>
> (1999, p. 74)

When a problem or symptom is magnified out of proportion rather than dealt with realistically, or when a problem persists or grows more serious in spite of efforts to solve it, it is probable that triangling and the projection process are active. Bowen's further insight was that an acute problem, symptom, or illness becomes chronic when "it slips unnoticed into a usefulness in the family" (Bowen, 1990). The problem becomes chronic when it begins to serve some function in the relationship system. It may become a focal point for the collective reactivity of the family, a rallying point for family unity, an overshadowing concern that draws attention away from other areas, or an avenue for enhanced functioning of some members. Caring for others can be emotionally fulfilling and socially praiseworthy, yet when the caretaker begins to do for others what they are able to do for themselves and the recipient succumbs to a helpless posture, a boundary has been crossed. Over time the fusion undermines the functioning of the more vulnerable person despite empathy and good intentions.

After first describing this process in families, Bowen went on to observe the same process on a larger scale in societies. He saw certain groups in the society as most likely to become objects of the projection process:

> These groups fit the criteria for long-term, anxiety-relieving projection. They are vulnerable to become the pitiful objects of the benevolent, oversympathetic segment of society that improves its functioning at the expense of the pitiful. Just as the least adequate child in a family can become more impaired when he becomes an object of pity and oversympathetic help from the family, so can the lowest segment of society be chronically impaired by the very attention designed to help.
>
> (1978, p. 445)

Edwin Friedman took his understanding of Bowen theory to his work as a religious leader, teacher, and writer to illuminate his observations of emotional process in religious congregations and in society. He was struck by the growing popularity of the concept of empathy, especially in the training of leaders. While he acknowledged that "being responsive to others, and perhaps even sharing their pain exquisitely . . . is heartfelt, humanitarian, highly spiritual and an essential component in a leader's response repertoire" (Friedman, 1999, p. 179), he also expressed concern about the regressive results of the overuse or misuse of empathy. Consistent with Bowen's thinking, Friedman drew an important distinction between empathy and responsibility:

> The focus on "need fulfillment" that so often accompanies an emphasis on empathy leaves out the possibility that what another may really "need" (to become more responsible) is *not* to have their needs fulfilled. Indeed, it is not even clear that feeling for others is a more caring stance (or even a more ethical stance) than challenging them to take responsibility for themselves.
>
> (1999, pp. 179–180)

The same anxiety-driven relationship patterns that are involved in symptom development and impairment of certain members of a family or a society are also involved in the way that families and societies try to help their symptomatic members. Despite good intentions, some efforts to help do make problems worse. People become caught in repetitive ways of responding that don't work, yet are unable to envision more flexible and creative options. When one or more members have sufficient knowledge about the emotional process and its mechanisms to observe it in the family, and especially to observe and modify their own parts in it, the family gains a better chance to calm down and make thoughtful choices.

123

Differentiation of Self in Helping Relationships

Differentiation of self encompasses altruism and empathy, but goes beyond the emotional level. With increasing cognition, humans evolved the capacity to balance automatic emotional responses with thinking, and, with this, the ability to understand the needs of others at a more complex level and to consider the longer-term consequences of expressing the instinct to help. The effort toward differentiation of self involves discernment of needs in context, awareness of one's history and the automatic programming acquired in one's own family, management of those automatic responses, and increasing responsibility in the way one offers help and asks for help. The following statement from Michael Kerr is an elegant summary of the ideal balance between thinking and feeling that one strives for in the helping relationship, on both the giving and receiving sides.

> When the intellectual system has the option to operate independently of the feeling system, it is possible for an individual to do for himself without being selfish and to do for others without being selfless. This becomes possible when behavior is based more on principle than on the obligatory pressure of the feeling system.
>
> (1988, p. 335)

Principles are the expression of one's "best thinking." In times of relative calm, one works out the beliefs, convictions, and action positions that serve as the "the beacon in the storm," to steer one through times of stress, intensity, and confusion. This preparation can make the difference between offering a "quick fix" that hazards making things worse, or offering de Waal's "targeted help," accurately tuned to the reality-based needs.

In earlier writing on the subject of help (Ferrera, 1999), I offered a set of principles that came out of my effort to respond thoughtfully to one of the most difficult problems in my family, my younger sister's diagnosis of multiple sclerosis and subsequent years of illness and disability. My sister was in her thirties, married with a houseful of young children and a career as a church organist when the illness was diagnosed. The illness took a steady downhill course. Each exacerbation reduced her functioning and called for increased care. Over several years, she became severely impaired and received intensive medical care at home. She died at the age of 62, having shown extraordinary adaptability and will to live in the face of daunting physical limitations and losses over almost 30 years of illness.

At the time of Katharine's diagnosis, I also was in my thirties, married, with a houseful of children. In addition, I was beginning a master's degree in social work and was newly acquainted with Bowen theory. My position as responsible oldest daughter, underscored by several other factors and patterns in the family, had steered me toward the role of family caretaker. Over the years I had focused my helpfulness on whichever family member my mother was most worried about. With the onset of my sister's illness, the stage was set for me to become a "super" caretaker.

Looking back, I know I fell short of my "best," but I also believe I spared my sister and family what might have been my "worst," the automatic overfunctioning reactions that are my deep legacy from the family multigenerational past. Over the years, the principles have held solid and it has been useful to consult them on many occasions of heightened anxiety. I revisit them here with a few further thoughts.

First, *remember the power of calmness*. The contagion of anxiety and its impact on an emotional field is well known. Calmness is also contagious. The person who can keep a perspective, focus on facts, think before acting, and remain somewhat, even by a few degrees, calmer than others becomes a resource to the family or group. After exhausting every option for changing others and solving a problem, I remind myself that the only thing left is to manage my own anxiety and hopefully transmit a degree of calmness to others. It helps to recall MacLean's wisdom about playfulness being a marker of mammalian behavior, and Friedman's idea that while we must face the seriousness of the problem, we must also watch out for the problem of the seriousness: "In an atmosphere where everything is dire, a vicious cycle develops. As loss of playfulness destroys perspective, the seriousness 'uptights' everyone further, thus circling back to escalate the reactivity of members to one another" (Friedman, 1999, p. 84). Sometimes when I went to see Katharine, she would be the calmest person in the room. I would come in with my rushed, serious focus on "what needs to be done," and she would greet me with a joke.

Second, *stay in contact*. This is not as easy or obvious as it sounds. Distancing is an automatic and ubiquitous response when anxiety is raised. Feeling overwhelmed by a problem or a need, not knowing "what to do," may lead one to retreat and do nothing. When this happens, the ill or impaired person has a double problem: living with the illness and being stayed away from. "Just show up," is something one can do even when feeling inadequate to handle a problem. Bowen often spoke of the importance of being "present and accounted for." Third, *relate to the whole person*. A diagnosis does not define a person. There is more to a person than her illness or problem. As Katharine's illness progressed, it became harder to find the strong and gifted woman I had known, and our sister relationship was submerged at times by our roles as the helper and one being helped. Ultimately, she taught me more than anyone what a deep inner core of strength and spirit looks like.

Closely related to the third principle is the fourth: *respect the autonomy of the other*. All of us are vulnerable to loss of self under pressure. Illness or impairment add greatly to the ordinary pressures of life, putting one in a position of increased reliance on others, often limiting one's freedom and privacy. Faced with such challenges, people show varying abilities to maintain autonomy, and helpers show varying levels of sensitivity to know when help is needed and when it is better to stay out of the way. My sister came to need increasing physical care, but she did not need people to think for her. She had choices with regard to how she thought about her life and how she dealt with the illness.

Fifth, *give information without telling others what to do*. With illness or impairment, an individual's world shrinks. Energy is pulled into day-to-day survival; there is less time, energy, or capacity to attend to the larger world. Family, friends, and helpers are a resource when they bring information that allows a confined person to stay in contact with the world, especially information that is relevant to personal needs and choices. The challenge I found was to manage my own investment in what my sister and family did with the information. What I considered a gem of information might or might not be of interest to them as they constructed their own solutions.

A profound lesson in emotional neutrality and self-awareness is offered by Loretta Nowakowski, a nurse whose practice focused on caring for elderly and frail people. She speaks to the subject of being neutral amid the intensity of health care systems:

> The question of resources would become very different if we gave people time to think over a decision. We are not to assume what the patient needs or wants. As professionals, we are consultants. It is the patient's life to manage.
>
> (Nowakowski, 1996)

Nowakowski's ability to convey relevant medical information to her patients in a neutral way allowed even very ill patients to come forward with their own decisions about life and death matters. What she saw convinced her that "an organism can hear important things about itself as long as there is life" (Nowakowski, 1996).

Sixth, *define one's own position and limitations*. Grandiosity may be part of the desire to help. In fantasy, one seeks the power to save others; in reality one has definite limitations. An emotional "I-will-be-all-things-to-you" was my initial response to Katharine's illness. It was a slow and humbling learning process to discover how little I could actually do against the powerful forces driving a serious illness. Yet that "little" was an important little. If I could offer support and interest for what it was, not expecting it to change anything very much, I could stay connected. If I allowed myself to become overtaxed, I might burn out and be tempted to cut off. As I shifted my focus from trying to solve the problem to defining what I realistically could and could not do, my choices became clearer. I became somewhat more open with her about the realities of my life and my availability to her. To follow this principle requires facing the possibility that one's limits may be reached before the needs of the other are met.

Seventh, *allocate resources in a balanced way.* One of the most basic yet daunting jobs for a family, and for a community and a society, is to provide resources to care for the needs of its members. Another is to distribute resources equitably amidst a multitude of complex, competing demands. Emotional process is ever-present in the way these challenges are addressed. Emotional intensity focuses on those with illness, impairment, and other problems as "special," which can mean that they become the objects of intensive investment of resources, or, at the other end of the spectrum, they can be discounted or stigmatized. Both extremes push the individual toward an isolated position.

The real problem is not so much the lack of resources, but the anxiety about resources. When anxiety is managed well, a family or helping system can be amazingly creative about finding and using resources. With a cooperative mix of talents and ideas, a variety of people making a variety of contributions, the needs become manageable. People become more confident that there will be "enough to go around," and that they can live within the limitations of their resources.

Eighth, *stay connected with every member of the system.* With increasing anxiety, a family or helping system can become polarized, a divided system with people taking sides on questions of how much help is needed, and what is the "right" way to help. The more involved caretakers may become critical toward the "uncaring" ones who are not doing enough while the "outsiders" may resent the "insiders" who don't include them.

The beauty of a system, especially when it is operating calmly, is that each member has a unique contribution to make. As years went by, I saw members of my family engage in Katharine's life in ways that I could not have done, or even imagined doing.

To follow the eighth principle, one also needs the ninth: *stay in contact with objective thinking and objective thinkers.* Bowen believed firmly that humans were capable of thinking objectively about themselves, even about close-to-home personal issues. He developed a disciplined approach and a theory to provide a guide to objective thinking. One needs sufficient knowledge of history and context to see the bigger picture, and then one needs knowledge of the emotional system to understand that picture. The quest for objectivity has led the curious all the way back to multigenerational family history and evolution to gain a broad perspective. Regular contact with this body of knowledge and regular contact with thinkers and writers who have achieved a reasonable level of objectivity and emotional neutrality are valuable resources for one who aspires to think more objectively. Open any page of Bowen's book *Family Therapy in Clinical Practice* (1978), and you will make contact with objective thinking and emotional neutrality.

Tenth, *work toward open relationships.* Bowen defined an open relationship as one in which the partners can communicate a high percentage of personal thoughts and feelings to one another. Relationships are often most open in the early stages when positive attraction is strong. As conflictual issues emerge, partners tend to become more guarded, editing sensitive subjects out of the conversation. As communication shrinks to fewer and fewer "safe subjects," people come to believe, "We just can't communicate!"

The open relationship is marked by interest, respect, and appreciation for the other as an individual separate and different from self. Differences are not divisive; they are seen as part of the individuality of each person and a source of richness in the relationship. Kerr observes, "When people can listen without reacting emotionally, communication is wide open and differences are an asset . . . not a liability" (1988, p. 188).

A relationship is open to the extent to which partners can see, hear, and understand one another in a relatively objective and accurate way, free of projection, bias, criticism, pressure, and anxiety. Roberta Gilbert describes openness as a quality of higher functioning families:

> People are aware of what they think and can express that accurately and appropriately to others. They can wait to speak, when necessary, until they are sure of what they think.
> They are also open to hear what others think. . . . Defining of self is not telling the other what to do, it is a statement about self—an "I-position." The openness of the relationship system insures that everyone in it knows pretty much what everyone else thinks about most important topics.
>
> (1999, p. 98)

A climate of calmness gives people a better chance to think; thinking leads to clarity; clarity leads to knowing one's convictions and where one stands; knowing where one stands and having the courage to communicate it is the work of developing the "I-position." If people could recognize that their best thinking is also their best contribution to their families and communities, they might be more encouraged to speak their thoughts.

To be seen, heard, and understood is a deep human desire. When this level of human contact is achieved, it is enormously calming and healing. People bring out the best in one another. When the best thinking and resourcefulness in one connects with the best in another, there is a creative opening up of possibilities and solutions beyond what any one person could have envisioned.

Concluding Comment

Nature has endowed humans with an impetus toward altruism, a capacity for empathy, a highly evolved brain, and a force for differentiation of self. The beauty of differentiation is that it is a process designed by nature that allows us to move a degree or two "beyond nature," toward understanding and addressing dilemmas that are inherent in the biological roots of human behavior. The work of differentiation encompasses balancing automatic emotional responses with thinking, considering the relationship of needs to resources, of costs to benefits, of intentions to actual outcomes, of immediate urgency to longer-term consequences. The work of differentiation requires discernment of complex issues and careful definition of principles. At our best, we find the graceful balance between responding to one another's needs and respecting one another's strength and autonomy.

Bowen wrote:

> Man has a responsibility to those less fortunate. Responsible man fulfills such responsibilities automatically. If the most influential segment of society could work toward the differentiation of self, it would automatically spread through the less influential segments and really benefit the less fortunate segment and raise the functional level of all society.
>
> (1978, p. 450)

REFERENCES

Bowen, M. (1978). *Family therapy in clinical practice*. New York: Jason Aronson.

Bowen, M. (1982). Subjectivity, Homo sapiens, and science. *Family Center Report, 4*(2), 1–4.

Bowen, M. (1990). Chronic illness in family adaptation. Paper presented at the *Symposium on Chronic Illness: Implications of Bowen Theory for the Study of Health and Illness*. Georgetown Family Center. Washington, DC.

Coetzee, J. M. (1990). *Age of iron*. New York: Random House.

Darwin, C. (1871/1981). *The descent of man and selection in relation to sex*. Princeton, NJ: Princeton University Press.

Dawkins, R. (1976). *The selfish gene*. Oxford: Oxford University Press.

de Waal, F. B. (2008). Putting the altruism back into altruism: The evolution of empathy. *Annual Review of Psychology, 59*(1), 279–300. doi.1146/annurev.psycho.59.103006. 093625

de Waal, F. B. (2009). *The age of empathy*. New York: Three Rivers Press.

Ferrera, S. J. (1999). What is help? A theoretical and personal perspective. *Family Systems, 5*(1), 44–55.

Friedman, E. H. (1999). *A failure of nerve* (E. W. Beal & M. M. Treadwell, Eds.). Bethesda, MD: The Edwin Friedman Estate.

Gilbert, R. M. (1999). *Connecting with our children*. New York: John Wiley & Sons.

Hamilton, W. D. (1964). The evolution of social behavior. *Journal of Theoretical Biology, 7*, 1–52.

Hrdy, S. B. (1999). *Mother Nature*. New York: Pantheon Books.

Kerr, K. B. (1999). The projection process in health care systems. *Family Systems, 5*(1), 71–80.

Kerr, M. E. & Bowen, M. (1988). *Family evaluation: An approach based on Bowen theory*. New York: W. W. Norton & Co.

Lassiter, L. L. (2008). The regulatory function of the triangle. In P. Titelman (Ed.), *Triangles: Bowen family systems theory perspectives* (pp. 63–89). New York: Haworth Press.

Lassiter, L. L. (2011). Others. In L. Margulis, C. Asikainen, and W. Drumbein (Eds.), *Chimeras and consciousness* (pp. 71–90). Cambridge, MA: MIT Press.

Low, B. S. (2000). *Why sex matters.* Princeton, NJ: Princeton University Press.

MacLean, P. D. (1978). A mind of three minds: Educating the triune brain. In *Education and the brain* (pp. 308–342). Offprint from the Seventy-seventh Yearbook of the National Society for the Study of Education. Chicago, IL: The National Society for the Study of Education.

MacLean, P. D. (1982). The co-evolution of the brain and family. *Anthroquest, 24*(Winter), 1, 14–15.

MacLean, P. D. (1985). Brain evolution relating to family, play, and the separation call. *Archives of General Psychiatry, 42*(April), 405–417.

MacLean, P. D. (1990). *The triune brain in evolution.* New York: Plenum Press.

Mayr, E. (2001). *What evolution is.* New York: Basic Books.

Nowakowski, L. (1996). Lecture presented at *Family Health Services' Bowen Theory Conference: Anxiety and Organizations in Today's Society,* Houston ,TX.

Ridley, M. (1993). *The red queen: Sex and the evolution of human nature.* New York: Macmillan.

Trivers, R. (1985). *Social evolution.* Menlo Park, CA: Benjamin/Cummings.

Trivers, R. (1971). The evolution of reciprocal altruism. *Quarterly Review of Biology, 46*(1), 35–57. doi: 10.1086/406755

Trivers, R. (1972). Parental investment and sexual selection. In B. Campbell (Ed.), *Sexual selection and the descent of man 1871–1971* (pp. 136–179). Chicago, IL: Aldine.

Trivers, R. (2002). *Natural selection and social theory.* New York: Oxford University Press.

Wilson, E. O. (1998). *Consilience: The unity of knowledge.* New York: Alfred Knopf.

II

DIFFERENTIATION OF SELF IN
THE THERAPIST'S OWN FAMILY

6

DEFINING A SELF IN FAMILY, PROFESSION, AND SOCIETY

Peter Titelman

Differentiation of self, the cornerstone concept in Bowen theory, is a universal human process—the integration of the instinctual forces of *individuality* and *togetherness*. This process is usually complete by the time a young adult leaves home. *Defining a self* refers to the intentional activity of an individual, usually under the auspices of coach or consultant trained in Bowen theory, of differentiating a self in his or her family—the nuclear family, family of origin, and extended family. The terms *differentiating a self* and *defining a self* are essentially synonymous (Bowen, 1978a, p. 541).

Each of us lies along a universal continuum in our capacity to separate thinking from the emotional expression of reactivity. In Bowen theory, emotion is the automatic, instinctual life force that binds individuals in a family and subsequently in nonfamily groups and organizations. Achieving a higher level of functioning in one's family involves the ability to reflect on and control one's emotional reactivity in family relationships. This same capacity enables us to define ourselves in our professional relationships and our relationships in the wider society. One's efforts to define a self in these three spheres are inextricably intertwined.

What follows is a description of my own efforts to define a self in family, profession, and society from 1972 to 2014 from the perspective of Bowen theory.[1]

Defining a self is a lifetime project—one that is never complete. I will describe certain major nodal events in the life of my family that offered fortuitous opportunities to pursue this work intentionally. Differentiating a higher functioning self involves periods of progress, stuckness, and, at times, regression. Energetic periods are followed by lulls in this nonlinear lifetime effort.

Efforts to Define a Self in the Family: 1972–2014[2]

The events focus especially on the primary triangle[3] in the family of origin, on dealing with the illness and death of parents, on the value of rituals surrounding death, and on bridging emotional cutoff in the extended family.[4]

Death Rituals and Their Value: A Bowen Theory Perspective

A ritual is a set of actions, religious or secular, that generates symbolic meaning. Individuals, groups, or entire communities can enact them, publicly or privately, in formal or informal settings.

Bowen (1978a) described the importance of ritual in dealing with death. Death rituals allow the family and larger social networks to acknowledge death without denial and without isolating the family from the community. "[T]he best function of a funeral," he wrote, "is served when it brings relatives and friends into the best possible functional contact with the harsh fact of death and with each other at this time of high emotionality" (p. 331).

Family death rituals, including the presence of significant members of the larger community, are enacted along the continuum of differentiation of self of the family. At the lower end of the continuum the ritual will be more inflexible, more rote, and will involve a higher level of emotional reactivity. At higher levels on the continuum, family rituals are more flexible and less emotionally reactive—that is, less impulsive and out of control. They are more expressive of the individuality of family members, rather than being driven by emotional fusion in the family or by societal patterns and expectations.

This description of the function of rituals applies equally to religious, secular, traditional, and nontraditional death rituals. The advantages of certain ancient traditional rituals, or newly created ones, depend on the levels of differentiation and chronic anxiety that undergird the way those rituals are expressed and experienced by families and communities.

A Brief Family History

The Family of Origin

I was born in Los Angeles and lived there until age 11 (Figure 6.1). My sister is four years older than I am. My father trained and practiced briefly as a lawyer, he then worked as a labor organizer and, later, worked in retail businesses. When I was 11 we moved to western Pennsylvania and my father took a position in his family's business. Three years later he became national sales manager of that company and we moved to New York City.

My mother started a private elementary school in Los Angeles, helped start a community mental health center in Pennsylvania, and was director of a college-based elementary school in New York City. My parents retired in their mid-fifties and moved to the south of France, where they lived the rest of their lives after I went to college.

I attended a Quaker college in Indiana and got my PhD in psychology in Pittsburgh, where I met and married my first wife. After graduation we moved to western Massachusetts and had a son and a daughter. We separated

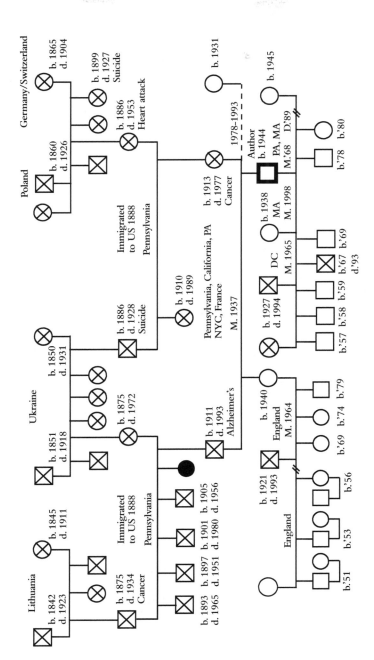

Figure 6.1 Titelman Family Diagram

after 20 years of marriage and divorced in 1989. After a three-year courtship, I remarried in 1998.

My sister went to college in Vermont and spent a semester in England, where she met and married a man and henceforth lived. She had three children and three stepchildren. Her husband died of cancer in 1993.

The symptom patterns that controlled fusion in our family were: 1) reciprocal over- and underfunctioning, with my mother in the overfunctioning position and my father in the underfunctioning position (she worried about him and took care of him; he was depressed); and 2) projection of anxiety onto a child: I received the brunt of my parents' anxiety, expressed as concern about my intellectual and emotional functioning.

The Paternal Extended Family

Judging from the stories that my parents, uncles, aunts, and older cousins told me, my father was a bright, charming youngest child with four older brothers. He was born after the miscarriage of a girl. His mother, a strong and stoic woman, came to the United States from Belarus. After having four sons, she desperately wanted a daughter. After my father's birth, the doctor did not tell her for three days that her newborn was a boy. As a baby he was initially dressed in girls' clothes. In his primary triangle he was fused with and babied by his mother; they were in conflict with his father. The latter was a playboy with a history of infidelity who enjoyed exotic cars and made his own wine. He started a sportswear business. My father and three of his older brothers exhibited some of their father's behaviors.

One of those uncles described my father as always the sensitive, emotional one in the family, the brother who needed to be protected. My father was the only one of the five brothers who went to college. Under pressure from his father, who was dying of colon cancer, he became a lawyer. Unhappy with the practice of law, he later became a labor union organizer and political radical. Eventually he grew disillusioned with politics and joined the family sportswear business, founded by his father, and owned by the middle brother.

The Maternal Extended Family

My mother was the younger of two sisters. Her mother considered her "the cute one" who would go into theater. Her mother saw her sister, F, as more intelligent, and she went to an Ivy League college. Their father, himself an Ivy League graduate, was described as "very sensitive." One day in 1928, when he was 42, he shut the doors and windows in his kitchen and turned on the gas. My mother was 13 at the time.

She told me this story in 1974, when I was 30. It was F who first came upon the scene. Their mother and grandmother were out of town. F smelled gas coming from the closed kitchen and ran next door to get help from an aunt. She tried to conceal the grim truth of their father's death from her younger sister.

My aunt's decision to become a Red Cross rescue worker, and my mother's decision to focus on the emotional life of children, may have been responses to their father's suicide. My mother's mother was a resilient and warm woman who started a bookstore and raised her daughters effectively in spite of her husband's death.

The Family Projection Process

In the three years following my first learning of my grandfather's suicide, I began to reflect on how the family projection process worked over three generations. I came to see how I had received the brunt of the family anxiety from the interlock of my mother's and father's families, not just from my mother. Both grandfathers underfunctioned emotionally and both grandmothers overfunctioned.

The projection of anxiety had three components: 1) Males were perceived as weak, females strong. The significant nodal event was my grandfather's suicide. 2) My mother took care of my father and naturally worried that if she didn't do so he would become more depressed, dysfunctional, and potentially suicidal, since she had experienced her own father's suicide. I believe this accounted for my mother's constant watchfulness and overprotectiveness. 3) Finally, I was a male in a family of vulnerable males.

On the maternal side of the extended family the projection process settled on my mother after the suicide of her father, as she was more sensitive than her older sister. Her anxiety took the form of overfunctioning for males, specifically my father and myself.

On the paternal side of the family, projection settled on my father as the spoiled, sensitive youngest child. And I lived out my father's position as the babied one, while my father managed somewhat to extricate himself—or pretend to—from that position, passing it on to his son. My fusion with my mother paralleled my father's fusion with his mother.

In another kind of fusion, my parents and great-grandparents were first cousins. My father's mother was the oldest sister of my mother's father. I remember her as a strong, stoic character. In both families, the fathers were weaker and more "sensitive" than the mothers.

Family Reactivity to Death, Ritual, and the Effort to Define a Self

Avoiding death rituals that allow family and friends to grieve together and express respect for the dead has been a theme in my family.

When I was nine my maternal grandmother had a fatal heart attack. My mother told me that she had been taken to the hospital, but not that she had died. "She's okay," my mother said, and began to cry. A little later I learned that my grandmother had died. My father and I drove to the hospital so that he could sign the necessary documents while I waited in the car. My mother stayed home.

There was no funeral or other formal death ritual. A few family friends came to the house, bringing food. I never returned to my grandmother's apartment or saw any of her personal items again, except for photos of her. Perhaps my mother's inability to speak of her death and the avoidance of any funeral rite were related to her father's suicide and her reactions to his funeral, which involved an open casket in their home.

For many years I assumed that my grandmother had been cremated in Los Angeles, where we were living at the time of her death. No one told me that her remains were placed in the same cemetery plot where my grandfather was buried, nor did I know where the plot was located. It was not until 2011 that I came upon a photograph online of their gravestone and discovered that they were in Mount Carmel Cemetery in Philadelphia. As far as I know, my parents never visited the gravesite after my grandmother's death in 1953.

When my father's mother died in 1972 I went to her funeral with many extended family members, but my parents and sister did not. My father explained that he had visited his mother a few months earlier and it did not seem necessary to return to Philadelphia from France for the funeral. My sister was living in England. My father thus isolated himself from sharing the experience of loss and grief. Unresolved attachment, emotional fusion, and expression of undifferentiation may have also been factors of which I was unaware.

My parents explained their behavior by saying that death was a part of life and didn't have religious meaning for them. They and their parents were all nonpracticing Jews with a humanistic philosophy. My father had a bar mitzvah, but it was more of a social than a religious event. I agreed with my parents' philosophy, but also saw their way of dealing with death as indirect and lacking connection with family and community.

Bowen theory regarding the taking of I-positions as part of defining self in the family has enhanced my understanding of the importance of weddings, funerals, and other rituals. It was important to attend my paternal grandmother's funeral and to be present and accounted for in my extended family, although my father was not there. Dealing with death and the rituals around it was part of my effort to take I-positions. Further efforts on this theme will be described in a later section.

Efforts Toward Defining a Self in the Primary Triangle: 1973–1977

When I graduated from college in 1966 and went to graduate school in Pittsburgh, my parents moved to the south of France, where they lived for the rest of their lives.

In 1971 I began studying Bowen family systems theory and making a serious effort to apply the theory to defining self in my family. At Thanksgiving 1973 my maternal aunt came from Brooklyn, New York, to visit my wife and me. I was creating an extensive family diagram, and I pressed her for details of our family history for five or six hours. Her knowledge of names, dates, and other basic facts was extensive. Sometime afterward she let me know that I had worked her over mercilessly. It was a good lesson: Don't be overexuberant in questioning family members.

My initial focus was on my relationship with my parents. This led to a series of events that helped modify my relationships in the primary triangle of mother-father-son. I visited them in the summer of 1974 and found my mother concerned about my father's depression and worried that he might commit suicide. She wanted to go to England to visit my sister and her family and do some consulting work, but was afraid to leave my father alone. This was when she told me for the first time that her father had killed himself—because he was depressed about business problems, she thought.

She told me that on the way to her father's burial she had overheard two first cousins—brothers of her future husband—say that because my grandfather had killed himself the family might not be able to collect his life insurance. This left my mother in emotional turmoil. Her older sister, who was the first one on the scene, had said their father died of a heart attack.[5]

The revelation of my mother's painful past gave me a new, less reactive way of understanding her overprotectiveness toward both my father and me. I saw that her emotional process probably stemmed from unresolved feelings about her father's suicide.

On this occasion in the summer of 1974 my mother asked me, with some emotion, to talk with my father and help him feel less depressed. I responded that I did not see my father in the same light as she did, and that I did not think he was suicidal. This was an effort not to fuse with my mother's anxiety and not get triangled into my mother's agenda. I said she might be overconcerned about his well-being, and that it was important for her to do something for herself. I encouraged her to go to England without him, if he was not in the mood to go with her.

A few months later she did just that, to visit my sister and look for part-time consulting work. My father preferred to stay at home and garden; he was relieved not to have to tag along with his wife. She did in fact get work in England, thereafter consulting three or four times a year with the principal of a private day school.

By not colluding with my mother in her perception of my father as severely impaired, I made a deliberate move away from my usual position in the primary triangle. This detriangling move seemed to serve as a stimulus for my mother to become less anxious in relation to my father.

I made a plan to raise the issue of my grandfather's death the next time I saw my mother and aunt together. We met at a restaurant in London in

December 1975. I looked squarely at them and said, "How did my grand-father die?" They both kept to their previous stories, remaining calm and nonreactive to each other on this issue. Bringing up my grandfather's death with my mother and aunt was an effort to talk about my grandfather in an open and direct way. During this discussion my mother seemed less anxious than when I had visited her in France a year and a half earlier.

I resolved to spend more time one-on-one with my father and less time with my mother, without actually neglecting her, and did just that during my 1975 visit with them. Predictably, my mother sensed this movement toward my father. I tried to avoid engaging her in intellectualized discussions—an old pattern—that she experienced as a painful loss. Near the end of the trip, when we were alone one day, she said she missed talking with me: "You must be angry with me. You seem to be avoiding me." I managed not to become reactive, and she became less defensive.

I returned home, feeling successful at forging a closer relationship with my father while staying in contact but not fusing with my mother, even in the face of her efforts to make that happen. During this same period and continuing in 1976 I made great progress on my doctoral dissertation, believing that the work of defining a self in my family had played a part in being able to move toward completing a degree I had been working on for almost 10 years.

Efforts to Define a Self in Relation to My Mother's Illness and Death: 1976–1977

My wife and I returned to the United States early in 1976. Soon after, my mother wrote that she had seen her doctor, who advised her to take Provera (used in hormone replacement therapy and in treating some cancers) and then have a hysterectomy in March. She was cheerful about her medical condition. In fact, she had been diagnosed with uterine cancer, which she tried to conceal from me. I knew she was likely to hide the seriousness of her situation in order to "protect" me from worrying about her. I decided to call her while she was in the hospital, ask her how she was feeling, and then ask her directly whether the surgery had removed all of the cancer. She seemed relaxed and not defensive in response to my direct questions. She acknowl-edged the fact that she had cancer and reported that the surgeon said it had been completely removed.

That summer I went to Europe to see my sister, her family, and my parents. After attending a family therapy conference in England I spent a day and an evening alone with my mother in London. I felt a sense of warmth and con-nectedness with her, without the old fusion. There was some talk about my dissertation but little intellectualizing. She assured me again that her health was good and that the surgery had been completely successful.

I did not know it at the time, but that would be the last time I saw my mother before she died. My efforts to define myself in relation to my parents set the stage for finishing my dissertation soon after my return from that trip. Perhaps it also contributed to the position I took with my doctoral committee: I asked that they read my dissertation quickly and schedule its defense for the following fall, bringing closure at last to a 10-year process. I defended it on November 19, 1976. In her next letter my mother congratulated me and expressed her certainty that I would be "the best psychologist ever."

I was awakened early in the morning of January 28, 1977 by a call from my sister. Our mother had died early that morning in London. I had spoken to my mother on the phone less than a week earlier. She was depressed and wondered if she should see a therapist. In the throes of death, it was easier for her to see her problems as psychological rather than physical. Was this denial or a mixture of denial and the doctor's not being direct with her about her terminal condition?

My parents had told me that they wanted to be cremated and that they did not want funerals. I believed that preference arose from their experience of my grandfather's suicide and the open casket funeral in my mother's home. I knew, however, that I needed to see my mother's body in order to fully accept her death.[6] I expected that my father, sister, and aunt would not want a funeral, or a showing of her body, and that they would quickly cremate my mother. It was important that I communicate quickly to my sister my desire to see my mother's body before she was cremated. Before leaving for England I told my sister what I wanted and she agreed.

At the funeral home they brought my mother's body out of a freezer. She was shorn of clothes and makeup, wrapped in a white sheet. I kissed her ice-cold forehead. My father, sister, and aunt did not come to the funeral home. (Later I learned that my father had in fact spent several hours at the bedside of his dead wife.)

The ritual of viewing the body of a dead family member went against the grain of the family, but I knew I wanted to do it. Choosing to observe it was an I-position, a part of my effort to define myself in my family. It involved taking a position that dealt more directly with a reality that was different from that of my parents, sister, and aunt.

A week after my mother's death I returned to France with my father. He didn't know it, but I was carrying my mother's ashes with me. I had planned to bury the ashes under her favorite cherry tree at home. When I told my father about the ashes and asked him to join me in burying them, he was very emotional and he declined. I left the next day without burying the ashes.

The next summer, while visiting my father, he agreed to my plan. We buried my mother's ashes under the cherry tree.

A few years later I videotaped a conversation with my father about his family history (Titelman, 1981). At the end of the interview I asked him how he felt about our burying his wife's ashes and its meaning for him. He told me that he was very glad that we buried the ashes together.

Efforts to Define a Self in Relation to My Father's
Alzheimer's Disease: 1980–1993

My father began a happy new relationship in 1977, a year after my mother died. It lasted until his death in 1993. In 1980 I began to recognize in him the symptoms of Alzheimer's disease, including memory loss, cognitive confusion, and Sundown syndrome. Doctors confirmed the diagnosis in 1984.

During these years I was challenged to be my highest possible functioning self as my father increasingly directed his confusion, blame, suspicion, misunderstanding, and anger at me.

In 1982 I wrote to my father in France asking if he would be willing to provide temporary financial support while my new clinical practice, consulting, and teaching geared up. He completely misunderstood the amount of help I was requesting. Instead of the 500 dollars I asked for, he believed I had asked for 5,000 dollars per month. My father was angry; I felt confused and humiliated. I managed to avoid reacting emotionally and the situation was resolved, at least temporarily. But over the remaining years of his life my father continually imagined that I was taking advantage of him financially.

Within a year or two my father changed his will. He told his lawyer—someone I knew quite well—not to disclose the changes to me. I felt sad and disappointed that he did not trust me, but I realized that my father was in the grip of Alzheimer's disease. A few years later, when the lawyer was able to confirm my father's diagnosis, he oversaw a further change in the will, leaving one third of my father's assets to his partner, one third to my sister, and one third to me. My father left his house in France to my sister and me. This resolution seemed fair to both of us.

During those years—1980 to 1993—there were many difficult scenes where my father was uncomprehending, jealous, irrational, or angry, traits and behaviors that he had never exhibited before. At first I would be taken aback and have to struggle to control my own emotional reactivity, even though I knew that the disease had taken control of his personality and actions.

Two incidents were particularly painful. In 1987 I brought my father a copy of the first book I had edited. I was proud of this accomplishment and wanted to share it with him. When I handed him the book he didn't seem to know what to do with it. He looked as if he would tear it up, and I quickly took it from him. I had an unrealistic expectation that my father would congratulate me.

During another visit in the late 1980s, we went to a restaurant for dinner with his girlfriend. She and I were having a conversation. My father imagined that I was being overly intimate with her and he became jealous. He may have felt left out, as it was clear that he did not understand what we were saying to each other. I had known for many years at this point that his Alzheimer's was serious, yet initially I was taken aback. I had to think through how I could control my reactivity.

On January 28, 1993 my father died in France. I organized a burial ritual similar to the one that took place for my mother. My sister, my father's partner, and I had a chance to be with my father's body before he was cremated. We buried his warm ashes in the backyard of his house under the same cherry tree where he and I had buried my mother's ashes. I spoke briefly about my father's life. The burial ritual was short. My sister had to get back home to England to be with her husband, who had terminal cancer. He died six months later.

During my father's illness I worked hard to become less reactive to his attacks, fears, dysfunction, distrust, and helplessness, and not to cut off or get angry with him. My guiding principle was not to blame him but to keep in mind that the disease was running the show. Before the Alzheimer's my father had been a man of critical judgment, perfectionism, and fairly high chronic anxiety, besides being a loving and generous father. I now had to relate to a father who, for all practical purposes, had lost his "self." I tried always to keep in mind the "self" that my father had been before Alzheimer's had taken charge.

It took an enormous effort to relate both to my father's Alzheimer's disease and to my father as a person whose self had radically changed and diminished, yet remained my father in the past, present, and future. I had to make a distinction between the *self* and the *person* of the individual with Alzheimer's.

The self may be diminished and transformed through illness, but the person remains as a living being with whom relationships exist. I use the term *person* to describe the automatic existence of the biological and physiognomic gestalt of an individual human being from birth through death. In Alzheimer's disease, particularly when it has caused severe deterioration of the self, the person exists in his relationships with others through his functioning position (for example, father) and through past experiences with others.

Alzheimer's disease can be understood as part of a mental construct triangle. In this case there are two living individuals, the son and the father, as well as the disease. Although the disease is a living biological process, it functions impersonally in a triangle when one person relates to another with Alzheimer's disease as if the disease and the person are a single unit. This leads to the loss of the ability to relate one-to-one with the person who has the disease. In this situation the person and his disease are in the inside positions of the triangle, and the other person is in the outside position. For the latter to relate directly to the person with Alzheimer's, he must allow for the impact of the illness on the ill person's functioning, but he must also seek to remain clear that the person is not the disease. I worked very hard to maintain contact with my demented father in order to keep a human connection with him.

Bridging Emotional Cutoff in the Extended Family as Part of Defining a Self: 1980–2013

As I learned more about relationships in my paternal extended family, I came to see that my fused family of origin was a branch of a family characterized by major emotional cutoff (see Figure 6.2). I began to link the cutoffs in my paternal extended family to the emotional fusion in my family of origin (Titelman, 1987, p. 45). This awareness led to a shift in my thinking about the interlocking relationship between fusion and cutoff.

The period from 1980 to 2010 focused on more contact with members of my paternal extended family and on bridging cutoffs on that side of the extended family. My mother was dead and my father had Alzheimer's disease. My parents hadn't prepared me to be connected to, or even to know much about, my extended family beyond my grandmothers, uncles, aunts, and cousins.

I got to know a first cousin once removed, E., who turned out to be a great source for multigenerational history in my father's family and the cutoff in that family. I exchanged at least 30 letters with her and had many phone conversations. I visited her once in New Jersey, when I was living in Massachusetts.

I learned from E. that instead of having one great-uncle and one great-aunt, as I had believed, I actually had eight additional great-uncles and aunts, all deceased, about whom my father had never spoken. He may have had little or no contact with some of them. I learned that eight of my great-uncles and aunts used a different spelling for their family surname, and that my great-grandfather had four additional marriages following the death of my great-grandmother. I never met any of my great-uncles or aunts or their descendants from my paternal grandfather's side of the family until I met cousin E.

Clues about cutoff from three generations in the past, gleaned from the facts E. told me, turned out to be relevant to the cutoff between one of my paternal aunts and my parents, particularly my mother. These clues included: 1) females who married into the family were often in severe conflict, and 2) my paternal grandmother was described as looking down on her husband's family, which may have led to more distancing between my paternal grandparents and the grandfather's extended family. Cousin E. reported the following:

> Your grandmother was not very friendly with other women of the family. I always had the feeling that she felt superior to them.

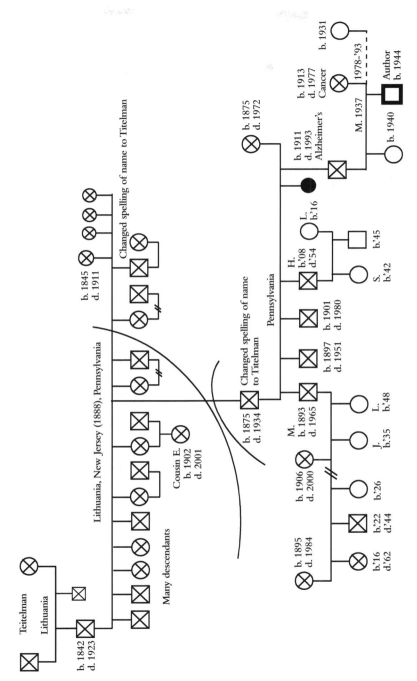

Figure 6.2 Cutoff in the Paternal Extended Family

I remember visiting your grandmother's home in what was called "Strawberry Mansion," Philadelphia, and she made us take our shoes off before we could go in the house. Of course the Japanese and the Muslims do that, but seventy years ago it was not done in Jewish circles in this country.

(Titelman, 2003, p. 116)

A decrease in religious and family rituals in my father's family paralleled an increasing level of assimilation, including moving away from the practice of Judaism by my father's father. A focus on business, professional life, the arts, and political involvement seemed to replace involvement with the extended family and religion.

In addition to the rich material about my father's extended family that I gathered from Cousin E., I bridged the emotional cutoff with my Aunt L., the wife of my Uncle H., my father's favorite brother, from whom he had been completely cut off for 38 years. I realized that I was the recipient of what I later designated as *secondary cutoffs*, that is, cutoffs from extended family members, as opposed to cutoff from one's parents.[7] (See Figure 6.2.)

I "inherited" the cutoff from Aunt L. from my parents. Although Uncle H. was my father's closest brother and my family lived only a couple of blocks from H. and L., there had been little contact between the two families. I had heard my parents describe Aunt L. as not being friendly to my mother, and as being a messy housekeeper and a disorganized person.

Following my father's death in 1993, I wrote to my first cousin, S., and she told her mother, Aunt L., that my father had died. Aunt L. wrote a letter of condolence to me, and we began an exchange of letters. In 1995 we had our first phone contact. I found her to be a sympathetic and humorous person. In 1999 I visited her in Los Angeles. This was our first face-to-face contact since the early 1950s.

I hypothesized that the cutoff between my parents and Aunt L. was a spinoff of the triangle that included my grandmother, mother, and Aunt L., with Aunt L. being in the outside position. Aunt L. described her mother-in-law as a housecleaning "terror," among other issues. She called her a "crumb detector." Aunt L. told me that my mother was more competent and accomplished than she, and that my grandmother favored my mother because she was her niece as well as her daughter-in-law.

This hypothesis turned out to be true. The cutoff between my parents and Aunt L. was caused by an interlock between two triangles: the mother-in-law and two daughters-in-law triangle, and the triangle of my parents and Aunt L. Via a third triangle, my parents and me, I inherited the emotional fusion of this segment of my family of origin. This three-generation process generated a cutoff between Aunt L. and me without there ever having been issues between us. After bridging this cutoff, my relationship with my humorous and warm Aunt L. has continued to thrive to this day.

I made a further effort to bridge cutoff with two first cousins, the older of whom I may have met when I was very young. They are the two daughters of Uncle M., my father's oldest brother, from his second marriage. Uncle M. was the black sheep in my father's family of origin. He was cut off from his siblings when he left his first wife and remarried. My aunt and my first cousins were secondarily cut off respectively from their extended family. My effort produced positive contact with Cousin J. and Cousin L. and between them and their half-sister J. and her family, as well as the larger extended family on our paternal side. When in 2003 I initiated and helped organize a family reunion, the first ever in my father's family, these two cut-off cousins participated. I have stayed in contact with both of them and have developed a meaningful relationship with one of them.[8] (See Figure 6.2.)

In the last few years I began to turn my attention toward the extended family, both dead and alive, in the biologically shared family of my paternal grandmother and maternal grandfather—the family in which both my great-grandparents and my grandparents had first-cousin marriages. It took over 30 years for me to shift my focus away from my paternal line to this paternal-maternal line. I made written, phone, and in-person contact with one second paternal-maternal male cousin, H., and I wrote and phoned a female second paternal-maternal cousin, D (see Figure 6.3).

In the spring of 2014 I visited the cemeteries in Philadelphia where my maternal grandparents and great-grandparents, my maternal great-aunt who committed suicide, and my paternal grandparents and great-grandparents are buried. It was meaningful to see for the first time the graves of the ancestors, particularly the maternal grandparents whom I had only discovered in 2011 and who had been buried under the same stone. I visited a cousin, D., and her family, whom I had not seen in 56 years. This trip was an effort to connect in person with cousins from the side of the family who were related to my mother's father and my father's mother.

Further Efforts to Define a Self Through Death Rituals in the Family: 2008–2013

I had saved some of the ashes of my aunt, mother, and father. Many years after their deaths, in the summer of 2008, with my second wife, son, and sister I scattered those ashes in Cape Cod Bay and the Atlantic Ocean, where the spirit of place resides for me and my family. In the summer of 2011 I celebrated the hundredth anniversary of my father's birth with my wife, sister, and daughter at the places where those ashes had been carried out to sea. We shared stories and memories of my father. In the summer

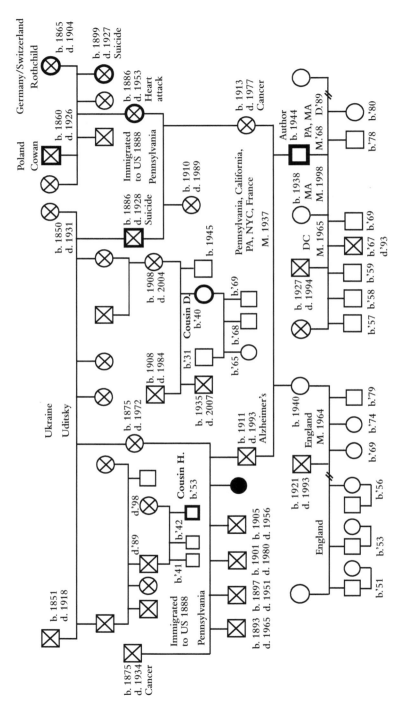

Figure 6.3 Maternal Extended Family Diagram

of 2013, we had a similar ceremony marking the hundredth anniversary of my mother's birth.

Defining Self in Profession and in Society

Differentiating a self goes beyond working on relationships in one's family. It is an intentional process that includes defining a self in one's professional relationships, and in one's larger societal relationships. The efforts in these three spheres are inextricably intertwined.

My Relationship With Murray Bowen: 1972–1984

The man whose theory guides my professional and personal life is Murray Bowen. My efforts to define myself in relation to Bowen began in 1984 with my decision to edit a book in spite of Bowen's opposition to the idea. Could I act on what I believed in the face of disapproval from the leader of my professional family?

My first Bowen theory teacher, Paulina McCullough, introduced me to Dr. Bowen at the annual Georgetown Family Systems Theory and Family Systems Therapy Symposium in Washington, DC, in November 1972. For many years our relationship consisted of Bowen generously answering my multitude of questions about his theory.

In the spring of 1977 I submitted an abstract for the annual Georgetown Family Center Symposium. Bowen wrote the following letter:

Dear Dr. Titelman:

. . . I will communicate my reactions to your abstract. If I perceive your premise, you have accurately picked up the degree to which I have failed to find biological models for the concepts. My effort has been a "reaching toward" the accepted sciences, in the far off hope it may lead out of the closed system thinking of the dogmas, the religions, and the philosophies, and into the more open system of the accepted sciences. A long-term goal is to work toward a viable conceptual bridge between the "social sciences" and the "accepted sciences.". . . Thousands of professionals are closer to your philosophical social science position than to the one toward which I strive, which implies that I am still pretty much social science but trying to keep the door open to the biological sciences . . . it gets real interesting when there is one with enough knowledge to debate "The Philosophy of Science" which holds that it has a firmer foundation than the accepted sciences, which are moth eaten with assumptions and untenable premises. That position has facts to it.

Thanks very much for sending the abstract. . . . I did want to respond to you with a personal letter rather than a routine letter.
Sincerely,
Murray Bowen, M.D.
Clinical Professor
Director, Georgetown Family Center
(Bowen, July 12, 1977)

In the spring of 1978 I sent Bowen a copy of a paper I had written entitled "Bowen's Family Systems Theory: Natural Science or Human Science?" (Titelman, 1978). Bowen wrote the following on November 9, 1978:

I have always been grateful for gifted people who can debate forever about each individual point about science and the nature of man, and about anything that provides a polarity. One of the most productive debates was a gifted philosopher with good points to prove that "science" is mushy and inexact and that good philosophy is more scientific than real science. He was on target as long as he could find a target. . . . Not too many people are interested in this kind of subject matter. I think the profession will profit from your kind of thinking. Keep on working. I will be interested in hearing about the kind of modification in theory that emerges from your efforts. It was good to see you at the recent Georgetown Symposium.
Sincerely,
Murray Bowen, M.D.
Clinical Professor
Director, Georgetown Family Center (Bowen, November 9, 1978b)

In 1981 I published a modified version of that paper in the journal *The Family* (Titelman, 1981). It was a critique of the biological underpinnings of Bowen theory from a psychological philosophical perspective. Bowen was going to do a training day on November 8, 1981 for the Family Living Consultants of the Pioneer Valley in Northampton, Massachusetts, where I was co-director. A friend told me that Bowen had commented on my paper in his talk at the Georgetown Symposium on Family Theory and Psychotherapy on November 8. His remark illustrated his own way of being differentiated.

Here's what Bowen had said: ". . . Peter's going to keep his position. He's never going to give it up, and I'm not going to give mine up. So he sharpens my thinking by being Peter. . . . He's got his ideas and I've got mine" (Bowen, 1981).

By 1983 I had come to agree with Bowen that the natural systems evolutionary perspective is a necessary and valuable underpinning of Bowen theory. This change took place through listening to a variety of presentations on evolution and natural systems and seeing how they fit with how human families function.

In 1983 I invited Bowen to do a training day on family of origin in Northampton the following spring. Bowen responded:

> . . . A day on family of origin is little enough time for the subject. People tend to hear the family of origin as a simple technique engrafted onto antique psychological theory. The whole family of origin thing runs into problems when people operate out of technique alone. I will work as hard as I can on my day there to make it into a good day for you and your group.
> Sincerely,
> Murray Bowen, M.D. (Bowen, August 2, 1983)

The training day was a good one, and Bowen was pleased with how it had gone. He wrote: "For me, the day in Northampton was a plus. I think the session with S. was effective" (Bowen, March 18, 1984). These were all straightforward and mutually respectful exchanges.

An Unintended Opportunity to Define Myself in Relation to Murray Bowen: 1984–1989

Initially, in August 1984, I wanted to put together an edited volume on Bowen theory, training, and application. I sent a proposal to Jason Aronson, among other publishers. Aronson wrote back that he would be more interested in a book on the therapist's own efforts toward differentiation of self in the family of origin and extended family.

I made the mistake of thinking that Bowen would be interested in having a chapter reprinted in this collection and, without checking with him, I included Bowen's original anonymous paper on his own differentiation of self efforts in the manuscript. Aronson read the papers in one night and got back to me quickly and enthusiastically, encouraging me to publish the book with his company. When I contacted Bowen, he was understandably upset that I had not checked with him first before showing the table of contents to other potential contributors and to Jason Aronson. It was naïve and irresponsible of me not to have done so.

Over the course of a year and a half Bowen and I corresponded about the proposed project. Bowen told me that a book of stories of therapists' own family efforts would be too subjective and narcissistic, and that he wanted no part of it.

I learned several years after my book was published that Bowen had posted a negative letter about me on the bulletin board of the Georgetown Family

Center. Two faculty members decided to drop out of my proposed book, expressing anger that I might publish a book that betrayed Bowen in some way. Another faculty member spoke calmly with me, saying that, while he liked the idea of being a part of the book, it would put too much pressure on him in regard to his relationship with his mentor, Bowen.

I removed Bowen's chapter and the chapters of the two other disenchanted contributors, as well as the chapter by the writer who would have liked to contribute but who weighed the emotional costs and benefits and decided to drop out. I appreciated the latter's honesty and lack of emotional reactivity in his stance when declining.

I had some sleepless nights, feeling anxious at the possibility that I would be out in the cold without contact with Bowen and the Georgetown Family Center, the citadel of his theory and training. Bowen wrote an angry letter that I received on January 18, 1985. I wrote back to him:

> Dear Murray,
>
> Thanks for the quick letter. I received it today. I appreciate the frankness and willingness to share your beliefs about my proposed book on the therapist's own family. I have always taken very seriously what I hear you saying. I still believe that sharing some of the papers I have proposed would be a plus. I understand your decision not to want your paper to be included. . . . Since all of the papers had already been previously published, I thought the positives outweighed the negatives. . . . I look forward to hearing from you.
>
> Sincerely,
> Peter Titelman (Titelman, January 18, 1985)

On September 9, 1985 I wrote the following letter to Bowen after receiving another critical letter from him:

> Dear Murray,
>
> Your thoughts about my project on family of origin gave me a lot of food for thought. They helped me to . . . clarify my own thinking. I want to apologize for having included your paper in the original proposed table of contents without clearing it with you. I was very caught up in the enthusiasm of Aronson's interest in doing such a book. . . . I have let all potential contributors know your position about the book on own family. . . . I look forward to attending the Georgetown Symposium and seeing you there.
>
> Sincerely,
> Peter Titelman (Titelman, September 9, 1985)

Bowen wrote the following letter back to me on October 5, 1985:

Dear Peter:

Your recent letter stimulates this. I am not inclined to take much time for such, but maybe you can "hear" a little my objection to a book that is theoretical rather than personal. In my opinion the main contributions were differentiation of self—family diagrams—the nature of the emotional system—triangles—etc.—finally integrated into a composite system after a dozen years. In those years it was a guess the world might not "hear" that divergence for a century or more. Should work stop until the world "heard"? A critical decision was to "keep going" and add several appendages including "family of origin."

A number of pro and con controversies went into the 1966–67 decisions about presenting the "family of origin" ideas. There was a hope that focus on "own" might reduce the "hearing" lag time. The initial response was fairly good but the "own" thing stimulated subjectivity, and almost totally obscured the theoretical base [that] made it all possible. There have been numerous regrets about the "right" answers, within their own heads. There was a microscopic gain from Anonymous,[9] but individual distortions prohibited potential therapeutic gain. The "fad" of the flood was overwhelming. Further explanation was no more effective than stemming floodwater with a hand shovel. Basic concepts are no more than discarded words. People faddishly "go home" and perfunctorily react as they did in childhood. The situation is little better than genealogical people have done through the years. The societal situation is similar to the great religions with conflicting sects and cults. Inability to "hear" beyond subjectivity may be increasing the "lag" time.

I played my own part in the distortion, when Georgetown Symposia permitted a few "own family" papers. The Symposia resembled carnivals or religious camp meetings. They were popular but the professional dignity was lost in a sea of subjectivity. When "own family" papers were curtailed, a semblance of professionalism returned. There were dozens of requests to reprint the Anonymous paper. I refused, but I did follow publication amenities about reprinting other papers. I opposed the publication of books of "own family" papers back in the 1970's. None were published. It seemed to be an easy and distorted way for editors to get their names in print, and for publishers to capitalize on the distorted fad.

Systems ideas are too new for final judgment, but I believe that some version of natural systems ideas will ultimately show one way into the future, if we can stay on principle and avoid the glitter of subjectivity and popularity. When you and Jason Aronson chose the opposite direction, it left me out. When you sent letters for publication approval, the Family Center followed strict publication protocol and left the decision to the individual contributor. Some, without thinking, went along with the popularity of getting their name in print. If they chose the popularity direction, they created a dilemma within the Family Center.

The past several years the training programs, and the Symposium, have focused more on basic concepts that finally gave being to "family of origin" ideas.

Sincerely yours,

Murray Bowen M.D. (Bowen, October 5, 1985)

As I began to receive negative feedback about the book project, my goal was to make my decision about whether to go ahead with it without emotionally cutting off from Bowen and other important members of my professional family. This meant taking an I-position in the service of being a more differentiated self. I was anxious about this—not surprising in the context of being a "youngest pleaser" in my own family of origin. My greatest anxiety was not fear of rejection, however, but the fear of failing to do a *good enough* book.

I had more sleepless nights considering the possibility of personal and professional rejection. I decided that giving up the book would be an undifferentiated action. My effort was to *own* and take responsibility for the book project, attributing the ideas to the founder and original teacher of the theory, Murray Bowen, but acknowledging that it represented my interpretation of Bowen's theory. I was aided in keeping on track by being outside the inner emotional orbit of Bowen family systems theory, the Georgetown Family Center in Washington, DC.

After explaining my goal to those who disapproved, I decided to follow my chosen course without discussing it further with them. I stayed in contact with the disapproving leader and did not cut off. After *The Therapist's Own Family: Toward the Differentiation of Self* was published in the fall of 1987, I did not discuss the book with Bowen and did not expect feedback when I sent a copy of the book to him. I never lost respect or positive feelings for Bowen. My aim was to try to be fairly objective regarding criticism of my project, not reacting emotionally, and not cutting off from the disapproving ones through counter-criticism or personal attack.

By not becoming reactive in the face of disapproval, I tried to put into practice what I had learned from Bowen and Bowen theory. I strove to stay on my self-directed course when I encountered the following threefold reaction, which Bowen described as predictably occurring when an individual takes an I-position in the service of a differentiating effort:

1) We disapprove of what you are doing;
2) If you don't give it up, you are hurting your professional family and the theory;
3) If you don't give up your effort, you will not be a part of this professional family.

I was able to maintain personal contact with Bowen and have a respectful relationship with him. In May 1986, the year before the book was published, I was at the symposium put on by the Center for Family Consultation in Chicago and Bowen was present. One evening the presenters and Bowen were sitting around after dinner and I had an opportunity to spontaneously encourage Bowen to talk about his days at the Menninger Foundation. Those who were there said they had never seen Bowen open up with anecdotes and stories the way he did that evening.

In June 1986, at the Pittsburgh Family Systems Theory Symposium, I presented material from the book in Bowen's presence. I experienced little reactivity in myself or from Bowen.

In the spring of 1989 I was invited to present at the Georgetown Family Center monthly Professional Lecture Series on the topic of incest. It meant a lot to me that Bowen, who was very frail by that time, attended the meeting. I thought Bowen might have sensed that I was feeling some anxiety, as he chose to sit next to me. I appreciated that gesture. At the end of the presentation Bowen and I walked out of the meeting together.

Defining self in one's professional life through I-positions, while continuing to maintain a one-to-one relationship with significant mentors and colleagues in the midst of important triangles, without attacking, cutting off, or triangling, can be a valuable part of differentiating a self. It is a process that can interlock with defining self in one's family, and it can increase, or solidify, functional self, at the least, and possibly increase the level of basic self, although that is not clear until the end of a life course.

Taking an I-position with significant others who are disapproving, in either one's own or professional family, is not fun, but no one ever said that defining or differentiating a self would bring universal approval.

Efforts to Define a Self in the Context of Society

I believe that while the family is viewed as the most emotionally driven system—compared with professional, occupational, or larger societal systems—emotional process in society is equally if not more fraught with chronic anxiety, undifferentiation, and emotional reactivity. Lower levels of differentiation and high levels of chronic anxiety in the context of societal emotional process, particularly in times of societal regression, produce potential or real threats of the possibility for the extinction of the family and its larger group, be it religion, ethnicity, tribe, state, or nation of the larger group.

Defining self involves, among other dimensions, knowing what one believes and where one stands on principles. It involves taking I-positions, taking action stands based on what one believes. It comes out of the solid self—one's core beliefs—not beliefs that are appended to self to please or go along with one's family, colleagues, countrymen, or ethnic or religious affiliations, in order to be a part of the togetherness whose views the individual may not truly share.

In the realm of society, two of my principles are: 1) speaking truth to power or authority when the rights and security of an individual, group, or country are under siege from other(s) who have disproportionate power or control over them; and 2) holding myself responsible for my own actions in society. I can only control my own actions, but I am interlocked with those family and nonfamily members with whom I am in close contact. I believe the above principles should be undertaken with a modicum of emotional neutrality and without attacking or cutting off from others who may disagree with me.

This section of the chapter describes two areas in which I sought to define myself at the level of societal emotional process by putting my beliefs into action. The first involved participation in the Southern civil rights movement in young adulthood, and the second was my response to the Israeli-Palestinian conflict over the past decade.

In my family of origin there was a strong belief in the value of upholding civil liberties and civil rights. My parents had been political radicals from the 1930s through the early 1950s. My father as a young adult had been a civil liberties lawyer and a union organizer, and my mother was also politically active. She was an educator who founded a progressive elementary school in Los Angeles. I incorporated those family values into my own belief system and at a young age began to act on them.

I attended my mother's elementary school in Los Angeles, and later, in New York City, I attended a progressive high school in Harlem. The latter was racially integrated and many of the families held progressive political views and values.

The North Side Center, a youth center run by Kenneth Clark, was located on the floor below my high school. Dr. Clark was the psychologist whose studies of African American children in the South demonstrated that the self-images of African American children were impoverished compared with those of Caucasian children. This was demonstrated by African American children's negative perceptions of black-skinned dolls in comparison with their positive perceptions of white-skinned dolls. Meeting Clark, and knowing that his study was a significant piece of evidence leading to the Supreme Court's decision in 1954 to end segregation in public schools across the South, made a deep impression on me.

In 1958, my high school took in Minnijean Brown to finish her high school education. She was one of the nine African American students who first integrated Little Rock High School in Arkansas in 1957. After she responded emotionally to the racist taunts and abusive behavior from white students she was expelled.

Efforts to Define a Self Through Participation in the Southern Civil Rights Movement

In my senior year of high school in 1962, I participated in the Tom Paine Discussion Club. There I heard Tom Hayden, an activist and one of the founders of the Students for a Democratic Society, describe his experiences in McComb, Mississippi, working on voter registration with the Student Non-Violent Coordinating Committee (SNCC). I was inspired by Hayden's talk.

In my first year of college, 1962–1963, I began to follow closely the civil rights movement in the South. In the spring of 1963 James Bevel, an important organizer for the Southern Christian Leadership Conference, visited my college campus, where I met him and the Freedom Singers, a group that came out of SNCC. I decided to volunteer for the Student Non-Violent Coordinating Committee in the summer of 1963. At that time SNCC was focusing on both desegregating public accommodations and challenging voter registration discrimination. My parents, who shared my values, were supportive of this decision, but they expressed concern about the danger of the endeavor.

I believed that it was important to put beliefs into action, even though I was fearful of facing physical danger from angry white Southerners.

In June 1963 at age 19 I flew to Atlanta, joining other volunteers and SNCC staff at Koinonia Farm in southwest Georgia for training in nonviolence. I was then sent to the SNCC project in Albany, Georgia, a bastion of segregation that Dr. Martin Luther King and his colleagues were unable to change. The SNCC group consisted of local adolescent and young adult volunteers, black and white, and three or four full-time staff. They were housed in the homes of African American families who were willing to give them room and board as well as moral support.

My fellow volunteers, staff members, and I met daily at the SNCC headquarters and mapped out our activities and strategies for the day. I did door-to-door canvassing and encouraged adolescent and adult African Americans to attend mass meetings at local black churches and to consider joining nonviolent efforts to seek admittance to segregated public accommodations, such as the public swimming pool and the movie theater. At these meetings SNCC workers, local leaders, and ministers would speak to the crowd, and everyone would sing freedom songs.

Working together with others for something I believed in deeply was a significant experience in becoming a more defined self. One is more of a self when one can take an action on behalf of one's beliefs, particularly when threatened by others who hold dearly to opposite views. Neither attacking nor withdrawing in the face of fear was challenging.

I was jailed in Americus along with two other SNCC workers. More than 100 local youth demonstrators and a few SNCC workers were jailed in Albany. The jails, like all public facilities, were segregated. In "Georgia Justice: A Report from Albany," the *New Republic Magazine* (Roberts, 1964) described what took place at the trial. The demonstrators

> . . . testified that they were walking on a dirt path, which served
> as a sidewalk, two abreast, making no noise, on their way to a mass

meeting and that Chief Pritchett came up and arrested them. He testified that they were sitting in the street blocking traffic. The testimony of five Negroes and two "outside agitators" didn't carry much weight against the testimony of the chief of police, so it was $193 or 30 days.

Three white SNCC workers, including me, were taken out of the Americus jail in the middle of the night and put in a van. It was a frightening ride, as we did not know where we were going. Finally, we were placed in the Albany jail in a cell with two Northern white soldiers stationed at a local army base who had been arrested for drunken and disorderly conduct. Laurie Pritchett, the police chief, told the soldiers that they would get out of jail sooner if they beat up the "nigger-loving communists" in the cell with them. One of my co-workers and I fearfully crouched on one of the bunk beds. The third co-worker, an ex-Marine, stood his ground. This encouraged the soldiers to have at him. He did not fight back, but continued to stand his ground. The attackers, frustrated, gave up.

Then we went on a hunger strike. Every day we went out on the work detail, riding on the back of a city truck, cleaning the streets. As the truck began to move, we were forced to run after the truck and jump on when it started off.

After seven days in jail I was bailed out by my parents. I felt ambivalent about leaving my co-workers still in jail. My mother spoke with me after I got out. She said that although she was proud of me, my father was being pressured to get me to return home by an older brother who owned the family business. This uncle was influenced by criticism from a company salesman whose territory included Albany, Georgia. Apparently my working for civil rights and being arrested was bad for business. My father did not actually put pressure on me to return home, but my mother did, and I gave in to her. As a result, I didn't complete my summer volunteer work. I was aware that while I wanted to stay through the summer, I did have anxiety about the potential for danger. I saw my decision as lacking courage, and as a regression in my effort to be a more clearly defined self.

I spent the rest of the summer of 1963 working in the New York City office of SNCC, alongside Stokely Carmichael and others. I attended the August 1963 civil rights march on Washington at which Martin Luther King gave his "I Have a Dream" speech, and I made up my mind to return to the South to participate in the movement for equal rights and opportunities for African Americans at a future time.

In 1964 I spent the winter term of my sophomore year in college in an off-campus program in Washington, DC. My fellow students and I spent considerable time lobbying congressmen at the time that the 1964 Public Accommodations Law was being pushed through Congress by President Lyndon Johnson. It became law on July 2, 1964.

While in Washington, I wrote a lengthy paper (Titelman, 1964) identifying Southern segregationist congressmen and senators who held powerful positions and who were vulnerable to being defeated in the upcoming elections. I sent this paper to the Southern Regional Council, an organization whose mandate was to support, with grants from foundations, the increase of African American voter registration in the South. Wiley Branton, the director of voter registration at SRC, informed me that my research was useful for the 1964 voter registration drive, and for getting out the vote.

In the summer of 1965, I made good my promise to myself to return to the South. I worked for the Child Development Group of Mississippi, a Head Start program that was staffed, primarily, by civil rights activists. I was placed in the center in Rolling Fork, Mississippi. There I coordinated a reading readiness program. Part of the agenda included staying up all night, taking turns with other staff members, being on the alert for attacks by white Southerners who were threatening to shoot at the center. Though somewhat anxious, I was able to complete my summer commitment. In addition I was able to manage my relationship with my parents, who were more anxious than I was about my going back to the South.

My belief that all humans should be respected and treated equally was ingrained in my family. For example, my parents took in a Japanese American adolescent to live with the family in Los Angeles because her parents had been sent to an American concentration camp during World War II. This value was truly incorporated into my life through personal relationships, readings, and reflection. I did not believe my civil rights activities were undertaken to please my parents. I chose to witness and be counted in relation to what I believed. At the same time, it may also have been partly the effort of a youngest, dependent child to separate from, or become less emotionally fused with, his parents, particularly his mother. To the degree that that was a factor in my choice, it might be described as an automatic effort to be a more defined self. My involvement in the civil rights movement might be described as a limited effort, since I was not financially and emotionally independent from my parents. And I had not yet been in contact with Bowen theory. Therefore, the effort to define a self was not as robust as I wish it had been.

Efforts to Define a Self Through Participation in the Quest for a Just Solution in the Israeli–Palestinian Quagmire

I became interested in the Israeli–Palestinian dilemma in 2000, when my son majored in Middle East Studies at college, spent a term in Jerusalem, where he studied Arabic, had both Israeli and Palestinian professors, and then spent five years living in Syria, with trips to Egypt and Yemen along the way.

Through my son I became aware that the struggle between Israelis and the Palestinians represented a serious threat to world peace. Their conflict highlighted in general the problem of man's difficulty in recognizing the humanity of the Other, be it focused on differences of religion, ethnicity, culture, or the territorial imperative. I decided to work on behalf of a just peace between the Palestinians and the Israelis.

After the initial exposure to the issues from my son and my own reading about the Israeli-Palestinian situation, I joined a group that sought a just peace for both parties and the right of Palestinians to have their own state, alongside Israel, or alternatively for both parties to live in harmony in one state.

I began an effort to apply Bowen theory to the emotional process in society in the context of the Israeli-Palestinian situation, using the concepts of differentiation of self, chronic anxiety, triangles, the emotional projection process, emotional cutoff, and other components of the theory. I gave presentations and read papers at Bowen centers, exploring the issues of territoriality and the spirit of place, triangles, and the intersection of chronic anxiety and differentiation of self in the context of the conflict over land, water, religion, ethnicity, and language in the region.

I became involved in providing long-term support to a small community center in Nablus, West Bank, that offers programs to Palestinian children and families. I traveled to the West Bank and Israel in 2005–2006 with the Faculty for Israeli-Palestinian Peace. In 2012 I made a second trip to the West Bank. It included presenting a workshop for Palestinian psychologists and other health care providers at An Najah University in April 4, 2012. The topic was "Serving a Community Under Siege: Individual, Family, and Community Perspectives." Its focus was on how psychiatric caregivers cope with living under the siege of the Israeli Occupation and how they manage to lend a hand to individuals who have been traumatized through imprisonment and sometimes torture at the hands of the Israeli Defense Force occupying the Palestinian territories (the West Bank and Gaza). I explored how Bowen theory might be useful in understanding the chronic anxiety that is concomitant with the experience the Palestinians are undergoing, as well as that of their families, and the community as a whole.

I struggled to find the balance between the principle of *neutrality* and its application in what I perceived as a significant imbalance in the power relationship between the nation of Israel and the Palestinians, who do not have a state or a nation and who live in the Israeli militarily occupied territories of the West Bank and Gaza.

While believing that chronic anxiety underlies the issue of power between the Israelis and the Palestinians, I also believed that the *disproportionate power relationship* existing between a country and an occupied territory, or between two countries, is a factor in many international relationships and conflicts.

Defining self in society and in the family intersected when I held different positions from those of several family members and colleagues in regard to the Israeli-Palestinian dilemma. My effort was to be able to hold my viewpoint about the Israeli-Palestinian dilemma without becoming reactive and emotionally cutting off from them in the face of their own emotional reactivity. This involved gaining a greater degree of neutrality, seeing how different branches of my family varied in their religious or nonreligious views and practices, and understanding the varying political views within my extended and multigenerational families.

An example of my neutral interaction with one family member involved a written exchange with a cousin with whom I had bridged a secondary cutoff. She sent me a video that I perceived as presenting Israel as the victim of Palestinian terrorism. It did not show the reciprocal nature of terrorism between the two parties. I wrote back to my cousin that I opposed terrorism, but that I believed the terrorism was a reciprocal process. I explained that I believed Israel had disproportionate power in relation to Palestine, and that the United States and Israel reside in the inside positions of a triangle, while the Palestinians, locked in the occupied territories of the West Bank and Gaza, are in the outside position. I concluded as follows:

> I yearn and stand for the security of Israelis and Palestinians in which both peoples, and they are cousins, will end their "domestic abuse" and find a way to live in harmony. Both peoples are never going to be forced to leave that piece of territory that represents a homeland for both peoples and is rooted in the human instinct, that he shares with many other species, territoriality, and in man's subjective response to his sense of the *spirit of place* in relation *to* his homeland in the face of the real or imagined threats of extinction by the Other. . . . I know our experience and thinking varies on this subject but you are my cousin and I value our relationship, after bridging what I call a long secondary emotional cutoff, based on our families of origin and extended family history.
> I send my love to you and S.,
> P. (Titelman, 2011)

My cousin responded in kind:

> Hi P.,
> Thanks so much for your nice, long letter! It has helped me to understand where our opinions diverge on the issue, and we are of course in total agreement about terrorism and our prayer for world peace. I'm hoping that sometime in the next couple of months I can read the book you recommended.
> We send our love to you and T. and are thankful that our "cousinship" is still going strong.
> Hugs and Ribbits, J. (Cogan, 2011)

Dialogue with other cousins who were more aligned with Israel also took place.

I was able to control my emotional reactivity to their position with which I strongly disagreed. My effort was to define my position on an important societal issue without trying to force these family members to "join my side."

Summary

In this chapter I have tried to describe my efforts to define a self, beginning with the work of differentiating a self in the primary triangle, followed by work in the extended family, and through an understanding of the multi-generational family system that precedes the living members of the family emotional system. Defining a self in one's family is a foundation for raising one's level of differentiation of self. To be robust, however, this work includes defining or differentiating a self not only in one's family but also with significant nonfamily members, including work or professional colleagues, and within the community and larger society within which one lives. Defining or differentiating a self, and being a self, should include all the significant arenas of an individual's involvement in the world in which he or she lives.

I have aspired to raise my functional level of differentiation over more than 40 years, but I know that evidence of having increased my basic level of differentiation can only be ascertained over a whole lifetime, and possibly the lifetime of future generations.

NOTES

1 From 1971 through 1973 I was part of a family therapy training program at the Western Psychiatric Institute and Clinic in Pittsburgh, Pennsylvania, where one of the faculty, Paulina McCullough, had been a student of Murray Bowen. I was also co-leader of a therapist's own family consultation group initiated by Lois Jaffe at the Irene Stacy Clinic in Butler, Pennsylvania, for 18 months in 1974 and 1975, and a participant in an advanced Bowen theory seminar led by Paulina McCullough in 1980 and 1981.

2 I have chosen to write in the first rather than the third person in this chapter, as I am describing my own efforts to define a self. At the end of his own chapter "On the Differentiation of Self," Bowen (1978a) wrote: "I had little reservation about this public report. As families move from the compartmentalized, less mature world of secrets and foibles which they assume they are keeping under cover, and into the world of permitting their private lives to be more open and as a possible example for others to follow, they grow up a little each day" (p. 520).

3 For a description of the concept of the emotional triangle, see "Concept of the Triangle in Bowen Theory" in *Triangles: Bowen Family Systems Theory Perspectives* (Titelman, 2008, pp. 16–33).

4 Some of the material presented in this section and the section "Bridging Emotional Cutoff in the Extended Family: 1980–2013" is similar to more detailed accounts presented in *The Therapist's Own Family: Toward the Differentiation of Self* (Titelman, 1987a, pp. 317–347) and *Emotional Cutoff: Bowen Family Systems Theory Perspectives* (Titelman, 2003, pp. 111–138).

5 I gained access to my grandfather's death certificate in 1988; it confirmed that his death had in fact been a suicide.

6 Having seen Bowen's powerful videotape "Family Reaction to Death" (1972), I realized that seeing the body of a family member who has died was important in the process of accepting death.

7 "A primary cutoff takes place within the primary triangle, it involves an individual in relation to one or both of his or her parents. A secondary or derivative cutoff takes place between an individual and a sibling, grandparent, uncle or aunt, or cousins. This form of cutoff takes place within secondary triangles that spin off from or are interlocked with the primary parent-child triangle. Secondary cutoffs, based on interlocking triangles, can be described as indirect or 'inherited,' and are based on multigenerational emotional process. Some cutoffs are inherited in the sense that an individual has no direct face-to-face contact with a particular individual" (Titelman, 2003, p. 25).

8 For a more complete description of my efforts to bridge emotional cutoffs in my extended family, see Titelman (2003), "Efforts to Bridge Secondary Emotional Cutoff," in P. Titelman (Ed.), *Emotional Cutoff: Bowen Family Systems Theory Perspectives* (pp. 111–137).

9 "Anonymous" is a reference to Bowen's anonymous chapter originally published in *Family Interaction: A Dialogue Between Family Researchers and Family Therapists*, edited by J. Framo (1972, pp. 111–173). It was presented at the Family Research Conference, 1967. This chapter was reprinted in Murray Bowen's selected papers, *Family Therapy in Clinical Practice* (1978), entitled, "On The Differentiation of Self" (pp. 467–528). This chapter is Bowen's description of his effort to define himself in his family of origin.

REFERENCES

Bowen, M. (1972). "Family reaction to death." Videotape. Georgetown Family Center. (Producer). Available from www.thebowencenter.org.

Bowen, M. (1977). Personal correspondence to Peter Titelman, July 12, 1977.

Bowen, M. (1978a). *Family therapy in clinical practice.* New York: Jason Aronson.

Bowen, M. (1978b). Personal correspondence to Peter Titelman, November 9, 1978.

Bowen, M. (1981). Toward understanding the origin of the Bowen theory. Paper presented at the *18th Georgetown University Symposium on Family Theory and Psychotherapy.* Washington, DC, November 8, 1981.

Bowen, M. (1983). Personal correspondence to Peter Titelman, August 2, 1983.

Bowen, M. (1984). Personal correspondence to Peter Titelman, March 18, 1984.

Bowen, M. (1985). Personal correspondence to Peter Titelman, October 5, 1985.

Cogan, J. (2011). Personal correspondence with Peter Titelman.

Roberts, D. (1964). Georgia justice: A report from Albany. *New Republic Magazine, 28*(3).

Titelman, P. (1964). Negro voter registration and national politics. *Prism 1–7, 1961–1967.*

Titelman, P. (1978). Bowen's family systems theory: Natural science or human science? In P. G. McCullough, S. K. Rutenberg, J. C. Carolin, and P. Titelman (Eds.), *Second Pittsburgh Family Systems Symposium (1978): Collection of Selected Papers* (pp. 10–33). Pittsburgh: Western Psychiatric Institute and Clinic, University of Pittsburgh.

Titelman, P. (1981). Toward an existential-phenomenological alternative to the biological foundation of Bowen's family systems theory. *The Family, 9*(1), 53–60.

Titelman, P. (1981). Videotape interview with Leonard R. Titelman, January 1, 1981.

Titelman, P. (1985). Personal correspondence to Murray Bowen, January 18, 1985.

Titelman, P. (1985). Personal correspondence to Murray Bowen, September 9, 1985.

Titelman, P. (1987a). *The therapist's own family: Toward the differentiation of self.* New York: Jason Aronson.

Titelman, P. (1987b). Family reaction to death in a family. In P. Titelman (Ed.), *The therapist's own family: Toward the differentiation of self* (pp. 317–347). New York: Jason Aronson.

Titelman, P. (2003). Efforts to bridge secondary cutoff. In P. Titelman (Ed.), *Emotional cutoff: Bowen family systems theory perspectives* (pp. 111–138). New York: Haworth Press.

Titelman, P. (2008). The concept of the triangle in Bowen theory. In P. Titelman (Ed.), *Triangles: Bowen family systems theory perspectives* (pp. 16–33). New York: Routledge.

Titelman, P. (2011). Personal correspondence with cousin J. C. 2011.

Titelman, P. (2012). "Serving a community under siege: Individual, family, and community perspectives." Presentation at An-Najah National University, Nablus, West Bank, Palestine, April 4, 2012.

7

APPLYING DIFFERENTIATION OF SELF IN ONE'S FAMILY

Phillip Klever

The author experienced an unprecedented dip in his mood in October 1979, when he was 28 years old. This was perplexing to him, since he had been experiencing success in all areas of his life and had been feeling "on top of the world." His wife was four months into her first pregnancy, which had been planned and was greeted with excitement. In addition his wife, his parents, and he had just returned from a 10-day trip to Europe, which included the first visit to his maternal grandfather's birthplace in Denmark and to the home of his former American Field Service "brother" in Italy. The trip was fun and surpassed expectations. In May of that same year he took action on his goal to start his full-time clinical private practice, which was off to a stable beginning. And during the summer he played the lead role in the production of a community theatre musical. He felt that whatever he touched turned to gold.

He decided to consult with a family-oriented psychiatrist to understand what was happening. He went into that consultation with a mindset that the family system had an important influence on a person's functioning. In 1974 the author had been introduced to Bowen theory (Bowen, 1965) in a graduate social work class on family therapy. Of the theories to which he was introduced, Bowen theory had the most appeal and made the most sense with its focus on the multigenerational family. Having grown up in the matrix of his mother's active involvement with her extended family, he had an intuitive pull toward a theory about the larger family. In addition he had five years of applying family systems thinking in his clinical work.

In the consultation what emerged as contributing factors to the author's sagging mood was his anxiety about becoming a father, which was related to unresolved emotional issues in his relationships with his parents, and his tendency to avoid being a defined self. The pregnancy brought these emotional issues to the forefront. He saw this time as an opportunity to take another step in growing up in his family of procreation and in his family of origin.

The Family

The author was the fifth of six children. He was the youngest for five and one fourth years when the last child was added to the litter. He grew up on an Iowa farm of 160 acres that his maternal grandfather bought from the original homesteader in 1910. His father and mother married in 1937 and had their first child, a daughter, in 1939. They went on to have a son in 1941, a daughter in 1944, and three more sons in 1949, 1951, and 1956. The author's parents lived on this farm during the 10 years covered by this report, and the author lived in Kansas City, which was four and a half hours away (see Figure 7.1).

The Mother

The author's mother, who was born in 1917, was the youngest of seven children. She had four sisters and two brothers. She went to Iowa State University for a year and then taught at a country school for two years before her marriage. When she married in 1937, she became a farmer's wife, which meant helping with some of the farm work, as well as taking charge of the many tasks of homemaking. Community service was an important value to her, so she was involved in many volunteer and community activities. She was often selected to be the president or chairperson in these groups. Even in her family of origin she functioned as a leader and organizer for frequent family gatherings. For some members in her family of origin she was also a confidant. In each of these settings she led without raising her voice. Her older children sometimes described her as controlling and dominating. Her way of getting her point across in a disagreement was to tell a story. In 1967 she was employed as the activity director of a county program for senior citizens, where she worked until her death in 1989.

The Father

The author's father was born in 1911, and was the ninth of 12 children, three girls and nine boys. His next older brother died before the author's father was born, so the author's father was the oldest of the last four sons. Like his wife, he was raised on an Iowa farm about seven miles away from his wife's family farm. His father died when the author's father was 18 years old, so with the cooperation of his brothers he helped run his parents' farm. When he and his wife married, he farmed his wife's family farm and bought it two years later in 1939 when her father died. He retired from farming in 1973. He was a slow-paced, steady, hard-working man of few words.

The Parental Marriage

The father and mother were usually cooperative in the work of managing a farm and raising a family. The author's father was responsible for planting,

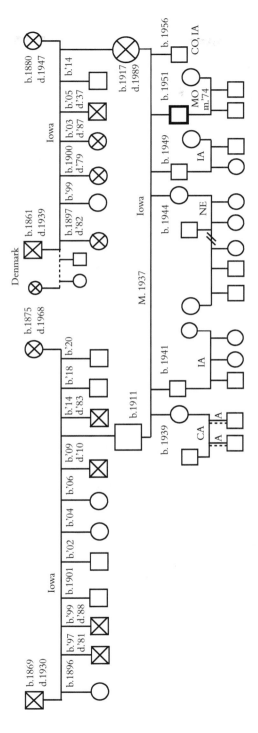

Figure 7.1 The Klever Family Diagram

tending, and harvesting the crops and taking care of the cattle, pigs, and sheep. During the first 20 years of their marriage the mother helped with chores, such as milking and raising and butchering the chickens. She was also the one responsible for gardening, homemaking, and parenting. She was clearly in charge of running the family, and in almost all ways the father seemed to defer to her. There were daily rituals of connection for the mother and father. Usually all three meals were eaten together, as well as occasional mid-morning or mid-afternoon lunches. They always slept together and occasionally demonstrated affection in front of the children. From the time of the father's retirement until the mother's death in 1989 he helped her behind the scenes with her work with senior citizens by carrying supplies or driving the elderly on trips. While the author's parents had daily involvement with each other, their level of openness with each other was uncertain to the author, due to the father's usual quietness around him.

Their occasional moments of tension erupted in several areas of their marriage. She would complain to him about his part of the farmstead being unkempt or not up to her standards. This complaint would especially be registered when the pigs or cows broke through a fence into the mother's garden. The author remembers his mother expressing this type of complaint to her husband at the breakfast table and him storming out of the house to take care of it. In turn, the father would occasionally comment about his wife's eating. (She was overweight.) One time the author remembers his father saying to his wife at the breakfast table, "My God, why are you putting so much sugar on your cereal!" His wife immediately got up from the table with tears in her eyes and walked away.

The Mother–Son Relationship

The author and his mother held a positive view and feeling about each other throughout his childhood and adolescence, even though they seldom verbalized those feelings to each other. He would occasionally report events and happenings in his life, but he did not talk with his mother, or anyone else, about his thoughts and feelings. Although he has some memories of upsetting his mother during his preschool years while playing wildly with his next older brother, pleasing and accommodating his mother became second nature to him. He sensed her pleasure with his leadership roles in high school, as well as his academic, athletic, and musical success, though she seldom expressed her pride directly. He remembers that his mother seldom corrected him during his junior high and high school years, and they almost never had conflict with each other. One exception occurred when he started high school. She wanted him to join the Future Farmers of America organization because of her admiration for the teacher and her esteem for the FFA organization. The author had no desire to join. In spite of some internal tension about disagreeing with her, he told his mother his decision.

His oldest sister left home for college when he was six years old. This began the theme of struggle with separation between his mother and three older siblings for the rest of his time at home. Seeing and hearing his mother's disappointments, sadness, frustrations, and distress with his three oldest siblings, he felt pulled even more to please his mother and to be a good boy. During a summer day when he was about 14 years old his mother was visibly upset about one of his older sibling's dating habits. While ironing the laundry she said through her tears that she hoped he would never do what this sibling did. He thought he would never upset his mother in this way.

While the author and his mother had these close feelings for each other, he also had the desire to distance and separate, a natural maturing process. When he was five, his youngest brother was born. The author remembers telling his family on a drive in the car that he was glad he was not the baby of the family anymore. He had just started kindergarten and felt more desire to become a big boy. In addition, there was more room in the family for him to grow up with his mother's focus on the new baby. Also, in preadolescence and adolescence the author was embarrassed about his feeling of closeness to his mother and made every effort to not be seen as a mama's boy. This feeling increased his desire for distance in their relationship.

The Father-Son Relationship

The author and his father in many ways had a distant relationship during his childhood and adolescence. They seldom talked to each other and usually had an overt calmness in their relationship. Neither asked the other about his day or thoughts or feelings. During his childhood and adolescence the author never turned to his father for help or direction for anything in his personal life. At nine years old the author was expected to help his father and older brother with the farm work. His oldest brother had left home for college the year before. Helping with the farm work involved milking cows, feeding and caring for pigs, chickens, cows, and sheep, shoveling manure, castrating pigs, fixing fencing, baling hay, and helping with crop and field-work. He especially enjoyed milking the cows and was responsible for that chore when his father and/or brother were busy with fieldwork. The author helped with morning and evening chores before and after school unless there were conflicting extracurricular activities. Parts of the weekend and summer were also expected times for the author to help his father. Cooperating in doing this farm work put the author and his father in daily proximity, which was a way that they got to know something about each other with little talking.

In spite of the usual calm, the father-son relationship had occasional overt and covert tensions. His father was sometimes frustrated with the author's lack of competence in doing fieldwork. His brothers seemed to have a more natural interest in and competence with using tractors and machinery. In addition the author experienced his father as a poor teacher in that he would tell his son to do a task in the field without instruction. If the author asked his father for directions, the father would say, "Just go do it." A more pervasive tension developed in the author toward his father in preadolescence. About that time the son began to see his father as unintelligent, a poor communicator, an inadequate husband, and at best an average farmer. The son was sensitive to his mother's occasional frustrations with her husband and seemed to absorb her frustrations with him. The son never expressed this negativity or contempt directly. Instead it intensified his disinterest in his father and his sensitivity with his mother. One example of his disinterest occurred when his father explicitly asked the author to go with him to town to sell the pigs that they had just loaded into a truck. This was unusual for his father to offer a direct invitation. The son declined and thought: "that's the last thing I want to do."

A summary of the primary triangle begins with the author absorbing some of the parents' tension and distance. This occurred through the mother and son's mutual responsiveness and overly positive perceptions of each other and through the father and son's distance, as well as the author's negative view of his father. The son's perception that his father was not a "good enough" husband for his mother contributed to the fusion in the mother-son relationship and the shape of the triangle.

The Older Brother and the Interlocking Triangles

The author's next oldest brother, who was 20 months older, was an important person in the author's day-to-day childhood experiences. His brother was attractive, engaging, and often outgoing. When others were present he brought energy to the room. The author in contrast tended to present a more serious, quiet presence and to hold back and watch his brother interact with others. During much of their childhood and some of their adolescence they were each other's primary playmates. They played farm, sports, and board games and watched television with each other. Though they usually had separate chores, they also worked with each other on the farm. They were similar sizes as they grew up and were often called "the boys." On a few occasions others wondered if they were twins.

Their relationship was often cooperative with occasional tension, competition, and fighting. When the author was in junior high, he refused to physically fight with his brother anymore and decided to avoid any controversy with him in part because their mother had expressed distress with this sibling rivalry. In retrospect his refusal to fight did little to reduce the underlying tension and probably aggravated it. One factor that intensified the rivalry was the somewhat unclear pecking order. In addition, during junior high and high school the author got somewhat better grades, played on the football team for several years (his brother, who was more interested in sports, thought he was too small to play), and was cast in the lead role in several plays and musicals. The older brother was conflicted about his younger brother's successes. The older brother seemed to be proud of his younger sibling's accomplishments, yet was unaccustomed to the author out-shining him and seemed to feel diminished by this turn of attention to his younger brother during high school.

Another key aggravation to the sibling relationship was the mother's dif-ferential relationships with the two boys. She was occasionally critical of the author's brother and conveyed unverbalized positive feelings for the author. The brother felt that "Mom likes you better" and that the author took his mother away from him when he was little. The author was aware of this, and a few times during adolescence the author would confront his mother about being critical of his brother. When the author's brother was an adult, he asked his mother about having favorites. She said, "It's only natural for a mother to love all her children, but to like some children more than others." The brother said, "I rest my case."

Another key component of the interlocking triangle was the father's closer relationship with the author's older brother. This will be described in the next section because the author only had a vague understanding and aware-ness of the relationship between his brother and father until he began his effort to differentiate a self in his family.

Working on Differentiation of Self

The Primary Triangle

The author realized that his mood was related to his position in the pri-mary triangle with his parents. He began to see the impact of the distance with his father, of his overly positive view of and oversensitivity toward his mother, and of perceiving his parents' marriage through his mother's eyes. The author's reading of Bowen theory in graduate school and throughout this period (Bowen, 1978), psychotherapy consultations in 1979–1980 and 1988–1989, and ongoing discussions with his wife helped to shape his under-standing of the emotional process and to give direction to the effort to grow up a little more. (His wife was in Bowen theory training during much of this 10-year period.) One of the first steps in becoming a more mature self was assuming a more adult position in his relationships with his parents, getting to know each of them as individuals, and developing one-to-one, person-to-person relationships (Bowen, 1978). In this effort he hoped to learn more about himself, the emotional process in his family system, and the reciprocal influences between them and himself. Before this time he had seldom been consistently intentional about his family relationships.

For the author to become more of an adult and individual meant chang-ing how he thought about and interacted with his father, mother, and their marriage. He saw how his distance and negative view of his father and his fusion and positive view of his mother reciprocally influenced his relationships with both of them. He began by applying these ideas in his relationship to his father. Before this the author seldom talked with his father. If the author called his parents' home and his father answered the phone, which was unusual, his father almost immediately turned the phone over to his wife. If the author did happen to ask his father a question when the three of them were in a room together, his mother usually answered for her husband. So to develop a one-to-one relationship meant finding a way to deal with his mother's interference and the author's passivity toward each of them. The author implemented several steps. When he called his parents, he requested to talk with his father as well as his mother. During occasional visits the author also made a point of talking with his father and showing an interest in what was going on in his life. This created much anxiety for the son. He thought, "What am I going to say? What if my father doesn't have anything to say, what do I do then?" He also had to push past the immature feeling of not wanting to know more about his father.

Early on in this effort the author asked his father to show him where the author's father had lived during his childhood. The author's plan was to use this as an opportunity to talk with his father alone about his history. The son thought that going on a drive and seeing tangible places would be easier than a face-to-face conversation about his life. He asked his father to do this alone. The son knew that if he did not make it explicit his mother would probably come along and take charge of the excursion. The author was anxious also about his mother's potential distress with being left out, but he knew this was a beginning exercise in worrying less about her emotions. He also thought that if he stayed in steady contact with his mother, her reactivity probably would be minimal.

When the author arrived alone at his parents' home, his father was ready to take him in the car to show him a part of the father's history. He took the author to the farms he had lived on growing up, to his parents' and paternal grandparents' graves, and to his paternal grandparents' farm. The author took pictures. Though anxious at first, he and his father had a relatively relaxed time and good discussions about his history. The son wondered if his mother planned the excursion, or if his father put this short day-trip together on his own. To the son's pleasant surprise his mother seemed happy and at ease when they returned. The author thought that maybe she understood his need to know his father better.

This marked one beginning change in the triangle. From that time on the author and his father interacted with each other with less intrusion from the mother. The author persisted in being interested in his father's life and in telling his father about himself. While his father continued to be a "man of few words," during this 10-year period from 1979 to 1989, he gradually talked more about what was going on in his life. Though the son could behaviorally make this change, some of his old perceptions and feelings of his father were reshaped more slowly. The author was frustrated that his father almost never initiated contact toward him. He would think, "Why am I the one who always has to initiate?" Then he reminded himself that the goal of this effort was not to change his father but to work on his own part in the relationship. This relationship provided an opportunity to reduce his passivity and emotional distance. He believed that if he could manage the anxiety in becoming a more defined person with his father, his assertiveness and effectiveness in other relationships would also improve. He also reminded himself that his father was in part a product of his own multigenerational family emotional process. The author remembered his paternal grandmother as being a "woman of few words" and the author's father seldom interacting with her in a personal way. The author's mother was the one who communicated more with her mother-in-law.

The author also began defining or differentiating a self in his relationship with his mother. The first step was reflecting on the nature of his relationship with his mother both past and present and observing their interactions and his thoughts and feelings. Many of his reflections about the period leading up to 1979 are presented in the previous section. He also began to think about how he defined himself on important emotional issues in the family. His tendency was not to say what he thought, especially if his viewpoint might upset his mother. He usually waited to be asked and seldom interjected himself during his mother's stories about other people or her life. The author decided to inquire more about his mother's history and her family of origin. She seemed interested in telling stories about her family, since she had a strong interest and involvement with her family.

During his consultations with the psychiatrist he realized that one area of undifferentiation between him and his mother centered around his singing. She derived much pride in his singing at church, for her senior citizen's program, and at community events. Whenever he made visits home, she arranged for him to sing. Almost without thinking he accommodated her requests. But as he reflected more about this dynamic, he realized that he had never stopped to think about whether he wanted to sing. He gave little weight to his preference. The unspoken dynamic was that if she wanted it, he did it. With this awareness, he told his mother that he wanted to take a break from singing in her community, and that if she wanted him to sing for her at home, he would be glad to sing for her. He was quite anxious about the impact on his mother of his taking this position. It felt selfish. She was upset, never asked the author to sing for her, and told a story to indirectly illustrate her feelings. An adult sibling group, who were neighbors, played together in a musical group, but the sister decided to stop participating. The author's mother expressed her viewpoint that it was too bad that the sister wasn't willing to share her talent.

The author had some success in telling his mother what was going on in his life and in listening to his mother's stories about her life. He observed, though, that the stories were often about other people she was involved with. Her thoughts or feelings were often implied, but not stated directly. When he attempted to clarify her thoughts on the subject, she seemed uneasy or dodged his inquiry. He also noticed that sometimes when he would tell her something about himself, she would tell a story of her own or change the subject. Maybe she was unaccustomed to his being more personal with her or maybe she sensed his anxiety in being more of a self with her. This pattern of interaction usually threw him off, and he could not find a way to stay engaged with her on a personal level or to tell a story of his own. He noticed his inability to think flexibly on his feet when he was with her. While the author made some progress in developing a one-to-one personal relationship, his occasional difficulty in bridging the distance between them lasted until her death.

Another part of the author's attempt to differentiate a self with his parents was having a more systemic view of his parents' marriage. Through his consultations he realized how his parents were in a reciprocal relationship with each other, with his father in a passive position and his mother in a dominant position. While this arrangement seemed to occasionally cause distress between them, overall it actually worked quite well. With this understanding the author felt more detached about his father's passivity and his mother's dominance and responded differently when comments were made about his mother's "controlling" nature. With a bit of humor he would say that it seemed they were a good fit for each other and actually had a cooperative marriage.

Another change in the author's way of thinking was seeing more clearly the multigenerational influences on his mother's overresponsible nature, her fusion with her mother, and her feelings about the author's next older brother. She said that when she was living with her parents as the youngest child, she felt responsible for most of the household responsibilities. She saw her mother as old and needing help, while the author's mother was young and industrious. Early on she was groomed to take on an overresponsible position with her mother. She also became a leader to many in her family of origin, and some turned to her during times of crisis or decision-making in their own lives. During visits from 1979 to 1989 she disclosed to the author's wife that she had been hospitalized and received electroconvulsive therapy sometime between 1945 and 1947, the year her mother died. In an effort to know his mother better, the author said to her once that it must have been hard for her when her mother died. She said that her mother's death was not hard, but somewhat of a relief. She added that the hardest time was when her mother lived with her from her father's death in 1939 until her mother's death in 1947. Her mother had diabetes and did not follow the protocol for her care. In addition, the author's mother wondered if her mother had a mental problem because of her pronounced fluctuation of moods. The mother's father saw mental problems as a weakness of character. The mother also told the author once that the only child she had concern about having mental problems was the author's next older brother.

The Interlocking Triangles With His Brother

The author's next oldest brother had a strong influence on how the author's primary triangle functioned, so this relationship was key in becoming more of a self in his family. The effort to differentiate a self with his brother involved observing more closely their interactions and his own thoughts and feelings in their one-to-one conversations on the phone and in their family visits. The effort also meant being a more defined self that was dictated less by old habits. One dynamic the author noticed was the brother acting as though he were inferior in some ways to the author. During one visit the brother's wife said that he usually got depressed after a visit with the author's family because he felt that the author was doing better than he. The author seemed to have a better house, be more successful, and have a happier marriage. One time he told the author's wife that she reminded him of his first fiancée, whom he deeply loved and who broke up with him.

Another related pattern was his brother's tendency to present his problems or troubles and the author's effort to help. The author saw how this perpetuated their positions in the family. The author was reinforcing a one-up position by treating his brother as the one with the problems and the author as the one who had his life together. This was a continuation of the tainted perceptions developed in the relationships with their mother and father. With this awareness the author began to stop helping his brother in their conversations and to listen, to ask questions to understand him better, and to act as though the brother had the wisdom to solve his own problems. The author also made an effort to be more open about the struggles in his own life, his uncertainties, and the important issues in his family. This again gave the author practice in being less passive and a more defined self.

Another challenge for the author was that his brother often seemed disinterested in interacting. He would need to get off the phone, not have much to say, or not seem to be listening. The author tried just to observe it, to avoid the automatic inclination to withdraw, and to take advantage of the times when his brother was in a receptive mood. At other times the brother could be engaging, especially when other people were a part of the interaction. When this happened, the author noticed that he automatically became quieter and took an outside position in the group, just as he had when he was younger. This awareness sometimes helped him to be intentional and to stay involved in the relationships.

Another step the author took was to be clearer with his mother about how he saw his brother's and his own strengths and weaknesses. One time his mother expressed a concern about how his brother was handling a financial decision and the author presented his viewpoint about his brother's competence in the situation. The goal was not trying to change his mother's mind or to defend his brother, but to present his own perception.

In 1987 his father and mother were planning to celebrate their fiftieth wedding anniversary, which was often a big celebration in their rural Iowa community and in his mother's family. The mother asked the author to be the MC for the program for the celebration. He immediately felt tense because he knew his brother would be upset for being slighted, and once again his mother was putting the author in the spotlight. The author said that he needed to think about it. He then told his parents that he was willing to do it, but that in his opinion his brother would be better suited to be the MC. His brother had a more naturally inviting and energetic public persona than the author. His parents had the brother be the MC, which he executed with his positive energy, while the author took leadership for organizing the program.

Before this effort the author did not have a clear picture of how the father-brother relationship worked, other than that they worked together comfortably. The brother did more of the fieldwork than the author and had more enthusiasm about farming. In one conversation he told the author that he tried to keep the author from getting involved with their father by keeping him from doing the fieldwork. For example, the brother would volunteer to do the plowing or discing to keep their father from asking the author for help. The author had no idea that was happening. This helped the author to see how that relationship contributed to the distance between the father and the author.

Another illuminating communication was between the author and his father on the phone, when the father mistakenly called the author "Huck." Huck was the father's next younger brother, whom the father teased growing up. Huck, a salesman with an interest in music, was the father's only brother who had a white-collar job. The author's insight was that his father shared a similar sibling position (older brother of brothers) with the author's older brother and maybe identified with him, and maybe he saw Huck and the author in similar ways. The author noticed how the father seemed to light up when the author's next older brother was around. The author had not been conscious of that before. These observations of the relationship between his brother and father helped the author to understand how his brother held more of an inside position with his father, and how the author held a more outside position. In 1990 after the mother's death, the father made the author's next older brother and younger brother the executors of his will. This seemed to be another indicator to the author of the closeness his father had with the author's brother.

Family Relationships Outside the Interlocking Triangles

The author realized that his distant and passive relationships with his larger family were an extension of his childhood way of relating. He saw that it was time to take an adult position in his family. This involved establishing one-to-one relationships with his siblings and with as many extended family members as possible. Another recommendation from his Bowen theory coach was to be present for important family events, such as weddings, funerals, baptisms, and moves. These events could lead to more interaction, family stories, and objectivity about the family system. Implementing these ideas, especially one-to-one interactions, was emotionally difficult because of the anxiety it provoked. First, it was new, so it was unfamiliar. Second, it raised his fears about being more of a self. "What if they don't really want to talk with me or want me to visit?" "What do we talk about? What if there are silences?" The author was immature in knowing how to carry his part of a conversation and in managing the potential anxiety in a family relationship. Part of the purpose in taking on this challenge was to become more of an individual and more adept at regulating his emotionality in close relationships.

The first part of this effort was to develop one-to-one relationships with his siblings. This included more frequent phone calls and making visits occasionally without his spouse or children. Leaving out his wife in these interactions made sense because he could have let his wife's outgoing personality fill the interaction space while he became more passive, just as he had tended to do with his older brother. Going alone he couldn't hide in someone's shadow. He clarified that he was making a solo visit because he wanted to have some time with them by himself occasionally. This was awkward for the author and his siblings at first, but then it became an accepted way of being with each other.

During a visit to his oldest brother, the author said that he wanted to have a more open, personal relationship with him. His brother said he did not think family members could be friends with each other. Thinking on his feet, the author said that he didn't agree, that he thought family members could be like friends with each other. This was a major change for the author to be so clear and direct about his own viewpoint. This reflected his conviction and thought about this issue. Over the years the author and this brother have developed an open, personal relationship. In developing improved relationships with his siblings, the author has not just focused on personal issues. He shared activities, kept a sense of humor and play, and chatted with them about each other's interests or about world events. A Bowen theory coach told him that working on these relationships is 90 percent contact and 10 percent differentiation of self.

Another awkward change was the author's curbing his gossiping about other family members and keeping the discussion primarily about himself and the family member who was present. When they would start reporting or complaining about other family members, the author would either listen, attempt to give his best objective viewpoint of the talked-about family member, change the subject, bring the discussion back to himself or the member present, or ask if he/she had talked with the family member about his/her thoughts. Several family members expressed frustration with his not joining in to talk about others in the way he had before.

The author made contact not only with his siblings but also with his aunts, uncles, and cousins, who were usually 20 to 60 years older than he. He felt anxious initiating contact with most of these people because he had never had his own relationship with them. He had watched his parents socialize with these family members, but seldom shared more than a greeting or goodbye. Without exception each person was responsive and welcoming of his initiation of contact. The benefits of phone conversations, letters, cards, and visits with these extended family members were not only learning to face his own anxiety about taking an adult position in the family, but also learning more about each family member and the family system from a perspective other than his mother's. For example, one of his mother's maternal first cousins gave her perspective on his maternal grandparents' marriage. She described his grandfather as tending to dominate his grandmother, and said they had some tension in their marriage in part due to the 15 years difference in their ages. His mother had never discussed the tension in her parents' marriage with the author.

The Period Leading to His Mother's Death

In the fall of 1987 the author received a call from his next older brother. He said, "You better call Mom. I just talked with her, and she is real depressed. I didn't know what to say. You've dealt with this in your work." The author instantly felt tense and concerned about his mother. He noted that his brother seemed to be "passing the ball" to him to help his mother. He resisted the urge to call his mother immediately, to rush in and help her. He knew he was full of emotion and needed a day to think as clearly as he could. The next day he called her. She was crying and saying that she was "good for nothing" and that she didn't feel like doing anything. She said that it started when she felt overwhelmed while preparing a luncheon by herself for a neighbor's family and friends. She felt that it tipped her over her limit.

He was to find out how the work he had done in his family of origin prepared him to handle a period of higher family anxiety. From his learning about differentiation the author developed some ideas to guide him through this time. The first was to use his thinking to work with the emotional reactivity in himself and the family. The second idea was to listen to his mother without giving too much advice or to not act like the expert because of his anxiety and because he was in the counseling field. Third, he knew he needed to stay in regular contact with his father. Fourth, he kept in contact with each of his siblings to hear their thoughts and to share his perspective about how this was affecting him and his understanding of his mother's depression. His fifth idea was to develop his best objective understanding of what contributed to this symptom and its effect on the family, so that he might counterbalance the inevitable emotional forces in himself and the family.

He thought about the changes that had occurred in his mother's life and the family. The last of her three sisters who lived in her community had died that August. They had talked regularly with each other. His single, younger brother had just left for an extended trip around the world. His mother had turned 70 in May, and over the years she had indirectly expressed concerns about aging. She had described her mother's difficulty with functioning in the last seven years of her life. The author's mother was still working at her job and had no plan for transitioning from the demands of her work. He described these facts as possible stressors that might be affecting her low mood. He also stated that there was a history of depression in her family that may have contributed to this symptom. In addition, he conveyed that he did not have the answers for what to do or why this was happening and that his mother and father had many strengths to pull themselves through this.

Talking with his siblings was useful to him. These conversations helped him reduce his anxiety and to know more about his five siblings. His oldest brother said that he was reluctant to call his mother about this because he didn't want to bother her. His sense was that it was best to give her time to work it out on her own.

One pleasantly surprising interaction happened with his father during the first week of talking with each other. When the author expressed interest in how they were doing, his father firmly and clearly said, "We're going to be just fine." The author had no memory of his father ever making a statement like this to him before. Usually his father was more passive or undefined and let his wife do the talking. The author heard the implied boundary-setting message as, "You don't need to worry. Your mom and I will take care of this problem." The author was also probably more receptive to his father's strength.

During this time the author was finishing writing a book on marriage that had been accepted by a publisher. His concern about his mother was a distraction from his writing. He considered stopping his personal goal to publish this book, so that he could focus on helping his mother and his family. Then he realized that acting on this urge would probably not be helpful to anyone. His knowledge about differentiation instructed him to stay on course with his goals and to stay connected to the family as he proceeded. He believed this approach would probably be more helpful to everyone involved, so he finished his book.

Several months later his next older brother reported job problems, high blood pressure, and long-standing marital problems, leading to his wife separating from him for two days. This was a perfect invitation for the author to assume a "helpful, one-up" position with this brother. With this in mind the author made every effort to focus on his brother's strengths, as well as the struggle. When he talked with his brother, he listened and empathized with him about how hard marriage is and described a few of the problems in his own marriage. He went on to say he thought that his brother and wife would probably work this crisis out because they always had before. Instead of trying to help his brother, he held on to the mindset that they were fellow travelers in the ups and downs of life.

The following spring, in May 1988, the author visited his mother's brother, who was three years older than his mother. His Bowen theory coach recommended the visit to his maternal uncle during this time of higher family anxiety related to his mother's depression. This maternal uncle revered his sister. The author wanted to get to know this uncle more, to learn about his history, and to find out if he was prone to depression as well. The talkative uncle freely shared his history and revealed that he also had times of being depressed, especially because of his worry about money.

In November 1988, his mother was diagnosed with acute mylosetic leukemia, a few days after her youngest son returned from traveling. She decided to pursue treatment in the city in which the author's next older brother lived. He and his wife provided a place to stay and emotional support in the ongoing cancer treatment. On the day that she was diagnosed she received a letter from the author about the issue of his singing. In the letter he let her know that he was ready to say "yes" sometimes to her requests for him to sing for the community. He had realized that he could think through what he wanted to do and not have to reflexively try to please his mother. He sent the letter with no idea that his mother was sick until he received the call about her diagnosis from his younger brother. The next day he called his mother and she said that she had received the "brown letter," a reference to the unpleasantness of the letter. The author was surprised because he saw the letter as having a positive message and opening up the relationship, which he told her in their conversation. But discussing the letter was secondary to dealing with the news of her diagnosis. During the three plus months until her death his singing was never again discussed. His focus in the relationship was to be interested in her thoughts and feelings about her illness, her life, and her dying, and to be open about his own thoughts and feelings in those areas. He largely succeeded in that goal, though she was increasingly quiet in the last month and a half of her life.

During her three-month illness the concept of differentiation was a guide to the author. The author continued regular, open contact with his mother, father, and siblings. He tried to stay aware and thoughtful in the midst of family emotionality and reactivity and to define himself on important issues and decisions. He saw this as an opportunity to observe himself and his family under higher stress. One time occurred in the hospital during the first week of her illness, when she was given her treatment options. Five of her six children and most of their spouses stood around her bed to discuss her treatment decision. She asked the group, "What would you do?" Immediately, several family members said that she needed to do what she thought was best and that they would support her decision. This was also the author's first thought. Then her oldest son said, "I think you know we all will support your decision. But you want to know what each of us would do, if we were in your position." She said, "That's right." He went on to say that at his age he would have the treatment for the chance to live. She turned to her husband and asked, "What do you think?" He said, "You don't want to know what I would do." She said, "You wouldn't have the treatment, would you?" He said, "You know me too good." She then went on to say that she's always been a fighter and that she didn't want to give up. She decided to have the more aggressive treatment for an improved chance to live. The author was struck with the clarity of self in those who spoke and in his quietness during that discussion. He assumed his more typical listening position in the family togetherness.

A sibling discussion around the kitchen table on the day before the funeral gave the author more understanding about family patterns. The author's oldest brother said that one of his mother's strengths was that he felt special to his mother. Then the author, his sisters, and youngest brother each said they had the same feeling with their mother. After a pause the author's next older brother said, "I never felt that way growing up." During his marital crisis in 1987 his mother told him that she was proud of him. He said that his mother's words made a world of difference to him. The author suddenly had a mixture of feelings and thoughts. First, he was surprised that most of his siblings also felt special to their mother. He thought that he was the only one in that position and that it was a marker of the fusion between his mother and him. This was a relief and began to give him another perspective about the complexity of fusion. Second, he felt awkward about his brother's feeling with his mother in contrast with his five siblings. While this wasn't new information, it confirmed the author's perception of the emotional process in the family triangles.

Conclusion

The author's application of the concept of differentiation of self was useful in taking a step in growing up in his family. The concept directed him to develop more adult, personal relationships with his family. This step required him to get a better handle on his anxieties in relationships, his emotional reactivity, and his tendency to be too passive and undefined with others. Developing a more objective view of his family system, the interlocking triangles, and the reciprocal influences between his family and himself were part of the cognitive guide. In addition, because the current family drama is shaped in part by the past, he learned about the multigenerational history as a way to broaden the lens, to reduce anxiety, and to develop a more objective view of his family and himself.

REFERENCES

Bowen, M. (1965). The use of family theory in clinical practice. *Comprehensive Psychiatry, 7*, 345–374.
Bowen, M. (1978). *Family therapy in clinical practice.* New York: Jason Aronson.

8

DIFFERENTIATION AND REMARRIAGE

A Thirty-Year Journey

Anthony J. Wilgus

The effort to differentiate a self in the nuclear family and the family of origin can be a lifelong endeavor. Along the way, typical life events ensue, some expected, some unexpected. Departures from the family home, marriage, career selections, and geographical moves alongside an unplanned pregnancy, chronic illness, and premature death provide potential opportunities to more clearly define the non-negotiables by which an individual strives to lead a principled life. But there are complications.

When two individuals make a commitment to spend their lives together in matrimony, there is little anticipation that this relationship will end in divorce. Yet the demographics of marriage in the United States indicate that this will occur quite frequently (Divorce updates, 2012). Despite this peremptory rupture of the pair bond, a significant percentage of those couples will remarry, divorce, and then remarry again (Kreider, 2005). For good or for ill, it appears that some humans have learned little from the prior relationships that will be of value in sustaining future relationships. Given these relationship challenges facing the human over the course of a life, might a long-term commitment to the process of differentiation make a difference?

Remarriage after divorce or death is fraught with a unique set of challenges. Bowen theory affords another way to conceptualize the success or failure of these marriages. It is the thesis of this chapter that a sustained effort over time toward differentiating a self in the family relationship system can have a beneficent impact on remarriage. Examination of the author's life over 30 years suggests that this long-term endeavor ultimately contributes to calmer, more thoughtful, and ultimately, more stable remarriages. (Hereafter, Mr. W will refer to the author while other names and identifying data have been altered.) Employing a life development approach covering more than six decades of Mr. W's life, the chapter begins with a brief description and analysis of his family of origin incorporating concepts from Bowen theory. This segment encompasses the period in his life through early adulthood in which he had his first marriage and a divorce and no exposure to Bowen theory or any of its concepts. Next, there will be substantial discussion covering Mr. W's 25-year second marriage, a period in which he embarked upon an extensive journey to incorporate the concept of differentiation, ranging from an introduction to the theory in graduate school to a prolonged attempt to differentiate himself in his important relationships with the concomitant impact upon the trajectory of his life. With a life course now infused with a modest awareness of the family emotional process and his part in that, the third part of Mr. W's life covers the period after the death of his second wife and his subsequent marriage to another individual followed by a chapter synopsis. The author contends that the stability found in the second marriage and the orderliness that led to the third marriage is an outcome of a conscious, determined commitment to apply the core concepts from Bowen theory in a life.

Goals Defined by Mr. W

The process of differentiation has many facets. In a personal recollection of the author, Dr. Murray Bowen laid out the challenge succinctly: "The most grown up thing that you'll ever do in your life is to develop a person-to-person relationship with each individual in your family" (Bowen, personal recollection, n.d.). This "person-to-person" relationship was one in which both parties were able to communicate their thoughts, feelings, and fantasies to each other with minimal reactivity or involvement of third parties, especially when anxious. Of course, while the maxim may be simple and unambiguous, the actualization of those wise words is not. To the extent that even minute progress transpires in the living out of these simple and complex observations, the person engaged on this path will have the opportunity to lead a more stable and orderly life. One manifestation of this outcome happens in the course of the marriages of the individual under study, Mr. W, resulting in less likelihood of fragmentation and divorce and in the ability to negotiate life's vagaries. Grounded in a little more thinking, a little less reactivity, and founded on solid principle, remarriage can "go the distance."

Strategies Employed by Mr. W

Learning was a critical component of a 30-year commitment beginning with the introduction of these ideas in an MSW program in the mid- to late 1970s. Subsequently, Mr. W enrolled in the postgraduate training program at the Georgetown Family Center for two years, followed by continued study, attendance at Georgetown's annual symposia, and the presentation of papers in symposia devoted to Bowen theory. The threat of a job loss and a marital separation occurred in 1987, culminating in the securing of a faculty coach from the Georgetown Family Center that continues to the present.

The pragmatics of differentiation entailed a host of strategies. Written correspondence, regular phone and email conversations, greeting cards, and individual and family face-to-face visits were ways to initiate and maintain contact. Presence at key family events, including family reunions, baptisms, weddings, funerals, graduations, illnesses, and other nodal occurrences allowed for Mr. W to be present and accounted for in the midst of a sometimes anxious family process. The use of a personal journal along with the drafting of goals for family visits coupled with a modicum of genealogical research also proved useful.

Family of Origin: Birth to 21

Mr. W, the eldest brother of a brother and two sisters, grew up in a relatively intense togetherness-oriented family (see Figure 8.1). His parents met in Asia as World War II ended. They had a whirlwind courtship of six weeks and left the husband's family somewhat perplexed at the rapidity of the marriage. Interestingly, Mr. W's parents were not only youngest siblings in their respective families but both of them still lived in their family homes with their widowed mothers at the age of 30. Mr. W's mother left the land of her birth, never to return, as she moved in with her new husband and his mother in the Midwest. In nine months, Mr. W (described by his father as the honeymoon baby) appeared, followed by his brother 11 months later and a sister in another 11 months. When Mr. W was approximately five years old, his parents secured a small home in the same community and the final child, a daughter, arrived. Mr. W's father worked as a laborer in a local factory, moving into the position of a foreman after a number of years. Mr. W's mother never worked outside of the home.

Describing his parents' marriage as one that was highly fused, he noted that over the course of their 62-year marriage they never spent a night apart, save for short hospital stays. Fueled by a significant degree of emotional cutoff from his mother's family in Asia and his father's overly compliant relationship with his own mother, the couple negotiated the anxiety with conflict, impairment in the mother, and the involvement of Mr. W in his parents' marriage. As the eldest son, Mr. W carried a special importance to his mother due to the fact that sons were not only important in the land of her birth but also due to the preponderance of females in her own family of origin (out of 15 children by her father, 12 were females, and only two males lived to adulthood). Consequently, the isolation of Mr. W's mother from her mother and siblings who were scattered throughout the globe and with whom she had relatively minimal contact, essentially initiated by a few of her siblings, contributed to an overpositive focus on her firstborn. While adhering to the typical profile of an eldest brother of brothers and sisters described by Toman (1976, pp. 153–156, 160–163), Mr. W not only was academically successful but also became his mother's confidant, hearing stories of her difficulties with her in-laws and her sense of isolation.

From his earliest memories, Mr. W recalled the intensity of some of the disputes between his parents that centered around three pivotal figures: the paternal grandmother, her son, and his wife. Having been coddled by her

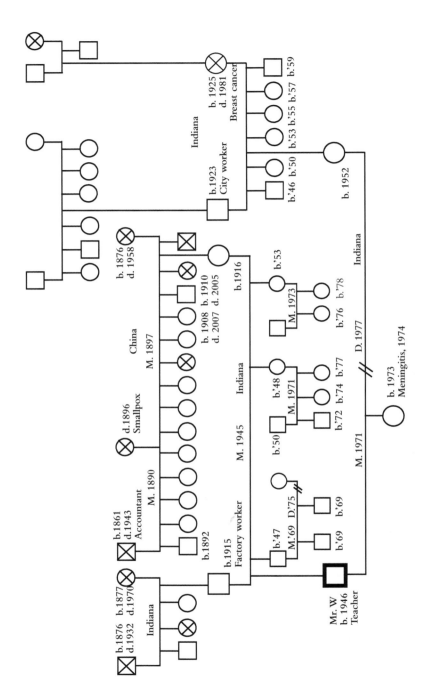

Figure 8.1 Family of Origin and First Marriage Diagram

own mother as a "sickly youngest child," Mr. W's mother had hoped to lean on her new husband in similar fashion. The husband, however, did not provide the degree of attention that his wife required, since his own mother also made demands upon him. When this significant in-law triangle could no longer contain the anxiety, Mr. W's mother would then regale him with negative stories about his father and his father's inattentive and insensitive family. As a young boy, Mr. W felt sorry for his mother, siding with her in her misery, whereupon conflict would emerge between him and his father. This pivotal triangle in Mr. W's family of origin shaped his initial career and future relationships with women.

Growing up Catholic near a Jesuit university in Asia, Mr. W's mother recounted warm family stories about her family's relationship with the priests from this institution. Absorbing the tales of these heroic men, Mr. W soon declared to his family and to others that he was planning to became a priest and a member of the Society of Jesus at that. What is informative here and an indication of his own level of undifferentiation from his parents was the fact that he maintained that he had made this decision at the ripe age of five years old. Of course, he received much attention and adulation from his mother and others for this vocational path, resulting in his entrance into a Jesuit seminary immediately after high school.

Despite being limited in his ability to separate himself from his mother and father, Mr. W initially found seminary life fulfilling. Continuing to excel academically, he pictured himself on the path toward being a Jesuit missionary, not unlike those storied figures told to him on his mother's knee. The Jesuits taught him the joys of scholastic rigor, building upon the legacy of the Christian Brothers who mentored him in high school. But as he advanced in this regimented and ascetic life, doubts appeared relative to one vow that he had taken, that of chastity. Exposed to women on a college campus in his fourth year of training, Mr. W, who had forgone dating in high school due to his impending vocation, became aware of the other sex. This crisis of faith, exacerbated by his involvement with a coed while still in the seminary, led to the angst-provoking decision to exit the religious life. When informed of this departure, Mr. W's mother withdrew and became silent while his father exploded in anger. A possible interpretation of this move might be that Mr. W was attempting to define a life course for himself, apart from the hopes and dreams of his parents, particularly his mother. The degree of reactivity implicit in his leaving the seminary, however, suggests that this was not the case inasmuch as the choice was rooted in his infatuation for a young woman.

Early Adulthood and First Marriage: 22 to 30

Now professionally adrift, Mr. W secured a position as a special education teacher in a major metropolitan area despite the absence of any background in this area. Perhaps recalling the words of his father relative to dating women of another "race," that is, "Be friendly but not familiar," Mr. W catapulted into an intense relationship with an African American woman, asking for her hand in marriage after knowing her just a few weeks, a strategy that his father had also employed. While this relationship eventually terminated, Mr. W was successful in piquing the ire and consternation of his parents. He found their strident opposition comforting at times, giving him a false sense of bravado and pseudo direction.

This rebellious stance fired his relationship with his future first wife, an African American woman from his hometown and the third of seven children in a similarly intense and anxious family. They, too, vehemently opposed her involvement with an older white man, and an elopement followed. Huddled together in an "us against the world" position, the newly married couple left the area for a large Midwestern metropolis where the husband had secured a scholarship for graduate school, majoring in Afro-American and African studies. During this time, Mr. W was geographically and emotionally distant from his parents and his siblings. There were routine visits home and while his parents had voiced their displeasure with the marriage, they did not exclude him and his wife from the family home. Their eldest son, once the family success story, now mystified his parents. Trips home were routine and perfunctory, often including shouting matches with his father over the volatile issues of the times such as race and politics. His mother remained in the background as relationships in that primary triangle shifted. Mr. W was now in the outside position with his parents in an alliance with each other.

Not surprisingly, tensions soon heated up between Mr. W and his wife, resulting in a pattern of his avoidance of any potential conflict (emotional distance) and her frustration when trying to make some kind of contact with him. These difficulties abated when the couple moved into a large house with seven other individuals (mostly fellow graduate students). However, an unplanned pregnancy and the birth of their daughter, the completion of graduate school, and the move back to the couple's home community contributed to their destabilization. Not having addressed his fusion with his own parents, Mr. W and his wife separated after a little more than four years of marriage. Following a brief but failed attempt at reconciliation, the wife initiated divorce proceedings, leaving Mr. W with the convenient self-serving story that his wife was the one who wanted the divorce. Their immaturity and the inability of both parties to see their part in the relationship contributed to a more extreme version of the emotional cutoff that was present with both of his parents. After all, divorce is a form of running away behavior from an individual that once held importance in a life. By this time, Mr. W was almost 30 years old.

Adulthood and the Second Marriage: 31 to 55

Having relocated to a college town where his first wife had moved following their initial separation, Mr. W attempted to land a job. Perusing the employment ads, he found himself drawn to positions that required an "MSW."

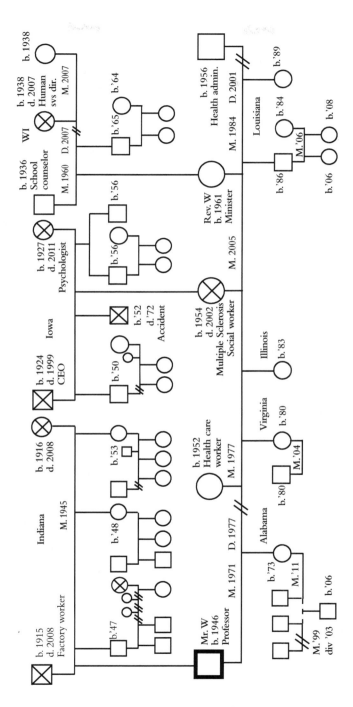

Figure 8.2 Family Diagram of Adulthood and Subsequent Marriages

Uncertain of this degree, he did some investigation, discovering that the university did indeed offer a Masters of Social Work, whereupon he applied and gained admission. Recalling his father's reminiscences about drifting through life without much career direction, Mr. W felt an affinity for his father's predicament. His father had attributed this aimlessness to the fact that his own father had become ill when he was 12 years old, later dying when he was 16. Indeed, Mr. W would occasionally hear his father describe his youth as one characterized by growing up "without a father." He was still unaware of a concept like the multigenerational emotional process, which might have provided some understanding of his own situation. Undifferentiation can also manifest itself in career aimlessness, a path reminiscent of his father's self-described meanderings.

Recently separated from his first wife and waiting for the finalization of the divorce, Mr. W spotted an attractive woman at the graduate school orientation. Repeating the pattern of a rapid courtship employed by his parents and himself in his first marriage, Mr. W actively pursued this woman. Somewhat responsibly, he informed her of his prior marriage and of his two-year-old biracial daughter. Somewhat blindly, he also contended that he had definitely resolved his first marriage, assuring his future second wife that he was now ready for another relationship. He did not know at this time just how little he actually knew, which certainly seems to be a key factor in the collapse of second marriages (Marano, 2000). Within a year of meeting his future second wife and six months after his first marriage ended, Mr. W remarried in August 1977. In typical distancing fashion, Mr. W did not inform his former spouse of this marriage, and she only learned about it when she spotted the wedding ring on his finger when he was picking up his daughter for a visitation. This added to already festering resentments between them.

The new Mrs. W, the youngest sister of brothers as well as an older sister of brothers, was more than seven years younger than her husband, in this, her first marriage (see Figure 8.2). She came from a prominent and economically affluent family. Although academically gifted, Mrs. W was the projected-upon child in her family of origin. Her fusion with her mother would play out in fractiousness. Her mother described herself as "walking on eggshells" in her daughter's presence, a tension that had erupted in Mrs. W's teen years in full force. The premature death of a favorite older brother who served to buffer some of the relationships in the family only added to the anxiety. Generally, conflict in this family remained underground, with humor and verbal banter utilized as ways to establish both a connection and distance.

Early in their dating relationship, problems emerged and the couple sought help from the university counseling center. The bulk of their disagreements stemmed from Mr. W's unresolved issues from his first marriage, with his wife now making claims that he married her "on the rebound." They would verbally fight about the role of his former spouse in their lives and the regular visits with Mr. W's daughter. On one occasion, the three-year-old daughter asked her new stepmother, "Do you hate my mommy?" She answered that she really did not know the little girl's mommy and could not hate her, to which the child responded, "Well, my mommy hates you," illustrating the new sets of triangles that stem from the unfinished business of a first marriage.

In the graduate program in social work (1976–1978), Mr. W first learned of Bowen theory in courses taught by a respected professor, now considered one of the pioneers in social work. Captivated by the content, Mr. W began collecting information on four generations of his family for a special seminar with this professor, coming to the realization that he knew little about his parents' respective families of origin. He did discover the obituary of his maternal grandfather, a man who died in Asia three years before Mr. W was born. The words in the opening of the obit stated that this man was "better known in his community as a social worker," a revelation both startling and humbling. There was a budding realization that somehow this ancestor whom he had never met but about whom he had heard countless stories was somehow shaping his life, a life that he had formerly thought he was determining for himself. He also came to see the distance in his mother's family, never having met some of her siblings and their children.

In this seminar, each graduate student had an opportunity to present his or her family diagrams to the class, with Mr. W being the final student. Cluttered with information and people, Mr. W smugly reviewed his family diagram, ending the presentation with a flourish. He still recalls a classmate's observation: "All the other students had numerous questions for the group, but you had none." In retrospect, he would later come to realize just how little he knew about how families actually operate and that compiling large amounts of data is not necessarily equivalent to differentiating a self in the family of origin. Nonetheless, Bowen theory resonated in his brain in a way that no other material did. In discussions with the faculty member, he came to understand his significance to his mother, as Mr. W became the repository of the emotional residue of her home country and family. He began asking questions about the theory, only to be informed by a classmate that the Georgetown Family Center offered a postgraduate training program in Washington, DC, for out-of-town professionals. Recalling that information subsequent to graduation, Mr. W enrolled in this program between 1979 and 1981.

At the conclusion of graduate school in 1978, he contacted his mother's older half-brother, a man with whom she had not had contact since leaving Asia in 1946. This was Mr. W's initial attempt to bridge an emotional cutoff in the family, naively believing that his mother would be delighted that he made contact with this sibling. Much to his surprise, Mr. W's mother began telling him negative stories about this brother and the ways in which he had disappointed their father. This was new information. Undeterred, he made the visit anyway intrigued about his mother's parents, whom he had never met but about whom he had heard numerous overpositive accounts. Warmly received by this newfound family member, Mr. W made inquiries about his mother's parents, siblings, and life in her home country. Speaking openly, his uncle painted a very different picture of their family of origin, describing Mr. W's maternal grandfather as a distant and aloof man and the maternal grandmother as a somewhat vindictive stepmother who clung to her own biological children, particularly her eldest daughter and Mr. W's mother (she was the youngest, after all). He would continue this relationship with his uncle, later meeting cousins and other family members who had formerly been strangers. When this uncle celebrated his fiftieth wedding anniversary with his wife, Mr. W was there. And when this uncle died, Mr. W attended the funeral over the protestations of his wife, the only member from his own side of the family to be present. Forging a relationship with this man gave Mr. W a deeper understanding of the concepts of emotional cutoff, triangles, and the difficulties of trying to separate a self from his mother. Moreover, Mr. W had begun the "baby steps" toward appropriating a theory, a way of thinking for himself. It was not easy.

His involvement in the postgraduate training program at the Georgetown Family Center amplified his insights. Patterns that were present in his first marriage began to appear in his second marriage. Managing anxiety expressed by emotional distance and his wife's tendency to defer to him in the one-down position, Mr. W saw similarities in his own parent's marriage. Where a prominent triangle for his parents had been that between his father, his father's mother, and his mother, an active triangle included himself, his current spouse, and his former spouse. Prior to deciding to have a child, Mr. W's current wife expressed great concern that he would not love "their child" as much as he loved the child by his first marriage. While these concerns dissipated with the births of two daughters in 1980 and 1983, Mr. and Mrs. W negotiated the togetherness forces between them with a fair degree of distance. After 10 years of marriage, Mr. W's increasing unhappiness with his employment followed by a crisis at work coupled with Mrs. W's growing dissatisfaction with her husband's remoteness from her erupted in her request for a marital separation. Reeling from the problems at work and his wife's unhappiness with their marriage, Mr. W sought professional help from a coach at the Georgetown Family Center in 1987.

It is important to note that Mr. W had embarked upon a more structured effort to differentiate a self in his family of origin and in his marriage from the beginning of his involvement in the postgraduate program in 1979. Faithfully attending the annual symposium sponsored by the Georgetown Family Center, he had begun to make visits to his parents and siblings on a regular basis. At times, he would take his entire family. And then, he would have an agenda for solo visits, including: 1) attendance at key family events that he formerly would have missed; 2) visits of his father's older brother and older sister, spending time alone with each of them and hearing different perspectives on his father's family of origin; and 3) trying to change his position in the parental triangle, that is, trying to secure some alone time with each parent. Additionally, he established more regular phone contact and correspondence with his mother's family who were scattered throughout the globe.

What is also noteworthy was an exercise to clarify his religious beliefs in 1981 as an attempt to more clearly define a solid self, the non-negotiable component not sacrificed for the sake of harmony. Growing doubts about the devout faith of his birth led him to conclude from this exercise that he had *no* religious beliefs that came from within him and that he had embraced beliefs that belonged to his parents and other ancestors. Despite the unhinging of self that this precipitated, he did discover confidence that he would find a way that would make some sense to him and that he could embrace more completely. In the mid-1980s, he was introduced to Unitarian Universalism, which made increasing sense to him. His growing knowledge of evolutionary theory, the importance of the rational and emotional parts of the human, and his limited comprehension of Bowen theory suddenly provided a better "fit" for him in this faith tradition and with the way he wanted to live his life. This would later become a bone of contention in his family of origin and family process would play out on the canvas of his newfound religious beliefs.

Of import at this juncture is that despite almost 10 years of familiarity with Bowen theory and some effort at implementing some of these concepts in his own personal life, Mr. W still found himself and his wife in a crisis. If he had any illusions about the prospects that Bowen theory would provide a "quick fix" for his predicaments, he was sorely mistaken. Involvement in the coaching effort contributed to a careful reconsideration of his professional career. A major employment shift and corresponding geographical move led to some calming of the anxiety in the couple. He took a stance with his wife about her request for him to move out of the family home by suggesting that if she was so unhappy, she could leave. This led to a brief increase in tension followed by a period of calm when she perceived that he was serious about this position. Where he formerly would have acquiesced to his wife's wishes, just as he did when his first wife asked for a divorce, he found a way, although still anxious, to remain on the scene. Standing his ground made a difference, however small at the time. Yet the relationship process continued to play itself out in predictable, if not entirely understood, ways. Mrs. W began experiencing fatigue, numbness in her extremities, and bladder problems, conditions to which she attributed to her pregnancies in 1980 and 1983. Preliminary tests in the mid-1980s confirmed a neurological condition, followed by a more definitive diagnosis of multiple sclerosis in 1989, the period after the family relocated to another state for Mr. W's new job. It might be that the overfunctioning and underfunctioning reciprocity in her marriage to Mr. W and a continued process of fusion with her family of origin were factors in this diagnosis.

Throughout the initial 10 years of his marriage to his second wife (1977–1987), Mr. W had regular visits with his eldest daughter who lived with her mother about one hour from the family home. When she turned 14, however, her mother moved to the South to pursue a relationship and a job opportunity, taking their daughter with her. Mr. W's relationship with his former spouse remained tense and conflictual, and he did his best to keep contact to a minimum save for conversations about the logistics of visitation. In the meantime, this daughter began to exhibit a host of psychological symptoms, resulting in a three-month psychiatric hospitalization when she was 11. When the fusion with this daughter became intense, Mr. W's former wife would contact him, indicating her sense of being overwhelmed and looking to him for respite. The move resulted in an exacerbation of the daughter's symptoms, leading the mother to request that the daughter live somewhere else. After an ill-conceived attempt to live with Mr. W's sister, the daughter came to reside with Mr. W and his family in 1989, raising the level of anxiety in that unit. Bowen theory would prove invaluable here.

The triangles common in divorce surfaced in anxious fashion with Mr. W being most reactive to his second wife's apprehensive response about the inclusion of his daughter in their home, particularly with her concerns about the impact upon their own two daughters, now ten and seven. Consultation sessions with a coach versed in Bowen theory contributed to a rather ingenious solution. Mr. W secured an apartment down the street from the family home where he and his eldest daughter would temporarily reside. His alternating between two domiciles relieved some of Mrs. W's concerns over the next two years. While other family members and friends were critical of this arrangement, Mr. W determined that this was the most efficient alternative at the time, given the status of the relationship.

Prior to living with her father and his family, Mr. W's eldest daughter had exhibited psychological symptoms leading her own mother to be concerned for this daughter's safety as well as her own. Threatening to harm herself and her mother, the now 16-year-old daughter who had been hospitalized at 11 was receiving psychiatric care, including psychotropic medication. When this adolescent came to live with her father, she had several questions for him: "Are you going to make me see a psychiatrist?" "Are you going to have me put on medication?" Guided by Bowen theory, the father responded directly: "The only person who is going to see a psychiatrist is your father. I know that you have threatened suicide in the past and I want you to know this. There is nothing that I can do that can really stop you if you want to take your own life. However, if you do that, you will contribute to a life of terrible sadness for your mother, your father, and your sisters that is the legacy of suicide." The daughter seemed baffled and relieved by this communication.

Sticking to his word, Mr. W employed the coaching sessions to manage himself in the midst of these anxious times. And the eldest daughter who had been doing poorly in a high school in another state pulled up her functioning. There was never a hint of suicidal talk again. She graduated from high school with a 3.00 average, involving herself in the choir. She secured a part-time job at a fast food restaurant. And she was admitted to a competitive college in the Midwest where she would later graduate, continuing to spend the bulk of her summers with her father's family, now in the family home. Perhaps the diminution of the intense fusion between the daughter and her mother (she was the only child, her mother had not remarried at this point, and the two of them were geographically removed from the extended families) and Mr. W's growing conviction in his own beliefs provided more "wiggle room" for this teen. Free of some of the intense focus and no longer the primary focus for absorbing anxiety (for example, Mr. W's second wife had physical symptoms), she had space to do a little more of what she needed to do at this stage of her life.

Mr. W's mid-life career shift in 1987 progressed well, despite the typical transitional tasks accompanying such a move. The family had handled the addition of the new family member and the geographical move, with the three daughters progressing nicely in their schooling. Mrs. W took a position as a social worker in a nearby community, leaving Mr. W to deal with the responsibilities of caring for the children before and after school, preparing many meals, and getting them to their varied activities. Given the fact that his employment left him with the summers relatively unencumbered, he developed more of a relationship with his three daughters in addition to gaining some respect for the work that women do with their offspring. He consciously continued his work on himself within the context of his family. When a potential job offer arose in a different part of the country, Mr. W turned it down on the basis of wanting to stay in geographical proximity to his own family of origin as well as that of his wife. Realizing the strands of emotional cutoff paired with physical distance in his mother's family, Mr. W opted to seek employment in a place that was equidistant from his family and his wife's family. Bowen theory provided a framework for making these important life decisions.

In the early 1990s, there was a pileup of stressful events that would take a toll on this family. Mrs. W's employment ended due to a cessation of a grant that subsidized her position, and she began to experience an increase in symptoms of multiple sclerosis. Now a college student, Mr. W's eldest daughter suffered a violent sexual assault while visiting her mother. She recovered from her physical wounds but the emotional residue remained. Nonetheless, she returned to university in the fall of that year, progressing with her studies. Overwhelmed by the rapid succession of major crises, Mr. W's functioning deteriorated and he became involved in an extramarital affair. His knowledge of Bowen theory, his 15-year effort at defining himself more clearly, and his ongoing coaching were not enough to inoculate him from becoming symptomatic. In the midst of this collapse, he recalled Dr. Bowen's observation, "Why is it that the human has to fall down a manhole before he realizes it's not a good idea?" (Bowen, personal recollection, n.d.).

Trying to extricate himself from this hole, Mr. W once again turned to Bowen theory. He recalled the importance of an open relationship system with important people in his life, the prerequisite of a person-to-person relationship that Dr. Bowen had described. He embarked upon a series of specific moves in his relationship network that countered the magnitude of the feeling process that was running through his being. Feelings dictated running away from Mrs. W, escaping with another woman to begin an exciting new life (the limbic system is not the seat of logic). Feelings pulled him toward secrecy, covertly avoiding mention of this relationship. And these beguiling feelings swamped any comprehension of his responsibility to the group, namely, his wife, his children, his organization, and the respective extended families. While he was totally incapable of quelling the passions now aroused in his mid-brain and some of the behaviors that followed, he made a sliver of a thinking decision that ran in the face of intense feelings. He decided to disclose the affair to the important people in his life, a choice rooted in Bowen theory.

Initially, he told Mrs. W about the affair. Devastated by this disclosure, she somehow found the capacity to tell her husband, "If you're in love with this woman, perhaps you should move in with her." Taken aback by her unpredicted response, he found the prospect of moving in this direction undesirable. They decided instead on a marital separation, a period that lasted six weeks with the emotional fallout continuing for at least two to three years. Prior to moving back with Mrs. W, he terminated the sexual relationship with the other woman, but the turbulence in that relationship and in his marriage continued. Mr. and Mrs. W together discussed the marital separation with their 12-year-old and 9-year-old daughters, evoking tears and distress from all parties. Continuing on the path of opening up this highly emotional event, Mr. W informed his parents, his siblings and their spouses, and his wife's parents of what had happened. In spite of the well-deserved criticism and recriminations heaped upon him, he found a small measure of relief in having the affair out in the open, a posture suggested by Bowen theory.

In the middle of the marital separation, Mr. W, in desperation, made a phone call to his former wife. Not wanting to replicate the emotional cutoff that occurred in his first marriage via divorce, Mr. W plaintively asked this woman from whom he had been divorced for almost 16 years and with whom he had polite but tense interactions in that period, "What was I like to live with?" This woman would later tell him that she was tempted to hang up the phone but that there was something in his voice that touched her in its authenticity. So she told him. She described his distance from her and the frustration that she experienced in trying to make a connection with him in addition to his overfunctioning on her behalf, and Mr. W suddenly realized that he was functioning in the same manner with his second wife. And it was not dissimilar from the ways in which he functioned in his family of origin, overfunctioning in relation to his mother and keeping his distance from the togetherness pulls in his family of origin. This auspicious phone conversation proved to be a turning point not only in Mr. W's relationship with his current wife but in his relationship with his former wife, who would turn out to be a resource not only for him, but his entire family over the subsequent years.

Energized by the outcomes of this disclosure, Mr. W expanded his attempts at openness to his mother's surviving brother and sister. Traveling to the city where these individuals lived, Mr. W visited each of them. His maternal uncle was a formidable figure in the family, well known for his opinionated views on the world. Mr. W himself had been the recipient of some of his uncle's critiques and over the years had repeatedly attempted to make a connection with him. Letters that he sent were not answered in those early attempts and phone calls were brief and strained. He did not realize that he had been the subject of some conversations between his mother and her brother, resulting in some of the beliefs that his uncle had of him. With some trepidation, he spilled out the entire unsavory tale to his uncle, anticipating the expected condemnation of this unspeakable behavior. Instead, his uncle sat next to him, listened without interrupting, and then patted him on the knee, saying, "I know that you will do the right thing." There was no advice on what that "right thing" happened to be, no shoulds or opinions. The uncle gave him a vote of confidence instead, astonishing the confused nephew and leaving him to figure out just what the right thing actually was. Bowen theory was instrumental in this effort.

Similarly, Mr. W took his maternal aunt to lunch during the same period, again sharing his marital difficulties with her. Again, instead of commenting upon the affair, this woman gave him her views of the young Mr. W and his relationship with his mother. The aunt declared, "When you were a boy and a young man, I never liked you all that much. You seemed like a snob. I thought that my sister was wrong to speak about your priestly vocation at such a young age as she coddled you, making you out to be so important." Surprised to hear these keen observations, Mr. W found that his honest telling of his current life's struggles resulted in his aunt's newfound discovery of her nephew as she summarized at the end of their luncheon, "After speaking with you like this, you're not really that bad after all. You're human." While years of hard work were still ahead for Mr. and Mrs. W as they repaired their marriage, these difficult and rewarding encounters with a former spouse, an aunt, and uncle were an integral part of that reconciliation.

As Mr. and Mrs. W slowly and agonizingly began to address the unaddressed issues in their marriage, they recommitted themselves to each other. Mr. W openly apologized to his wife's parents for not only the pain that he had caused their daughter but also the upset for both of them. In a magnanimous gesture, his father-in-law counseled, "That's water under the bridge. Your wife needs you now." And she did, indeed, for her symptoms of multiple sclerosis began to accelerate, in no small measure due to the marital difficulties that they had endured with the husband's affair. Mr. W came to see that for a time his feeling self had taken charge of his thinking self. Making the effort to distinguish thinking from feeling and then choosing to move in the direction of thinking proved daunting for Mr. W, but not impossible. But it took time. And it took hard work. With a way of thinking about the world that provided an anchor in the midst of life's storms, Mr. W found some degree of courage that was to fortify the family for what was to occur.

Mr. and Mrs. W faced the obstacles of the wife's increasing physical deterioration in the mid- to late 1990s. On their twentieth anniversary (1997), they renewed their vows to each other. They both played a critical role in the establishment of a new Unitarian Universalist congregation in their community, the first in the city's history. Mr. W's employment situation stabilized and he was fortunate to have a schedule in which he could provide care for his wife. Efforts at differentiation did not cease as the family grappled with the wife's multiple sclerosis. Outcomes of his earlier efforts emerged in novel forms. His former wife now became active in his family, applauding the recovery of his marriage to Mrs. W. She visited his family, staying with all of them and developing a relationship with the two younger daughters. Eventually, his former spouse remarried and attended the high school graduations of Mr. and Mrs. W's daughters just as Mr. and Mrs. W celebrated the college graduation of his eldest daughter with her mother and friends. Mr. W, citing his understanding of Bowen theory, shared with his former wife that more mature people do not get divorced. Insightfully, she promptly replied, "If we had been more mature, we would never have gotten married." There is wisdom in that statement. At one graduation party, his former wife offered to feed his current wife so that Mr. W could visit with the guests. Mrs. W's father was amazed by the sight of his daughter being fed by this woman who formerly had an apparently adversarial relationship with the family. When he commented upon her kindness, she simply replied, "Well, I love this woman." Not everyone in the family, however, appreciated the presence of the former spouse in their midst. Mr. W's parents and siblings were quite critical of her involvement in the family, but he held his ground striving not to defend his actions nor attack them for what they believed should happen. Again, the courage of his convictions, forged by Bowen theory and tried and tested in important family relationships, offered Mr. W a growing clarity about how he wanted to live his life, even with the disapproval of important others.

Mr. W's parents continued to be a resource and a challenge to him. The togetherness forces in the family of origin played themselves out on the canvas of religious beliefs. Mr. W's father and mother had a terribly difficult time with the fact that their son no longer practiced the faith in which they raised him, Roman Catholicism. Over the years, verbal battles occurred primarily between father and son, with Mr. W perceiving his father to "get on his back." Typically, he would defend himself or mount a counterattack on his parents' beliefs which only maintained the tension and corresponding distance between them. Triggered by his father's inquiry on whether or not Mrs. W had been baptized, Mr. W decided to address the issue in a letter to his father. Chronicling their relationship from his point of view, the son took a position with his father while recognizing his importance in his life. He had come to the realization that he was similar to and different from his father, which allowed him to be a tad more thoughtful and also clear in where he stood on matters of faith. Although his father never verbally acknowledged the letter, there was a palpable loosening up of their relationship. Now in his fifties, Mr. W could finally be in the presence of his father and mother without having the kneejerk response to run away either internally or physically. Small progress can take decades of work.

As Mrs. W's health declined, Mr. W found it important to formulate and implement some core principles for his life, part of the differentiating effort. For instance, he held to the following: "There is a human being behind every symptom, and that person is not defined by an illness. Every effort will be made to connect with the thinking, feelings, and fantasies of that individual." Even when his wife had difficulty in speaking and even when neurologists diagnosed her with highly impaired cognitive functioning, Mr. W believed that she was still present. When he told her, "Honey, I know that your brain is still working and that you still understand everything that is going on around you," she would reply, "Yes, I do." He also believed that she had the ability to participate in the decision-making process on both major and minor issues. When the opportunity arose for a trip to Hawaii even though she was confined to a wheelchair and no longer able to walk, Mr. W would ask her if she wanted to stay in the Midwest or take the trip to Hawaii to which she immediately responded, "Go to Hawaii." And they did, despite the consternation and concern of some family members. While there, he wheeled his wife to a beach to watch the sunset, kneeling next to her and holding her hand. As they watched the sun sink into the Pacific, she leaned over and whispered, "Thanks for taking me to Hawaii." And when the time came that her body was so compromised that major surgery was proposed, a possible but risky option, Mr. W again explained the situation to his wife, asking for her input but not expecting an answer. But she uttered a dismissive sound at the prospect. When he asked her if she wanted to die, again not expecting a response, he heard a soft assent. Mrs. W died peacefully at home in 2002, surrounded by her daughters, her mother, her husband, and her two college friends. Influenced by Dr. Bowen's article on death (Bowen, 1978, Chapter 15), Mr. W engaged his daughters and friends and family members in the construction of the funeral service, having an open casket and a church service. His former wife was there, and people remarked upon the resilience and strength of the family. What they did not know was how an attempt to adhere to Bowen theory made this possible.

Later Adulthood and Third Marriage: 55–Present

Mrs. W died in the twenty-fifth year of their marriage and Mr. W, now 55, had no intentions of remarriage. Instead, he devoted himself to spending time with his daughters, visiting his parents and extended family members who were still alive, and recommitting himself to his profession, which eventually entailed some academic publishing. Saddened by the death of his wife, he was content to be a presence in the lives of his family and a force within his profession. He was a little more deliberative and reflective and a little less reactive. Of course, well-meaning people offered plenty of advice: Sell that big house now that your children have left home and start dating again, you're still a young man. At times, he was not beyond reproach from his children. In the midst of a particularly difficult holiday when he was difficult to be around, one of his daughters reminded him, "You're not the only one who lost someone here." That accurate reminder was invaluable in showing how his family could be a resource for continued learning.

In the mid-1990s, Mr. and Mrs. W had been among the original 10 founders of a church in their community as mentioned earlier. In 1996, the church obtained a grant to subsidize a student minister, a woman who befriended his wife and daughters. In fact, when she departed the church after nine months, the two younger daughters made a request, "When we grow up, would you be the one to marry us?" Never before or since had anyone made such a request. Over the years, Mr. W had provided letters of reference for this now ordained minister as she moved throughout the country in pursuit of her studies and her first pastoral appointment. When his second daughter indicated that she was engaged, she asked her father about the whereabouts of that minister and he put his daughter in touch with her. She agreed to officiate at the daughter's wedding. Additionally, Mr. W had learned that this woman whom he had admired so much along with his wife and daughters had been divorced for several years. Perhaps surreptitiously or not, the daughter seated the minister across from her father at the rehearsal dinner and at the wedding reception. Quite unexpectedly, Mr. W was smitten. It had been two and a half years since his wife had died, and he had not dated at all. But that all changed.

Rev. W, Mr. W's third wife, was an eldest sister of a brother, the first time he had ever been involved with an eldest. His prior two wives had been younger sisters of brothers, a compatible mix. The challenge of relating to an eldest like himself was new territory for both of them and the fact that Mr. W grew up with younger sisters and Rev. W grew up with a younger brother helped mitigate some of the potential rank conflict inherent in their eldest positions. They would currently describe their relationship as a working partnership, each with their own areas of expertise and an understanding of the opposite sex. All parents readily embraced the prospect of their marriage. Mr. W's father joked that his son had "finally found religion" inasmuch as he was marrying a minister. Coming from a conflict avoidant family with a fair degree of emotional cutoff in her father's family and fusion in her mother's family, Rev. W and her husband incurred some of the typical transitions associated with new relationships. The differentiating effort that Mr. W had made to that point continued to offer direction.

After the wedding of his daughter in 2004, Mr. W, ignorant of the relationship status of the minister other than knowing that she was unmarried, wrote an introductory letter in which he expressed his interest in getting to know her and spend time with her, even though she lived on the East Coast. A whirlwind courtship ensued, recalling the history of his parents' courtship and that of his two marriages. Some things never change, it would seem. As he began to see this individual, he informed his daughters, his dead wife's mother and brothers, and his parents and siblings. To a person, they were positive and enthusiastic, as were his friends and colleagues. When the couple married in May 2005 (almost three and a half years after Mr. W's wife's death), his second wife's entire family was present along with his children, parents, siblings, and friends.

Knowledge of the common triangles in divorce was invaluable. Much to the surprise of his future wife and her parents, Mr. W contacted her former husband. In addition to wanting to detriangle from the tensions between his soon-to-be wife and the man to whom she had been married for 16 years, bearing a son and a daughter now ages 19 and a half and 16, he wanted to let this man know where he stood relative to the daughter who had remained in the custody of the mother. Mr. W indicated his support for this man's position as the father, pledging to support that role in any way possible. Rather than seeing himself as a future stepfather subsequent to the marriage, he conveyed the notion that he was the mother's husband, a more benign role with minimal expectations. Somehow, the very act of meeting with this man toned down the relationship intensity that often follows remarriage. Word traveled throughout multiple sides of the family, opening the door for future communications, some a bit tense, others calmer. Most recently, his wife's former father-in-law died somewhat suddenly. Taking Mr. W off guard, his wife suggested attending the funeral and went out of her way to be a gracious host to her former spouse and his new wife, offering the use of their home in that community where she had formerly lived. Seeing people that she had not seen in more than 10 to 15 years, Rev. W was received with great warmth and affection. Later, her daughter texted Mr. W, ". . . just wanted to personally thank you again for supporting the family . . . and offering the home. . . . It meant a lot to all of us to have you and Mom there." Mr. W believes that the groundwork for this occurred seven years earlier when Bowen theory provided a way through an anxious network.

Mr. W and Rev. W experienced major life transitions in the aftermath of their marriage in 2005. Her parents announced a divorce and her 19-year-old son declared his intent to marry following the unplanned pregnancy of his girlfriend. Later, Rev. W's father remarried and her mother died suddenly. Mr. W's eldest daughter also had an unplanned pregnancy and his former wife remarried. Mr. W's parents died within eight days of each other. Despite the onslaught of these significant family happenings, the couple negotiated the often difficult path as partners, committed to living the rest of their lives together.

Conclusion

Exposure to Bowen theory opened up new vistas for Mr. W. There was nothing magical, simple, or easy about this new perspective. Knowledge accrued slowly, even when Mr. W thought that he knew more than he actually knew. Making the typical mistakes of a novice, he continually stumbled, attempting to "convert" other family members to Bowen theory, only to be humbled by his family's ability to stay ahead of him. Yet, he stayed the course. When problems arose in his second marriage and the thinking part of himself got submerged by the feeling part, he almost repeated precisely what he had done in his first marriage. The limbic pull to run away and "start over" was astonishingly compelling. Making a choice to adhere to principle instead of feeling was the most difficult thing he had ever done to that point. Decades of painfully reducing some of his own emotional cutoff with a multitude of family members, of struggling to discover where he stood on key issues in his life, and of seeing the important triangles of which he was a part eventually contributed to a reversal of fortune. Sustained and guided by Bowen theory that culminated in his commitment to adhere to a way of life that made sense to him, Mr. W and his second wife kept the promise "till death do us part." While caring for his wife had its own set of challenges, Mr. W found it effortless. In the final years of their life together, he would indicate that it was possible to fall more deeply in love again with one's spouse.

Unlike previous times in his life, Mr. W did not rush into another relationship after the death of his wife. The process of differentiating a self with all of its ever-present challenges was now part of the warp and woof of his life. While the courtship of his third wife contained the predictable limbic pulls that are present in this phase of a relationship, Mr. W proceeded with a certainty and a conviction borne of knowing who he was and who he wanted to become. Already, this eight-year relationship has weathered intense family storms. Regardless, Mr. W knows the outcome. Differentiation does make a difference, even if it does take 30 years.

REFERENCES

Bowen, M. (1978). *Family therapy in clinical practice*. New York: Jason Aronson.

Divorce updates: Divorce update and rates in 2011. (2012). Retrieved from http://divorcerate2011.com/divorce-updates.

Kreider, R. M. (2005). Number, timing, and duration of marriages and divorces: 2001. *Current Population Reports* (No. P70–97). Washington, DC: U.S. Census Bureau.

Marano, H. (2000). Divorced? Don't even think of remarrying until you read this. *Psychology Today*. Retrieved from www.psychologytoday.com/magazine/archive/2000/03.

Toman, W. (1976). *Family constellation: Its effects on personality and behavior* (3rd ed.). New York: Springer.

9

BOWEN THEORY AS A GUIDE TO DEFINING A SELF OVER A LIFE CYCLE

James C. Maloni

Introduction

The Bowen approach to psychotherapy and its concommitant theory were introduced at a personally vulnerable time in the author's individual and family life cycle, but it has had tremendous impact ever since, currently spanning 40 years of his 73-year life. Its influence shifted the author's view of development from a facile individual emergence to a complex and interdependent process that is subject to numerous predictable and unforeseen events.

The guidance afforded by this theory is a continuous reminder of the common phrase "one is not in this alone." At the same time, this contextual framework does not alter the larger goal of mature living in order to increase one's ability to manage life and to emphasize responsibilities over rights in relation to self and others.

A central concept of this theory, differentiation of self, emphasizes self management of emotions and the utilization of intellectual reasoning in decision-making. The theory painstakingly describes obstacles in this process. These obstacles include multigenerational factors that counteract and limit the ability to live one's life via a planned and thoughtful process. A systematic study of these obstacles is crucial to the realization of such maturation. Learning how to observe, monitor, and manage the anxiety and reactivity that manifest such obstacles is central to this endeavor.

These impeding obstacles manifest themselves in various ways. One primary way in which they are elucidated is through family relationships. These relationships contain the most intense emotions available for human interactions. They originate in family of origin circumstances and transfer to nuclear family situations. For example, the marital relationship reflects a similar level of fusion that existed between the two individuals and their respective families of origin. In addition, according to Bowen theory, the two people who marry are operating at similar levels of basic functioning; i.e., their basic levels of differentiation (emotional maturity) are essentially the same.

Apparent differences in functioning in a marital couple are explained by interactive dynamics. They are referred to as functional versus basic levels of differentiation, or manifestation of pseudo-selves. Couples who are married to each other are said to trade and borrow emotional self from each other, which explains how one individual in this relationship appears to be functioning better than the other one. The degree of this individual's over-functioning is similar to the extent of the other's underfunctioning. The trading and borrowing from each other is based upon a similar foundational level of differentiation. Although the basic level of differentiation is very similar, the functional level varies according to the relationship-driven borrowing and trading of overt daily functions and activities from each other. This constitutes automatic and unspoken teamwork that naturally evolves from the intense closeness of two or more emotionally intertwined people.

This chapter describes how the author was first introduced to Bowen theory. This was associated with difficulties in his first marriage that led to his wife initiating marital therapy. It so happened that the therapist chosen for this endeavor utilized Bowen theory in her work. After an initial adjustment to this approach, the author eventually incorporated this theory and therapeutic application into his personal and professional life. This occurred in the context of three years of marital therapy, followed by a period of eight years of relative stability in his personal life. A major focus on family of origin work was involved during this period of time.

However, a significant modification in the author's work situation and offspring leaving home for and graduation from college will then be discussed. Also, the wife's professional mobility will be described along with the eventual divorce and his remarriage. Particular details of the divorce will be described in relation to similarities in his maternal grandfather's life. This grandfather died 12 years before the author was born.

Transmission of such emotional processes occurring primarily through the maternal family branch will be highlighted. The significance of this position, based on observation, is particularly striking in this situation. The maternal grandmother did not meet her eventual husband until after these events had occurred in his life. Also, the author's mother had become a young adult prior to learning about these earlier events in her father's life.

The author learned this information concerning his maternal grandfather almost 20 years before his own divorce. Apparently, knowledge of earlier facts may be useful but insufficient in preventing the repetition of family history events. This points to the depth of how emotional processes are transmitted across family generations. This also relates to the difference between basic and functional levels of differentiation, which is fundamental in Bowen theory. Information and cognitive development are necessary but not sufficient ingredients for the type and/or level of emotional maturation involved in basic levels of functioning.

First Marriage

Seven years into this author's initial marriage (1972), his wife notified him of her substantial dissatisfaction with their relationship. She further informed him that marital therapy would be required in order for her to remain in the marriage. The author, who was 33 years of age and having received his doctorate in clinical psychology four years earlier, was experiencing considerable success in his professional work. By most conventional standards, his professional functioning would have been considered to be at a high level. Married, with two healthy young sons attending school in an upscale suburban district, his personal functioning also seemed quite satisfactory. Likewise, his wife, then age 29, a post-baccalaureate level registered nurse quite involved in this achievement-oriented community, was also functioning at a high level. Just as water seeks out and moves to the lowest possible level, this marital relationship exhibited a gravitational pull toward the most vulnerable components of its individual and family functioning. All the earlier successes and achievements were dwarfed, and shifted from significant to somewhat irrelevant, when confronted with such serious difficulty in this vital family relationship.

The subjectively life-altering request from his wife, which quickly led to an intensive three years of marital therapy, shifted the author's psychological posture from "riding high" to sitting in "a two down" position. The first involved entering marital therapy from a context that included an early emphasis on his shortcomings and vulnerabilities. The second "down position" was the sudden immersion into a new and unfamiliar family systems approach to marital therapy employed by their therapist.

This type of shift in one's life circumstances is instructive regarding the Bowen concept of differentiation, with a particular focus on the distinction between basic and functional levels of differentiation. From a functional level standpoint, this author's initial achievements as a new PhD psychologist, husband, and father were quite impressive. However, the concept of basic differentiation is more attuned to the subtleties and complexities in human functioning. It measures functioning more sensitively and thoroughly at all levels, and most especially in its underbelly, where marital issues often reside.

While dissatisfaction in a marriage could be viewed as a subjectively driven individual perception, it is more likely a manifestation of stress and anxiety evolving into symptoms that are embodied in one or more relationships. In addition, from a Bowen theory perspective, it indicates a substantial level of fusion in the marital relationship. This emotionally driven closeness can readily shift from positive to negative. This is often fueled by increased complexity and stress in the circumstances surrounding the marital/family situation.

The marital problem and subsequent therapy set up the author's initial exposure to the Bowen orientation toward family therapy. This introduction would evolve into the author's primary way of conceptualizing human behavior and subsequently applying this framework in his psychotherapy with individuals, couples, and families.

The three years of marital therapy appeared to stabilize the author's marriage for several years. The eventual separation and divorce may reflect the difficulty in making a significant increase in basic levels of functioning/differentiation in spite of considerable effort on the part of both spouses. Also, in this particular family, the offspring had grown from elementary age school children into college graduates. By this time, they were in a better position to initiate financial independence. In addition, the wife's professional career had developed quite successfully.

From a theoretical point of view, a substantial level of fusion in a marriage does not inevitably lead to separation and divorce. However, the absence of chronic physical or emotional dysfunction in a spouse and a relatively low level of projection onto the offspring left the marriage susceptible to absorbing and binding the stress and anxiety in the family. Thus, the combination of high marital fusion and the marriage being the primary "shock absorber" for the family stress lent itself to an increased tendency with this couple toward divorce. Also, "the increase in women's emotional and financial autonomy" during the second half of the 20th century probably contributed to more physical separations and divorces than had occurred previously, and was most likely relevant to this family's situation.

The author's introduction to the Bowen approach to therapy also set the stage for his focus on family of origin as the primary method of monitoring and managing self and significant relationships. This broadening of the focus from nuclear to extended families also de-intensified the emotional heat on the marriage for the author and his wife, at least for a period of eight years from the mid-1970s to the early 1980s. This broader focus may have raised the functional levels of differentiation for these two academically oriented individuals. Learning a new way to think about psychological and family issues perhaps provided some additional "spark" for them as they involved themselves in nuclear family activities.

Basic and Functional Levels of Differentiation

Bowen theory and application to therapy provided the author with a systematic method to study and learn new ways to engage with family of origin over an extended period of time. Although this constituted some new knowledge and experience, it most likely did not bring about change in his basic functioning (Bowen, 1978, p. 371). Some functional shifts contributed to improvements in managing daily life for several years in the nuclear family. The author and his wife's positive response in learning a different way to think about family processes also added temporary stability to their life situation. This acquisition of new components of pseudo-self shifted the fusion in a positive direction for a substantial period of time. Thus, increases in functional levels of differentiation most likely explain the relative stability in this marriage for an eight-year period from the mid-1970s to the early 1980s. Although this constituted a functional versus basic level of change, the psychological work involved in this process was substantial and involved something more than a temporary bandage repair. The nature of a substantial process in a marital and nuclear family context, which does not end in a successful product, is difficult to categorize. Nevertheless, a functional shift in an important relationship such as marriage can be significant in spite of its temporary outcome.

During the early 1980s, the author went from part-time to full-time independent practice of clinical psychology. This involved leaving a work setting that had provided a supportive relationship system to a situation of relative isolation. In addition, this move triggered a high level of stress and anxiety for the author regarding financial uncertainties. The latter put direct and indirect pressures onto the marital and nuclear family system. This occurred at the same time that the wife's career was advancing at a rapid pace, but without predictable financial gains for the family. Also, the family life cycle included two adolescent sons who were soon to leave home to enter college.

Conventional wisdom sometimes gives preference to the conclusion that a long-term and dedicated knowledge-based effort in combating marital and/or family problems should and will result in a successful outcome. In some situations, such as the one described in this chapter, individual preferences, family history, and life cycle circumstances appear to have been stronger adversarial forces than the efforts for long-term gains and maintaining sufficient calm in these family relationships.

Bowen theory is very clear that basic change does not occur easily, and when it does, often with the assistance of coaching, the change is more incremental than substantial. The absence of substantial change in basic self is a fact of life. Expectations for self and others often run counter to this reality. These unrealistic expectations have been reinforced by an emphasis on self help forms of psychological intervention, which first became popular in the 1960s and 1970s when this author was coming into the field. It is easy for this author and colleagues to unintentionally blend their understanding of Bowen theory with their earlier exposure to these self help and mind-over-matter approaches to human behavior.

This author's marital separation, which led to divorce, occurred more than 20 years ago. During this period of time, he has made progress in managing the anxiety and emotional reactivity that this reality triggers in him and in other people. The effort in this chapter to describe how the events occurred in his life is a beneficial process. This case study is a good illustration of how even a well-coached effort does not compensate for fault lines well beneath the surface. Hopefully this chapter will help more to clarify this reality rather than to further fuel the emotionally based expectations that enlightened psychological efforts can overcome multigenerational patterns steeped in the blueprints of nature. The hope that nurture can trump nature may be appropriate for some endeavors such as stemming or reversing certain medical diseases. Possibly such endeavors can benefit from the assistance of and congruence with societal priorities.

College Graduation—Marriage Dissolution

Although the marriage appeared to regain some positive energy soon after both sons left home for college, the author's wife initiated the divorcing process after the second son graduated from college. This occurred two years after she had relocated 300 miles from the Pittsburgh area to pursue a post-doctoral fellowship in Nursing Research. Although an observer could readily predict such an outcome based upon the previously described marital dysfunction, combined with moderately long-term geographical distance, the author was essentially unprepared for this life event. On the one hand, the geographical distance had reduced the level of marital conflict as both parties attempted to "put the best foot forward" when interacting with the other. On the other hand, the practice effect of dealing with routine disagreements was more limited under these conditions. Also, the wife had been demonstrating a low level of tolerance for any display of negative responses emanating from the author. The author had also become less tolerant when the wife expressed uncertainty about the future of the marriage.

Thus, for the author, a predictable life event (sons graduating from college) was associated with his perceived unpredictable event of formal separation and impending divorce. The author's difficulty in anticipating and hesitancy in accepting divorce was partially conditioned by an old school Italian Roman Catholic view of marriage. Also, and perhaps even more influential, was a similarity in pattern of the divorce of his maternal grandfather (to be described in a later section). The relevance of this event, two generations earlier, is its probable emotional impact on the author's experience of his divorce. The latter nodal event, which occurred on the horizontal axis of the author's family life cycle, likely generated more emotional intensity due to the similar event having occurred on the vertical axis of his family life cycle (McGoldrick, Gerson, and Petry, 2008). Whenever an event, which had previously occurred in the history of the extended family (vertical axis), is later repeated in the nuclear family (horizontal axis), the emotional intensity is usually heightened in relation to this event. Individual awareness of the earlier event is not a necessary condition for this process to occur. This multigenerational emotional transmission process resides in the recesses of individual awareness. It is steeped in the visceral mangroves of the evolving family relationship systems, and is often transmitted via the maternal axis. The qualitative nature of the maternal perception and her management of the family emotional processes associated with the event is a significant variable regarding the degree of intensity for later generations.

Incorporating the Bowen Framework

As discussed earlier, the author's introduction to Bowen theory and method of clinical application occurred in the context of marital issues that required an immediate commitment to receiving professional assistance. The latter took the form of an approach that was new to this author, and as such, was perceived initially as requiring a form of forced feeding; because total intellectual and emotional attention to this approach could possibly go a long way toward saving this marriage. Sometime in the first year of this new exposure, motivation to pursue this approach was developing a life of its own, and was no longer viewed only as a practical necessity. Clearly an appetite had developed for Bowen theory, as this was becoming the author's primary way of thinking about his personal and professional life.

The Bowen focus on extended family processes was compatible with the author's early emotional programming in an immigrant Italian family. His absence of direct exposure to his mother's Germanic family background did not diminish the impact of its emotional imprint. Bowen theory would prove to be instrumental in explicating this important influence. It was also beneficial that the author's two parents lived in good health for more than 20 years after his introduction to Bowen theory. Primary sources, such as two living and lucid parents, are a significant asset for this type of family research.

The author remarried three years after he was formally separated and divorced from his first wife. His parents were still living and they had maintained their mental faculties. This was also a major advantage for this remarriage, as they became acquainted and gave their blessing to the marriage and to this wife's offspring. The latter was an important factor in the integration process of remarriage and blending of families. The author's mother died 31 months after this second marriage, and his father lived for an additional 42 months.

Although remarriage and blending of families have offered their own considerable challenges, it does appear that the author's previous family work has been transferable and useful to the current situation. Increased knowledge about and added hands-on experience in navigating multiple intersections in relationship processes have proven to be particularly relevant. This has been applied fairly effectively to the complexities associated with remarriage and the reality in this situation of requiring partial or intermittent blending of families. This includes some additional patience and less reflexive responsiveness to unpredictable and unexpected situations that emerge in everyday living.

This second, 18-year marriage has probably also benefited from more than half of its duration involving retirement from employment for both parties. Associated with this have been numerous opportunities for stimulating forms of travel. This included a 15-week semester at sea experience, which occurred soon after retirement. This early post-retirement exposure to broad cultural and educational experiences has elevated the intellectual level of discourse for author and wife. In addition, this has proven to be useful in follow-up travel and educational situations.

In this second marriage, the author has learned to focus somewhat more systematically on the triggers for anxiety and emotional reactivity, especially in a close relationship. Prior to retirement, he was learning how to be more thoughtful when exiting stressful work situations and transitioning to personal areas of his life. Most likely these newer behaviors reflected situational shifts rather than major changes in the author's life.

The opportunity to effectively manage the loss of the long-term first marriage and remarry at the age of 55 contributed significant subjective components in the author's life. Clearly, the "one down" position associated with marital rejection was replaced with an enhanced sense of favorability to the other in the second marriage. There was also a short period of time in between the two marriages that allowed for personal healing. The latter occurred rather quickly and appeared to be sufficient for the author to regain his customary sense of well-being and positive self-perception. The processes described above most likely reflect functional shifts rather than basic changes. These shifts involved added flexibility in managing ambiguity and complexity associated with relationships.

In summary, the relative absence of daily stress and anxiety coupled with new opportunities and experiences since retirement have contributed to important functional shifts for the author. As alluded to previously, these shifts contain some increased flexibility in managing relationship processes. The relative absence of stress afforded by retirement for more than half of the duration of this second marriage probably does not provide the necessary conditions to test basic change from the first to second marriage. This conclusion is also heavily based upon adherence to Bowen theory, which emphasizes that basic change in human functioning occurs only in small incremental ways, and often does not occur at all. This component of the theory is consistent with the author's clinical experience.

Maternal Family System

The author had virtually no firsthand contact with his mother's family of origin, except for a few meetings, as a young child, with his mother's maternal aunt Harriet (see Figure 9.1). Nevertheless, the work with his mother in regard to her extended family proved to be valuable. This occurred not only through mother/son collaboration, but also in reference to specific content concerning her father's life. Approximately one year after the author began his professionally coached family of origin study, his mother revealed to him that her father, a United Brethren minister, had been married prior to his marriage to her mother. Along with the youngest of their three sons, the first wife had apparently made a sudden exit from the family home in order to be with another man. This event constituted a major news story in a rural area

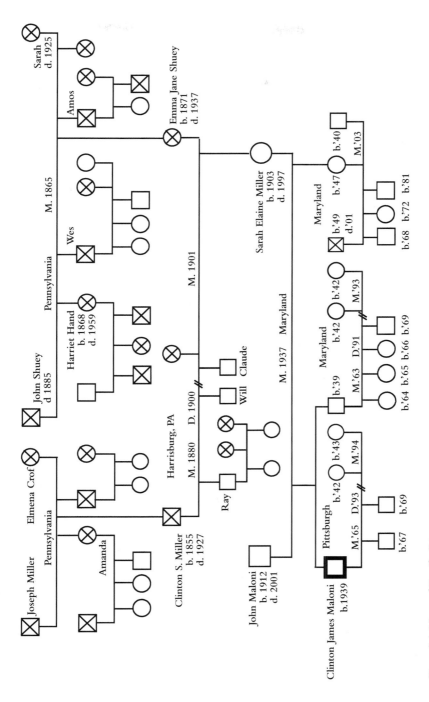

Figure 9.1 Maternal Family Diagram

of east central Pennsylvania during the last decade of the 19th century. It was the newspaper article that informed the author's mother of these dramatic details in her father's life that had occurred almost 30 years earlier. Having learned of this indirectly and accidentally as a young adult, she had kept this three-generation family secret from her offspring up until she informed the author. Passing on the secret information about the father apparently was an important by-product of her increasing commitment to the family-oriented research she was working on with her son.

His mother's self-initiated offering of this dramatic information, one year into his family research, added substantial depth to the inquiry. As alluded to previously, this would also be relevant information as the author was undergoing his own divorce 20 years after he had acquired the information about his grandfather. At this latter time, the author did a videotaped interview with his mother regarding this subject matter. He utilized this interview in two professional presentations. He described his efforts in gaining increased neutrality, as he was attempting to manage feelings of failure regarding his divorce (Maloni, 1993).

Maternal Influence and Differentiation

Murray Bowen observed that significant multigenerational emotional processes are usually transmitted primarily via the mother. The previous case example of the author's maternal grandfather's divorce supports this observation. This example also highlights the significance of the mother as transmitter of emotional processes, regardless of the degree of direct contact between her offspring and her family of origin. Apparently it is how the mother has managed this process that determines what is transmitted to her offspring. Thus, in the case of the author's maternal grandfather's divorce, the emotional processes relating to this event were most likely transmitted from the maternal grandmother to her daughter (author's mother), who in turn passed on her version of it to her offspring. This transmission process occurred primarily in covert ways. The only actual conversation that the author's mother had with her parental family members regarding this divorce was with her mother once she had discovered the information on her own. She and her father never discussed this subject, which was probably not unusual for that historical period of time.

It is difficult to determine the objective impact of the author's mother's decision to reveal this information. Most likely, this was part of an expanding mother/son level of communication, which would have a productive ripple effect on the author's overall family of origin work. This may also have been helpful to the author in achieving the goal of increasing his neutrality concerning his own divorce. This goal was somewhat complicated by a togetherness process whereby some family members and friends aligned themselves with his position during the divorce. Similar to the circumstances in his grandfather's divorce, the wife's initiating and relocating roles evoked sympathy and overly simplistic conclusions. Viewing these husbands as the victims in abandonment situations was an equally standard reflexive reaction for both the end of the 19th and 20th centuries.

Although the evidence is limited to the author's mother's portrayal of the earlier events, there is a possibility that history was repeating itself in regard to the similarity of circumstances. It does appear that the minister grandfather and therapist author were both perceived as victims in each of their divorces. Considerable focus on work in a human service profession, coupled with inattention to the nuclear family, was a possible emotional gravitational pattern for the author and his grandfather. If the portrayal of the 19th-century events regarding the grandfather's divorce is accurate, the parallels would be striking, even though there were almost 100 years separating the two life events.

The discovery of the grandfather's divorce, along with other information regarding emotional patterns in both maternal and paternal family systems, contributed to the author's commitment to Bowen theory both personally and professionally. This commitment took various forms and included numerous presentations at local professional meetings for more than 35 years. Several published articles and chapters of similar subject matter have occurred over a 20-year period.

Initially the focus of the author's family of origin work (or effort to define self in the family) was on the paternal side. This included a chapter on some parallels between the author and the previous two generations of Maloni males (Maloni, 1987). The presentations have also included a focus on how the author's German mother emotionally became an "adopted" member of her husband's Italian family (Maloni, 1980). Her role as a principal buffer of conflict and stress in her in-law family system reflected her mother's position with her own husband (author's maternal grandfather) and various relationship systems in his life. The latter included members of his various church communities, some of whom utilized her for physical and emotional support.

The author's family of origin work has repeatedly navigated a rich labyrinth of interlocking triangles. Having a fraternal twin brother imprinted and normalized the triangular nature of life, which included teaming up against their mother to insist on equal treatment on relatively insignificant matters. Subtlety and complexity characterized close relationships with parents, paternal grandmother, and paternal uncles and aunts. The author and his brother utilized competitive patterns between their father and his mother to obtain some preferences in food choices, which was an important theme in this extended Italian family. Bowen theory was an important guide in later developing a deeper understanding of these earlier realities in the author's extended family.

Becoming acquainted with his mother as an individual, separate from his father's extended family, was facilitated by a theory-based systematic effort.

This effort included numerous hours of independent researching of her extended family system. The unearthing of her buried biological family was an important aspect of this process. This added to the available family information, as well as helped to engage the author's mother more fully in the process. The numerous years that had transpired since she had direct experience with her extended family (except for the occasional visits with her Aunt Harriet), her long-term immersion in the in-law family, and the cutoff from the remains of diminishing family after her Aunt Harriet's death, had limited her access to certain aspects of this past.

The author's family of origin work with the maternal system added subtle components to the knowledge of his mother. These components provided some new glimpses of her as daughter and only child in a religiously oriented German and Pennsylvania Dutch family. Another side of her emerged as she described her warm and close relationship with her early widowed "earthy" maternal grandmother, whom she was named after, and in whose home she greatly enjoyed spending individual vacation time during the summers as a child. Her descriptions of time spent with this grandmother indicate increased levels of freedom and spontaneity. One of the author's mother's favorite examples of this was that "she allowed me to have coffee."

The author's application of Bowen theory in his clinical work spanned some 30 years until his retirement at the end of 2002. The 10 years following retirement have involved the author's application of Bowen theory to societal issues, primarily his study of two African nations. There has been long-term compatibility between this theory and the author's intellectual interests and emotional orientations. It is probable that this relatively stable marriage (between author and Bowen theory) has contributed to the author's functional level of differentiation. More specifically, this theory has been an important catalyst in aiding the author to consolidate his strengths and to manage his vulnerabilities and limitations more efficiently.

Post-retirement

It has been 10 years since the author retired from employment as a clinical psychologist. His interest in applying Bowen theory to societal issues was triggered two years before retirement. This occurred when he became acquainted with students from Rwanda who were studying at a local college in his community. Some of these students had lost parents and siblings in the 1994 Rwandan genocide. Thus began his interest in this genocide and in learning more about Rwanda in general.

Retirement provided time and new opportunities to focus considerable attention in this direction. After spending several years concentrating on Rwanda, he expanded his study to learning more about South Africa. In particular, the primary focus in this area was on the accomplishments of Nelson Mandela as well as issues related to leadership succession following the one-term Mandela presidency. This study of Rwanda and South Africa evolved into eight presentations to professional audiences who also have been specializing in Bowen theory and therapy.

During a brief discussion in 2009, the author was reminded by his frater-nal twin brother that their deceased mother would look on this work quite favorably. This reminder suddenly broadened the context regarding the ini-tial stimuli and triggers for this area of interest. Their Philadelphia-trained maternal grandmother, a registered nurse, had imprinted her global focus onto her daughter (their mother), who in turn had passed this to the genera-tion following her. Once again the horizontal axis (Rwandan students) was accompanied by a strong vertical trigger (grandmother to mother to author), which most likely accounts for the author's continued attention to and inter-est in this area of study.

There has been similarity and some variation in the goals of the international focus across the three generations. The author, his mother, and grandmother have shared an interest in attempting to identify the ingredients necessary to improve the welfare and quality of the lives of people living in underdeveloped nations. While his mother and grandmother utilized a religiously driven social justice model to advocate for people in need, the author has attempted to apply Bowen theory as an additional lens in studying similar phenomena.

Societal Process and Emotional Neutrality

In utilizing a Bowen systems approach to psychotherapeutic work with individuals, couples, and families, one is expected to maximize his/her level of emotional neutrality. Mastering Bowen theory, clinical supervision, and supervised efforts with family of origin are considered to be prerequisites for increasing one's neutrality in this work. Observing societal processes appears to be both similar and different from working with clinical families from a Bowen perspective. Learning how to manage self and reduce subjective reactions in the latter should be at least somewhat helpful in the former. The discipline involved should have some generalizing effect in the broader arena of society.

The author has discovered in his work on societal processes, as well as in discussions with peers, that societal triangles provide strenuous workouts when attempting to manage one's subjective reactions. The subtle intricacies of pseudo-self combined with the complex thickets of societal–political realities provide a relentless level of opposition to this endeavor. The idealization of a Nelson Mandela and the reflexive dismissal of a Thabo Mbeki (Mandela's suc-cessor), Robert Mugabe (long-term president of Zimbabwe), or Omar al Bashir (president of the current North Sudan) appear to be part of the natural process of emotional reactivity, particularly when the work continues for a protracted period of time. Expectations that ineffective or destructive self-serving policies on the part of these public officials will run their course in a limited time period promote the subjective reactions of disappointment and emotional fatigue. This is especially salient while observing, writing, and teaching about continued violence and state-sponsored criminality in these countries. The ability to utilize even a comprehensive theory that addresses the fundamental nature of the emotions driving such behavior is vigorously tested during this form of study.

Societal processes and triangles also provide a difficult challenge for this author due to his lack of educational and informational background in such fields as political science and world history. Although Bowen theory is broad enough to incorporate a concept such as emotional process in society, the author's ability to adequately apply it to his interest in specific African nations is somewhat limited.

The author's reactivity to educating himself about blatant governmental corruption and to numerous leaders' refusal to relinquish their positions and allow for succession is partially due to inattention to the Bowen concept of emotional process. More specifically, the pattern of intense commitment to holding on to leadership positions in other countries is best understood as a form of survival instinct, regardless of whether this is actual or perceived in reality. The depth of the Bowen concept of emotional reactivity, which includes physiological processes, is quite adept at addressing such long-term historical realities as tribal and ethnic territoriality issues.

Another possible explanation for the author's difficulty in maintaining neutrality when confronted with intense societal emotional processes is the fluctuating nature of functional differentiation. The absence of a professional network focused on this area of interest combined with less discipline in post-retirement habits contribute to some erosion in daily emotional functioning in the arena of studying societal emotional processes.

Nevertheless, and in spite of these limitations, the pursuit of research in these areas of societal process continues. Bowen theory also continues to serve as a useful guide in this endeavor, as it had been for 30 years of clinical work. The attainment of emotional neutrality was somewhat more advanced during that period of clinical work. This was due to various relationship and situational factors, as well as a reasonably sufficient level of basic functioning.

REFERENCES

Bowen, M. (1978). *Family therapy in clinical practice.* New York: Jason Aronson.

Maloni, J. (1980). Adopted by the spouses' family: The burial of biological family. Paper presented at the *Pittsburgh Family Systems Symposium.* Western Psychiatric Institute and Clinic. Pittsburgh, PA.

Maloni, J. (1987). At least three generations of male distancing. In P. Titelman (Ed.), *The therapist's own family: Toward the differentiation of self.* New York: Jason Aronson.

Maloni, J. (1993). Learning as a byproduct of failure in a long-term effort. Paper presented at the *Pittsburgh Family Systems Symposium.* Western Psychiatric Institute and Clinic. Pittsburgh, PA.

McGoldrick, M., Gerson, R. & Petry, S. (2008). *Genograms: Assessment and intervention.* New York: W. W. Norton.

III

DIFFERENTIATION OF SELF IN CLINICAL PRACTICE

10

A LONG-TERM COACHING PROCESS

Differentiation for Client and Coach

Katharine Gratwick Baker

This chapter describes a long-term coaching relationship between a client and a coach, the author of the chapter, as each of us worked toward higher levels of differentiation of self over a 29-year period, 1984 to 2014. For the purposes of the chapter, a "coach" is defined as someone who offers one-on-one consultation to a client while he or she works to enhance his or her functioning in close relationships, at work, and in the wider community. The goal of therapeutic work with a Bowen trained coach, in the most general sense, is that clients learn to reduce their anxiety and reactivity while raising their level of differentiation of self in their closest relationships. They are also coached to reduce triangling, overfunctioning and underfunctioning, and cutoff as responses to anxiety in their most significant relationships. A corollary to these goals is that the coach, without discussing the details of his or her own life, must manage his or her own anxiety, maintain neutrality, stay detriangled, and keep clear interpersonal boundaries in order to be effective in facilitating the client's ability to realize his or her goals. The reciprocity between coach and client over time requires that they both work on self in the context of an exploration of the client's emotional functioning. Unlike more traditional, individually focused therapies, the emphasis is not on the relationship between the client and the coach, nor on the client's potential emotional dependence on the coach, but rather on their ability to maintain separate, autonomous, though still connected selves during their work together. The real changes in the client's life happen outside the sessions, but the planning and strategizing about change and its effects happen in the sessions.

The Client

The client was born in 1946, and had her first appointment with me in the fall of 1984, when she was 38 years old. The coaching appointments initially took place in the outpatient psychiatry department of a large health maintenance organization (HMO) in Washington, DC, where I was employed and the client was a member. Later we met at my Washington office when

I opened a private practice. Since 1997, after I moved to western Massachusetts, sessions have taken place primarily on the telephone.

The client had two children who were ages 4 and 7 when the coaching started. She had separated from her husband in 1981 after 14 years of marriage. He had become romantically involved with a man, and they were divorced in 1982, although they maintained good contact with each other after an initial period of upset. They had joint custody of their children, who spent alternate weeks with each parent. In 1983 they had sought joint counseling with a child psychiatrist to help them develop a consistent approach to co-parenting in the context of one parent being homosexual. Her husband's male partner occasionally joined this counseling, as the children grew up.

The Coach

When the coaching began, I was 46 years old and had recently started working at the HMO after being employed for several years in the social work department of an inpatient psychiatric hospital. In my new job I had replaced a psychiatric nurse who had retired and passed on her substantial outpatient client load to me, including the client who is the subject of this chapter. I had received a master's degree in social work in 1975, and was working on a clinical doctorate at a local university. I had been married for 18 years and had three young adult stepsons, then ages 25, 26, and 27, whom I had raised from early childhood because their mother had died in 1963. I also had two biological sons who were 15 and 17 years old at the time the coaching began.

The Client's Family of Origin and Extended Family

The client had grown up in a small town outside Boston. Her father (see Figure 10.1 for all family members), age 65, was in good health and was the principal of a successful management consulting firm he had founded with an inheritance from his mother. The client's mother, 66, was also in good health. She had been a day care director before marrying the client's father, but did not work outside the home after 1943. She supported and participated in several charitable and civic organizations in the local community.

In the nuclear family in which she grew up, the client was the oldest of four siblings, who were all college graduates. Her brother was learning disabled, impulsive, and intensely attached to their mother. In the primary triangle the client's parents were somewhat distant from each other, and the client described herself as being closer to her father than to her mother, although he apparently called her "meatball" as a child, and there had been considerable parental focus on her weight as she grew up. Both parents grew up in Cleveland in upper-middle-class Protestant families. Her father was the second of three siblings and, like his father, was somewhat irresponsible

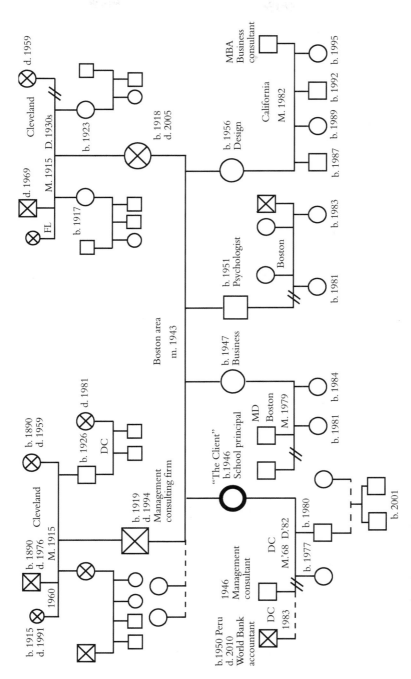

Figure 10.1 The Client's Family Diagram

about money management, even though he ran a financial consulting firm. The money in the family came from his mother.

The client's mother was also the middle of three siblings. Her father had been the mayor of Cleveland, and he had divorced his wife and moved to Florida with a second wife when the client's mother was a teenager. The client's first younger sister (one year younger than she), a publisher, had divorced her first husband, and then remarried a doctor in 1979. They had two children in this second marriage. They lived in the Boston area near the client's parents and were comfortably affluent. The client's brother (5 years younger), a psychologist, divorced his first wife (with whom he had a daughter), remarried his second wife, a speech therapist, and also lived near the client's parents outside Boston. Like their father, he had difficulty managing money and frequently accrued large debts. The client's youngest sister (10 years younger), had worked as a recruiter and fundraiser for the American College in Switzerland before marrying a businessman in 1982. Like her mother she had four children and did not work outside the home after her marriage. She and her husband lived an affluent life in California.

The client met her future husband when they were both 12 years old, as he was a friend of her first cousins on her father's side of the family. They remet in December 1967, while she was in her junior year of college, and he was a senior. They fell in love, became engaged in April 1968, married in September, and went to Fiji with the Peace Corps in October 1968. When they returned to the United States from Fiji in 1971, they moved to Cleveland, where the client finished her undergraduate studies and her husband taught in an elementary school. In 1972 they moved to Washington, DC, where the client worked in the public school system and began a master's degree in education, while her husband studied international business. He subsequently began to work for her father's firm in mergers and acquisitions. They divorced in 1982 after 14 years of marriage.

Preliminary Assessment of the Client's Functioning

At the time the coaching began, the client was extremely anxious about being single. She had begun dating a series of men, and had contracted herpes from one of them. She had sought psychotherapy in order to have an opportunity to talk through her life situation and make plans to stabilize her life as a single woman. She was *professionally high functioning* and was in training for a leadership position in the local school system, where she earned a good income. Her father helped her out financially from time to time, especially with the purchase of her home in Washington, but otherwise she was *financially independent*. *Cutoff* was not a response she used when anxious. On the contrary, she tended to move toward *adaptation and fusion* when under stress. She was in regular contact with all her family members, including parents, uncles, aunts, siblings and their spouses, her cousins on both sides of the family, and her in-laws. She frequently talked with them on the telephone, wrote letters to them, and got together with them for vacations and holidays. *Members of the extended family* were a consistent and generally positive emotional resource for the client throughout the coaching.

She also maintained regular *contact with her ex-husband*, and supported a shared-custody model of parenting with him because, as she said, "he is their father and I'm not going to cut [the children] off from him," although in the early 1980s in Washington, DC, it might have been easy to cut off children from a gay father. Together they took responsibility for raising their children, enrolling them in a bilingual international school and reaching agreements with each other on family behavioral rules as the children grew up. Both children did well academically, had lots of friends, and adjusted smoothly to the weekly transfer from one parental household to the other.

Except for a series of herpes outbreaks that may have been *stress* related, the client was in good health. She swam laps in a pool at a local gym every day and was slim at the time the coaching began, although she began to put on weight soon thereafter. Weight had been a chronic problem for her stemming from childhood, and she also described it as "a buffer protecting me from intimacy."

Over the years the client repeatedly identified three factors or "pebbles in her shoe" that both generated and intensified *anxiety* when she was unhappy about other parts of her life. These "pebbles" were her weight, her limited financial resources (in comparison with her siblings), and her lack of an intimate partner with whom she could share her daily life (as her siblings did).

Preliminary *evaluation* defined the client as a high-functioning individual who was well connected to her family of origin, although she was going through a destabilizing period in her life at the time the coaching started. *Prognosis* for restabilization and continued high functioning was good.

The Coach's Family of Origin and Extended Family

I grew up outside New York City, in southern Connecticut, and was the second of five siblings (see Figure 10.2 for references to my family). My father, trained as a medical doctor, had worked as an educator and principal of several private secondary schools in the New York area before retiring in 1967. He had died of congestive heart failure in 1982. My mother was a retired elementary school teacher, as well as an occasional actress in community theater, but was a somewhat arthritic 78-year-old at the time the coaching started.

Like the client, I did not incline toward cutoff in response to anxiety, and was well connected to my parents, siblings and their spouses, nieces, nephews, uncles, aunts, cousins, and in-laws. My siblings were all college graduates, active professionals, and married with children. They spent vacations and holidays together, and communicated regularly through letters, telephone,

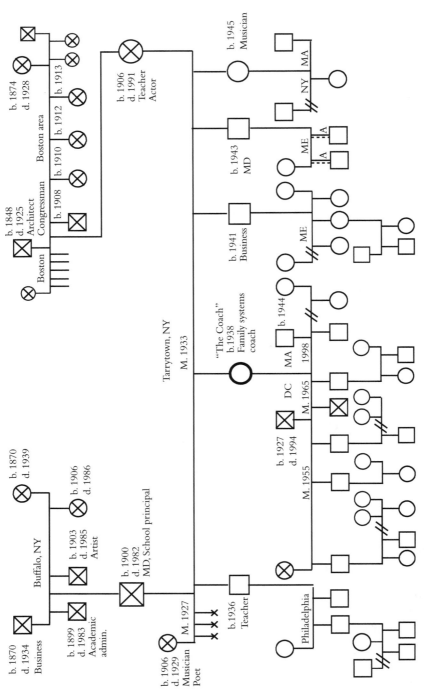

Figure 10.2 The Coach's Family Diagram

and e-mail (in the later years of the coaching). Like the client, my inclination when anxious was to adapt to significant others and move toward emotional fusion with them.

I was happily married to my husband who had been a widower with three small sons when I met him in 1963. He was in the U.S. diplomatic service, and had had a number of international assignments during our marriage. We had a wide circle of friends and colleagues, and our co-parenting of five sons was relatively smooth, although I did more hands-on parenting than my husband because of his long work hours at the State Department, and a traditional division of responsibilities in our marriage.

The Coach's Functioning

At the time the coaching began, my three young adult stepsons had all graduated from college and were living independently. I had two teenage boys at home and my husband held a demanding position at the State Department. I had received a master's degree in social work in 1975, and in 1984 had nearly completed a part-time doctoral program. I received a PhD in social work in 1985, and soon thereafter began to immerse myself in Bowen family systems theory, which I studied intensively for four years, from 1985 to 1989. Like the client, I was in good health and exercised daily. I managed stress and anxiety through an overfocus on my children and some adaptiveness in my relationship with my husband. Creative writing, music, exercise, and a high level of involvement in the local community were important, positive aspects of my life.

A Brief Review of the Client's Life Course From 1984 to the Present

The client's life course will be examined in a number of areas: 1) her relationships with extended family members, including her parents and siblings; 2) her relationships with her maturing children; 3) adult relationship themes, including her ongoing relationship with her ex-husband and his gay partner; 4) her health; and 5) her work and financial issues.

Relationships With Extended Family

A major issue for the client was the illness and death in 1994 of her father, who had been a powerful force in her life. As much as three years before his death, when he was first diagnosed with a blood disorder that developed into leukemia and congestive heart failure, she spoke often of her fear of losing him. Although he continued to work in his financial consulting business, he became depressed and physically weak, and her mother was very protective of him. His death at age 75 followed a major heart attack and kidney failure. After his death it became clear to the family that he had not managed his business effectively. Although generous-hearted, he had lived beyond his means, and he had left his wife with significant debts. The family resolved the problem of his debts through the sale of their vacation property on Nantucket to a large conservation foundation. This sale provided for the family's continued access to the property for the next 30 years, while paying off their father's debts and establishing an escrow account that generated enough cash to support their mother for the rest of her life. The client, her mother, and her siblings were responsible for keeping the property in good condition until it was to be finally passed on to the conservation organization in 2024.

The client was deeply saddened by the death of her father, whom she described as a "safety zone," unlike her more distant mother. In the primary triangle, she had experienced herself as being on the inside with her father, and with her mother on the outside. The desire to be on the "inside" of emotional triangles was a continuing theme in her relationships with her siblings and children throughout her life, and the coaching often focused on her learning how to be a comfortable observer on the outside of emotional triangles.

The Nantucket property became a touchstone for emotional issues with her mother and siblings in the difficult years after her father's death and throughout the ensuing years of coaching. This was a closely connected family, and their shared vacation home was a focal point for emotional fusion amongst them. As the oldest sibling, the client focused on "keeping the channels open," although she and her brother and sisters each had different needs and interests in the property. Her mother functioned as a kind of "buffer" between the siblings until her death in 2005. After that the client took the lead in arranging annual family meetings regarding management of the property, keeping track of family expenses, and setting up family vacation usage schedules, but shared management became increasingly contentious.

Money issues have always been significant for the client, as she has had fewer financial resources than her more affluent siblings, and she was frequently reactive when it seemed to her that decisions about the shared vacation home were based more on emotion than thinking, particularly for her brother.

Over the years the client and her sisters lost interest in spending time in the family house (an old cottage without electricity) on the island, and they resented having to contribute financially to maintaining it so that their brother could enjoy it with his family and friends. His closeness to their mother and his "specialness" as the only boy in the family made it particularly difficult for the client and her youngest sister to "take him on," and the third sister fully supported him until her own financial situation changed in 2011. As siblings they were generally "conflict averse" and the three sisters feared cutoff from their brother, who argued that the Nantucket property was an important legacy from their father. The sisters believed that their warm relationships with each other were their father's most significant legacy, rather than the Nantucket cottage, but they had difficulty presenting this perspective convincingly to their brother until after their mother's death. During coaching sessions I strategized with the client about how she could take leadership in toning down the multiple interlocking triangles that were central to their sibling conversations during this period, and the client tried hard to be calm and consistent as she and her siblings worked to resolve their differences while staying connected to each other.

During the 11 years between her father's and mother's deaths, through frequent visits and telephone conversations, the client focused on changing the imbalance in her original primary triangle. She wanted to develop a stronger connection with her mother, although she often felt that there was "an impenetrable glass wall" between them. In 2001 her mother sold the family house outside Boston and moved to a retirement community. In the fall of 2003 she developed a brain tumor, but initially responded well to chemotherapy. The client talked with her daily and spent a week with her on Nantucket during the summer of 2004. She said her mother was a "role model for graceful aging," but also described their continuing "dance of closeness and distance." When she asked her mother during that last summer visit if she had any regrets about their relationship over the years, her mother reflected for a moment and then said she was sad that the client "had always been overweight." The client managed not to react negatively to this comment, and later told me that, "this is how we are."

Her mother died at the end of March 2005, and the client described a "tsunami" of reactivity in the family following her death, with her brother developing serious financial problems and gaining an enormous amount of weight, his stepdaughter breaking her engagement, the client's first younger sister becoming emotionally very upset, and her youngest sister and husband living apart from each other for a while. For the client the loss of her mother was not nearly as emotionally disruptive as the loss of her father had been, and she felt better prepared for it, perhaps because of her mother's protracted final illness. I suggested that the client read Bowen's chapter "Family Reaction to Death" (Bowen, 1978), and this gave her ideas about how to talk openly with her siblings about their mother's death after it occurred, and how to take note of what Bowen described as the "emotional shock wave" that often follows the death of a family leader. The client realized that there was a four- to six-month "window of opportunity" for more family openness after her mother's death, and she took full advantage of this.

Relationships With Her Maturing Children

The client had a long-term, stable, shared custody arrangement with her ex-husband, from the time of their marital separation in 1981 until the children left for college. The two children lived in both homes on alternate weeks, and this arrangement worked well. A considerable part of the coaching over the years focused on the children's behavior and development, their reactions to a new partner with whom the client became involved, their own friendships, and occasional minor adolescent mishaps. Both children did well academically and socially at a bilingual international school in Washington, and then both went to Vassar College. At college her daughter (b. 1977) was diagnosed with chronic narcolepsy at the age of 20. This illness shaped her post-college career path, as she chose to pursue a doctorate in rhetoric with the hope that she could become a writer and college professor, both professions in which she could have some control over her unpredictable sleep patterns.

This young woman had a number of long-term, significant, heterosexual relationships while she was growing up, and then in her early thirties became romantically involved with a woman. The client was upset by her daughter's health and sexual identity issues but, with my encouragement, she worked to become more neutral and nonreactive to them. The sexual identity issue was particularly difficult since it stirred up the client's memories of the period when her husband had left her for a same-sex relationship. The client increasingly realized as her daughter became an adult that she could not take care of her anymore or "fix" the issues that concerned her, although she sometimes thought of her daughter as a disabled child because of the narcolepsy diagnosis.

In the primary triangle for this adult daughter, the client is on the outside, and the girl and the client's ex-husband are on the inside, which is uncomfortable for the client. Coaching in recent years has focused on the shifts in triangles that inevitably evolve in parenting adult offspring. The "impenetrable glass wall" that the client had often felt existed between herself and her mother seems to have reemerged in the relationship with her adult daughter, and the client works to understand the part she has played in creating the wall. As she currently describes it, she was always highly reactive to her mother's focus on the fact that she was an overweight child, and she distanced emotionally from her mother because of the anxiety and vulnerability this triggered in their relationship. The glass wall was something the two of them both created and participated in so that she could protect herself from her mother's negativity. She was never able to completely eliminate it as an adult, although she initiated weekly telephone conversations with her mother after her father died.

The glass wall with her daughter began to develop when it became clear that her daughter preferred her ex-husband's family of origin to her own. Apparently that family offered an emotional environment in which her daughter felt safe and comfortable, and the client was reactive to this, describing herself as feeling hurt. She would then become overbearing and would ask her daughter too many intrusive personal questions, which inevitably led to more distance between them. In coaching sessions, she practiced new ways to relate to her daughter by expressing thoughts and feelings about her own life rather than being covertly judgmental about her daughter's life.

Her daughter eventually began a tenure-track job in the University of California system, and the client helped her move across the country and get settled in a new community without being intrusive about her daughter's decisions.

The client's son (b. 1980) also went to Vassar College. In the fall of his junior year his girlfriend became pregnant with twins and, in spite of the fact that he ended his intimate relationship with her while urging her not to keep the babies, she decided to continue the pregnancy. She came from a funda-mentalist Christian family in Nashville, and her family strongly encouraged her to maintain the pregnancy. Two identical twin boys were born in June of 2001, and the client's son decided to assertively claim his fatherhood. He was present at the birth and held the boys when they were 10 minutes old.

The client's son finished college, graduating *phi beta kappa*, and started a successful career in film production based in New York. At the same time he managed to send child support payments to the mother of the twins, and traveled regularly to Nashville to visit them, in spite of their mother's initial resistance to his involvement. In the more than 10 years since their birth he has been an active presence in their lives and has included them regularly on family vacations. Both he and the boys' mother have had a number of serious romantic relationships with other people, and they have often had conflicts with each other with regard to care of the boys, but they continue to work fairly effectively as co-parents (as did the client and her ex-husband), and the twins appear to be thriving.

The client was actively supportive of her son's responsible involvement with the twins after they were born. Both she and her ex-husband traveled to Nashville with him several times so that the mother's family could see that he came from a viable, loving family. In recent years the client per-ceives her son as somewhat emotionally distant from her, preferring a closer relationship with his father. Again in this triangle, as with her daughter and her ex-husband, she is in what she experiences as an uncomfortable outside position. I have encouraged her efforts to respect her adult children's desire for more emotional separateness, but to work on detriangling by maintain-ing a solid, shared-parental connection with her ex-husband. This work is ongoing.

Because she had been very close to the children when they were little, being in the outside position in the triangles with their father challenges her to think about her part in these patterns. A long-term goal is to stay as con-nected to them as they permit her to be, but also to become more neutral and less reactive to them individually.

Adult Relationship Themes

The client had a number of relatively short-term relationships during the first seven years of the coaching, but frequently expressed feelings of loneliness.

Toward the end of 1991, she became involved with a widowed colleague who had a teenage daughter and worked in a different part of the school system. The relationship developed rapidly, and she soon introduced him to her family of origin and her children. She liked his "confidence, clarity, and exclusivity." At the beginning of the relationship she described him as "brilliant, with great insights," and she felt "safe with him because he listens."

Within several months, however, she began to become irritated by him, his "clutchiness," need for reassurance, and his desire to marry her because "we're good for each other." When he was anxious, he would move toward her and become what she experienced as demanding. She described fearing a "loss of self" with him. A year and a half after they met, after many ups and downs, the client continued to pull away and to say that she "couldn't get into a life rhythm" with him. At that point he put an ad in a local magazine and began to "explore other options." In January 1994 he sold his house, took a new job in California, and eventually remarried someone else.

The client felt a mixture of relief and sadness at the ending of this relationship, but did not resume regular dating, although she said she again felt "lonely." She said there were "no models for being single" in her family, and was distressed at her lack of intimate companionship. The issue of togetherness versus individuality in her relationships was not resolved, and she continued to experience this as a major lifelong concern.

In parallel to the client's efforts to form an intimate adult relationship, she continued to be closely connected to her ex-husband and his partner. Their co-parenting was a central focus for all three of them throughout the children's years in school and college, as well as during their young adult years. The client's ex-husband had worked as a financial consultant in her father's firm during the early years of the marriage, and until 1990. Throughout this period the client described feeling that he was "a black cloud" hanging over many aspects of her life. She felt that he "intruded" on her, and "created a layer" between herself and any intimacy she might want to develop with someone else. She wondered if she could "define a self" in relation to him and she felt that his turning out to be gay was "the ultimate deception." She was frequently extremely angry with him, and he with her, but they continued to co-parent together and to occasionally travel together as a family. His partner was a calm, peace-making presence in what she came to describe as their five-member nuclear family.

When her ex-husband's partner died of cancer just before Christmas in 2009, the client picked up the ashes with her ex-husband, helped him organize a memorial service, and two months later traveled with him and the children to visit the partner's family in Peru. When her ex-husband had a serious biking accident in Paris in May 2010 and was medically evacuated back to Washington, the client visited him daily in the hospital and at a rehab center for more than three months, taking him his mail and newspapers, and acting as a "central switchboard" for him, his family, and friends as he recovered. Although she sometimes felt exhausted, depressed, manic, and even taken for granted, she was definitely "present and accounted for" in this important relationship throughout the crisis. He in turn became a confidant and advisor to her over time as she negotiated the Nantucket property issues with her siblings. She believes that in family issues he has become and will continue to be her most significant life partner.

Health Issues

The second "pebble" in the client's shoe was her health, with a specific focus on her weight. Throughout the coaching, she continued to bring up concerns about her weight that stretched back into her childhood, when her tendency to gain weight had disturbed her parents. She frequently noted that her brother was also overweight as an adult, but because he had been a skinny little boy and an athletic adolescent, he had never thought of weight as a problem, even as a heavy adult. Throughout the coaching, the client would occasionally lose several pounds, attempt to "take control" of her eating, and exercise sporadically but not consistently. She was glad that her husband and her later partner accepted her body as it was. The new partner was obese himself, so he did not criticize her. But she did fear rejection from other men and articulated the idea that, for her, obesity was a protection against intimacy. She recalled that a neighborhood teenager had paid her and her younger sister to do "sexual things" with him when she was about 10 years old, and she thought this might have been a factor in her ambivalence about sexuality as an adult.

Other health concerns were a hysterectomy in 1992, herpes lesions that continued to appear occasionally until 1995, medication for high blood pressure in 1999, medication for prediabetes that she took for only three months in 2002 because of an adverse reaction, and medication for cholesterol in 2003. In 2009 she was diagnosed with severe sleep apnea and started to use a continuous positive airway pressure (CPAP) machine, which helped her sleep more soundly.

In 2011, at the age of 65 and on the advice of her primary care doctor, the client began to consider some lifestyle changes that would improve her overall health profile. She started exercising more regularly, took yoga training, ate more thoughtfully, weighed herself daily for the first time, and began to lose some weight, not through dieting (which she resisted), but because of her new lifestyle choices. She had never wanted her weight to be a central component of the coaching, but she reported her concerns regularly over the years, and began to make calmer, less reactive moves in the direction of improved self-care as she got older. The coaching strategy on this theme was to follow the client's preferences in terms of agenda and focus. When the client was ready to discuss lifestyle changes, I expressed interest in her thinking and encouraged her to make responsible decisions that would improve her health.

Work and Money

When the coaching began, the client was in a training program to become a public elementary school principal. In 1987 she achieved this goal and became the principal of an elementary school with a high percentage of children from immigrant and low-income single-parent families. She has remained the principal of that school for more than 25 years, through staff changes, budget cuts, layoffs, lawsuits, external reviews, and national educational policy changes. She weathered changes in superintendents, PTA complaints, severe overcrowding in her building, and reviews of "poor morale" from her staff. She received challenge grants, went to leadership conferences, initiated a mentoring program, had a mini-sabbatical to England for five weeks in 2006, and in 2007 participated as an expert on a national panel that examined children at risk for behavior problems. She has been a consistently serious, responsible leader in a very stressful work environment.

Starting in 2009 she began to talk with her union about retirement and took two seminars that focused on retirement. She wanted retirement to be an intentional rather than a reactive choice, and she approached the decision and its timing thoughtfully, knowing that she would wait to occupy herself with interesting activities when she was no longer running an elementary school. She had always loved her professional work and had considerable anxiety about leaving it, not knowing what she would do next. When she did leave the principal position at the end of June 2013, she decided not to call herself "retired," but to describe herself as being in an "encore" phase of life, as she sought new and challenging professional projects.

The third "pebble" in the client's shoe throughout the coaching process has been her anxiety about money. She traced it back to a period in childhood when she was nine years old and her father was unemployed for 14 months. She picked up on and apparently internalized her parents' financial anxiety at the time, and this became a theme for her in adult life. She frequently said she "felt out of control financially" and compared herself unfavorably with her more affluent siblings. She described her father and her ex-husband as generously "extravagant big spenders" and her mother as "frugal and miserly."

The client made a reasonable salary as a public school principal, her parents paid for her children's summer camps, her father helped her buy her house (although she refinanced the house and took over the title before he died), her ex-husband paid for the children's college tuition, and she inherited a significant sum from her mother, but she never felt she had "enough" to be able to relax about money. She frequently mentioned that she needed to work with a financial planner, but never identified one with whom she could be comfortable, and she framed much of her anxiety about retirement in terms of the insufficient money she would have to live on. In recent years she began to consult with her ex-husband with regard to financial decisions, and his expertise was reassuring to her. Her coaching goal in this arena was to recognize the sources of her anxiety in long-time family patterns and to develop a calmer perspective about her ability to live comfortably within her means, regardless of how that might compare with her siblings' resources.

A Brief Review of the Coach's Life Course
From 1984 to the Present

My life course will be examined in a number of areas that overlap with the client's concerns, though in less detail. Attention will be paid to similarities in our life experiences where I had to manage my reactivity, keeping clear the issues that were my own and those that belonged to the client. These included 1) our relationships with extended family members, including parents, siblings, and a shared vacation home; 2) our relationships with our maturing children; and 3) adult relationship themes following the ending of our marriages through divorce (the client) or death (my first husband died in 1994). As noted above, both the client and I have a tendency to respond to anxiety with overadaptiveness, triangling, and fusion rather than with cut-off. I have therefore had to curb my own responses to the client's tendency toward fusion, and challenge myself as well as the client to take separate, self-defining positions when appropriate. I also had to guard against a tendency to give advice to the client when it seemed that we had been through similar experiences, but to provide time and space in which the client could find her own solutions to her life issues.

Relationships With Extended Family

My father had died in 1982, and my mother died eight years later in 1990. My experience with the sequential deaths of both parents made it possible for me to connect with the client as she went through similar parental losses. I had also spent considerable time before my mother's death working to improve that relationship, and, like the client, I was somewhat prepared for the loss when my mother died after a brief illness.

My parents had a family vacation home on an island in Maine that they had passed on to my four siblings and me in the 1970s, so the five of us had experience in managing the property while our parents were still alive. We set up a trust for the property, and then converted it to a limited partnership, attempting to keep a boundary between our relationships with each other and our shared business management of the property. We were fortunate that, unlike the client and her siblings, we did not to have to face the necessity of sale of the property in order to cover debts and provide for our mother's support after our father died.

In spite of these more favorable circumstances, I developed a conflict with a younger brother around planned construction of an additional small house contiguous to the family land shortly after our mother died. This fact helped me understand the source of the client's triangles with her younger brother and their mother when he wanted to continue to have access to the Nantucket property after their mother's death. Like the client, I preferred to be on the inside of family triangles, and the conflict with my brother provided a learning experience in being in the outside position. My three other siblings worked hard not to take sides in this conflict, and over a period of years my younger brother and I exchanged letters and had long conversations in which we expressed our differing views. Eventually we decided that staying connected in the context of disagreement was more important than "winning or losing" a specific battle about the vacation property.

This conflict with my brother may have been part of an "emotional shock wave" following our mother's death, but hers was not an unexpected death at the age of 84, and all the siblings functioned reasonably calmly as a sibling team after it.

Relationships With Her Maturing Children

My biological children and stepchildren were significantly older than those of the client, and I had been through their numerous adolescent ups and downs, their departures for college, their young adult marriages, two divorces and two remarriages, as well as the birth of grandchildren by the time these parenting issues arose for the client. Like the client, I co-parented relatively smoothly with the children's father while the children were growing up. However, in young adulthood one of our sons developed a mental illness that ended in his death, and in later years, following my first husband's death, several of my sons developed life-threatening medical illnesses that caused me and my extended family enormous anxiety and pain. I had to work to manage my anxiety, to avoid triangling with other family members, to accept being on the "outside," to recognize that my children were adults who had to make their own decisions, particularly around medical treatment issues, and to acknowledge to myself that familiarity with Bowen theory does not protect one from family disasters and tragedies. I sought my own coaching from another Bowen-trained therapist in order to keep myself on track for a number of years. What I learned about self-management in relation to adult offspring helped me provide perspective when the client's daughter was diagnosed with narcolepsy and later formed a lesbian relationship, and when the client's son's college girlfriend became pregnant.

Adult Relationship Themes

A continuing theme for the client was her loneliness and lack of a life partner after her divorce. I faced a similar situation when my husband of 29 years died of cancer in August 1994. Because of my own experience, I was able to talk with the client about the difference between being "lonely" and being "alone," focusing on how one takes care of self, manages close friend and family relationships, and maintains positive energy, without the mutual interdependency and intimacy that can come from having a life partner.

After deeply grieving my husband's death and participating in coaching with a Bowen-trained therapist for almost a year, I began to socialize again, met a new partner, moved to Massachusetts, and remarried in the summer of 1998. Unlike the client, I was not encumbered with anxiety about a marriage that had failed, and I had a positive view of the future in a new relationship. The balance of togetherness and individuality that had been particularly hard for the client in her marriage and in her later relationship with a boyfriend worked more smoothly for me. Ultimately the coaching focused on the viability of life spent without an intimate partner, of learning to be alone without being lonely, and of recognizing that the anxiety driving the search for a new partner can generate lapses in judgment and mistakes that are often hard to undo.

Summarizing the Coaching Process

When the client first began to meet with me, our sessions took place weekly. After several months, when the client's anxiety was less intense, our sessions became less frequent, and we met once every two weeks for several years. Eventually our sessions fell into a monthly rhythm that continued to the present. During times of crisis, we met slightly more frequently, but in general the monthly meeting schedule was useful for the client as she worked to manage her anxiety and raise her functional level of differentiation.

In 2013 the same themes continue to be present for the client (weight, money, loneliness), but they generate less anxiety for her except when other issues (such as management of the Nantucket property or relationships with her adult children) become active, and then she brings up these three "pebbles in her shoe." In general, though, she is less reactive to them and more accepting of them as factual aspects of her life that she can manage reasonably well. Her weight is lower since she has begun to exercise more regularly, and she is less anxious about money since she consulted with a financial planner in connection with her impending retirement. She is less relationship dependent and more accepting of her life situation, although she says she still yearns for a life partner to share her life with through "pillow talk." In general one could say that her functional level of differentiation has increased over time as her anxiety has decreased, and her management of the ups and downs of life is smoother. The peaks and valleys are not so high or so low.

Overlapping themes for client and coach include the deaths of both parents, the ending of marriages and formation of new relationships, parenting young adults, managing self through the challenges of our children's illnesses, connecting to grandchildren, sibling relationships, and shared family vacation property, as well as the age-appropriate issues of aging and contemplation of impending retirement. A major challenge for me in addressing these overlapping themes has been to maintain neutrality and decrease reactivity as the client and I have made similar or different life choices. I have had to work hard to raise my own functional level of differentiation, although, for both of us our basic levels can only be defined at the end of our lives and through observation of the functioning of our children and grandchildren.

Over- and underfunctioning have not been major concerns in the coaching work because neither the client nor I seem to have managed anxiety with those patterns of reciprocal behavior. The essence of monthly coaching sessions has been to provide the client with an hour in which she can think and talk about the major themes in her life while strategizing about the work she will do with regard to herself in her closest relationships. The sessions provide her with the opportunity for an open expression of thoughts and feelings in a neutral, long-term one-on-one relationship, and a chance to plan her life's direction. She has worked to develop strategies for detriangling with her siblings, ex-husband, and children, and she has focused on managing her reactivity in significant family and professional relationships. She has sporadically kept a journal to track her management of major issues, and she has read a number of books and articles on Bowen theory. She also writes summary annual Christmas letters that address the themes in her life. I have kept detailed notes from our sessions together for almost 30 years.

Current Functioning of Client and Coach

The client retired from her job as the principal of a challenging public elementary school in June 2013, and is now focusing on where she will put her creative energy in her next phase of life. She thinks about her health and aging, but she is strong and clear thinking, and wants to continue to be productive. At the age of 68, she is not in an intimate partnership, although in recent years she acknowledges that she is deeply emotionally connected to her ex-husband particularly around parenting and sibling issues. She was also significantly and constantly available as an emotional support to him during the final illness and death of his male partner, and during his own long, slow recovery from a serious biking accident. Her relationships with her siblings continue to be generally stable, in spite of their differences with regard to the disposition of the family's property on Nantucket. The siblings continue to discuss their parents' legacy, three out of four of them believing that this legacy is embodied in the values inherent in their relationships with each other and their children, rather than in the property. The client has been more assertive with her younger brother since her mother's death and more able to challenge his demands that the disposition of the Nantucket property go his way, regardless of the financial and emotional impact on his sisters. I have encouraged the client to clearly define an I-position on this issue, articulating her own needs to her brother, as well as the long-term, multigenerational needs of the family.

I continue to work in my private practice and to be politically involved in my local community in Massachusetts. At the age of 75, I am in good health, exercise daily, and have been in a satisfying marriage with my second husband for 15 years. I am also positively connected to my siblings, adult children, and grandchildren, all of whom are fortunate to be able to spend time together at our family vacation home in Maine. My younger brother and I have put aside our conflicts with regard to the family vacation property, though who knows what struggles may erupt when we decide to pass the property on to the next generation. I work to manage my anxiety with regard to my adult children's health, maintain my neutrality, stay detriangled, and keep clear interpersonal boundaries in the important aspects of my life.

Future Directions for Coaching

Monthly coaching sessions primarily on the telephone will continue for as long as the client finds them useful. Both the client and I continue to work on self, including physical self-care, managing our anxiety and reactivity in significant relationships, participating responsibly in larger societal arenas, and searching for meaning in life as we age.

REFERENCE

Bowen, M. (1978). Family reaction to death. In *Family therapy in clinical practice* (pp. 321–337). New York: Jason Aronson.

11

DIFFERENTIATION OF SELF AND NEUROFEEDBACK

Integrating Top Down/Bottom Up

Priscilla J. Friesen

> Man can "know" something intellectually a long time before he "knows" it as part of his being.[1]

This case study demonstrates how neurofeedback[2] can be used to assist people in their efforts to decrease chronic anxiety and to better operationalize differentiation of self. Unlike more traditional consultation using Bowen theory, the consultation process described below involved the use of neurofeedback, which can potentially enhance a person's ability to resolve chronic anxiety. In essence, neurofeedback reflects patterns in the individual brain that have developed in the family of origin in preceding generations. This multigenerational process simply lives in one's being, becoming a part of "self"—from synapses to sentences. Given the way this process shapes every aspect of a person's development and organization, it comes as no surprise that the effort to manage one's reactivity is indeed challenging.

Bowen developed a way to apply his theory that involved a focus on developing self-awareness and observation of the emotional system, so that a person could change his or her automatic relationship patterns and manage reactivity. This occurs on a psychological level and involves a process of becoming "aware" of how reactivity impacts one's functioning. It is a "top down" process where the prefrontal cortex (top) is recruited to better manage relationship patterns, to develop a systems perspective about relationships, and to develop principles to guide behavior. Although this intentional effort to manage self is an essential component of differentiation of self, it addresses only one level of reactivity—from the top down.

Neurofeedback provides an additional way for an individual to become "aware" of how reactivity impacts his or her overall functioning. This technology gives feedback to the brain about a level of physiological reactivity that is not accessible through self-observation and cognition alone. It is a "bottom up" process insofar as it interrupts the reactivity of brain patterns at deeper levels of brain organization that exist outside of conscious awareness. These brain patterns developed within the same multigenerational context as the prefrontal cortex, making them intricately linked together, each influencing the other. Because neurofeedback has the potential to interrupt this more basic reactivity, from the bottom up, it offers a way to maximize a person's effort to become more resilient in the face of life's challenges.

In this chapter, *reactivity* refers to the markers of life's responsiveness within a person and between people. This includes patterns of physiology, psychology, perception, and behavior. Bowen theory describes variation in reactivity as influenced by the emotional system relationship processes over the generations. In this sense, all reactivity is emotional. *Anxiety* is the uniquely individual perceptual experience of life's challenges embedded within a person's emotional position in the relationship process. *Chronic anxiety* is then the sustained patterned reactivity that is reflected in less flexible recovery in the physiology and more rigid threat-based perceptions that lead to more inflexible behavior in relationships.

Differentiation of Self: Top Down/Bottom Up

Differentiation of self is a central concept of Bowen family systems theory and the focus of the consultation process. The process of increasing differentiation of self involves a person's effort to change, or interrupt, the deeply embedded inflexible relationship patterns that are shaped by the multigenerational family process. These patterns are integrated on all levels of an individual's organization, from the information processing of the prefrontal cortex, to the deeper automatic processes of the brain's central nervous system. Over one's life course, day-to-day adaptations produce patterns that are automatically occurring in a person's physiology, psychology, and brain. This reactivity exists within a person on multiple levels and represents not only a lifetime of responsiveness to life's challenges, but also an accumulation of adaptations from previous generations. This emotional architecture takes shape in both a person's relationship patterns and in the functioning connections of his or her brain.

Understanding how patterns of reactivity exist in the "top" and "bottom" levels of an individual's brain organization provides a way of thinking about differentiation of self and the entrenched nature of emotional reactivity. Inherent in this idea is that levels of emotional reactivity in the brain correspond with levels of differentiation of self. For example, at a higher level of differentiation of self a person's brain is able to more easily shift from one state to another. As a result, such individuals tend to get less bound up in repetitive states and are able to shift out of negative and unproductive thinking more easily. A person's ability to think (top) is better integrated with the automatic processes in the brain (bottom). People with higher levels of differentiation of self have a kind of flexibility that extends beyond the effort to be less—they simply are less reactive. This is consistent with the concept of differentiation of self and supports the idea that patterns of reactivity exist within every part of the individual's being, from physiology to psychology to behavior.

Working to increase one's differentiation of self requires tolerating the disruption and subsequent anxiety caused by shifts that occur in essential relationships. The brain must reinterpret its perception of threat and reorganize itself. An important component of the process involves making an effort to enlist the prefrontal cortex in overriding one's automatic reactivity. This is a challenging endeavor because there are powerful multigenerational patterns built into the deepest levels of brain development. Inhibiting the force of these patterns is difficult to sustain and often requires an extended effort. Neurofeedback is able to assist a person's effort by giving information to his or her brain about this deeper level of reactivity. The feedback the brain receives helps to interrupt the entrenched patterns that operate on a level outside of awareness. This bottom up process decreases the level of threat perception that has developed over the generations, as well as over the individual's life course. The outcome is a decrease in chronic anxiety that can be observed in less physiological reactivity and that, through a bottom up process, can potentially generate less psychological reactivity.

Case Study

Ms. Pratt was 50 years old and unmarried at the time of the consultation. She was a creative video producer. She was initially seen in 1997, while living with a man. Although she was interested in marriage at the time, he was not. This relationship followed an unsuccessful first marriage. After it ended she lived abroad for a time, and eventually returned home to Washington, DC. She was financially independent and co-owned a home in Italy with her mother.

My consultation with Ms. Pratt spanned 15 years, from 1997 to 2012. During this time, there were four distinct periods. Each consultation period revolved around a relationship with a man, and involved similar relationship themes and sensitivities. The fourth consultation was initiated in 2010, at a time when Ms. Pratt was experiencing intense emotional distress and reactivity. This was not surprising given the fact that her relationship at that time was with the childhood friend who had been instrumental in helping her stop her participation in molestation by a neighbor at the age of five. The intimate involvement with this man activated a level of emotional reactivity present during that earlier time period. Although the reactivity was dormant at a conscious level, it was influencing the level of intensity with which she conducted her entire life (see Figure 11.1).

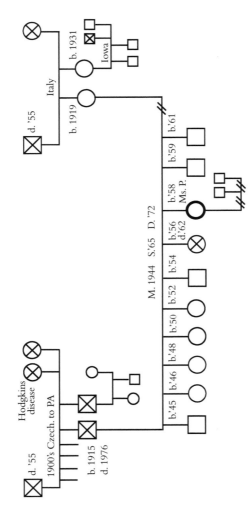

Figure 11.1 Ms. Pratt's Family Diagram

Family of Origin

Ms. Pratt was the eighth of ten children from a large Catholic family, most of whom lived in the local area. She was the youngest of five living sisters, with two older brothers and two younger brothers. A sister immediately older than Ms. Pratt had died of leukemia at age six, when Ms. Pratt was five years old.

The parents married in 1944 and formally separated in 1965. Her father's alcohol abuse played a significant role in the violence that often erupted between her parents. The father would also beat the oldest child, a son, and intimidated the older sisters. Although she did not directly experience the violence, she was present during these episodes and was significantly affected by them.

The separation and divorce of the parents occurred two years after the early death of Ms. Pratt's sister, Marian, who had been sick with leukemia for two years. This was the focus of the family's life when Ms. Pratt was three to five years old. It was during this time period that Ms. Pratt was repeatedly molested by a neighbor.

After her parents' separation in 1965, Ms. Pratt's mother supported the family as an entry-level government worker. She took back her maiden name and referred to her former husband as "Mr. K" to the children. She vilified him and refused to have her children mention him or acknowledge him as their father in her presence. She saw herself as a victim and blamed her husband for her unhappiness. Her negative attitude extended to all aspects of her life.

Paternal Side

Ms. Pratt's father grew up in a poor coal mining family in Pennsylvania. His parents had emigrated from Czechoslovakia at the turn of the century. In contrast to her older siblings, Ms. Pratt had little contact with her father's family. Although she knew that her father was on the younger end of at least seven siblings, she was unaware of his actual sibling position. She had personal knowledge of only one of her father's siblings, Tom, who had children. Her grandfather had died in 1955, and thus Ms. Pratt was able to deduce that her grandmother, who died from Hodgkin's disease, had died prior to 1955, because she knew that her paternal grandfather had remarried after being widowed.

Maternal Side

Ms. Pratt's mother was the older of two daughters spaced 12 years apart. The younger sister had two sons and resided in Iowa with her second husband, whom she married after her first husband died. Ms. Pratt had more knowledge and personal familiarity with this side of the family. Her maternal grandfather died in 1955 (the same year as her paternal grandfather's death), when Ms. Pratt was 2 years old. Her maternal grandmother lived until she was 98 years old, when Ms. Pratt was 28. This maternal side of the family was from Italy and Ms. Pratt continued to have contact with her extended family members who still lived there. This contact, which began during childhood trips with her mother, eventually led to their buying a house together in Italy. Ms. Pratt continued to visit Italy yearly.

Ms. Pratt was a young adult when she developed an independent relationship with her aunt, her mother's younger sister. Her mother continued to portray her own family and sister as having a negative influence and was disparaging about them.

Presenting Problem

Ms. Pratt extended her friendship to Matt, her childhood friend, who had been recently divorced and in a compromised financial situation. Initially he lived in her home in exchange for his handyman skills. Their friendship eventually became intimate. Over six months, the financial and emotional imbalance in the relationship began to undermine its stability. The relationship ended, but this connection with Matt aroused an intense reactivity fueled by her history. Unlike her experience in previous periods of consultation, Ms. Pratt was no longer able to deny that her reactivity, which had developed within her turbulent family, continued to live on and manifested itself in her current functioning.

During this period, Ms. Pratt experienced an increase in night terrors that had been constant companions since her childhood molestation. She lost weight, was unable to concentrate on her work, and drank more. She also had exaggerated fears while conducting her professional life. Going into new and unpredictable situations provoked a heightened and sustained level of reactivity. It included becoming easily overwhelmed, relying on others, being overreactive with her staff, and developing physical symptoms such as incapacitating headaches and muscle pain.

Consultation

The three earlier consultation periods (1997–1999, 2003–2004, 2006–2008) focused on issues either around a relationship involvement or a breakup with a man. In each of the previous consultations, the broader context of the family, including early life experiences and present-day family relationships, was explored. The focus of consultation was centered on her recovery from a relationship disruption and/or working to manage herself in the present. She read voraciously about Bowen theory. We discussed her family patterns repeatedly. In these sessions, she did decrease her anxiety around relationship disruptions and was able to move on with her life. However, the basic relationship patterns that included those with her mother, her father, and her siblings were only discussed, but not fundamentally addressed in a way that would promote emotional integration and a change in her way of relating to men.

The fourth consultation (2010–2012) also involved a relationship with a man. However, it was Matt's connection during the crucial time period in the Pratt family (when she was ages three to five) that brought an intense reactivity to the surface. The significant place Matt had had in her life during the illness and death of her sister, in conjunction with protecting her from molestation, was central. This process highlights the way a present-day relationship with a person who has been a part of an emotionally charged moment in the past can activate reactivity and bring to the forefront issues that have previously been outside of a person's awareness. Although a high level of reactivity has been a part of all her intimate relationships, this relationship gave Ms. Pratt an opportunity to connect that reactivity to her own family history, to become more factual about it, and to be less reactive in her present-day relationships.

Each consultation period with Ms. Pratt centered on the sensitivities and responsiveness she was experiencing within relationships. This inevitably involved her personalizing the problems, along with an inability to "see" the reciprocal nature of relationships. It was difficult for her to get beyond either taking the blame for the problem or seeing the problem as being in the other person. These sensitivities were amplified in the relationship with Matt and seemed to be more distinctly linked to the reactivity of her past with the present. The perceptual patterns established in the past continuously influence the relationships in the present. It is not often, however, that the coupling of the past and present is so apparent.

During the three earlier consultations, Ms. Pratt had had a great deal of animosity toward her mother, while at the same time, she felt obligated to respond to her mother's demands. It was difficult for her to set limits with her mother without feeling guilty. She adopted the perspective that her father was the "demon" and believed he had no redeeming qualities. She was not interested in talking about him.

The relationship Ms. Pratt had with her nine siblings was complicated and involved juggling alliances and polarities. As the youngest sister of sisters, she was sensitive to how her older siblings saw her and she frequently felt dismissed by them. The posture of blaming others, so characteristic of her family, could be seen in her siblings' resentment of their mother and the excuses they made for not participating in her care. As a result, Ms. Pratt ended up with the sole responsibility for her mother. Not surprisingly, the more she overfunctioned in relationship to her mother, the more demanding her mother became.

Neurofeedback

Unlike previous consultations with Ms. Pratt, this fourth consultation exclusively included the use of neurofeedback. During this process, electrodes are attached to both hemispheres of the brain and the person receives auditory and visual feedback while thinking, talking, and reacting. Although this feedback is mostly out of conscious awareness, it enables the brain to receive information about itself and to interrupt the inefficient patterns that have developed over time. The feedback impacts the nature of a person's thinking, responding, and integration of thought. This integration is simultaneously occurring at physiological, psychological, and cognitive levels during the session. Training occurs both while focusing attention on the feedback and/or during conversation with family or consultant without conscious attention to the feedback.

Neurofeedback (or brain wave biofeedback) provides moment-to-moment factual information about the brain's electrical communication system faster than information received through conscious awareness. For example, the brain interacts with the information it receives during the training at 256 times a second, significantly faster than is possible through cognition. The Zengar feedback is experienced as a slight hesitation in the music that simultaneously affects a visually moving image on a monitor. This hesitation engages the brain's "orienting" response in a way that is similar to when you hear a new sound and immediately focus your attention on it. The brain is continuously prompted to reorient and refocus based on a real response in the present, rather than to the automatic patterns rooted in the chronic anxiety of the past. Based on the feedback it receives, the brain has the opportunity to adjust its response and thus become less stuck in patterns such as overreactivity or underreactivity. Over time, the brain learns to shift states more easily, which enables it to be more engaged in the present and more efficient. This has implications for how a person's perception is organized and what is perceived as a threat. A brain that is more flexible and efficient is better able to respond to the present reality and is less governed by the fixed patterns of the past.

In this case, Ms. Pratt had adapted to living through the tumultuous time in her family. The developmental agenda for a three- to five-year-old includes the development of self-regulation. If the illness and death of the sister and molestation had occurred at a different age, the brain would have adapted to a different stage. Her emotional perspective was that her mother failed to stand up for her, as Matt had done. This perspective continued to be a part of her lifetime adaptation. This is an example of the way chronic anxiety colors a person's perception and subsequent functioning. The patterns of adaptation throughout development are built into the physiology, emotion, and perceptual states that serve as a template for adult life.

It is this level of the organism's reactivity that is affected by the neurofeedback. A session often includes a person thinking and talking about his or her life dilemma as the neurofeedback interacts with the conversation—thought and emotion. The feedback is continually engaging the brain during the conversation in ways that interrupt the reactive patterns below the level of awareness. It is important to remember that these reactive patterns are the foundation upon which thoughts and perceptions are built. When these basic reactive patterns are given the opportunity to reorient based on present feedback, a less reactive platform develops enabling new thinking and perspectives to emerge. This promotes the integration of automatic brain responses and thought. In other words, the neurofeedback training interrupts the reactive brain patterns while the conversation frames how to think about the life challenges in an integrated systems way leading to more productive action for self.

The quality of the conversation with Ms. Pratt was different during the neurofeedback training session. Other factors, such as the cumulative impact of consultation over the years, as well as the importance of the issues activated by Matt's presence, may also have contributed to the outcome. During earlier consultations, Ms. Pratt had been unable to answer questions about the facts of her family history. However, after becoming introduced to neurofeedback, Ms. Pratt built an accurate chronology of the history of her family and her early life. This included important facts around the deaths of both maternal and paternal grandfathers in 1955, and the illness in her next older sister, Marian, the following year. This clarified for her the level of anxiety she grew up in and the way it impacted her life course. She came to understand that her father's violence toward her oldest brother was a manifestation of chronic anxiety within her nuclear family. Rather than blaming her father, her mother, or her siblings, she could step back and see more dispassionately how the family system operated. She was able to better understand how each of her siblings responded, and how this relationship reactivity had impacted their lives. Ms. Pratt's critical attitude toward her mother for not protecting her from the molestation was neutralized when she was able to place it in the context of her mother and family dealing with the illness and death of her sister. Neurofeedback enabled her to discuss and engage in the multigenerational history in a way that fundamentally altered her level of chronic anxiety and reactivity.

Ms. Pratt invited her mother and one of her sisters to a consultation with her in 2011. Her 90-year-old mother, newly adapting to blindness from macular degeneration, described life from her perspective, including how difficult it had been during the illness and death of her daughter, Marian. She had been pregnant during this time and was overwhelmed by the demands of her children and her husband. In this overwhelmed position, she tolerated the violence both in the marriage and the violence that her husband directed toward her oldest son. Despite the fact that she divorced her husband following the death of her daughter, her anger toward him never ended.

During these conversations with her mother, Ms. Pratt was listening and asking questions while connected to the neurofeedback electrodes and training. This process decreased Ms. Pratt's anxiety and enabled her to be more sympathetic to her mother's rough edges, and thus to be less reactive and critical toward her. Hearing both her mother and sister describe life from their perspectives allowed Ms. Pratt to see them as individuals with a different viewpoint that she could now understand. The neutrality she acquired enabled her to define herself more clearly with her mother about what she would and would not do. As her reactivity decreased, her view of her mother changed. Rather than experience her mother's financial assistance as manipulation, she came to see her mother's aid in the purchase of her home as a genuine apology for her mother's inability to protect her during the time that she was molested.

Perhaps these conversations and the change in her perspective could have happened without the neurofeedback. The fact is, however, that this change did not occur during the previous consultation periods. Neurofeedback seemed to provide Ms. Pratt with the flexibility to entertain a more difficult level of conversation and perspective than she had had in the past.

Things also began to change in the sibling relationships. She defined herself more clearly with her sibling group, giving suggestions to them about ways they could help and share in the responsibility for their mother. These interactions led to gradual shifts in their behavior.

Although the mother was legally blind, and less able to function independently, she continued to live on her own. Ms. Pratt was no longer overfunctioning with her mother and was better able to think through how to reasonably function as one of nine siblings. When she began to communicate more clearly and firmly with her mother, her mother became more appreciative and more respectful of her daughter's time, making requests rather than demands. Most importantly, Ms. Pratt was no longer governed by guilt regarding her mother.

Ms. Pratt's attitude about her father also changed. She began to rethink the experiences she had with her father in the past. As she became less critical of him, she began to realize that she had overreacted and misinterpreted past interactions with him. Ms. Pratt told her mother she was going to talk about her father even if her mother did not like it, and that she would refer to him as "father," not "Mr. K." She informed her siblings of her plan. Despite their negative reactions, she continued to maintain a more neutral attitude about her father and even placed a framed photo of him in her living room.

Ms. Pratt's father died in 1976 of heart disease. Only one of Ms. Pratt's siblings, a brother, maintained consistent contact with their father following the divorce and was with him when he died. A senior in high school, Ms. Pratt was the oldest of three remaining children at home when he died. When told about her father's death, her mother pointed to an obituary and said, "The bastard died to spite me just because I finally got a decent increase in child support." Although the mother did arrange for a private viewing for the three children at home, she refused to let them attend the funeral, as she did not want them to "be around all that trash from Pennsylvania."

In her search to discover the facts of her family's life, Ms. Pratt directed questions to her older sisters. Unlike before, when she felt her opinions were dismissed, she began to experience more mutual respect. The relationship she had with each of her sisters became more flexible and easy and they even celebrated their first sisters' weekend together.

Ms. Pratt's Evaluation

Ms. Pratt described her experience with neurofeedback in the following ways:

> I was not interested in neurofeedback for the first few time periods that I sought your help. It was not until I became severely depressed that I was willing to try it. I figured if I was miserable enough to go walking in the woods and hope to be murdered, then why not neurofeedback.
>
> I immediately noticed an improvement in my sleep patterns. Very shortly into the process I began to notice a decrease in the nightmares that have troubled me since childhood. As our process continued, eventually the nightmares went away completely.
>
> It has enabled me to hear you. It decreased the anxiety so that I could hear what you were saying about theory and family. When I did not need to spend all my time defending myself, I could look at myself.
>
> You told me for years not to take things personally. Intellectually I understood what that meant. But I could not internalize it. In the flight or fight choice, I always chose fight . . . and fast. In the early weeks of neurofeedback it just sort of clicked. Don't take it personally! The whole need to take action about every little fearful moment sort of dropped away. It is easier to stay calm and see the facts. I attribute that to neurofeedback.

Ms. Pratt's involvement with her childhood friend brought to the forefront the way chronic anxiety of the past can live in the present. It may be that this linking of the past with the present provided the impetus and clarity for her to take on her life in a more substantive way. This opportunity, coupled with neurofeedback, was instrumental in her ability to fundamentally change her functioning. This change occurred not only in her interactions in her family but also in her physiology, her perceptions, and her emotional states. This might also be referred to as a top down/bottom up process.

Outcome of Consultation Including Neurofeedback

- Ms. Pratt's physiological reactivity changed. Her night terrors are gone, as are her headaches;
- Ms. Pratt experienced herself differently. She can see the part the other person plays rather than only seeing herself as the "problem";
- Ms. Pratt increased her ability to separate her "emotion," as in experiencing something as her responsibility, from "thinking," as in seeing the part both she and her partner play;
- Changes in her fear state enabled Ms. Pratt to not only think about Bowen theory as an intellectual process but to also integrate it into her psychology, her physiology, and her actions;
- She experienced changes in her reactivity to her father and she was not a part of the "group hate";
- The changes in her relationship with her mother included no longer being governed by guilt and having the ability to evaluate her mother's realistic needs;
- She was able to see the reciprocal nature of relationships;
- She observed changes in the relationship with her siblings. She became a respected participant in her sibling group rather than being either the "little sister" or the only sibling who cares for mother;
- There were changes in her anxiety about cleanliness. She now has a dog.

What Is Brain Efficiency?

Unlike traditional neurofeedback equipment,[3] the Zengar system developed by V. Brown is unique insofar as it is not focused on symptoms but rather on optimizing the brain functioning by improving the central nervous system's flexibility, resilience, and stability. The goal of this neurofeedback system is to promote resiliency in the brain by giving it feedback about the coordinated efficiency of 16 different frequency variables simultaneously. It measures the nature of the reactivity of the communication systems of the brain. The feedback occurs as an interruption of sound when the brain's communication patterns are overreactive or underreactive. This slight interruption orients the brain to the functioning present. From a Bowen theory perspective, overreactivity and underreactivity in the brain are associated with chronic anxiety patterns. These patterns are manifested in the deeply rooted emotional system of the individual and can be seen in the behavior, physiology, emotions, and cognitive patterns described in Bowen theory. This level of reactivity is a deeper and quicker level of "behavior" that can be observed through increasingly capable computing systems. "Behavior" in this way can be likened to the movement of a sea squirt in relationship to a current in the water. It is a more fundamental action of the organism. Although speculative, it may be that the neurofeedback provides a glimpse into how differentiation of self is observable in the brain.

Examples of Information Neurofeedback
Sends Back to the Brain

- How reactive or integrated the senses are with each other and how emotionally responsive they are to input (for example, a startle response when hearing a sudden sound will be different between people, as well as different when their eyes are closed or open);
- The manner of emotional integration of memory (for example, how reactive the brain patterns are when thinking of early activating events);
- How the patterns in the brain are below awareness and seem to reflect the chronic anxiety or the drumbeat of responsiveness to the room, the consultant, and the facts of life at present;
- The impact of the training can decrease in reactivity in all of the above patterns, including a difference in the relationship reactivity; it can also include the ability to be more open to experiences that were "shut down," overly inhibited or unavailable, as well as decreasing the over-reactivity of the system.

Neurofeedback: Individual Thinking Versus
Systems Thinking

Although Bowen theory and Zengar neurofeedback grew out of different disciplines, there is a synergy between the two perspectives, which is based on a shared systems orientation. Both conceptual frameworks were radical departures from the mainstream thinking that had preceded their development. And both made conceptual leaps from individual thinking to systems thinking.

In the field of neurofeedback, the dominant perspective is individually oriented and symptom focused, where the problem is within the person and the intention of the neurofeedback is to change the brain to become more "normal."[4] In contrast, Zengar neurofeedback is based on the idea that the brain is a system. Although the details of the technology go beyond the scope of this paper, it is based in the ever-changing dynamics of a system. The technology of Zengar neurofeedback does not rely on targeting designated areas for treatment, any more than a systems theorist would focus on one individual without considering how his or her functioning is a product of the emotional unit. This represents a radical departure from individual neurofeedback, in much the same way that Bowen theory represented a radical departure from individual theories.

This system orientation is built into the way Zengar neurofeedback impacts all sets of brain frequencies simultaneously (as an interacting unit), without targeting a specific frequency that has been designated as a problem.

In other words, the feedback responds to the variability of the electrical brain signals that can reflect, for example, the overreactivity and underreactivity of the communication system in the brain. This is comparable to the overreactivity and underreactivity between individuals in a family relationship system. With this systems-based feedback, the outcome of the neurofeedback training results in a broader, system-wide alteration in reactivity, such as either decreasing overreactivity or increasing underreactivity. This goes beyond simply working to be calmer in a relationship system. Zengar neurofeedback can potentially impact the chronic anxiety that has manifested itself in the brain as over- and underreactivity of electrical activity that evolved within the family multigenerational system. The feedback is constantly interacting with the individual's brain functioning as the brain learns to decrease the extremes of the overreactivity and underreactivity from moment to moment. This involves an interruption of the overreactivity or underreactivity of the deepest and earliest brain processes that are associated with survival and the threat response. This interruption allows the brain to learn the difference between "realistic" responses and "unrealistic" ones. The perception of this distinction is at the core of differentiation of self. The ability of a person to relate to a situation based upon the reality of the present rather than in the adaptations of the past is critical to increasing flexibility and increasing differentiation of self. Neurofeedback interacts with the brain functioning that has evolved from the emotional process of the family system within that individual. This is a central difference between individual neurofeedback and systems-based Zengar neurofeedback.

Regardless of the type of neurofeedback equipment used, the potential for increased awareness and change may be greater when it occurs with a consultant who can think of the individual as someone who reflects the reactivity within a multigenerational family system. Individual neurofeedback technology can be used to learn about self in the system by a consultant who is "thinking systems." This means that the consultant interprets the individual's brain functioning as a reflection of relationship reactivity rather than as a quality of the individual. For example, rather than describing brain function as "attention deficit disorder," the consultant sees the inability to focus and distractibility in the context of how that brain adapts to relationships. In addition, the consultant frames the reactivity as providing an opportunity to become less automatic and more "realistic" or intentional in relationship issues. In this case, awareness is required to accomplish the brain training goal along with the integration of the brain experience in the relationship system. However, Zengar neurofeedback allows a person to experience the *system* of the brain *that is below awareness*. As the brain receives information about itself, it begins to automatically make corrections and interrupt the pathways of reactivity. In many cases, the subtle shifts that occur through Zengar neurofeedback enable people to make connections that their reactivity blinded them from seeing previously. They are simply less reactive over time, living in each moment with less sense of threat or chronic anxiety.

Bowen family systems theory suggests that the development of the individual occurs within a multigenerational family context. This generation-to-generation development is the vehicle for the variation in reactivity present in each individual within each nuclear family. Increasing differentiation of self addresses both the intentional effort and one that interrupts the more basic level of reactivity. One process includes awareness and occurs through observing self, managing reactivity, and acting with intention. The other, which occurs outside of awareness and can be assisted by neurofeedback, interrupts a more basic reactivity level. Integration of the two promotes the most efficient process for differentiation of self.

The method of therapy that developed from Bowen's theory was based on the available knowledge about the brain prior to his death in 1990. At this time, neurofeedback was in its infancy and systems-based neurofeedback was not developed until 1998 (Brown, 2012a, 2012b). Bowen's method was primarily designed to stimulate awareness of self in the family emotional system and to manage one's reactivity while working toward functioning with clearer self-definition in relationships. The advances over the last 20 years in understanding how the brain develops and is organized permits new knowledge to be incorporated into Bowen theory. Since Zengar neurofeedback is optimizing the integration of the brain, outside of awareness, it might be thought of as a "bottom up" process. Zengar neurofeedback has the potential to contribute an additional way of optimizing one's functioning in the effort toward increasing the level of differentiation of self. This way of thinking is consistent with assumptions from Bowen theory.

The Family Brain

The effort to think about the family emotional system, while relating to the individual, is an inherent challenge in learning Bowen family systems theory. Using neurofeedback, under the broader umbrella of Bowen theory, inevitably involves the ability to adapt technology to a relationship context. This involves seeing how the reactivity pattern within an individual's brain represents a template for the family relationship system. The patterns of individual reactivity reflect unique brain patterns but they also reflect the emotional position that individual has in the family relationship system. This leads to the conceptualization of the "family brain" as a central component of the neurofeedback training. In other words, the training is affecting the nature of the family's relationship reactivity, as seen in the individual, rather than simply affecting individual symptoms.

When I began to utilize the Zengar systems-based neurofeedback in 2000, the connection between the family and the brain expanded exponentially—both in what I have learned and in what I have observed in consulting with individuals and their families. Zengar's neurofeedback system provides immediate feedback on the nature of reactivity in the brain. Decreasing reactivity at this pre-awareness level of the individual affects the broader relationship reactivity. This has enabled neurofeedback to become a family learning tool. All members of a family can use it to increase a system's flexibility more quickly than through one individual's effort.

Principles Based on the Idea of the Family Brain

- A person's entire multigenerational system lives in each moment—in the present;
- Basic perception is an extension of how a person organizes him/her self in every moment of every day;
- Each of us is organized, physiologically, emotionally, psychologically, and perceptually in an emotional position in our relationships. A person's perception of the world is the basis for his actions. All levels of a person operate in a position in the basic triangles at play in family relationships;
- When doing neurofeedback the brain processes the facts about itself. This is comparable to a person "seeing" or "experiencing" the family as a system.

Conclusion

Neurofeedback will likely continue to increase in efficiency and accessibility in the near future, making the potential to increase individual and family functioning a reality. This modality addresses the level of activity that operates below overt behavior. Discussions of differentiation of self usually involve only the "top down" process, with little appreciation for the "bottom up" processes that are the underpinnings of the structures for reactivity. Although we all want to be able to be less reactive in significant relationships, it is a difficult position to sustain over time. This disconnect has partially to do with the way the organism retains and holds within itself the chronic anxiety and challenges of the past. The ability to be in a one-to-one relationship necessitates a capacity to be fully engaged with significant others, with a poised appreciation for the moment. Neurofeedback facilitates the process, or integration, by enabling the brain to work with—not against—the shifts that are operating on the cognitive level.

Acknowledgment

I am deeply indebted to my colleague of 35 years, Margaret Donley. This chapter is an outstanding example of how ideas evolve in relationships. Ms. Donley's ability to organize the complexity of ideas and bring them to written form helped me articulate the connection between Bowen theory and neurofeedback. I am deeply indebted to what our relationship has contributed to Bowen theory.

NOTES

1 Bowen, M. (1978). *Family therapy in clinical practice*. New York: Jason Aronson, p. 441.
2 "Neurofeedback" in this chapter refers to the systems-based neurofeedback developed by Valdeane Brown, NeurOptimal by Zengar. www.zengar.com.
3 Other neurofeedback systems are designed to "normalize" the individual brain, thus decreasing symptoms. Most neurofeedback is based on this individual perspective, which has dominated research in the field.
4 This is established by assessing characteristics of frequencies and locations in the brain by a matrix of electrodes or measurements. This is typically done through an evaluation process where the problem is diagnosed and a treatment plan is established. The clinician guides the training process. The client then works to control his brain wave activity to meet the established goals.

REFERENCES

Bowen, M. (1978). *Family therapy in clinical practice*. New York: Jason Aronson.
Brown, V. (2012a). www.zengar.com.
Brown, V. (2012b). Personal communication, June 8, 2012.

12

DEFINING A SELF

A Long-Term View

Ann V. Nicholson

Defining a self is a complex task. It requires motivation, discipline, perseverance, courage, and knowledge of Bowen theory. The human, like other species, is highly sensitive to changes in his physical and emotional environment.
It is usual for people to seek therapy when the environment they live and
work in becomes more threatening. The rising anxiety and stress can moti-
vate people to learn new ways of thinking about how families function, to
observe patterns of behavior in one's interactions with important others, to
regulate one's automatic responses, to study one's part in the family relationship system, and ultimately to differentiate a self from the emotional system
of which one is a part.

Bowen theory views the human family as a natural system guided by the
same instinctual forces that govern all life forms. With its focus on function versus a focus on pathology, symptoms are viewed as evidence of one's
functioning within the emotional system, as well as evidence of the functioning of the system as a whole. Bowen theory equates the emotional system
with the automatic instinctive processes that guide living organisms. Where
some organisms may respond to social hormones or other chemicals, humans
respond most intensely to interactions within their family group, their closest attachments. Dr. Bowen observed these interactions among families in
his research unit at the National Institute of Mental Health as well as in his
clinical practice.

To think of the family unit as a system, with all component parts influencing and responding to each other, sets the stage for understanding the
complexity of differentiation of self. It was Bowen's genius to see what others had been unable to see, that the system instinctively functions in ways
that can undermine the functioning of one or more members in order to
enhance the functioning of others. The level of threat (real or imagined)
operating in the system activates this process, which serves to strengthen the
group, allowing for a greater chance of survival and reproductive success.
While beneficial to the group, this process is costly to certain individuals

within it. Triangles and interlocking triangles become activated in a process that for the most part occurs outside of awareness. Level of differentiation influences one's vulnerability to the triangle, as well as the degree of sensitivity to emotional pressure. The use of the triangle mechanism by the family unit is also influenced by level of differentiation because families perceive threat and respond to emotional pressure differently at different levels of differentiation.

The effort to alter one's functioning in important triangles requires knowledge of the "two-or-more-against-one process" (Lassiter, 2008, p. 64), along with an awareness of one's sensitivity to emotional pressure and a growing ability to regulate self. Over time, one can observe the degree to which their functioning is guided by the group rather than their own inner compass. Principles defined from within the individual, not in response to group pressure or one's multigenerational programming, are an important part of being a defined self. The goal of therapy is to assist people in the effort to develop their individual guidance system. That, in turn, will allow them to regulate feelings and the need for approval and closeness, and establish their own thinking based on a more factual assessment of their functioning within the family unit. A disciplined and consistent effort contributes to the process of becoming a more thoughtful and responsible self.

This chapter focuses on the effort of one individual to define a self in her nuclear and extended family. The therapy process has occurred over a 22-year span. Bimonthly or monthly sessions were the norm for the earlier years, with less frequent contact over subsequent years (see Figure 12.1).

A Long-Term Effort to Define a Self

The initial contact occurred following the psychiatric hospitalization of the client's youngest sister. The client, Dr. A, who lived in Europe, was looking for a referral for her sister and family, who lived in New England. In a brief conversation regarding Bowen theory, particularly focused on how each member of the family influences and is influenced by all other members, Dr. A became intrigued and shortly thereafter began her own course of therapy. No other family member has been seen, with the exception of her preadolescent son (many years later) and her second husband. They were each seen individually for two sessions. Clinical sessions with the client for the most part were by telephone, given the geographical distance.

Dr. A first contacted the therapist in September 1989. She and her husband, Dr. B, were living in England, where they met. Both were physicians and both taught at a prestigious university. Both maintained a clinical practice in their respective fields, public health and neurology.

The couple met in October 1984 when Dr. A was doing postgraduate work at the university where her future husband taught. They dated for seven months, lived together for two years, and married in March 1987.

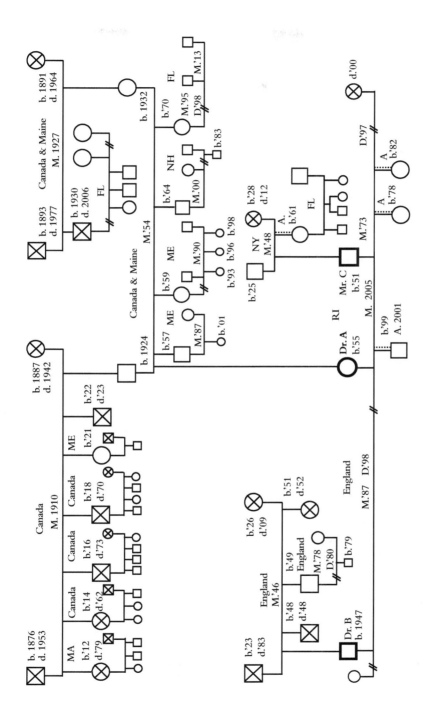

Figure 12.1 Dr. A's Family Diagram

Dr. A noted her decision to marry was "based on an incredible need for the other." The attraction for both had been immediate and intense. This was the first marriage for Dr. A and a second marriage for her husband, Dr. B.

Stage I: Jockeying for Self

At this stage each pressured the other to cave in and neither was willing to yield to the other.

Dr. A described the marriage as conflictual from the onset. "It's like a roller coaster with periods of calm closeness followed by intense conflict and a lingering aversion to the other." She was aware that the level of conflict was out of proportion to the reality of the problem. Dr. A could see that both spouses were highly sensitive to their emotional environment. Any shift in the togetherness or added stressor could lead to an outburst by one or the other. Dr. A noted how difficult it was for her to do anything independent of her mate. Hence, participating in her hobbies or interests was regulated by her husband's response and her sensitivity to it.

Within a year of marriage Dr. B's drinking was more evident, and there was some early indication that his performance at work was faltering. He had always been a high achiever and was well respected both in academic and clinical settings. He began missing class and clinical appointments and was occasionally unprepared for professional meetings. Negative feedback from his professional community became an added source of emotional pressure. The presence of symptoms was evidence of his vulnerability in the marriage and sensitivity to the emotional system. It was also evidence of the rising level of threat (real or imagined) in the system.

Dr. A had few friends in England and her husband socialized at work but never invited friends to their home. In many ways the relationship was quite insular, with both spouses reserving their energy for the relationship with the other.

Dr. A revealed little to her extended family, although there was regular phone contact and visits once or twice a year: "My energy goes to finding closeness elsewhere, not in the extended family." Dr. A noted she had always been highly sensitive to her mother's emotional state, and her mother's disapproval would be a major threat to self: "I didn't want to hurt her."

Dr. A also spoke to the projection process: "I was a very shy child. My parents described me as a very passive baby and they wondered how I would make it in the world."

Murray Bowen described the projection process in this way: "The family projection process refers to the mechanisms that operate as the parents and the child play active parts in the transmission of the parental problem to the child" (Bowen, 1978, p. 127). The problem begins in the mother with a projection of her unsureness (in whatever form) onto the child, and the father's support of the mother's projection seals the process.

By January 1990, Dr. A could see more of her part in interactions with her husband and described the marriage as calmer. She reported occasions when she was not interested in conflict and "it dissipated automatically."

Stage II: Early Efforts to Define a Self

Dr. A began planning for a trip home for her first sister's wedding in April 1990. Her plan was to give herself three days with her family before her husband's arrival. This was a shift in the couple's pattern, as they always traveled together, and she expected her husband to react negatively. She was aware of her automatic response to yield to the important other, "almost erasing self in order to accommodate the other." She saw herself as unable to deal with the hurt, threats, or anger of the important other. Not knowing how to manage self in this arena, she would automatically yield to avoid the discomfort. The visit home was an attempt to follow through on what she wanted to accomplish for herself, independent of her mate. Her goals were to have time alone with important family members and to avoid yielding to emotional pressure. This time she was successful, a solid first step in carving out time alone with each parent and a paternal aunt. She observed how difficult it was for her to act on her own without her spouse and his guidance.

Dr. A made another trip home in November 1990 without her husband. She saw how she was controlled by the family group and at times was unable to think. She noted there was an emotional pull within her to remain colorless in the presence of the group. She was more aware that her inability to function for herself was not just a problem in her but was part of her functioning position in the family. The therapist asked how the group influenced her capacity to think. She began to see how automatic it was for her to become what the family expected her to be. She had a new appreciation of the emotional process in her family of origin and her part in it. By December 1990, Dr. A reported she was operating more out of her own thinking but feeling alone, sad, and empty.

By February 1991, there was an increase in conflict in the marriage, and evidence of the over/underfunctioning reciprocity became clearer. Dr. B's functioning continued to decline with wider fluctuations at work and an increase in irresponsible behavior in the marriage, particularly in terms of finances and drinking. Marital conflict had increased to the point where Dr. B was hitting and pushing his wife as anxiety reached unmanageable levels. Dr. A reported her goal was "to get her husband to leave her alone." The more she distanced from him, the more he pursued her. Her nonverbal cues reflected her contempt and disgust. Both spouses were unable to regulate self and each lost any ability to control their reactions or responsiveness to the important other.

As Dr. A became more aware of the reciprocity in the process, she could track when the interaction was apt to lead to physical violence. She had a plan in place and frequently stayed in a hotel until she regained control of self. When she was able to shift her focus from her husband to "what do I need to do to regain control of me," she was able to think and plan and respond to the reality of the situation.

Dr. A realized that as the threat level in the environment increased, the potential for violence increased as well. Her husband's performance at work was erratic and he was frequently reprimanded for absences and low productivity. In this environment, he drank more and had increased difficulty managing his finances. Routine expenses were ignored. Dr. A saw how she participated in this process by relieving her husband of responsibility and functioning for him or by ignoring her own responsibility and misreading the environment in the marriage. Dr. A talked of how much she wanted to believe her husband and thus ignored facts that revealed the irresponsibility in each spouse. She saw herself as highly vulnerable to her husband's rationalizations and noted, "I feel weak, as though I can't stand up."

When the bank moved to foreclose on their property, Dr. A saw her part more clearly. The couple was in debt. The more her husband spent, the more she saved, and often gave him money when he was without. She was plugging holes in a dike in a frenzied state of activity. Both were responding to the increased threat in the environment and this influenced their behavior.

Dr. A began to take actions to protect her own finances and opened an individual bank account for the first time. Although she said she would not continue to support her husband when he ran out of money, she was unable to act on this for quite some time. She began to define herself around less threatening issues. Dr. A noted she had often been disarmed by her husband's words or perceptions and failed to focus on facts. Dr. B at this point had been forced to take a leave from his academic and clinical positions due to his erratic and irresponsible behaviors. Dr. A became more reactive to her husband's neediness and less focused on self. She was both attracted and allergic to his neediness. In this environment, Dr. B began drinking more and Dr. A's mother began to pressure her to divorce.

Dr. A asked, "What is the difference between cooperation and accommodation?" The therapist responded with two thoughts. Accommodation is associated with an emotionally driven feeling response that over time would accentuate the over/underfunctioning reciprocity. Cooperation implies a basic respect of both parties to function and move toward a solution with a view of implications for the short and long term. How will this action benefit me or the group and what is the cost? Cooperation is reflective of more mature functioning. The ability to regulate self would be directly related to the capacity to cooperate. The ability to assess one's environment more factually also influences this process. Studying this process in other species may help one's understanding of it in the human. What does cooperation look like in the natural world? What are the factors that interfere with cooperation in nature? Dr. A began to research the behavior of other species and has maintained an ongoing interest in the study of natural systems. She noted, "It helps to focus on facts."

In December 1991, Dr. A moved into her own apartment, believing she would be in a better position to work on self if she had her own place. This would be one of many attempts. She continued to give her husband money in spite of frequent efforts to regulate her behavior. Each spouse fueled the unreality of the other. The impact of unemployment was not experienced by Dr. B to the degree that his wife continued to provide for him and in essence function for him. Dr. A, in turn, functioned in ways that supported her husband's underfunctioning and enhanced her own. Her own career was moving forward in a number of areas: promotions, grants, and awards. Her husband was out of work indefinitely. It is often difficult for people to see the reciprocal nature of this pattern. Although the emotional process is outside of awareness for the most part, people can learn to bring more of it into awareness, using Bowen theory as a guide.

Dr. A focused on patterns in her parents' marriage. Focusing on the previous generation is a way to gain some level of objectivity and broaden the field of study. She saw her father as the symptomatic one and her mother in the caretaking or overfunctioning position. When she observed her father yielding to his wife in response to emotional pressure, she was able to see her own functioning more clearly. Dr. A also researched the history of alcohol problems in her extended family. Her father had three siblings with alcohol problems, as had his father for a short period of time. Two maternal great-uncles were rumrunners. This became an opportunity to discuss family relationships with each of her parents and gave Dr. A a clearer picture of her own emotional programming and her acute sensitivity to triggers in her marriage.

Dr. A continued to plan visits home and correspond with relatives. In July 1992 she told her husband, who was unemployed at the time, that she could not afford to take both of them to visit her family in Maine. He would have to be responsible for his share if he wanted to come. Dr. A went alone.

In this visit Dr. A again experienced her stuck position in her family. She had the sense that she had no freedom to move or think. This speaks to the degree of group pressure and her innate sensitivity to it, limiting her ability to rely on her own guidance. Dr. A observed her tendency to see herself in a negative light, insecure and inadequate in some way. She would feel jealous of another family member's ability, or appearance, or apparent sureness and then see herself as lacking in that way. This time she could make a distinction between a feeling and a fact. This is an important change when one is able to see the difference between feeling inadequate and being inadequate. Increasing one's ability to separate thinking from feeling is key to the process of raising one's level of differentiation.

Many people experience an emotional response following an important family trip. Dr. A found herself with an unexplainable feeling of sadness.

Upon her return home, she found her husband calmer, more cooperative, and sober.

In October 1992, Dr. A stopped giving any money to her husband. Her husband blamed her therapist. Often the family views a change in a family member as the result of therapy rather than the result of the person's own effort. This usually happens when the client has been overly positive about the therapy or the theory. Dr. B reacted to his wife's stated position and began drinking. The interactions were emotionally charged but did not lead to violence. It was only when her husband hid her personal journal that she lost all ability to self-regulate, and returned to the old togetherness, in heated conflict.

In November 1992, Dr. A tried again and said no to a request for money. There were four to five days of angry outbursts by her husband but no violence. Dr. A noted, "I am as immune as I can be to all the noise." Then there was the predictable shift to positive and engaging behaviors by the husband in a pressured plea to join the old togetherness. This is where Dr. A was most vulnerable and she slipped. This process would repeat over and over again. The therapist suggested she go back to the drawing board and prompted her to consider the following: what is your responsibility? What does it take to continue to work at this until you succeed in your effort to be more of a self? You now have a better picture of your vulnerability to praise, love, warmth, and acceptance. How difficult it is to stand alone and be a self!

By May 1993, Dr. B was back to work and paying an equal share of the monthly expenses. At this point, Dr. A could get herself into a neutral position more often. The problem was in staying there. When she was neutral, the couple was able to talk more openly. Dr. A reported that her husband began to see a pattern in his work history from overinvesting to cutting off. This same pattern was also apparent in his two marriages. Dr. A was more aware of her own intensity, describing it as an inner volcano. She could see how conflict absorbed it and shifted her focus toward her husband and away from self.

By August 1993, Dr. A noted there was a marked decrease in marital conflict and when it did occur it did not escalate beyond manageable levels. Dr. B began to reconnect with colleagues and friends and was maintaining a part-time work schedule. Over time, Dr. A found herself locked into the togetherness once again, being for the other rather than thinking for self. Hence, she paid less attention to her money, leaving it available for her husband to use irresponsibly. This was always a clear indication of reduced functioning on Dr. A's part. With increased togetherness, each spouse moved more instinctively. That ultimately clouded thinking and reduced the ability to regulate self. More questions followed on the part of the therapist: What makes money so toxic? Could Dr. A learn something from her family regarding the use and abuse of resources? At what point does she become so vulnerable in the emotional field that she loses her capacity to self-direct?

The goal was to get more objective regarding the emotional process and her responsiveness to it. Money in and of itself was not the issue. It was the emotional environment that was influencing Dr. A's behavior as well as that of her husband. Hence when the threat level increased in the relationship, the behavior of each spouse shifted. The behavior automatically became less regulated and more instinctive. And this, in turn, influenced the management of the resource.

Therapy continued to focus on Dr. A's functioning in her family of origin. She had seen herself as the inadequate one in the family and decided early on that she could compensate for this "by being smart." Dr. A focused on periods in her life of over- and underfunctioning. She recalled that in her early years she would avoid trying out for sports or other activities based on her assessment that she would not be good enough. Hence her sense of self restricted her movement in the world. She noted she married a "superstar" in response to her feelings of inadequacy. In this relationship she was functioning better, but her husband's functioning plummeted. Each spouse borrowed from the other in order to function, but over time Dr. A gained and Dr. B lost functioning. Both participated in the process unwittingly and without intent. To the degree that one family member absorbs more of the undifferentiation, immaturity, or weakness in the system, the functioning of other members is enhanced. Level of differentiation influences one's vulnerability to this automatic process. The higher the level of differentiation, the freer one is to maintain self in the emotional system. Hence, there is less need to borrow self from others. Bowen theory guides one to raise his or her level of functioning without compromising the functioning of others. This is done by altering the part self plays, by gaining control of the automatic forces within self that drive this process, while remaining in viable emotional contact with the group. Becoming a more responsible self ultimately influences the functioning of the family unit and gives each member of the group a better chance, to some degree.

In her visit to the extended family in May 1994, Dr. A noted she was calmer and in control of self during the visit and upon her arrival home. She began to think differently regarding her overfunctioning, seeing it as disrespectful and undermining the resourcefulness of her husband. Again she took a position regarding finances, "I will not continue to support two adults." Dr. A noted that her husband was "so nice," that she quickly lost her platform for self, and yielded to his requests for money. Dr. A noted, "Money is the most evident manifestation of my overdoing."

In October 1994, Dr. B's mother had double bypass surgery. Anxiety intensified at this time and was sustained over the next two years. There were many complications that followed the surgery, eventually resulting in amputations of both her legs. Dr. B's automatic response was to distance via alcohol, avoiding responsibilities as the emotional environment became increasingly more threatening. Dr. A maintained frequent contact with her mother-in-law but was also able to remain focused on her own goals. She decided to move on her position to take an apartment for six months, having been unsuccessful at such attempts in the past. She did not think she could define a position for self while living with her husband. She thought this action would get her husband's attention as well as allow her to refocus on her effort to define her financial responsibilities to him and to the household.

Dr. A made her third visit home in that calendar year. More and more extended family members were contacting her directly rather than through her parents. She had made a consistent effort to open up contact with extended family, particularly with a paternal aunt and a maternal uncle. Both relationships gave her new insights regarding the emotional environment in her parents' families of origin. She could now see the multigenerational programming and what she inherited from past generations.

She could recognize, for instance, the jealousies and feelings of inadequacy that her mother had in relation to her mother's only sibling, a brother who was two years her elder and had been their parents' favored child. Dr. A could see that her uncle's two broken marriages, cutoff from his three children, and financial difficulties stemming from repeated, failed efforts to get rich as symptoms of his relationship with his child-focused parents. She also could see that her father, a much favored youngest, was often seeking approval from others and could become angry if approval was withheld, particularly by her mother. She learned how her father had restrained himself from pursuing desired opportunities, such as attending college, because of a belief that he could not succeed. With those new understandings of key members of the older generation, she started to see the problems that surfaced in her life and in her marriage as versions of what had occurred in the past.

Stage III: Progress in Defining a Self

In January 1995, Dr. A moved into her own apartment with a short-term lease. Her husband called daily, was in much better control, and was not drinking. In February, Dr. A was contacted by her former landlady stating her husband, who had remained in their apartment, was not paying his rent. After repeated phone calls, Dr. A firmly told her to talk to Dr. B directly as he was now her sole tenant. Dr. A never heard from the landlady again. This interaction was a turning point for Dr. A, marking a change in her thinking and acting.

Dr. B began to stay with his wife two to three nights a week. By May 1995, Dr. B was drinking more and Dr. A was beginning to react as she had in the past. Predictably, conflict intensified one week after Dr. B's mother was hospitalized for another infection, post-surgery. But this time, Dr. A could see the process, although she was still reacting to it to some degree. While her resolve to live apart from her husband weakened as her mother-in-law's condition deteriorated, she nonetheless was sufficiently outside the process to see the interactions more factually and assess her part more accurately. She had a better level of control over her reactions. One particularly enlightening moment occurred when her husband was staying in her apartment. He was very drunk and very angry and accused her of infidelity. Dr. A thought, "This is him, not me." She responded, "You should see the number of men I have lined up." Dr. A reported the tension dissipated immediately and her husband went to sleep. This was an important milestone, being in the emotional moment but outside of it (detached) at the same time.

Dr. A observed a significant triangle between her husband, his brother, and their mother. Dr. B was in the outside negative position with his mother and brother maintaining their inside position. "You never do enough for me" was the mother's message to Dr. B. Dr. A developed more of an appreciation of the forces influencing her husband's behavior and his need for her acceptance and approval. This was an important triangle that had a significant impact on the interactions in the marriage and Dr. B's functioning. This triangle (mother-in-law, husband, and brother-in-law) and interlocking triangle (mother-in-law, husband, and client) were not given sufficient attention in the therapy process at that time. This was influenced by how the therapist conceptualized the process based on her understanding of theory at that point. It also speaks to the importance of triangles in the in-law system that are often overlooked in therapy, given that the primary focus is on the client's nuclear and extended family.

Dr. B's mother's health continued to decline. A series of infections were followed by more surgeries and hospitalizations. Dr. B told his wife, "Within two days of my mother's death, I will kill myself." In the interactions that followed, Dr. A noted she communicated something different. She could now choose how to respond. The intense emotion and reactivity were not there. Each could say what he or she thought without the threat of emotional pressure. Dr. A noted she was freer than she had ever been. There was a change in her functioning and her husband was responding to it. This allowed both to be more open.

Dr. A reported that her husband thought he had a greater attachment to his mother than most people. He was convinced he had to leave work to care for her. He could not do both. Again this speaks to Dr. B's pattern of giving up self to enhance the functioning and survival of the other. In interactions that followed, both spouses were able to talk about their individual goals. Dr. A addressed her goal to have children and noted she needed to live in an environment where it was possible to support and raise children. She also talked of her long-term desire to return to the United States.

In December 1995, Dr. B's mother had her second amputation. Dr. A noted her husband was consumed by his mother's failing health. That same month, Dr. A's father had quadruple bypass surgery. Dr. A noted there was a lot of anxiety in her family focused on her father's health and her youngest sister's secret marriage to a Brazilian immigrant, an event that had greatly disturbed the system. All of this made the emotional environment highly challenging for both spouses.

In the winter of 1996, Dr. A noted that her life was on hold. Her goals regarding children and returning to the States were far from being realized. The therapist told her she could get off the shelf any time she liked. The therapist noted that one's management of self influences the outcome and asked: How much is putting yourself on hold an outcome of your functioning position in the family? How much does the group keep you stuck? How do you perpetuate that?

In March 1996, Dr. B stopped drinking. He was teaching again and functioning better, in spite of the fact that his mother remained in a critical state. What allowed for this to occur? It may relate to the shift in the marital environment, allowing each spouse to function a little more independently. By May 1996, however, Dr. B was hospitalized for an esophageal bleed while his wife was visiting her family in the United States. Dr. B (as reported by his wife) again questioned whether he could continue to live, as his mother's condition was not improving. He was able to talk with his wife on the most intimate level about life and death and his relationship with his mother. Dr. B noted, " I just don't know how to get out of this." Dr. A was able to listen with a level of neutrality and respect that had not been there before. A neutral presence at an anxious time is the essence of help.

In June 1996, there was a cluster of stressors. A friend of Dr. B's died suddenly. Dr. B's mother developed another infection and was hospitalized in the ICU. Dr. B returned to drinking and Dr. A developed a major sinus infection. Dr. B saw his mother daily. He had the sense she would not eat if he were not present. Dr. A noted, "How hard it is to function for another!"

In September 1996, Dr. B's mother had her final bypass. It was discovered that the original graft had fecal matter in it, indicating it was inserted poorly and had contributed to the repeated infections along with two nicks in her intestine. Later Dr. A had a conversation with her mother-in-law regarding her medical issues over the past two years. Her mother-in-law noted that she had never said, "Stop, find another way! I turned myself totally over to them [professionals involved in her care]."

The couple continued to discuss life goals for each of them. Dr. B reported he could not consider moving to the United States. Dr. A was convinced she would lose self if she continued to keep her life goals on hold.

The marriage was calmer. There was markedly less conflict. In the past year, Dr. A left the house once due to escalating conflict. Dr. A reflected on the nature of conflict in her marriage; each highly sensitive to the other, each pressuring the other to cave in, and each programmed to overinvest in the relationship. Dr. A realized she had given too much importance to what her husband said, especially in the presence of tension, "Once I gave it importance, it became important." Dr. A noted, "I realize now how much of a contribution I made to the marital environment." Many people have difficulty seeing that their action/reaction is as important in maintaining the conflict as the action/reaction of the other.

Dr. A continued to focus on defining a direction for her life. She stated, "It's the first time I am making a thoughtful decision. I don't expect my husband to change." She began to explore adoption possibilities in the United States. In February 1997, she made the decision that she would move forward with plans for self, knowing it would mean divorce. She began planning a separation from her husband. Although she had not yet shared her plans with Dr. B, something important had shifted in the relationship and Dr. B began to drink heavily and react violently. In July 1997, Dr. A told her husband she planned to go forward with the adoption. She was fully aware of what this meant for her life and for the marriage.

In September 1997, Dr. A stated she was a different person. She had her own apartment. Conversations with her husband were calm. Dr. B noted his wife's goals were important to her but he could not join her. Dr. A made plans to move on divorce.

She noted:

> In the past, believing something was based on no evidence. I took what my husband said at face value and based plans on that. I heard words but I didn't look at actions. I ignored the absence of evidence. I never wanted to take charge of my life. I went into relationships with limited information. I believed my husband would make my life better. My brain was not engaged.

The intense need for a relationship interferes with seeing or acting on reality. Since age 10, Dr. A was rarely without a boyfriend. Dr. A noted she would always need to watch her automatic responsiveness, her magnetic attraction to another.

Stage IV: Ongoing Efforts in Defining a Self

In January 1998, Dr. A filed for divorce. She focused on plans to leave her job and move to the United States. Her challenge became planning her own life outside of a relationship. She wondered how much of what she did was in response to emotional programming. She noted that in the past she could not be herself in her family of origin, "I hid myself." Therapy focused on a growing understanding of differentiation of self.

Dr. A noted similarities in her functioning position in her family and in her workplace. She noted that she was adored in both places but realized her popularity was dependent on functioning more for the group than for self. This became apparent as Dr. A prepared to leave her professional positions and made plans to move to the United States. Dr. A's mother wanted her to return to the family home and live with her parents once again. She had been away too long. Dr. A's boss promised promotions and a very large bonus if she would stay. The chair of her department said he would die without her. All of this was evidence of emotional pressure to be for the other. Dr. A could see this now and began to appreciate the power of the emotional system. Dr. A explored overvaluing and undervaluing in her family of origin. She saw evidence of it in her maternal grandparents' marriage, in the relationship between her mother and grandmother, and in her relationship with her mother. Dr. A noted it was natural for her to err on one side or the other. There was a marked lack of objectivity regarding self in the last three generations. She could clearly see her emotional programming and its impact on her functioning.

Dr. A moved to the United States in September 1998 and took an apartment near her extended family. Within the year she was feeling smothered in the family environment and noted it impacted her mood and her level of anxiety. She felt isolated in the clump. She was again face-to-face with the emotional system, responding to the pull to be accepted but wanting to be an integrated self in her family. Dr. A noted, "What I was made to do was be a source of energy for everybody else. I won't get anywhere if I don't toughen up in the face of disapproval."

Dr. A ultimately took a job in Rhode Island, where she continued to teach and work in her field. She began to feel more centered. She had established a relationship with a former male colleague, Mr. C, who was divorced with two children. There were many issues related to his former wife and the functioning of his two teenage children. Dr. A wondered how available he would be, given the intensity of the problems in his nuclear family.

Dr. A refocused on her life goals. She noted she had to fight with herself, "My body rejects what I am going to do," speaking to an increase in physical symptoms as she completed the application process for adoption. At the same time, interesting shifts were occurring in her extended family. One brother's wife became pregnant after 13 years of marriage. Another brother married after living with his partner for 7 years. It is common to see nodal events clump together in a family, which speaks to the influence of emotional forces on behavior.

In August 2000, Dr. A noted how anxious she was in the presence of her parents. She would recoil from her mother and align with her father. "My mother does dumb things that draw my father's ridicule," she said. Dr. A noted that she did similar things with her boyfriend. The therapist noted that the relationship produces this pattern, not the individual. Dr. A saw herself as paralyzed in the parental triangle: "I am not thinking for myself and pulled by forces that say be colorless, don't do anything to upset others." She said, "I think I cut myself off from life more than I had to in my family." Dr. A noted her mother was very sensitive and that she, Dr. A, reacted to that. Her acute sensitivity to her mother influenced her behavior. She would be what her mother wanted her to be, which may have been a small price to pay for having a less anxious mother in the past.

There had been a lot of anxiety at the time of Dr. A's birth. Her mother had married against her parents' wishes. Her mother gave up a college scholarship to marry and move to rural Canada, a place Dr. A's maternal grandmother had opted to escape. Dr. A reported her parents did not know each other very long before they married and she was born one year later.

Dr. A noted her anxiety level was greater since her divorce: "There is a lot of anxiety when I am doing something for myself." She had made several important life decisions and acted on them, which could also account for the increase in anxiety. Progress does not come without its price.

In July 2001, Dr. A was notified by the adoption agency that there was a possibility of adopting a two-year-old boy from Eastern Europe. The process moved quickly and Dr. A picked up her child in December 2001. Dr. A began to have fears about her son. "Will he be shy as I was?" she wondered. The adjustment to parenthood was reasonably smooth and Dr. A found her boyfriend and extended family to be effective resources.

Dr. A had been diagnosed with a fibroid cyst some years before and learned in March 2003 that it had grown by nine centimeters within the past year. Dr. A recalled experiencing stomach pains the first day of her home study (part of the adoption process). In May 2003 Dr. A had a hysterectomy and was diagnosed with ovarian cancer. Her uterus was full of fibroids with a necrotic granulosa cell tumor. This is a rare and slow growing cancer and all lymph nodes were clean. No further treatment was indicated.

By July 2003 Dr. A was clear that she wanted to remarry. She did not want to be a single parent. In April 2004 Dr. A and Mr. C set a wedding date for August 2004. In June Mr. C asked to delay the wedding due to important work commitments, as well as a publisher's deadline on a book he was editing. Dr. A noted these were facts and she went along with his request. Later she realized that she lost self with this decision. She could see that this delay had more to do with anxiety than the content Mr. C presented. Many unresolved issues were surfacing for Mr. C. He did not want to end the relationship but realized he was not ready to commit to marriage. Dr. A considered ending the relationship, but decided to remain and work on her own life. Dr. A noted:

"The issue is not the relationship, it is differentiation of self."

In July 2004, Dr. A heard from her former husband, Dr. B. She reported that he apologized for his behavior in the marriage. He said he could not understand how he acted the way he did. He had expected himself to be in charge and he "could not measure up."

At this point, 2004–2005, Dr. A was beginning to experience a little more emotional separation from her parents. She noted there had always been a lot of tension between her parents. Her father would clam up for weeks at a time and would not talk. "That drove mother around the bend," she said. Dr. A typically aligned with her mother, pushing her father out in the context of the triangle. On a trip to Canada with her parents, Dr. A observed this process and resisted the urge to calm her mother, leaving her parents to deal more directly with each other. To her father she said, "How do you keep your wife so interested in you? She is always talking about you." To her mother she said, "I am so impressed with all the energy you invest in your husband. I always wanted my husband to be as interested in me as you are in Dad." Over the years, Dr. A had talked at length regarding her position in the primary triangle and now she was moving differently, able to speak to the process between her parents without aligning with either one.

Dr. A also reported an activation of the triangle with her mother and first sister. Her sister had been quite negative regarding the adoption. She had been "the only breeder" in the sibling group for a long time. Dr. A noted her sister acted as though Dr. A would not know how to care for a child. She would give Dr. A instructions for the simplest of childcare tasks. Her sister presented as the expert and Dr. A reacted to this. In this triangle Dr. A had frequently been pushed to the outside position. Dr. A was sensitive to this but was now more aware of it. Her mother and sister knew how to do things and Dr. A was perceived as clueless, helpless, and inept in the domestic realm. Dr. A thought she had been programmed to be a single career woman without children. She noted that her mother and sister maintained a consistent disinterest in her career: "They could never understand my devotion to work." Dr. A wondered if her overinvestment in work was related to an unresolved issue for her mother, who had given up a college scholarship to marry and move to Canada. Dr. A had functioned outside the family program when she adopted, without a husband, and the system would predictably react.

Therapy involved continual teaching about the triangle and the emotional system. It is essential to deal with one's reactivity to being pushed out before one can effectively redefine one's functioning in the triangle. Doing what you want to do with your life can push you out of the group. This is the nature of the emotional system. The "triangle hypothesis" defines the triangle as a mechanism in the human species to regulate group members, albeit outside of conscious awareness, for the benefit of the group, even at the expense of some group members. It is effective to the degree that the individual is sensitive and responsive to emotional pressure. When an individual guides self, responding to direction from within self, no longer responding to the emotional cues of the group, the emotional system will react and push that individual to the outside position, a position of rejection. The expected response, according to the rules of the emotional system, is that the pressure of possible rejection will force the individual to return to his/her previous position of functioning for the group (ff. Lassiter, 2008, pp. 64–77). In time, Dr. A was able to understand the emotional system more accurately and moved to put her mother and sister together and self out and said, "I am so lucky to have two caring mothers to teach me."

Dr. A and Mr. C married in September 2005. Dr. A talked about the smooth relationship with her second husband. He too had a stormy and problematic first marriage and both on some level were invested in keeping their relationship smooth. Mr. C adopted Dr. A's son, Michael, shortly after they married. Dr. A described a more conflictual relationship with Michael "almost from the beginning." She described him as a willful child who looked like her former husband. Dr. A noted her son was the opposite of what she was like as a child: "I tried to be a blank slate." She saw her son as much more apt to question, demand, or even attack. In this triangle, the parents were often in the inside position, with Michael pushed to the outside position. Most of the tension was focused between Dr. A and Michael. To tone down the reactivity, the therapist suggested that Dr. A take the problem up a generation; talk to your mother and father, work on the triangle with your two parents, and explore parent offspring relationships in past generations. Buy the idea that the future is better served if you fix the problem in you rather than being busy with your son's attitude. Much time was devoted to discussing the projection process, as well as Michael's functioning position in the triangle. Although the therapist rarely included her own family experiences in her clinical practice, she began to describe her efforts with her nuclear and extended family. The therapist cited many examples of her interactions with her son and husband, and her ongoing efforts to regulate her response to emotional pressure and alter her functioning in the triangle, thereby increasing her tolerance for rejection and disapproval. It should be emphasized that personal material was introduced many years into the therapy process and with a client who had a solid understanding of Bowen theory.

In January 2006, Dr. A reported there was more anxiety in her marriage and noted a shift in her focus from child to husband. She had been working on her reactivity to her son and had some success. She was now in a position to pay more attention to her functioning in the marital relationship. With a decrease in the anxious focus on a child, one predictably sees an increase in tension between the spouses.

In September 2006, Mr. C reported that he had seen an old female friend and found it difficult to cut off the contact. In time he revealed he had been having an affair over several months. This woman, Sandy, was pressuring him to leave his marriage and marry her. Dr. A stated, "I fantasized who my husband was. What I am dealing with now is reality." Dr. A increased her contact with her extended family and her mother-in-law at that time. Dr. A learned that her father had an old girlfriend contact him shortly after his marriage. Her father had had a long-term relationship with this woman and she had ended it to marry someone else. She came back to him after he had married stating she had made a mistake. Hearing this was helpful to Dr. A. The personal interaction and connection with her father was calming. Somehow it seemed to lessen the toxicity of her husband's affair. Also, she talked about her marital difficulties with her mother, who reacted calmly. While she did not speak to her mother again at length about the affair, she found her mother's neutral presence an important emotional resource during that time.

The work she had done in defining a self in her family of origin had enabled a new level of closeness and respect between her and her parents.

The therapist told Dr. A that Sandy was not important. What was important was the marital relationship and her part in it. An affair is simply a symptom of a family relationship problem. No participant in an affair knows your husband as well as you do.

Sandy began to contact Dr. A. It would be automatic for a wife to be angry at the affair, but in this case Dr. A was able to respond to Sandy's interest in her husband without being critical of her or her husband. There were some light moments where Dr. A was able to introduce humor in her interactions with Sandy and her husband. Sandy had a particular interest in their new home and shared with Dr. A advice regarding colors and fabrics. Dr. A would take that information to her spouse: "Sandy thinks this is the best shade for the living room. I am so glad you are attracted to women with good taste. She is so helpful. What would we do without her?"

Her husband reacted intensely and told his wife she was never to speak to Sandy again: "This is no way to be married." The emotional system will react when one does not respond in the expected way, when one is not guided by the group but by self. Dr. A was not looking for an inside position with her husband or Sandy. She was guiding herself based on thinking and knowledge of Bowen theory. Dr. A was consistent in her effort to maintain her outside position in the triangle, while putting her husband and Sandy together in the inside position. Choosing the outside position in the triangle versus being pushed into it is a marker of differentiation. Within a few months, Mr. C ended the affair.

The triangle in the nuclear family intensified following the diagnosis of Mr. C's mother with ovarian cancer (stage IV) in October 2008. Massive doses of chemotherapy left her in a debilitated state. Unresolved issues between Mr. C and his mother surfaced. Mr. C made several attempts to connect with his mother but found the interactions overwhelming. It was at this time that he sought therapy for himself but chose not to continue after two sessions.

In this challenging and more threatening environment, Dr. A noted that most of the tension was now expressed between her and Michael, while the marital relationship remained smooth (a more fixed pattern in the triangle). She had become an astute observer of the triangle and her functioning in it. She was reluctant to give up the togetherness with her husband, but saw how it was influencing her relationship with her son and her son's functioning. Dr. A continued to work on the triangle with her own parents and had a growing appreciation of how much she was still defined by the emotional system. She talked of missed opportunities as a child and young adult and saw this same process repeating for her son. Dr. A noted in the presence of a challenge, she would withdraw into what was comfortable rather than pursuing options that would demand more of her. She saw her son following suit. She noted she was resistant to talking about this with her parents, but more so with her mother. Again the therapist talked of working this out with her mother to free herself: "You can't free your son unless you free yourself."

In 2009 Michael, now age 10, developed symptoms of persistent nausea and vomiting, which were affecting his school attendance and performance. He was diagnosed with lactose intolerance. His behavior at home could be provocative, and as tension escalated he would throw and break household objects or push his mother. Dr. A noted how much her son reminded her of her former husband, speaking to the unresolved issues in her first marriage. She could see how the triangle worked with Michael pushed to the outside position. The anxious focus on Michael kept him on the hot seat, while preserving the comfort of the inside position for each parent. Dr. A noted that since her husband's affair ended, he had been on board in the marriage. Each focused on Michael's symptoms (physical or behavioral) to the point that they would adjust their plans/schedule to accommodate Michael's level of distress. Each had an investment in securing the inside position. To the degree that most of the conflict was contained between Dr. A and Michael, Mr. C was able to maintain a calmer relationship with his son and the marriage remained harmonious.

The therapist spoke with Dr. A about decreasing her focus on her son and his symptoms. The therapist suggested she put Michael in charge of his symptoms. The symptoms were a good barometer of the emotional process. The therapist also focused on how a nice, comfortable, and friendly relationship with a spouse can interfere with one's effort toward developing a better level of differentiation. More questions followed: did her husband regulate her functioning by being "nice" and did she do the same with him? Did being nice become a form of pressure on the other to maintain harmony in the relationship? Could she even think different thoughts in the presence of emotional pressure to be nice? How much did her son's symptoms indicate an unresolved issue in the marriage or with her parents? How much impairment will the system require in order to produce better functioning in some of its members? Since this process is outside of awareness, it takes time to see the facts of one's functioning in the triangle.

Dr. A had some success in pulling back from Michael's difficulties and was freer to work on her own functioning in the triangle. She noted that she saw inadequacies in her son that were also in her and that served to intensify her reactivity. She could see that if she dealt with her own inadequacies she would be less vulnerable to responding to her son's perceived inadequacies. She asked, "How much of me do I project onto him?"

The challenge for Dr. A has been to give up the inside position with her husband and define a position for self freer from the emotional system. She has found it difficult to maintain her effort with her own parents, particularly as the demands of day-to-day life become more significant. The awareness of the emotional process with her own parents is clearly reflected in her many descriptions of it during the course of therapy. Putting that awareness into action is another step along the road toward increasing one's level of differentiation and reducing one's emotional need for the other to whatever degree that is possible.

At the time of this writing, sessions with Dr. A are infrequent. All three members of the nuclear family are functioning well. Michael is in a new school, and in good health with none of his former symptoms. Dr. A and Mr. C are functioning well in their respective careers and there are no significant symptoms in the relationship or in either spouse. The family, nuclear and extended, continues to provide opportunities in relation to Dr. A's effort to differentiate a self.

It should be emphasized that a long-term effort to differentiate a self is always ongoing. Life presents to everyone a series of problems to be solved. How you respond to them is influenced by level of differentiation. Some success in working toward or increasing level of differentiation gives one more flexibility in thinking, and more options to explore in solving life's challenges.

Conclusions

This chapter describes a realistic effort to differentiate a self and demonstrates the role of a therapist, trained in Bowen theory, in this process.

The Therapist's View

This client is among the more motivated. She stays with a problem long enough to figure it out. She was interested in Bowen theory from the onset and has become increasingly more knowledgeable over the years. The therapist has learned as much from this client as the client has learned from her. There is a clear reciprocity in the learning process, which makes clinical practice so rewarding. Anyone involved in a consistent, disciplined effort to raise level of differentiation also becomes involved in applying Bowen theory to other areas of their life and beyond (work systems, social systems, organizations, and society).

Increasing one's level of differentiation is a lifetime effort. The change in basic level may be small but significant, nonetheless. A consistent effort over time allows one to manage self differently than one's basic level of differentiation would have allowed. An individual learns to function in ways that are more responsible, more respectful of self and others, with a greater ability to adjust to changing environments and a more realistic perception of threats. The ability to observe the emotional process gives one the opportunity to know self and others more factually and accurately. There is less of a need to deny who self is. The human is an instinctual organism. His more developed cerebral cortex allows him to observe self and his sensitivity to the emotional system. Bowen theory, particularly knowledge of triangles, provides a way to chart one's course through the emotional system without sacrificing one's own functioning or that of others.

Dr. Bowen gave us the framework to know human behavior through the lens of science (the facts of functioning of the family unit) but he did not tell us what to do with it. That is up to the individual. How far you go with it is up to you. We can all deceive ourselves in thinking we are experts on Bowen theory or the functioning of the human family. How do you know what you do not know? How do you maintain a focus on what you do not know? How do you know when you differentiated a self? What are the data in the family to support this? Is change in you reflected in change in other important family members? Will your grandchildren benefit from your effort? Where is the evidence for that? Bowen theory gives plenty of room for questions and exploration, but each of us has a responsibility to keep our thinking grounded in fact and to watch for our own inevitable distortions. The broadness of Bowen theory allows for a lifetime of research and that is a gift in its purest sense.

Making a research effort out of your own life seems to take hold of some people, like Dr. A, and they cannot give it up. Sure, they may get lazy and comfortable at times, but there is always an issue in the family to get them refocused. Then they see that the emotional system is guiding them and they know they have the choice to respond to group pressure or continue their differentiating effort in the context of the triangle.

A Word About the Therapist

The theoretical evolution of the therapist is all-important. How do therapists maintain their capacity to think systems and what do they do to expand their knowledge base? Some things stand out as critical: maintaining contact with Bowen family systems theory via formal training programs, conferences, consistent coaching, continued and persistent efforts in defining self in one's nuclear family, family of origin, and extended family, the study and research of nonhuman systems, a persistent curiosity and openness to new ideas, a large dose of humility, and the courage to stay with a problem until you figure it out.

This therapist's consistent effort in using Bowen theory in her own life, in her nuclear and extended family, influenced her thinking about problems presented by clinical families. When the therapist was stuck in the triangles in her own family, hearing this client's effort could facilitate the thinking of the therapist, freeing her to move a little differently in her own differentiating effort. It is clear that therapy over time becomes a collegial effort: two individuals with a similar interest in theory and knowledge of the emotional system, reporting on their best thinking about the challenges inherent in membership in every natural system, be it family, organization, society, or nonhuman social systems.

REFERENCES

Bowen, M. (1978). *Family therapy in clinical practice.* New York: Jason Aronson.
Lassiter, L. (2008). The regulatory function of the triangle. In P. Titelman (Ed.), *Triangles: Bowen family systems perspectives* (pp. 63–89). New York: Haworth Press.

13

DIFFERENTIATION OF SELF IN THE PRESENCE OF CHRONIC FAMILY SYMPTOMS

Patricia Hanes Meyer

This chapter will demonstrate the importance of differentiation of self as the foundation for solid functioning in the presence of chronic family symptoms. To raise one's level of solid self, profound work is required. That effort includes strengthening the capacity to remain focused and to act on facts in the face of strong feelings within self. When the effort to become more mature occurs in the midst of chronic family symptoms, it is significantly more difficult because chronic family symptoms tend to increase anxiety and to sustain that high anxiety chronically. The presence of moderate to severe anxiety makes the task of focusing on facts, and acting on those facts, much more difficult.

The process of developing a more solid self requires learning about extended family history and emotional patterns, one's own emotional patterns, nodal events and their impact, and the triggers within self that launch the flow of immaturity. Such knowledge makes it possible to recognize the difference between facts and feelings and to be able to act on facts in the presence of intense feelings.

At no time over the years of developing Bowen theory did Dr. Bowen ever describe "phases" in the process of developing a solid self. However, as I studied Bowen theory beginning in 1970, and began to work to develop a more solid self, it became clear to me that there were four specific, completely intertwined phases of work in the process of developing a more solid self.

The first phase consisted of completing a meticulous and thorough study of one's extended family. In the process, myths and emotional reactions toward family members became clearer, which allowed a new level of objectivity about the extended family to emerge. For those who are able to develop more objectivity about family members and their patterns of functioning, a natural awareness of the patterns within self also emerge, leading to phase two. As observations of emotional patterns within self become painfully clear, so too does the clarity about what patterns would have to be changed if self is to function in a more solid way. The focus on building a strategy to change dysfunctional patterns within self begins in phase three. Phase four is the continuation of phases one–three for a lifetime.

Differentiation of Self: The Four Phases of Therapy

While no two individuals or family systems are alike, these four phases of Bowen family systems therapy are necessary for individuals to build a more solid self.

All individuals begin at some point in phase one, *the phase of learning about the history of one's family*. The goal of phase one is to build a road map of the significant facts and emotional patterns of the extended family. This knowledge provides a context for understanding the issues that self is experiencing in the present. In phase two, the focus shifts to discovering *the significant facts and emotional patterns of the self*. Some individuals never move beyond the symptom presentation and history taking of the extended family. Other individuals may be able to make observations of the extended family patterns but not be able to make those same observations about self. Phase three occurs automatically for those who have been able to gather facts about the extended system and also about self. It becomes automatically clear what *patterns in self have to be changed for the self to function in a more responsible, solid way*. Some individuals may be able to observe both the emotional patterns in the family and in self but are unable to take action to change those patterns. Additionally, there will be those who can objectively observe the family, and self, build and activate strategies to modify those dysfunctional patterns, but once they experience symptom relief they are no longer motivated to continue the effort. For those who are motivated, there will be a steady movement to develop *the capacity to live a responsible life, grounded on principles, responsibility for self, and respect for the reality of others*. This is a lifelong process.

Phase One: Discovering the Historical Facts and Emotional Patterns of the Extended Family

What occurs at the beginning of therapy is crucial. For the clinician, it is a delicate balance between meeting an individual or family where they are emotionally, the symptom focus, while also beginning to acquire knowledge about the individual and his or her family emotional system. The therapist must be mindful that the individual usually has come to therapy with some degree of fixed focus, anxiety, reactivity, and doubt that truly changing his or her reality is possible. If the therapist has respectfully listened and validated those emotional concerns, while calmly asking factual questions about the family of origin, an immediate connection is created.

A different picture emerges in therapy when the questions of a therapist connect with the emotionality of the family and its anxious concerns, when the questions and focus of the therapist are on target for the family or individual. Individuals frequently respond to a connected question with a comment such as "that was a good question" or "I have never thought about that before." There is an immediate thoughtfulness, although not necessarily a lasting thoughtfulness, at this early stage. Individuals frequently leave initial sessions visibly calmer, knowing that there is someone who has connected to their anxious concerns . . . in a way that is objective and neutral. The therapist has positioned himself or herself in this way to provide individuals with an opportunity to *think* about a problem in their families about which they have felt frantic and to *discover* their patterns of emotionality and their families' patterns of emotionality, in the context of knowledge about human functioning. The therapist's office, a neutral learning space, creates an environment in which individuals can be productive "learners," capable of building solid change (Meyer, 1998, p. 76).

The tasks of phase one include: stimulating curiosity about the individual's history, creating a thorough multigenerational family diagram filled with indicators of how the members of the family system are functioning, defining the emotional patterns of the system, and focusing on nodal events that have had an impact on the system.

The multigenerational diagram serves both the therapist and the individual. For the therapist, the diagram *is a road map* of what has occurred, its likely impact, and what will need to be resolved for the individual to become a more solid self. It reflects the emotional intensity between the generations. For the individual, discussing the diagram provides a connection between events and the emotions they engender between the people in the system.

Curiosity is crucial to the success of the effort. The lens widens through the accumulation of new facts and changes the individual's perspective on self and on the family. As the neocortex begins to *think in new ways* about old emotionally laden history, a new level of objectivity emerges that acts to lower anxiety. For many, emotional reactivity lessens through the process of thoughtfully reviewing the system and challenges long-held assumptions about self and the system.

What is occurring is that the individual is discovering the difference between *fact* and *feeling*. Kerr (Kerr and Bowen, 1988, pp. 30–33) provides an excellent description of the difference between facts and feelings. The individual learns that developing the capacity to *think about* emotional process in the family and in self provides an entirely new ability to act based upon facts, in spite of intense feelings. This capacity makes it possible to define the actions of self separately from the automatic feeling process and the ability to resist the automatic need for togetherness with others, for sameness, and for approval. At the same time, it provides the energy to stand alone on issues when necessary because the self accepts and understands the facts at hand and can remain focused on those facts in the presence of intense feeling.

The significance of accepting and understanding the difference between fact and feeling and acting upon that difference represents one of the significant contributions of Bowen theory. It is also one of the most misunderstood aspects of the theory. Over the years, Bowen theory's focus on searching for facts of functioning in the midst of intense feeling has been interpreted as being "against" and defocusing feelings in the therapeutic process. Nothing could be further from the truth. Bowen theory focuses the effort to become a *thoughtful* observer about the feeling patterns within self. It does not encourage the individual to re-experience or move into the feelings. Rather, it focuses on the facts of the feelings: *when* the feelings are triggered, *what* was occurring when the feelings were triggered, *what* have been the past emotional patterns of those individuals present in the current situation. These observations allow the individual to be fully aware of the intense feelings he or she is experiencing while remaining focused on the facts at hand. This distinction allows an individual to act on the facts thoughtfully while strongly feeling the associated emotions. The capacity to act on facts in the presence of intense feelings is the marker of a more mature self. In Bowen theory, solid self is built on a commitment to live based upon facts, principles, and responsibility for self, in contrast to living based on reacting automatically in the emotional field. That reaction may include feelings of sadness, anger, or physiological reactions such as a "knot in the stomach" or a pounding headache. Reactivity does not focus on the facts at hand, only on the feelings that are felt.

Discovering all the intense emotional patterns in the multigenerational history is critical for building maturity. Individuals will need to search for *opposite patterns* (compensation) as well as *patterns of repetition* (replication), since both represent repeating family patterns. Responding to intense patterns may emerge into behaving in an opposite manner—the daughter of a mother who yells when upset may be unable to yell "when the house is on fire." On the other hand, the daughter may become a yeller just as her mother was. When these patterns become clear and evident, individuals gain fresh perspective on the emotional dilemmas that brought them into therapy. Suddenly the problem at hand begins to make sense. The mystery is gone. And as current dilemmas begin to make sense, the overwhelming feelings about them begin to lessen. A frequent response will be "no wonder this is so hard for me." Things that make sense don't feel nearly as heavy or unchangeable.

The individual will need to develop a deep respect for the influence of nodal events, those events that engender high levels of emotion in any relationship system. One example would be the unexpected death of a young parent in the family as compared with the death of an elderly grandparent. Another would be the onset of a chronic disease in one member that creates significant impact on many other members of the family. Even more important is the effect of a *cluster* of nodal events on the system. These are several high-intensity events that happen in a short period of time. Loss of a job and loss of a parent within a few months would be an example. Ending a marriage and losing one's home would be another. With such events occurring at the same time, it is more difficult to thoughtfully and effectively respond to any of the events. There is a feeling of being out of control, or being unable to completely focus on any one matter satisfactorily because the other crises demand attention at the same time. Having respect for the power of a cluster allows the individual to become calmer and accepting of the multiple pulls on self to do the best one can do regardless of how complex and demanding the cluster is. Dr. Bowen described this process as "the emotional shock wave" phenomenon. Bowen theory allows the individual the perspective to determine which aspects of each issue are most crucial to be acted upon.

Discovering the functional patterns within self, the individual will no longer be so emotional, panicked, or defensive about current dilemmas. The individual begins to connect patterns within self with what has been discovered in the family history and family patterns. From learning Bowen theory, the individual now understands that what has been discovered in one's own family is, in fact, consistent with emotional process in all human families. This is not to say that the individual does not continue to be upset about his or her own dilemmas but they are now understood in a more objective manner, from a more thoughtful point of view.

Phase Two: Discovering the Historical Facts and Emotional Patterns of Self

In phase two the focus turns to the individual. With the same wide lens, the individual works to define his or her emotional patterns, those that replicate patterns in the family of origin and those that are opposite to patterns in the family of origin.

With the backdrop of extended family history, many become aware of the patterns in self naturally and often quickly. For those who struggle with viewing the family history factually, it is difficult to focus on self because the individual is caught up in blaming others or the environment for the dilemmas he or she faces. Individuals who can accept those facts begin to accept responsibility for their own lives and struggles. Understanding the factual evolution of the dilemma leads to possible choices of action as he or she assumes responsibility for the part that self has played in the problem at hand. The individual also gets clear about those aspects of the problem over which self has little or no control, including how others choose to respond. Accepting responsibility for self leads to a new level of self-respect, empowerment, and increased functioning. As with phase one, the individual who accepts responsibility for self often automatically begins to move toward formulating a structure for personal change. Knowledge of where functional change is needed naturally comes into focus.

Phase Three: Building a Strategy for Changing Self

Formulating a strategy for personal change is the focus of phase three. For most individuals, many months of therapeutic work discovering facts and patterns have occurred before they are ready to develop a strategy. Their strategy will be grounded in knowledge about human functioning. Bowen (1978, pp. 529–549) provides an excellent description of the process of building a more solid self.

Formulating a strategy for change is entirely different from using "technique," which is a specific action designed for a specific situation. Developing a strategy based on Bowen theory involves defining life principles that guide *how* an individual *assesses a situation, makes decisions,* and *takes action.* Formulating a strategy can guide an individual throughout his or her lifetime. Examples of life principles might be: 1) Whenever possible, attend all significant family events; 2) always act to correct an error in functioning such as failing to make an apology; 3) be very respectful of the emotional intensity associated with exits and entrances in and out of emotional systems. Such principles can allow the individual to use knowledge to guide decision-making. Thoughtful consistency in an individual tends to create trust from others, and gives predictability of what others can expect from self. An example would be: say what you mean, mean what you say. Emotional systems that have members who function with thoughtful consistency tend to be calmer.

Knowing the predictable patterns of an emotional system is the bedrock for a strategy of change. That knowledge makes it possible to know what tends to increase or decrease reactivity in the system. When anxiety increases in a system, thinking decreases and polarization and reactivity increase. When anxiety decreases in a system, the system becomes calmer and more flexible. The impact of knowing what will increase or decrease reactivity in a system will be demonstrated in the family case study discussed later in the chapter.

Further, the knowledge that has been gained in phases one and two, as well as remembering the principles one believed prior to the onset of acute anxiety, yield a new capacity for observation and thinking in the individual. This new capacity is very different from a specific technique developed for a specific situation. Cause and effect thinking is less effective than systems thinking when facing a complex problem.

Phase Four: The Lifelong Work of Solid Functioning

Phase four is the life work of changing self. Based on thorough knowledge of the system and of self, developing a strategy for changing dysfunctional emotional patterns is possible. Phase four is the work of thoughtful living as dilemmas are encountered. With a defined belief system, it is possible to say and to do those things necessary to have a deep sense of inner peace and pride in one's life journey. Making decisions based on seeking approval, or avoiding disapproval, can be significantly lessened and sometimes eliminated.

The flow from phase one through phase four is not a smooth one. New data and new crises will yield new, previously unknown data about the family emotional process. The new data lead the individual back to phase one: data collection and review of emotional patterns. The work at changing self continues.

Clinical Case

Mr. and Mrs. Morris entered therapy in the mid-1990s to focus on their stressed marriage. Mr. Morris had many complaints about the marriage, with the primary focus being the lack of intimacy, both physical and emotional. His view was that Mrs. Morris was obsessed with their son and therefore not available to him. Mrs. Morris was baffled and distressed by her husband's dissatisfaction. Her loss of fertility due to endometriosis had been a painful loss for her. As a result of the infertility, the couple adopted a son who was one and a half years old at the time. Within weeks of beginning therapy, Mr. Morris decided to separate, moved out, and quickly began dating. He remained involved in taking care of their young son, who by then was seven. Mrs. Morris continued on with the therapy, now as a single parent and as a single woman. She has worked for more than 16 years on differentiating a self in the relationship with her son. That work continues to the present.

Phase One: Discovering the Historical Facts and the Emotional Patterns of the Extended Family

Mrs. Morris adjusted to the separation reasonably well. In spite of difficulties with sleep, she adjusted to the responsibilities of maintaining her home, responsibilities of her demanding job, and responsibilities for her son. There was depression, sadness, and loss. As she was processing the end of her marriage, an ending she did not want, she was also constructing her family diagram and beginning to learn about the family patterns. She gathered facts about each family member for three generations, looking at the emotional patterns of each one and describing the history of what factually occurred in the life of each member (see Figure 13.1).

Mrs. Morris was the middle of three children. At the age of four, her mother committed suicide, leaving the children in the care of their father, who could be highly critical, had poor boundaries, and became physical with the children on occasion. He remarried shortly after his wife's suicide and had four additional children. The stepmother did not connect positively to her three stepchildren, which created additional trauma for Mrs. Morris and her siblings. Mrs. Morris was reported to closely resemble her biological mother, which may have been a factor in the negative relationship that

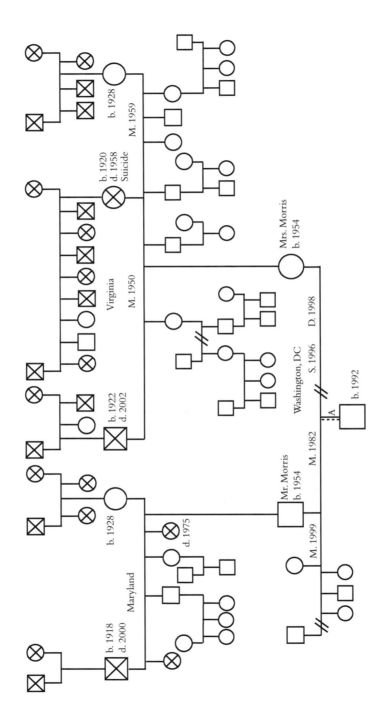

Figure 13.1 Mrs. Morris's Family Diagram

developed between her and her stepmother. There were varying degrees of tension between the two sets of children, between the stepmother and the stepchildren, and between the father and all of the children.

Mrs. Morris reported that her early adulthood was chaotic. She had not learned that her mother's death had resulted from a suicide until she was 24. Distraught by this new information, she went through a period of emotional distress that ultimately resulted in seeking the assistance of a psychiatrist. There were numerous relationships with men during this period and two overdoses.

Working on the family diagram was very fruitful for Mrs. Morris. She was able to begin to see functioning patterns among members of the family and to look at those patterns factually for the first time. Her typical response to the reactive relationship system and its chaos was to take whatever was said or done very personally, not understanding the reasons members of the family seemed to treat her so unkindly. Her relationship with her full siblings was positive although distant. Her relationships with two of her stepsiblings, the youngest sister and the brother above her, were very adversarial but better with the other two stepsiblings. The youngest stepsister was always critical of Mrs. Morris, which was a constant source of anxiety and distress for her. These relationships left Mrs. Morris with a strong feeling of "not fitting in" and being "less than other people." She struggled with feeling isolated, which increased the tendency to respond to interactions as personal slights.

Beginning to look at the functioning patterns of her father, stepmother, and siblings allowed Mrs. Morris to become more thoughtful. Over the next several months, she began to observe her own patterns of behavior, and her tendency to react began to decrease.

At the same time, Mrs. Morris began to observe the patterns of behavior in Mr. Morris. She could observe his role in his family of origin and now see how emotional behavior patterns from his family had played out in the marriage. By this point Mr. Morris had remarried and had three stepchildren. As he moved into a new marriage and became a stepfather, his involvement with his adopted son decreased significantly.

It is interesting to note that for all of the emotional struggles Mrs. Morris had in her family and personal relationships, her work history reflected a very different picture. In her demanding work as a consultant, Mrs. Morris was consistently very successful. Her work was technical in nature, and she brought to that work consistent, determined precision. Even in the year after the marital separation, Mrs. Morris received a significant promotion. The emotionality that was so draining in personal relationships was far less present on the job. Even in times of high stress due to high-level briefings, critique sessions, and unbending deadlines, she was able to stay on track and thrive. This is not to say that there weren't times of conflict with colleagues, or times when her feelings would be hurt. Both did occur but, in spite of them, Mrs. Morris kept her focus clear and successfully managed that process.

Phase Two: Discovering the Historical Facts and Emotional Patterns of the Self

Symptom Development in the Nuclear Family

Bowen theory describes three categories of symptoms that can develop within a nuclear family: 1) unresolved marital conflict, 2) symptoms within one of the spouses, and 3) symptoms in one or more of the children. The Morris family had a combination of all three categories. Families in which symptom presentation moves among the members are more flexible emotional systems. Families that present a fixed symptom in one child, for example, are more rigid emotional systems. The Morris nuclear family presented with marital conflict that ended in divorce, frequent medical issues in Mrs. Morris (although none became debilitating), symptoms of depression in Mr. Morris, and a significant child focus on the son.

The therapy focused specifically on Mrs. Morris's work regarding her relationship with her son, and on her tendency to overreact to others. Bowen provides a description of nuclear family process and the three arenas of dysfunction in *Family Therapy in Clinical Practice* (1978, pp. 376–379).

At the time of the marital separation, the adopted son was seven years old. His functioning was appropriate for a seven-year-old. However, several school personnel had observed that he was "different." He was active in sports, particularly baseball, and participated in Boy Scouts.

As the son became a preadolescent and a young teen, indicators of an exquisite sensitivity began to emerge. If the son felt pushed or pressured, he would push back or withdraw. He would react strongly to expectations. Clearly capable of learning and academic accomplishment, his grades vacillated from good to poor. In sports, he could have a good game, attend baseball practice, and then skip the next game. Mrs. Morris never knew what to expect and felt she was always walking on eggshells.

The acute sensitivity developed into deeper symptoms. He became depressed and highly emotional, refusing at times to attend school. Several different mental health professionals evaluated him, with assessments ranging from depression requiring medication to depression requiring institutionalization. The deeper symptoms set the stage for a couple of very traumatic years in which Mrs. Morris experienced acute anxiety about her son. The son was isolated and made statements about suicide. Interestingly, Mrs. Morris had experienced some of the same emotions after she learned of her mother's suicide. Mr. Morris remained minimally involved during this difficult period. Mrs. Morris had to be the leader. Mrs. Morris continued to overfunction and Mr. Morris continued to underfunction in relation to the son.

Mrs. Morris's work at observing functioning patterns in the family and in herself resulted in her becoming more able to observe and to know *how* and *when* to connect with her son. This knowledge emerged partly because she could learn from those communications that backfired and made matters worse. That learning might not have been possible had Mrs. Morris not become so capable of observing patterns within herself and within her family of origin.

The son survived the volatile years in which it was not clear whether he would make it without completely collapsing or committing suicide. His later high school years were chaotic, with periods of reasonable grades and functioning mixed with periods of failing to do work, take a test, or go to sports practices or games.

Phase Three: Building a Strategy for Changing Self

What happened during the "at risk" years? An effective medication was finally identified, as was an effective therapist for the son. Equally, or more important, was the leadership of Mrs. Morris, who became so knowledgeable about her own emotional patterns and those of her son that she was able to provide a stable, secure environment in which he could begin to build "functional feet" upon which to stand. For a description of Bowen's approach to defining a self see Kerr (1988, pp. 107–111). One additional factor was the therapist's work monitoring the anxiety of self before beginning any session with Mrs. Morris during the at-risk years. Before ever welcoming Mrs. Morris into the therapy office, the therapist evaluated the level and nature of anxiety within herself so that the therapist's anxiety would not be added to the emotional system of Mrs. Morris, a system already on overload, in which the son was at risk of an impulsive suicide.

The secure environment was built through times of high anxiety, trial and error, and ever-deepening knowledge about the family emotional system: both Mrs. Morris's emotional system and her son's emotional system. Understanding the difference between *"responsible to,"* and *"responsible for,"* was another helpful pillar of Bowen theory. Mrs. Morris became very clear on what her responsibility was *to* her son. That responsibility included providing a predictable structure in their home and managing her anxiety and energy. Her son had to have real responsibilities in his own life, and to participate on the team of mother and son managing a home, which included dogs.

Mrs. Morris developed an exquisite knowledge of when to *move in* and engage the son's emotional field, and when to *remain neutral* toward his emotional field. This knowledge allowed Mrs. Morris to get through reactive emotional times without pouring her emotional anxiety onto her agitated son. Had she done so, he might have plummeted back into risk of collapse or suicide. She learned that these were times to fix his favorite meals, to turn her back on how much he was watching TV or playing computer games. And she never applied pressure to function: "If he flunks this course, we'll figure out what to do next." None of the "failures"—failing a class, not getting into a college in a timely manner, not graduating on time—that can stir emotional anxiety in parents were options for Mrs. Morris. Had she reacted anxiously, the son would likely have returned to being "at risk." This knowledge was so real for Mrs. Morris that it was similar to the person who knows if he were to eat peanuts, he would likely die.

Moreover, Mrs. Morris learned how to work effectively with the emotional fields that surrounded her and her son. One critical piece was to connect with school officials. The son had an Individualized Education Plan (IEP) due to learning difficulties. Mrs. Morris experienced the full range of reactions to the teachers and counselors, including frustration, anger, and disappointment as they would underrespond to an issue with the son, or fail to follow through even when the plan they had agreed to had been appropriate. Just as she kept a neutral emotional field at home when the son was particularly challenged, Mrs. Morris learned to keep her contact with the school personnel neutral to positive but with a newly developed firmness. Further, she learned by observing her son's relationship with extended family members and which ones to encourage to get involved with him when needed. For instance, his paternal grandmother represented softness and sweetness for her grandson. While struggling with diabetes in her own life, the grandmother was consistently sweet in encouraging the grandson. During a period when the son was highly reactive, the paternal grandmother might be invited for dinner with no mention of the son's current emotional arousal. Mrs. Morris learned to reach out to the few families with whom the son was comfortable, and with whom he would enjoy himself. A couple of neighborhood families included fathers who naturally reached out to her son in "fatherly" ways, providing critical validation of his worth and value. Finally, Mrs. Morris developed awareness of the activities that worked well for the mother and son. For instance, she knew the son loved to hike, which she enjoyed as well. She learned to say: "it's been such a tough work week, I need to go hiking," and requested that he come also. In almost all cases, the son would participate, providing relaxed, enjoyable hours of connection.

The capacity of Mrs. Morris to connect to her son while minimizing her anxiety followed years of enormous work on learning Bowen theory and focusing on her own functioning. Bowen theory provides such a powerful process for change through the consistent focus on facts and the emotional patterns found within an emotional system. This allows a broad focus on a dilemma to encompass a wide range of facts. For example, Mrs. Morris struggled the most with her own immaturity when considering issues that the son had with the school, teachers and counselors, and his IEP. Her automatic reaction was to protect and defend her son concerning school issues and to be angry and blaming of school officials. What would occur in therapy sessions as each school issue arose was a review of the facts. The therapist's questions would include: "In what ways did the son contribute to the development of the problem?" Defensive answers would come from Mrs. Morris to questions such as "If your son is going to be successful in adulthood, what is it that he needs to learn or accept about the school's expectations?" "What is the reality of the teachers who have many students to follow?" "What response from you would encourage them to work productively with your son on this issue?" "What responses would lessen the likelihood that they will do so?" "How can you approach the meeting with school officials and your son that will maximize the best possible outcome?" "Knowing your tendency to get defensive, how could you approach the meeting so that you can be thoughtful, calm, and firm?"

Such therapy sessions followed hours of earlier sessions of respectful listening as Mrs. Morris would reflect on the problem at hand and her feelings about the current reality. She expressed a desire to criticize the teachers and counselors, and how unfair it all was to her son, who was struggling. There was significant validation in those early sessions about the strong feelings, the fact that the son was struggling, and that this dilemma was truly hard for him. For an individual to be able to hear and grasp the broad facts about her or his dilemma, it is crucial that the therapist validate the feelings. Then, focus on theory becomes effective, allowing the individual to become respectful of reactivity in the other and in self. That respectful knowledge about the predictability of emotional patterns allowed discussions about likely outcomes: if *action A* is chosen rather than *action B*. It would include facts about likely outcomes if path A is chosen rather than path B. Such discussions occurred with consistent acknowledgement that the daily dance between facts and anxiety is a struggle for everyone, including the therapist and the individual in the office.

The therapeutic process is a two-way process. Not only is the individual growing with new knowledge and the accompanying decrease in reactivity, but the therapist is as well. No two individuals are alike; they each approach the task of focusing on facts of an emotional dilemma in his or her own way. The use of an I-position or humor may be described in a manner that is unique and delightful. There can be mutual respect in the therapeutic process between the therapist and the individual. In the case of Mrs. Morris, it became clear that she was the expert in the room on when to, and when not to, define an expectation of her son.

With the combination of what Mrs. Morris had learned and acted upon, the miracle happened. The son graduated from high school *on time!* Literally, up to the day of the ceremony, it was not clear whether this would occur. There were numerous roadblocks in several of the classes that could have precluded the graduation. Mrs. Morris faced each "snag" with the same strategy of *when* to *define self* and *an expectation,* or *when to simply listen* as one by one the issues were resolved. Of course, high school graduation did not solve the son's functional difficulties. However, it was truly an amazing accomplishment for a teenager once at risk of not even living to graduate. On the day of graduation, it represented an accomplishment that placed the son on the same level as higher functioning teenagers headed straight to a good college.

He had graduated on time with his high school class. Needless to say, following the celebration, the son's future would continue to be a struggle, unlike that of many of his classmates.

Following high school graduation, the son enrolled in the community college system where he began pursuing basic courses. Several semesters later, he has achieved grades of "B" and "C," has dropped classes, dropped one semester, and started back again. This was not unlike his high school pattern except that his completed classes were because of independent self-management, getting up, getting to school on time, and doing his work while mother was away at her job and no teacher or counselor was checking on him. What remains ahead is to complete college, obtain a job, and continue to build independence. It is not yet clear how successful the son can be in these arenas.

By the time Mrs. Morris was ready to build strategies to address her emotional patterns in relationships, she had become very clear about the difference between facts and feelings. The phase one work of building a factual family history, and the phase two work of understanding her own emotional patterns, and historical events, prepared Mrs. Morris for beginning to change the dysfunctional patterns in her functioning. For those who can embrace the study of their own family history, the difference between fact and feeling becomes clear except, of course, when becoming acutely anxious, which makes the distinction much more difficult to keep in focus.

For Mrs. Morris, that work was particularly critical in the relationships with her husband, her father, her stepmother, her most difficult half-sister, and her son. In regard to the relationship with Mr. Morris, Mrs. Morris came to understand that part of her attraction to him had been because of his kindness toward her after she had had a series of late teen and early adult relationships that were not healthy or functional. With that kindness also came his neediness, passivity, and a frequent failure to be trustworthy in difficult moments. Not being there when needed, when emotional pressure became difficult or intense, was also a pattern. An example was when her son had a make-or-break project for a class and he had become so distraught under the pressure that he threw himself on his bed, cried, and withdrew. Mrs. Morris sat down on his bedroom floor and remained there for a long period, providing the son the security of her presence and assurance. In dramatic crises like this one, Mr. Morris often just left. Mr. Morris wasn't intending to be destructive in his behavior; he simply wasn't able to participate during the difficult times of the at-risk years. By the time the divorce became final, Mrs. Morris had come to realize that she would not want to reconcile with Mr. Morris had he wanted to do so. Nevertheless, accepting and adapting to his second wife and three stepchildren and watching a new world emerge for Mr. Morris was very difficult at times.

Mrs. Morris had desperately wanted more than one child. The first few times Mrs. Morris was around Mr. Morris and his new wife at family events, she became deeply sad and depressed. It took a long time before Mrs. Morris could respond to those "everyone present" moments with only mild or moderate discomfort. Never enjoyable, the joint events became more workable, and the discomfort was accepted as a part of the new reality. When events included inviting Mr. Morris's new family into her home, the hurdle was particularly distressing. However, that hurdle was eventually crossed several times by Mrs. Morris, resulting in a level of calm though uncomfortable acceptance.

Work to accurately understand her father's functioning was both very difficult and very freeing for Mrs. Morris. The facts painted a picture of a man who could behave inappropriately in expressing affection, though never inappropriate touching, which left Mrs. Morris feeling discomfort around him. He had a temper that could include verbal meanness and occasional face slapping. His alcohol use may have contributed to some of these physical actions. Yet, as her knowledge of his emotional patterns increased, she discovered that her father had suffered several major losses in his life, including the suicide of his first wife. He never appeared to recover from that loss. Mrs. Morris did not know whether that was because of guilt, lost love, or both. Prior to the suicide, the father had enjoyed a remarkable, highly successful job that required international travel. After the suicide, left with three young children ranging in age from eight to three, he could no longer leave the country for travel. Ultimately that career path came to an end. He never completely recovered from the ripple of the loss of his wife and his career. Finally, he found himself solely responsible for his young children's welfare and needs.

In the beginning, looking at the relationship with the stepmother was very stressful for Mrs. Morris. Four years old when her mother committed suicide, five years old when her stepmother joined the family, Mrs. Morris described feelings of bafflement as she sought to understand the negative tension in her childhood. She described her stepmother as having low self-esteem and depression, being overweight, and suffering high anxiety riding elevators or flying in airplanes. Mrs. Morris's mother was described as having been beautiful and having had a high IQ. Of the three original children, Mrs. Morris was told that she was the one who most resembled the beautiful mother. That fact did not help her relationship with the stepmother whom she described as insecure. Additionally, Mrs. Morris's high anxiety, exhibited by her need in childhood to keep her bedroom light on at night, made the stepmother nervous. There was an overall rejection by the stepmother and failure to connect with Mrs. Morris and her biological siblings. Further, the stepmother did not have good relationships with her own biological children much of the time.

The relationship with the youngest half-sister was and continues to be prickly. She is a successful lawyer who always acted as the leader of the siblings. She married a physician and they had three children. While living out of town, she would make pronouncements about what was or was not going to happen in regard to their parents. Of the four half-siblings, only two produced children. It had been emotionally important to Mrs. Morris to establish a relationship with the difficult half-sister's family, hoping for her son to have good experiences with his cousins. The half-sister rejected all attempts by Mrs. Morris to create time together. Because of the leadership status of the half-sister and Mrs. Morris's desire for closeness and connection, the half-sister's rejections were deeply painful to Mrs. Morris, who felt like a misfit in the family, even though she had better relationships with other siblings and half-siblings. Acceptance and approval from this half-sister was enormously important to her. Over the years of work on this relationship, Mrs. Morris made several more overtures toward the half-sister that were more effectively executed. Those overtures included several respectful, well-written letters attempting to build a connection. All overtures were turned down or ignored. Ultimately, Mrs. Morris developed a more factual view of the emotional patterns of the half-sister toward her and the rest of the family. Her feelings were no longer hurt by the distance and rejection. Indeed, if the half-sister were to come to town, Mrs. Morris would experience an increase in anxiety, but she was no longer hurt or wounded. She would regret that it couldn't be different and be annoyed at the half-sister's actions and statements but without being hurt. This accomplishment was of major importance because the approval of the half-sister had been of major importance. It was accompanied by new levels of self-respect that Mrs. Morris enjoyed. It was the result of her work with her blended nuclear family along with the significant level of responsibility and leadership that she now enjoyed within the family. She was much more free from the emotional need for approval and acceptance that had gripped her for so many years. In fact, her home became the center for family gatherings once the stepmother's functioning deteriorated. Those gatherings included the difficult half-sister on several occasions.

While observing the functioning patterns of the members of the extended and nuclear family, Mrs. Morris automatically began to observe her own reactivity to those various functioning patterns and to the arenas of her own dysfunction.

Mrs. Morris's parents lived locally, as did several of her siblings. The family system demonstrated chronic volatility and an abundance of unresolved issues were always present. Emotional reactivity was always occurring. Mrs. Morris moved back and forth, pondering her failed marriage, her nuclear family, and her extended family. The level of reactivity in the extended family provided a rich opportunity for observation. As she observed family members' functioning patterns, and gathered factual information about each one's reality, she became more thoughtful, less reactive, and more capable of taking actions in regard to the issues at hand. She became calmer and clearer about what she could do and what she couldn't do in the system, if she were to maintain solid boundaries on what was and was not her responsibility to the system. However, when the family reactivity was high, it was more of a struggle to be clear about what was occurring, how she was reacting, and what steps she needed to take to define her own responsibilities.

Mrs. Morris's efforts demonstrated the power of facts for those who seek them and the effectiveness of therapy based on Bowen theory. She exemplified the benefits of long-term therapy. Shorter therapy can have the outcome of a shift in the family's functioning in response to the work of one or more family members to become more thoughtful in their actions. Individuals can become knowledgeable about the family emotional process and their own patterns but may not be able to build a solid base for thinking and behaving. The family can operate at a calmer level until the next emotional issue arises. When it is possible to observe a family system, over long periods of time, it becomes apparent that there is, or is not, in fact, a more solid level of functioning. With Mrs. Morris, the capacity to move in and out of relationships without returning to the old pattern of taking difficult interactions personally and feeling rejected has been consistently observable.

Phase Four: The Lifelong Work of Solid Functioning

Mrs. Morris has made the commitment to remain focused on the functioning of self, day-in, day-out. That requires acceptance and respect for anxiety as well as determination to assume as much responsibility for self as possible so that functioning can be at the highest possible level.

Anxiety is crucial for survival. Without it the species could not experience longevity. It is anxiety that causes us to notice in our peripheral vision a nearby car driving too fast, to notice a subtle change in functioning of an elderly parent, or to notice a stranger approaching inappropriately. However, should anxiety become chronic, the forces that act to protect now become forces to wear down and compromise functioning. The medical literature is filled with articles on the negative effects of cortisol, the fight-and-flight hormone, when it chronically pours into our bloodstream. For one description of how the brain functions read MacLean (1990).

Our society today is surrounded with threats, those that are real and those that are imagined. To function at the highest possible level, one must be continually conscious of the role anxiety plays in day-to-day life. It is necessary to develop an overall strategy for living that permits the *self to control anxiety* rather than *anxiety to control the self.* One or the other will dominate. Kerr (1988, pp. 112–133) provides a detailed description of chronic anxiety.

Not only is it necessary to understand the power that anxiety can wield on functioning, it is also necessary to know its characteristics and to be vigilant in watching for those characteristics. One must know the behaviors within self that will emerge when anxiety spikes. This awareness allows the self to predict a likely spike, to prepare for it, and to minimize or prevent it from occurring. One must know subtle features of anxiety that create a slip in functioning so subtle that were the self not monitoring, the slip would not be noticed until symptoms emerged. What is required is a continual monitoring of the facts in our reality and the feelings that emerge from those facts, which create a lifelong struggle to act on facts in spite of powerful reactivity. Being focused on facts along with being aware of the intensity of anxiety within self, and in the surrounding systems, is the work of functioning as a solid self for the remainder of one's life (Kerr, 1988, pp. 132–133).

The Process of Long-Term Therapy
With Mrs. Morris

Mrs. Morris responded to Mr. Morris initiating therapy with a serious attitude. She was baffled by the nature and intensity of Mr. Morris's distress about the marriage. She was also deeply distressed by his determination to end the marriage and begin dating. Nevertheless, she worked hard from the beginning.

Mrs. Morris was able from the start to gather and organize the facts about the members of the family system. This process was done in spite of an anxious, emotional yearning for acceptance and approval that she had felt most of her life. The pull for togetherness was strong but so was her capability to think and observe. Mrs. Morris was able to accept the notion that no one functions poorly out of thoughtful choice. For example, the negative characteristics of her father could be attributed to his own childhood experiences as well as to his wife's suicide. Once she considered her father's poor functioning in light of the enormous impact of the suicide, she could build acceptance of him as he was. This did not mean that she now felt close to her father or that she now viewed his behavior as acceptable. It simply meant that she could accept him as he was.

Mrs. Morris on her own began to make the leap from the patterns she saw in the extended family to those she began to see in her own functioning. Sometimes defensive about her past reactions, Mrs. Morris was able to sit with the patterns she began to observe within herself. In fact, she was relieved to let go of the idea that the problems in her life came from others not accepting or approving of her. As long as she viewed the solution to her problems as being what others would or would not do, she was dependent on what others did. Accepting responsibility for her own behavior was a relief because it was something she could control. Letting go of blaming others was also a relief. Had Mrs. Morris seen herself as a victim, the changes that occurred would not have been possible. She realized that what she did or did not do made all the difference in what would occur.

The clarity that emerged with an orderly description of facts and patterns allowed Mrs. Morris to move naturally into developing a strategy for herself. Once it is possible to see predictable patterns in the emotional family, clarity about changes that need to be made in self emerges naturally. As Mrs. Morris could see her father's tendency to be critical under certain circumstances, that criticism did not feel so personal or so demeaning. As she was less "hurt" by the pattern, she was able to be firm and calm in her actions. The same was true in her relationship with her rejecting half-sibling. As patterns became clear, she wondered why it had been so important to have her approval and that this half-sibling's pattern of rejecting people was not just toward her but also toward other siblings. She accepted this pattern and might be annoyed by it but was not wounded. Further, she accepted that when rejecting moments occurred when she was under intense pressure in several arenas at once (a *cluster* of issues), such as when she had an issue at work, had not slept well, and had an issue with her son, her reactivity was stronger.

There was more difficulty in building a strategy for actions with her son. If the issue concerned the behavior of school officials, she struggled with the urge to defend and protect her son. However, when nonprotective action based on the facts was recommended, she would be able to calm her responsiveness and move to a more neutral position with school officials and with her son.

The lifelong work of building a responsible self, not blaming others, has only begun for Mrs. Morris. Her son is more than half through his local community college program. His college performance has been erratic, including dropping classes, and one entire semester. The son's social contacts remain minimal. However, he has successfully held a part-time job at a local department store for the past six months, requiring continual interaction with customers. The job has required her son to dress professionally and to manage expectations he has not previously faced. It is not possible to envision how much independence will be established in the future. Mrs. Morris appears to be at peace with this unknown reality, although she acknowledges that if her son were living independently, she would be inviting friends into her home more frequently.

Today, Mrs. Morris leads her life with a clear focus. Retirement is within sight but her economic situation dictates that she work for a few more years. She was able to make a move within her company away from a position requiring several major deadlines each year and enormous preparation of technical materials. The job had required hours and hours of intense study and learning about the technical topic, coordinating data from others into the final report, and briefing. With each of these deadlines came long hours and significant stress. The new position in the company carries its own stress. However, her workday has become normal in its length and in its demands, making several more years of work possible. Her new work environment encourages her tendency toward isolation, which is not favorable to her functioning or to her well-being. She has taken several actions to create consistent social contact, including rejoining an old car pool where the social contact had always been very satisfying. She saw the reality, knew its impact, and took the actions needed for her well-being.

The extended family continues to present issues and interactions that can be stressful and unpleasant. Mrs. Morris maneuvers through these interactions.

She clearly sees the emotional patterns of those around her and of the system and is able to predict likely reactivity concerning the stepmother's issues, such as preparing her home for sale. Over time, she has learned to identify where her leadership is appropriate, the tasks that she is capable of, and the issues and arenas to avoid. There is little reactivity to negative interactions with the family. During times of active engagement, her anxiety emerges, but she knows where her role and function need to be. She is relieved when these active periods with the extended family are over. However, she has no significant emotional reaction. Today, her home tends to be the gathering place for family meals.

Over the years, Mrs. Morris has remained in active contact with the family of Mr. Morris. This connection includes holiday meals and other social events. Holiday gatherings will usually include Mr. Morris and his new family. While not necessarily enjoying the interaction, Mrs. Morris can participate in these gatherings with little difficulty, even when they require that she welcome the new family into her home.

Summary

This chapter focused on how Bowen theory provides clarity about what occurs when an individual in any emotional system can know self and how his or her emotional patterns evolved from the larger family system. That knowledge includes clarity about the trigger points in self that activate the flow of immaturity (reactivity), grounding principles upon which to make daily decisions, and a respect for the reality of others. Nowhere is this clearer than in long-term therapy, where observation can reveal outcomes in a way not possible with shorter-term therapy.

The chapter presented an example of an individual who grew up in a family system in which there was trauma and consistently high levels of reactivity. This *emotionally driven* individual sought approval and needed to avoid disapproval. She chronically felt that she didn't *fit in* with others and those feelings propelled her to seek togetherness from people around her. From this state of yearning for emotional connection, she began the slow process of learning about the facts and patterns of functioning in her blended extended family. That effort focused on the difficult relationships she had with her father, stepmother, a half-sister, and her son. Once those family patterns began to emerge into an objective picture, she was able to see the way family members functioned in the context of their life circumstances, and her oversensitive reactivity began to dissipate. Further, her focus began to shift automatically to the functioning of self and her own emotional patterns. Having begun to observe the functioning of family members more objectively, she became less defensive, as patterns in self began to be clear and visible. By this point, her knowledge about human functioning had increased, thus lessening her blaming of others. Once the patterns in the family of origin and nuclear family and in her self began to be understood, she shifted her focus naturally toward what she needed to change. Strategy development began with *trial and error* actions that made sense based on the information that had been gathered. Mrs. Morris would attempt an action that made sense and evaluated its effectiveness. Sometimes the action was exactly what was needed and sometimes the action was not effective, requiring a new assessment and a new plan. In her family of origin, efforts to change patterns came rather naturally. With her son however, it was particularly difficult to change patterns. When she no longer picked up his responsibilities automatically, the trial and error began. Due to his ultra-sensitivity to feeling pushed by expectations, it took her a long time to learn *when to push* with expectations and consequences and *when to remain neutral*. She became adept at knowing when to challenge his reactivity and when to remain neutral. Moving back and forth between the two processes, addressing or remaining neutral, she allowed her son to slowly move from an *at risk emotionality* to a far more *functional emotionality* that included new levels of independence and self management following his graduation from high school.

At the time this chapter was written, it was not clear how much independence would be possible for the son. What was clear is that her son has not been at risk for several years, that he can move around the community connecting to others when needed. While he is still isolated in general, he has a capacity to interact with a small group of peers and adults with a new level of comfort. At the time this chapter was written, Mrs. Morris has made peace with the uncertainty of her son's future and is committed to remaining involved in his functioning while focusing on managing her own work and social life. Several years ago Mrs. Morris had a personal relationship that lasted for several months. Today, she is content with a social life of friends and family. Compared with earlier years, her anxiety is greatly reduced, and no longer a major factor in her day-to-day functioning. As Mrs. Morris continues her therapeutic work, her efforts to build a solid self, she readily understands that functioning is a clearly defined, consistent way of making decisions based on principle and facts. It is a lifelong effort that she is prepared to undertake.

REFERENCES

Bowen, M. (1978). *Family therapy in clinical practice.* New York: Jason Aronson.

Kerr, M. E. & Bowen, M. (1988). *Family evaluation: An approach based on Bowen theory.* New York: W. W. Norton.

MacLean, P. (1990). *The triune brain in evolution.* New York: Plenum Press.

Meyer, P. H. (1998). *Bowen theory as the basis for therapy.* In P. Titelman (Ed.), *Clinical applications of Bowen family systems theory* (pp. 69–116). New York: Haworth Press.

IV

RESEARCHING
DIFFERENTIATION OF SELF

14

CHALLENGES OF CONDUCTING BOWEN FAMILY SYSTEMS RESEARCH ON DIFFERENTIATION OF SELF

Randall T. Frost

Murray Bowen developed his theory of family emotional functioning in the course of doing family research. When he began a five-year research project from 1954 to 1959 at the National Institute of Mental Health, he designed a research plan to fit as closely as possible to other structured research in science (Bowen, p. 471).[1] He elaborated in great detail an initial hypothesis that "anticipated every relationship problem and every clinical situation that could develop" in the project that brought mothers and young adult schizophrenic patients to live together on a research ward of the hospital (p. 470). He wrote:

> The hypothesis also predicted the changes that would occur in psychotherapy. When research observations were not consistent with the hypothesis, the hypothesis was modified to fit the new facts, the psychotherapy was modified to fit the hypothesis, and new predictions were made about the results of the psychotherapy. . . . Any failure to change in psychotherapy was as much a reason to reexamine and change the hypothesis as any other unpredicted change. Strict adherence to this principle resulted in a theoretical-therapeutic system that was developed as an integrated unit, with psychotherapy determined by theory.
>
> (pp. 470–471)

Bowen wrote that the theory is a result of "the original research hypothesis modified and extended hundreds of times, with each modification checked many times in and out of the clinical situation" (p. 472).

Theories are meant to be continually tested, refined, and extended. Bowen theory is no exception. This chapter will discuss some of the challenges of conducting research on the central concept of the theory by describing the nature of problems to be solved for research design to reflect the operation of families as "living systems." The theory grew out of disciplined observation of family patterns of functioning that repeated predictably under similar conditions. Bowen wrote, "The theory is an abstracted version of what has been observed. If it is accurate, it should be able to predict what will be observed in other similar situations" (pp. 305–306). The combination of disciplined observation and the growing ability to predict family patterns of functioning led to the formulation of each concept of the theory. For research on differentiation of self to be valid, the same approach and methodology used to develop the theory as a whole should be used to test, refine, and extend the concept of differentiation.

Differentiation of self occurs on a continuum. In Bowen theory, differentiation refers both to the degree of fusion between intellectual and emotional functioning in an individual and the degree to which one self fuses or merges into another self in a close emotional relationship. According to Bowen theory, these two broad definitions of differentiation intertwine. The greater the relative differentiation between intellectual and emotional functioning in a family member, the more that person is able to maintain a greater degree of differentiation in relationships with other members of the family. Bowen believed that people fall on a continuum in the degree of fusion or relative differentiation in both domains. A major challenge for research on the concept of differentiation is to find ways to define more precisely differences in the degree of fusion or relative differentiation between emotional and intellectual functioning among different people and different families.

By emotional functioning, Bowen referred to behavior governed by the part of the human we share with the rest of life. The emotional system of the individual refers to the part of the brain that "handles the myriads of sensory stimuli from the digestive, circulatory, respiratory and all the other organ systems within the body as well as stimuli from the sensing organs that perceive the environment and *relationships with others*" (p. 372; italics added). The emotional system includes "all the automatic functions that govern the autonomic nervous system" and can be thought of as "synonymous with instinct that governs the life process in all living things" (Bowen, p. 356). The emotional system includes automatic functioning within an individual and in his or her relationships with others.

Bowen defined the intellectual system as a function of the cerebral cortex that "appeared last in man's evolutionary development and is the main difference between man and the lower forms of life." He characterized the intellectual system as involving the ability to "think, reason, and reflect, . . . which enables man to govern his life, in certain areas, according to logic, intellect and reason" (p. 356). The intellectual system enables the human to use careful observations about the world outside of self to correct more subjective impressions formed by the emotional and feeling systems.

Bowen defined the feeling system as a "link between the emotional and intellectual system through which certain emotional states are represented in conscious awareness" (p. 356).

The more intellect can function with a degree of separation from the feeling process, the higher the level of differentiation. Bowen wrote that the core of the theory "has to do with the degree to which people are able to distinguish between the *feeling* process and the *intellectual* process" (p. 355). This characterization of differentiation of self emphasizes the degree of awareness that people have of the difference between the thinking and feeling processes.

When people begin to work on improving their level of differentiation, one of the things they try to do is to become more aware of when they are reacting emotionally and when they are able to be more objective, better able to use their intellectual system to evaluate a situation. Just observing when anxiety is going up within self and when it is subsiding is a start on a research effort to improve one's ability to distinguish between the thinking and feeling processes. Anxiety can take many forms, and few people are aware of the many ways in which anxiety can manifest for them. People may distance or shut down when they become anxious; or they may be more prone to pick a fight, or to defer to their partner to avoid a fight. They may focus more on what is right or wrong about another member of the family when they are feeling anxious. They may develop telltale physical symptoms like a stomach ache or start drinking more. Better differentiated people are better able to recognize when they are functioning simply to reduce unpleasant feelings as opposed to being more factual and objective about what is going on in and around them. The effort to improve one's awareness of this difference between the intellectual process and the feeling process is a starting point for systems research on differentiation in the clinical setting.

As noted above, Bowen also defined differentiation as "the degree to which one self fuses or merges into another self in a close emotional relationship" (p. 200). What does it mean to fuse or merge into another self in a close emotional relationship? Emotional fusion is the opposite of differentiation. When Bowen came to view the family as an emotional unit, an organism in its own right, he was referring to the degree to which the functioning of individual family members was governed by the reciprocal functioning of the other members of the family. Whenever one spouse goes along with his or her mate, even when they disagree on a matter of importance, they are emotionally fusing or merging into a single entity who proceeds to "decide" for both of them. Or a couple who manage differences between them by focusing on one or more of their children fuse into a single entity in which parents become more comfortable in their relationship with each other by focusing on what is right or wrong with a child. A father may disagree with his wife's approach to parenting a child but remains silent rather than stir up conflict with his spouse. The child may then react automatically to the perceived two-on-one focus with rebellious behavior, providing more "justification" for parental focus on him or her. The emotional circuitry of parents and child fuse into a single unit that governs the repetitious pattern of interaction. Other children may simply comply with parental perceptions but then internalize the anxiety and become more vulnerable to physical, emotional, or behavioral symptoms. Systems research entails observation of such repetitive patterns of functioning in a family and the part each person plays in maintaining the automatic patterns. Such patterns reflect the degree to which one self fuses or merges into other selves in close emotional relationships.

The better the ability to distinguish between the thinking process and the feeling process in a close relationship, the better the ability a person has to observe the patterns of fusion in those relationships. Observing one's own part in patterns of fusion, in turn, contributes to the ability to distinguish between the thinking and feeling processes. When a father recognizes that his silence is contributing to the intensity of an emotional process between his wife and a child, he is one step closer to being able to modify his part in the problem. When a spouse recognizes that consistently deferring to her husband when she doesn't agree with him is contributing to her depression, she is one step closer to being able to modify her part in the problem. To conduct systems research on the concept of differentiation requires an "up-close" view to see the patterns and the way in which the emotionally driven thinking of family members helps to maintain the patterns. This clinical approach to research on differentiation parallels the methodology that Bowen employed in the development of the theory.

Bowen developed what he called a scale of differentiation to convey that the "basic" mix between emotional and intellectual functioning is on a continuum. In between the extremes of differentiation is an "infinite mix between emotional and intellectual functioning" (p. 362). He wrote he wanted to have a "reasonably accurate baseline for evaluating the functioning of people, for comparing them with each other, and for evaluating change over time." Bowen thought the scale of differentiation had been "used long enough, with enough people to make it a reasonably accurate method in the hands of those experienced in the variables" (p. 271). The scale of differentiation runs from 0 to 100. He wrote general profiles of people in the ranges of 0–25, 25–50, and 50–75, and a more hypothetical range from 75 to 100, sketching significant differences in the lifestyle of people in the different quadrants of the scale.

Filling in the continuum outlined by Bowen in his scale of differentiation is complicated by the fact that Bowen theory is a systems theory with two main variables. The level of anxiety in a person or the family is the second main variable of the theory in addition to differentiation of self. Bowen defined anxiety as an emotional response to a real or perceived threat. The degree of fusion between intellect and emotion and the propensity to fuse in a close emotional relationship is influenced by the level of anxiety in a person or a relationship system. The very meaning of the word "variable" is that its value is not absolute but emerges only in relation to other variables. So the higher and the more chronic the anxiety, the more feelings "fuse" with thinking and the more family members fuse into close relationships. At the same time, people and families vary in the amount of anxiety they have to experience to lose contact with their more objective thinking process and for the boundaries between self and others to dissolve into an emotional fusion. One family may adapt relatively well to the birth of a child without undue anxiety and without an increase in emotional fusion. In another family, the husband may react emotionally to the shift in his wife's focus from him to the child and become more critical of her. She may react to his criticism of her with criticism of him for not being more "supportive." He reacts to her criticism by emotionally distancing from his wife, who focuses even more on the newborn. The increase in anxiety precipitated by the birth of a child is sufficient to drive the development of a pattern of relating characterized by more conflict and distance in the relationship between husband and wife and a more intense level of involvement of mother with the developing child. In the first family, it may take several other stressors occurring at the same time to drive the family toward loss of objectivity and heightened patterns of fusion.

Increases in anxiety can affect what Bowen called *functional* levels of differentiation. The term "functional" conveys the idea that the degree of fusion between emotional and intellectual functioning is not fixed but influenced by the level of anxiety in self and in the family system. Bowen also defined what he called *basic* level of differentiation as an *average* of functional levels under calm and stressful conditions (p. 371). Basic level of differentiation varies among individuals and families. Different levels of anxiety can shift functional levels of differentiation above or below the basic level of differentiation for an individual (p. 432). Bowen considered the scale of differentiation as referring to the basic level of differentiation of an individual. He also noted that there is "a kind of average level of differentiation for the family which has certain minor levels of difference in individuals within the family" (p. 362). He suggested that it is possible to assign a functional level of self for an entire family determined by the level of (basic) self in the head of the family (p. 424).

However, the "basic" degree of fusion between thinking and feeling and the propensity to fuse in close relationships itself generates chronic anxiety. When the emotional fusion between two spouses plays out in the inability to discuss matters important to each for fear of conflict, the emotional distance that results creates its own chronic anxiety. When more conflicted couples consist of a member who can't stand the partner having a different opinion from their own, that expression of emotional fusion also generates its own chronic anxiety. Lower basic levels of differentiation generate more chronic anxiety than higher basic levels of differentiation. Families that generate more chronic anxiety are less able to adapt to stressors that generate additional acute anxiety. So the two main variables of Bowen theory reciprocally influence each other—heightened levels of acute anxiety can lower

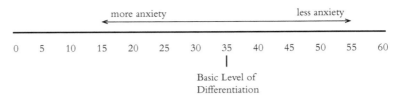

Figure 14.1 Functional Range of Differentiation

functional level of differentiation while lower basic levels of differentiation generate more chronic anxiety that renders individuals and families more vulnerable to stressors that, in turn, heighten acute anxiety.

The distinction Bowen makes between basic and functional levels of differentiation reflects the interaction of the two main variables of the theory. Figure 14.1 depicts an estimate of functional range of differentiation for a basic level of differentiation of 35. The more anxiety there is, the more the functional level dips below 35; with less anxiety, the functional level of differentiation rises above the basic level.

But how does one go about taking an average of functioning under different levels of stress to arrive at a basic level of differentiation for an individual? Moreover, an individual's functioning cannot be adequately assessed without also assessing the functioning of that person's nuclear family. One person's functioning can be enhanced at the expense of other members of the family. So what does it mean to take an average of the functioning of a person and that person's family over many decades?

One gauge of functioning is the number and intensity of symptoms that develop over the years in response to variable amounts of stress. And, in fact, one of the variables that reflects level of differentiation is the ability of people and families to adapt to stress. Bowen wrote that at the lower extreme of differentiation are people "less flexible, less adaptable and more emotionally dependent on those about them. They are easily stressed into dysfunction and it is difficult for them to recover from dysfunction. They inherit a high percentage of all human problems" (p. 362). On the other hand, those who are more differentiated and whose intellectual functioning can retain relative autonomy in periods of stress are "more flexible, more adaptable, and more independent of the emotionality about them. They cope better with life stresses, their life courses are more orderly and successful, and they are remarkably free of human problems" (p. 362).

Yet there is not a simple one-to-one connection with level of differentiation and the presence or absence of symptoms. Bowen notes:

People with the most fusion have most of the human problems, and those with the most differentiation, the fewest; but there can be people with intense fusion who manage to keep their relationships in balance, who are never subjected to severe stress, who never develop symptoms and who appear normal. However their life adjustments are tenuous, and, if they are stressed into dysfunction, the impairment can be chronic or permanent. There are also fairly well-differentiated people who can be stressed into dysfunction, but they recover rapidly.

(pp. 362–363)

If one were able to assess accurately both the amount of stress to which an individual and his/her family must adapt and the degree of symptomatic reaction to that amount of stress, it would be possible, over an extended period of time, to gauge variation in the ability of individuals and families to adapt to stress. Since ability to adapt to stress is one of the indicators of higher or lower levels of differentiation, a reasonably accurate assessment of ability to adapt to stress provides a way to begin to define more exactly where particular individuals and families fall on the continuum of differentiation.

The challenge for research is to be able to assess both amount of stress and degree of reactivity to stress. Stressors can be defined as events that place a demand on an individual and his/her family to adapt. Stress is defined as the amount of demand realistically placed on a family unit to adapt by a particular stressor or combination of stressors. Adaptation refers to how the individual and the family reallocate time, energy, and resources to meet the new demands placed on the unit by the stressor(s). At times, individuals and families are unable to adjust to the demands created by new stressors without impinging on the functioning of one another. The degree of impingement that occurs represents the degree of emotional reactivity to the stress.

Anxiety refers to the degree of emotional response to a real or perceived threat. Threat can range on a continuum from real to imaginary. Anxiety related to a genuine, time-limited threat can be adaptive. Anxiety related to an unlikely or imaginary threat can become more chronic and long term. The perception of threat is what distinguishes anxiety from stress when stress is understood as the amount of demand realistically placed on a family unit to adapt by particular stressors. Stressful events may or may not be perceived as a threat to a family member(s) or family relationship(s). For example, a promotion in the workplace usually represents a stress because it requires some adjustment in a person's functioning as the person takes on additional responsibility. The promotion, however, may not be perceived as a threat at all and create very little anxiety. In fact, the person may relish the challenge.

Developmental processes provide an excellent opportunity to assess the ability of a family to adapt to stress. Most thinking about the life cycle focuses on the developmental tasks of individuals as they grow older. Consistent with Bowen's conceptualization of the family as an emotional unit, life cycle processes like birth, adolescence, leaving home, courtship, engagement and marriage, divorce and remarriage, serious illness and death affect the entire multigenerational family. These are periods in family life when emotional-instinctual forces run high. How the family adapts to the new demands such events place on the unit provides a window on the family's ability to adapt to stress. The fact that every individual and family experience some, if not all, of these events means that the functioning of the same family can be evaluated over time and different families can be compared with one another for how they navigate the same kind of events.

As an example, adolescence is one of those times in family life that provides a good opportunity to assess the ability of a family to adapt to the anxiety created by the intensity of the emotional attachment between parents and adolescents. The more intense the attachment, the more anxiety is created by this period of rapid physical growth. The author has written a rough scale of variation in family functioning with adolescents that gives an indication of the range of variation that can occur around this life process. The scale has been written to parallel the scale of differentiation with particular reference to the adolescent period in family life.

Scale of Family Functioning With Adolescents[2]

0–10: Adolescents are emotionally "welded" to the family. There is essentially no opportunity for the adolescent to develop a self that is separate from the family togetherness. Adolescents develop severe emotional, physical, or social symptoms in relation to the intensity of family emotional processes, especially when they try to function apart from the family. Hard-core schizophrenia, alcoholism, and/or drug abuse are among the problems that can develop from this level of intensity. Parents are as emotionally bound to their offspring as the offspring are to them.

10–20: Adolescents are strongly bound emotionally to the family, with very little opportunity to develop a self that is separate from the family together-ness. Adolescents in this range may function without diagnosable symptoms if the family is unusually calm and solicitous. However, they are vulnerable to developing symptoms whenever the positive focus is modified by stressors in the family or by the normal process of trying to move away from home to establish their own lives. When symptoms develop, they are apt to become chronic, lifelong problems.

20–30: Adolescents in this range are highly sensitive to the approval or disapproval of important others, which compromises their ability to function as separate selves, especially when the family is more anxious. Adolescents in this range can assemble more of a "pretend" self than adolescents in the 0–20 range, but it is largely a self that is made up of ideas and behavior borrowed from others or assembled in opposition to the views of important others. Adolescents in this range are quite vulnerable to developing symptoms but they are less likely to be quite as severe or chronic as adolescents who are below 20 on the scale.

30–40: Adolescents in this range have more free intellect to assemble more of a solid self that is based on their own thinking than are people at lower levels, but they are still subject to peer pressure in many areas that they have not thought through for themselves. The friendship system is made up of people in this same range of functioning. Conflict with and distance from parents is not uncommon but it is less severe than at lower levels.

40–50: Adolescents at this level are more aware of the interplay between their own thinking and pressure from others but they are still vulnerable to the opinions of others in areas where they are ill defined. There are fewer such areas than for adolescents at lower levels of functioning. Adolescents in this range have more open relationships with their parents, with the exception of areas that are more sensitive for both. There is more flexibility to pursue personal areas of interest without undue parental focus, positively or negatively. Adolescents at this level are still vulnerable to symptoms under moderate levels of anxiety but the symptoms are fewer in number and more moderate in severity.

50–60: Families with adolescents at this level have lower amounts of chronic anxiety that permit adolescents to develop more of their own selves separate from parental anxiety. Adolescents in this group are more adventuresome without being reckless. Life is more of an adventure to be enjoyed than an "ordeal" to be endured. Under high enough pressure or stress, this group can still develop symptoms, but the symptoms are fewer in number and more moderate in severity and atrophy more quickly than for adolescents under comparable stress at lower levels of functioning. Parents worry less about adolescents at this level and trust them more.

60–70: Families with adolescents at this level have well-functioning teens, responsible to others and for themselves. They are not antagonistic toward parents or overly compliant. They have been assuming appropriate responsibility for themselves since they were very young and adolescence is a continuation of this early trend. They function very effectively even in difficult situations, balancing responsibility for self with responsibility to others. It takes a relatively high level of stress for symptoms to develop, and the symptoms quickly subside when the stress is relieved.

70–80: Adolescents and their families function at unusually high levels rarely found. Adolescents function up to their capabilities in all areas that they care about. While they are sure of what they believe on all important matters, they readily consult with parents and other knowledgeable people when making important decisions. They are able to evaluate the opinions of others and incorporate new information on its own merits without being unduly influenced by their relationship with the person providing the advice or information.

Similar scales can be constructed for each developmental period in family life. One avenue for systems research on variation in levels of differentiation is to characterize each family on a continuum for major life cycle processes over multiple decades. A higher level of adaptability at such times in family life is broadly consistent with higher levels of differentiation.

Of course, other stressors can occur at the same time as the family is moving through a particular life cycle period that may make family adaptation to the developmental challenges more difficult. A breadwinner may lose his or her job soon after the birth of a child. Or more than one life cycle process may occur at about the same time. For example, the death of an important member of the extended family may occur at about the same time as a young adult is attempting to leave home or more than one child may be going through adolescence at the same time. The presence of additional stressors during a life cycle period means that the additional anxiety created by the need to adapt to more than one stressor makes that period more challenging for a family than it would otherwise be. To arrive at a reasonably consistent estimate of the amount of stress placed on a family unit by more than one stressor requires the ability to rate all potentially significant stressors in order to arrive at the approximate total demand placed on the unit to adapt.

Holmes and Rahe (1967) and subsequently Miller and Rahe (1997) made such an effort. They constructed an inventory by asking hundreds of people to rate the relative amount of life adjustment required by various life events. The respondents were asked to estimate the intensity and length of time required to accommodate to a life event regardless of its desirability. They were asked to base their opinions on the average degree of adjustment required by the event rather than the extreme, since the researchers recognized that people vary in the degree to which they adjust with particular ease or difficulty to different events. Using marriage as an arbitrary number of 50, people were asked whether the readjustment was more intense and protracted than marriage. If so, they were asked to choose a proportionately larger number for that event. If the respondents decided that the event represented less intense and shorter readjustment than marriage, they were to indicate how much less by assigning a proportionally smaller number than 50. Holmes and Rahe relied on the fact that the subjective assessments of relatively large numbers of people provide a remarkably reliable quantification scale of the physical dimensions of objects (Henry and Stephens, 1977).

Miller and Rahe (1997) used the same methodology as Holmes and Rahe (1967) but added 44 events to the original 43 developed in the earlier study. Miller and Rahe reported that the "mean values from this scaling method have proven to be remarkably similar across a series of both American and cross-cultural investigations" (Miller and Rahe, 1997, p. 280). These life events inventories can help a clinician to factor in an estimate of the relative weight of other events occurring around the time of a life cycle event. They represent an effort to develop a consistent measure of the amount of change to which an *individual* must adjust.

The Holmes–Rahe and subsequent Miller–Rahe inventories, however, have limitations from a family systems perspective. People were not asked to assess the amount of adjustment required for a family unit but for individuals. To come closer to results useful for systems research would require a study asking respondents to estimate the amount of adjustment to events for an entire family unit. Even in the expanded inventory developed by Miller and Rahe, important stressors like the adolescence period are not included. Also, from a family systems analysis, a particular event can function both as a reaction to previous stressors and a new stressor in its own right. Divorce, for example, could come as a result of a buildup of anxiety evoked, in part, by previous stressors, as well as represent a new stressor to which the family must adapt. The effort to arrive at a consistent and valid estimate of the amount of demand a stressor or combination of stressors places on a family is one of the problems to be solved to help measure variation in the ability of individuals and families to adapt to stress.

Another challenge is to estimate change in the number and intensity of symptoms that develop in the wake of stressors. One way to approach this challenge is to develop operational definitions from minimum to severe for the categories of symptoms that Bowen theory identifies. Building on definitions originally developed by the Bowen Center for a family assessment guide and for the Family Database Project, the author has attempted to develop operational definitions for the intensity of emotional distance and conflict in marriage as well as for the degree of severity of social, emotional, and physical illnesses in spouses and children.[3] A comparison of the number and the intensity of symptoms prior to a stressor or stressors with the number and intensity of symptoms that develop six months to a year after the stressor(s) provides an estimate of family reactivity to stress. A comparison of the amount of stress with the degree of symptomatic response provides one measure of family adaptability to stress.[4]

Yet this approach omits the impact of stressors that may not rise to the level of symptoms.[5] An oldest daughter whose mother dies when she is a teen may give up on a personal goal to pursue higher education in order to care for her younger siblings. This outcome does not, in itself, represent a diagnosable symptom, but it does impinge in an important way on the self of the oldest daughter. Some oldest daughters may take the responsibility in stride and plan to attend university a few years later than planned. Other oldest daughters in the same situation may bitterly resent the imposition in a way that adversely affects their functioning in the future. Better differentiated families find ways to mitigate the adverse effects of stressors on family functioning, while families with lower levels of differentiation are more vulnerable. There are many ways in which families and individuals adapt to the demands created by stressors. The development of a new symptom or the exacerbation of old symptoms is only one possible outcome. A challenge for research on differentiation of self is to capture the full range of the ability to adapt to varying amounts of stress that, in turn, can help to fill in the full continuum of differentiation.

Variation in the ability of family members to pursue personal goals is another indication of basic level of differentiation. The more energy that goes into seeking love and approval and keeping relationships in some kind of harmony, the less energy that is available for self-directed goals (Bowen, p. 367). Like ability to adapt to stress, the capacity to pursue independent life goals provides another measure of level of differentiation. The author has developed a preliminary scale that attempts to describe a range in ability to pursue personal goals. The scale illustrates how it may be possible to take another indicator of level of differentiation and use it to flesh out more specific levels of differentiation, including goal-directed behavior at the higher levels of differentiation. (See scale below on goal directedness.) As in all research based on Bowen theory, there is an effort to minimize the use of self-report and rely on what people actually do when evaluating their functioning.

Goal Directedness

0–10: People have no discernible goals or goal-directed behavior at this level; the person appears aimless, incapable of formulating personal goals, tossed about by feelings in and around self; cognitive functioning is completely compromised by feeling.

10–20: People at this level are able to formulate a few general goals but the goals appear to have little or no relationship to the behavior of the person. What goals he or she is able to articulate are either absorbed uncritically from the environment or formulated uncritically in reaction to the environment. Goals readily change when the relationship environment changes. There is very little cognitive involvement in formulation of goals. They are almost entirely feeling-based.

20–30: People at this level are able to arrive at more specific goals that have a loose link to the behavior of the person. He or she is easily distracted from the pursuit of these goals, however, and makes little progress toward personal goals unless the person is in a low stress environment. People at this level are highly influenced by the opinions of others. Alternatively, they may have an intense goal focus to the exclusion of the ability to recognize the impact of their intense pursuit of goals on others. A little more cognitive involvement is discernible than in someone at the 10–20 level.

30–40: People are able to enumerate both short- and long-term goals more clearly and to actively pursue their goals. Under low/moderate pressure, the person loses focus but is able to recover when the pressure subsides. When anxiety increases, the person can feel torn between pursuit of personal goals and the claims of others on self. Personal pursuit of goals may impinge on spouse or children. A realistic balance between responsibility to self and responsibility to others is difficult to maintain. Cognitive influence on formulation of goals is discernible, especially during low stress periods.

40–50: People at this level are better able to set realistic goals for self and to work toward them. They require a moderate amount of stress to lose focus. They are better able to balance the pursuit of personal goals with responsible behavior toward others. They are less swayed by the opinions of others than someone in the 30–40 range. The thinking system is more involved in the formulation of personal goals, but under moderate stress the emotional system still overrides thinking.

50–60: People at this level are sure of personal goals and responsibility to others. They are able to adjust to most stressors without impinging on self or others. It requires a moderately high level of stress to lose track of personal goals and responsibility to others. The thinking system can override feelings so long as stress remains in the low to moderate range.

60–70: People at this level rarely compromise on goals important to self and the thoughtful pursuit of self-direction in life while remaining respectful toward others. They require a relatively high level of stress to lose track of personal goals and direction.

70–80: People at this level essentially never give way on matters of importance to self and self's direction in life, even under high levels of stress. They are able to persist in the pursuit of goals in and through the ups and downs of life. Nuclear family members are also able to pursue their own personal goals without loss of self to the others.

A set of important variables that help to determine basic and functional levels of differentiation are what Bowen called solid self, pseudo-self, and no self. Like many of the variables that make up the concept of differentiation, the variables of solid, pseudo-, and no self are best investigated in the clinical setting and by people working on differentiation of self in their own family. Solid self, according to Bowen, is the part of self that is made up of "clearly defined beliefs, opinions, convictions and life principles on which self will take actions even in situations of high anxiety and duress" (p. 365). Solid self is stable and non-negotiable. "Solid self refers to who I am; what I stand for; and what I will do or not do in a given situation." Solid self, according to Bowen theory, is formed slowly and can be changed from within self, but it is never changed by coercion or persuasion by others (p. 200). Solid self is the part of us that doesn't give way under pressure.

Pseudo-self, on the other hand, can be changed by emotional pressure (Bowen, p. 365). Pseudo-self is made up of beliefs and principles acquired from others and it is negotiable in relation to others to enhance one's image or oppose the other. Pseudo-self is the part of us that fuses with important others (Bowen, pp. 200–201). When we haven't thought through what we believe for ourselves,[6] we may defer to others to make decisions for us or we may anxiously pressure others to go along with our pseudo beliefs. In this sense, pseudo-self is a component of functional level of differentiation. People can use pseudo-self quite effectively to guide behavior when he or she is not overly anxious or under pressure from the relationship system. Functioning can be enhanced by pseudo-self but functioning can also drop when a person loses pseudo-self to others and becomes unsure of self, deferring to others as anxiety increases. The beliefs of pseudo-self are negotiable and subject to the vagaries of anxiety and pressure from the relationship system.

No self refers to very low levels of functioning in which there are not even borrowed beliefs a person can use to guide functioning. A person is completely rudderless in those areas of functioning in which there is not even pseudo-self that is available to draw upon (Bowen, p. 92). People are completely dependent on others to guide and advise them.

Murray Bowen believed "the level of solid self is lower and (the level) of pseudo self is much higher in all of us than most are aware" (p. 366). At very low levels of basic differentiation there is almost no level of solid self and not much pseudo-self (Bowen, p. 92). At 35–40 on the scale of differentiation there are "relatively low levels of solid self but reasonable levels of pseudo self, which is obtainable from and negotiable in the relationship system" (Bowen, pp. 201–202). At relatively high levels of basic differentiation, there is more solid self. According to Bowen,

> People above 50 [on the scale] have developed a reasonable level of solid self on most of the essential issues in life. In periods of calm, they have employed logical reasoning to develop beliefs, principles, and convictions that they use to overrule the emotional system in situations of anxiety and panic.
>
> (p. 369)

The amount of solid self contributes to a person's (and a family's) ability to adapt to stress. To the extent that solid self is formed by reflection on personal experience and a reasonably accurate appraisal of reality (also a hallmark of solid self), the self is better able to adapt calmly to challenging circumstances. The development of solid self presumes the disciplined use of the intellectual system to define the beliefs and principles that make up solid self. The definition of solid self reduces the degree of fusion in thinking and feeling in the areas of functioning where more solid self has been defined. And it reduces the propensity to lose self to relationships. When certain principles and beliefs are no longer negotiable, the better defined person can follow his or her own compass in those areas rather than a group compass. A teen who has thought through what he believes about taking drugs, for example, is not vulnerable to peer pressure to use if his beliefs are part of solid self.

Bowen used predictions about change in psychotherapy to test the theory as he went about developing it. The *theoretical-therapeutic system* that resulted continues to enable clinicians to make predictions about change in psycho-therapy. Clinicians are in a good position to conduct research on variables like solid self if they can exercise scientific rigor in the course of their work with families. For example, theory predicts the following about an increase in the amount of solid self:

- if a family member thinks through for self what he or she responsibly believes about an important area of his/her own functioning that had been previously ill defined;
- if a family member takes into account the relevant facts of the situation, including knowledge about the predictable function-ing of the family emotional system;
- if the level of anxiety in the family system is not already too high;
- if the person is able to take action on his or her belief in spite of the pressure from the relationship system and from within self to abandon the effort to be a more defined self;
- if the differentiating family member is sufficiently sure of the principle he or she is using to guide his/her behavior that the person can stay on course without distancing from the family, without engaging in an argument, and have a neutral response even to provocative comments, then the intensity of the fam-ily reactivity directed at the member to "change back" will increase;
- if the differentiating-one is able to maintain his position while staying emotionally close to the family and not reacting emo-tionally to the family's predictable reactivity. Once the family is convinced the differentiating member is not going to change back, then the family's reactivity will subside and the family as a whole will move to a slightly higher level of functioning as a result of the differentiating member's ability to put an increase in solid self into action.

The amount of solid self a person has thought through for self is an indi-cator of that person's basic level of differentiation. However, solid self can be discerned reliably only under pressure. Only when a person can act on his/her beliefs "in spite of pressure from the relationship system to main-tain the former level of amorphous no self" (Bowen, p. 424) does solid self reveal itself to be solid. A couple can discuss calmly the differences in their approach to parenting and the relative advantages of each until anxiety shoots up, at which time the differences get expressed in polarized debate. The polarization under stress is evidence that the beliefs about parenting represent pseudo-, not solid, self.[7] The presence and absence of solid self can become evident clinically as people report on their ability to act on their beliefs in their relationships with one another. Simply asking people questions about whether they stick to their principles under duress is an inadequate measure of differentiation. Bowen was clear that what people do is far more indicative of level of differentiation than what they say. Clinical research can document what happens when people begin to develop firmer opinions, beliefs, and principles and to act on them without reacting emotionally to the predictable reactivity of the family.

Testing predictions on the outcomes of increases in solid self also has the potential gradually to refine the variations in lifestyle represented by different points on the scale of differentiation. Families whose lifestyles can be described one way at the start of therapy can be characterized after a course of family therapy that includes an increase in solid self that satisfies Bowen's definition of that process. The before and after characterizations of family functioning can begin to document small but important increases in basic level of differentiation as a result of an increase in solid self. If enough clinicians following the same methodology assembled enough families, the variations in functioning before and after increases in solid self would potentially enable such families to be distributed along a continuum of functioning. The differences in lifestyle before an increase in solid self and after would capture small changes in basic level of differentiation that could be summarized and gradually used to refine the scale of differentiation.

An increase in solid self also affects the balance of what Bowen theory calls the individuality and togetherness forces in a family. These two counterbalancing life forces are part of the emotional system (Kerr and Bowen, 1988, p. 342). The life force for individuality is the instinctual drive to be an individual in one's own right, with one's own personal goals and direction in life. The life force for togetherness refers to the instinctual need for the approval, love, affection, support, and agreement of important others. An ideal balance between the two life forces according to Bowen is 50/50, with freedom to move in either direction depending on circumstances (Bowen, p. 277). The two life forces operate in reciprocal balance to one another—the greater the need for togetherness, the less drive for individuality (Bowen, p. 311).

The two life forces play out differently depending on the level of differentiation. At higher levels of differentiation, people are able to pursue their own personal interests and goals without impinging unduly on others' ability to do likewise. At higher levels of differentiation, the togetherness force gets expressed in the quality of emotional contact with others and genuine interest in their well-being. At higher levels of differentiation, people can be themselves and permit others to be who they are. The individuality and togetherness forces complement one another. At lower levels of differentiation, the togetherness force is increasingly more dominant. At lower levels of differentiation, the life force of individuality—struggling against the intensity of the force for togetherness—gets expressed in a more selfish way, pursuing one's own perceived interests without regard for the realistic impact on others, or readily giving up on one's own goals and direction in life. At lower levels of differentiation, the intense need for the other can result in making togetherness demands that do not respect others as individuals in their own right, and allowing others to make irresponsible demands on self.

Anxiety, the other main variable of the theory, also influences the balance between the two life forces. As anxiety increases in a relationship system, the perception of threat activates the forces for togetherness that tend to override responsible individuality. As anxiety decreases, the individuality/togetherness balance returns to the norm for a particular basic level of differentiation.

The principles of solid self inform how intellect manages the interplay of individuality and togetherness. What one comes to believe about responsibility to self and to others can come to influence how much energy is available to pursue individual goals and how much life energy is automatically deployed on behalf of others. The extent to which such principles have been thought through will influence the degree to which intellect can govern the interplay of these emotional life forces in a more adaptive fashion. An increase in solid self will upset the balance of individuality and togetherness in an emotional system. A woman who has made her only child and her husband the priority in her expenditure of time and energy begins to rethink her priorities after her husband leaves her for another woman. As she begins to recalibrate the balance between her responsibility to herself and her responsibility to others, her daughter, colleagues, and her former husband predictably react negatively to the change. Clinicians can predict in advance the emotional process that will follow even a slight shift toward individuality. By recording carefully the prediction and the result, clinicians can contribute to testing Bowen theory.

Clinicians can also help to discriminate the different mix of individuality and togetherness that accompanies different basic levels of differentiation. When a person can thoughtfully define more clearly his or her beliefs about responsibility to self and to others and act on those beliefs in a manner consistent with Bowen's definition of what it takes to increase solid self, he or she can increase his or her basic level of differentiation. Documenting the specific differences in the balance of individuality and togetherness before and after an increase in solid self can contribute to refining the scale of differentiation. Bowen described a clinical case in which

> [the husband] devoted weeks to thinking through his professional goals and future. His life energy went to individual goals rather than the previous goal of happiness. As his life energy was directed more to the responsible functioning of self, the wife pleaded, accused, attacked, and alternated over interest in sex and withdrawal of sex— all favoring a return to togetherness. He stayed fairly well on course, with only minor lapses in response to accusations that he was a terrible father, that his children were being harmed by his lack of

interest, that he was not capable of a close family relationship or an adequate sexual relationship.

The process reached a breakthrough during a noisy emotional outburst from the wife in which he was able to stay close. The following day the relationship was calm. The wife said: "One part of me approved of what you were doing, but somehow I had to do what I did. Even when I was most excited and angry, I was hoping you would not let me change you. I am so glad you did not give in."

There were a few weeks of calm before the wife started on a self-determined course. Then the husband was the petulant, demanding one. It was as if he had lost the gain from his previous efforts. Then came another emotional breakthrough and new levels of differentiation for both . . .

(1978, p. 222)

Bowen wrote that the pattern in which one and then the other changed continued in definite cycles over a three-year period. He also described other changes that accompanied the increases in differentiation:

Each was changing in relationship to families of origin, working through in crises similar to the crises between the spouses. Also, the husband began to find differences in his work situation that were resolved with a new and better job. In the course of psychotherapy the couple began to find old friends less attractive. They no longer liked the old social gatherings with gossip, the berating of other people, the intense emotional reactiveness between spouses in the group, and the bias and prejudice in those who crusaded against bias and prejudice. This reaction follows the predictable pattern of people choosing friends from among others with equivalent levels of differentiation. They found different friends with a different orientation to life while maintaining casual, pleasant, infrequent contact with the old friends.

(1978, p. 222)

This summary documents some of the changes in lifestyle that followed an increase in solid self and a shift toward more individuality in the marriage. Bowen's clinical report also documents an improvement in the ability of each spouse to pursue personal goals. All of these changes in lifestyle represent an increase in the basic level of differentiation for the couple. An accumulation of numerous clinical cases documenting the changes that follow an increase in solid self can both test hypotheses derived from Bowen theory and contribute to filling in continua of functioning that make up the level of differentiation. The different mix of individuality and togetherness that accompanies different basic levels of differentiation represents another such continuum.

Bowen theory provides other avenues to refine the scale of differentiation. Variation in basic level of differentiation is the result of a developmental process that begins with conception and ordinarily ends when a person leaves his or her original family to make one's own way as an adult. In children who emerge with a lower basic level of differentiation:

> Much of the mother's thinking, worry, feeling energy goes into "giving attention" to the child, to which the child responds by "giving" an equal amount of self to mother. This is in contrast to the better differentiated mother whose giving to the child is determined by the child's need and not the mother's anxiety. The amount of mother's "giving of self" to the child constitutes a programmed "need for love" in the child that will be manifested in the child's future relationships. The amount of "need for love" tends to remain fixed for life. The amount of reciprocal "giving and receiving" in the early mother-child relationship provides the first clue of the future level of 'differentiation of self' for the child. The parent–child relationship may stay in fairly calm equilibrium until adolescence when the dependently attached child attempts to break away from parents and form peer relationships.
>
> (Bowen, p. 275)

Not getting the amount of attention one is used to getting stirs up anxiety in both parent and child and can result in reactive behavior to try and restore the former balance of "giving and receiving." People emotionally programmed to need a large amount of attention—positive or negative—have their behavior governed by that need throughout life. As a result of this developmental process, people leave their family of origin with greater or lesser degrees of unresolved emotional attachment to the family. The more emotional attachment to the original family, the more the adult child also looks to others to "meet his/her needs" in specified ways. The more intense the need for the other, the more the fusion with the original family replicates in other important relationships. Bowen wrote, "The degree of unresolved emotional attachment (to parents) is equivalent to the degree of undifferentiation" (p. 534).

A closely related indicator of level of differentiation is the degree to which a person increasingly learns to assume responsibility for self in life. The process of learning to assume responsibility for self also takes place initially in the process of growing up, as parents turn over more and more responsibility to children to make their own decisions. The children gradually learn to regulate their own behavior and become less dependent on the family to "meet their needs." The more children learn gradually to take responsibility for self as they grow up, the better their level of differentiation and the less unresolved emotional attachment to the family. When this process is reasonably successful, the child develops a more separate self from the other members of the family while remaining in good emotional contact with them.

To the extent that this process is less successful, the person emerges from his or her family with a lower level of differentiation and a greater amount of unresolved emotional attachment to the family. The family plays its part in fostering a more dependent child. The functioning of parents is often enhanced by having a child whom they perceive as needing their help. When the family takes too much responsibility for a child's functioning, the child does not learn to take as much responsibility for his or her own self.

One of the most important nodal points in a course of family therapy occurs when members of a family begin to shift their focus of attention from other to self. When a member of a family can become more accurate about his or her own part in automatic patterns of family functioning, that person becomes less dependent on others to change. When such a shift in focus is directed by a more objective thinking process, the person is able to get beyond the emotional process of blaming self or others. When family members can modify their own behavior consistent with a more accurate way of thinking about their part in the problem, therapeutic outcome can begin to improve for the family. Clinicians can document the importance of a shift in focus toward responsibility for self by making a series of conditional predictions about therapeutic outcome. What does the clinician predict for a family in which one and then other family members become more and more accurate about their own part in the family problem and better able to modify that part? What would the clinician predict for the same family if they were less successful in shifting toward responsibility for self? Making specific, conditional predictions of therapeutic outcome linked to an increasing ability to take responsibility for self represents another opportunity for therapists to conduct clinical research on differentiation of self. People with better levels of differentiation assume more responsibility for self.

Bowen's concept of emotional cutoff provides another potential means to arrive at a "rough estimate" of differentiation in self (Bowen-Kerr Interview Series, 1980). Emotional cutoff refers to the way in which people distance from their family of origin to manage the anxiety created by the amount of unresolved emotional attachment the person has with his/her original family. The greater the degree of unresolved attachment to the original family, the more parents and adult children have a relationship appropriate to an earlier stage of development. Such relationships can become uncomfortable for both parents and adult children. A frequent way people manage the chronic anxiety created by the fusion to their family of origin is by a combination of physical distance and/or emotional isolation. The more intense the unresolved emotional attachment people have with their original family, the more extreme the use of mechanisms for cutting off and insulating self from the original family. Some people with the most intense unresolved emotional attachments never leave home. At this extreme end of the continuum, people may manage the intensity of the attachment by withdrawing intra-psychically into psychosis. People with equally intense attachments may manage the intensity of the attachment by leaving home and never making contact again. In between the extremes are people with less unresolved emotional attachment to their original family. People who feel they have disappointed their parents may feel inadequate around them and keep their contact infrequent and superficial to minimize their own discomfort. Less intense attachment requires lesser degrees of cutoff to manage the discomfort of the emotional fusion.

If the degree of emotional cutoff provides at least a rough index of a person's functional level of differentiation, clinicians can contribute to the ability to assess functional level of differentiation by establishing a baseline of the degree of emotional cutoff at the start of a course of family psychotherapy. The level of emotional contact with parents and other members of the extended family can be characterized according to the frequency of contact, the geographic distance from one another, the degree of openness with which family members communicate about significant developments in each other's lives, and the ability to speak person-to-person about self to the other who can reciprocate. Such indicators of emotional contact can provide a baseline against which to compare possible changes over time as people try to bridge the existing level of cutoff and begin to resolve some of the unresolved emotional attachment that fuels cutoff. Degrees of emotional cutoff, like differentiation, occur on a continuum. Progress in refining the ability to describe degrees of emotional cutoff can also represent progress in the ability to describe levels of differentiation with greater nuance.

The challenge of using the degree of emotional cutoff to estimate degree of unresolved emotional attachment is complicated, however, by Bowen's observation that it is possible for families with identical levels of differentiation to have different amounts of contact with past generations.

> One family remains in contact with the parental family and remains relatively free of symptoms for life, and the level of differentiation does not change much in the next generation. The other family cuts off with the past, develops symptoms and dysfunction, and a lower level of differentiation in the succeeding generation.
>
> (Bowen, p. 383)

How does one reconcile the seeming contradiction between degree of cutoff representing a rough estimate of differentiation of self and two families with identical levels of differentiation having different amounts and quality of contact with past generations? The distinction between functional and basic level of differentiation helps to resolve the potential contradiction between the two statements. The family that maintains viable emotional contact with its family of origin is able to maintain a higher *functional* level of differentiation than the other family that does not maintain contact with the parental family. The *basic* level of differentiation of the two families remains the same, but one family operates in the higher part of the range of functioning available to it, while the other more cut off family is more anxious and operates out of the lower end of the same basic range of functioning available to it. Figure 14.2 illustrates the interrelation between the degree of emotional cutoff with family of origin of a person at an assumed basic level of 35 and the estimated variation in functional level of differentiation, amount of anxiety, and vulnerability to symptoms in the adult child and his or her nuclear family.

Emotional cutoff is not defined simply by the number of contacts people have with parents or the geographic distance they may live from parents. Emotional cutoff can be reflected by all kinds of emotional distancing and other forms of emotional reactivity to the parental family while having contact with them.

Bowen theory maintains that there is a "specific amount of immaturity of undifferentiation to be absorbed within the nuclear family, which is fluid and shifting, to some degree, and which increases to a symptomatic level during stress" (Bowen, p. 477). The immaturity of undifferentiation in the nuclear family gets expressed in some combination of four mechanisms—marital distance, marital conflict, dysfunction in a spouse, and projection to one or more of the children. The absorption of a specific amount of immaturity in one of the mechanisms means there is less that has to be absorbed in the other mechanisms. If there is a specific amount of the "immaturity of undifferentiation" that gets absorbed in the four mechanisms, then the ability to measure the degree to which the mechanisms come into play provides a potential way to estimate basic level of differentiation.

Some of the immaturity of undifferentiation can play out in the relationship with members of the family of origin when people are in reasonable emotional contact with the original family. The immaturity that derives

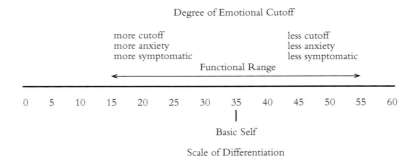

Figure 14.2 Degree of Emotional Cutoff

from unresolved emotional attachment—and the anxiety it produces—can be absorbed to some extent in highly supportive relationships in the family of origin as well as reactive ones. The more spouses are cut off from the original family, the more immaturity and anxiety generated by the unresolved emotional attachment there is that has to be handled in the nuclear family. Bowen theory holds that when spouses are able to reduce the amount of emotional cutoff with their family of origin, they can ordinarily reduce the amount of chronic anxiety in the nuclear family. This theoretical proposition can be tested clinically when people are successful in increasing the amount and quality of contact they have with their original family. Theory predicts that some of the anxiety in the nuclear family will lessen. The development of operational definitions to characterize the use of each of the four mechanisms ranging from minimal to mild, moderate, major, and severe can provide a more disciplined way to test the hypothesis that bridging cutoff reduces anxiety in the nuclear family over time.[8] If the intensity of one or more of the mechanisms declines, the hypothesis is strengthened.

Merely reducing cutoff, however, does not increase basic level of differentiation according to Bowen theory. Bridging cutoff is only a necessary first step toward defining a more solid self in one's family of origin. When a person is able to define more of a self in the original family in a similar process as outlined earlier in a nuclear family, the amount of immaturity and the chronic anxiety it produces is reduced whether with the original family or the nuclear family.

Three sets of variables influence the amount of anxiety a nuclear family has to contend with. The first variable is the basic level of differentiation itself and the amount of chronic anxiety generated by whatever the given basic level happens to be. The second set of variables revolves around how that chronic anxiety gets absorbed—in emotional cutoff and nuclear family emotional process. The third set of variables has to do with the number and intensity of stressors placing demands on the nuclear family to adapt. When basic level of differentiation does not change and the number and intensity of stressors on the nuclear family do not change, one can usefully investigate the impact of bridging emotional cutoff on the intensity of emotional process in the nuclear family as measured by possible changes in the degree of marital conflict and distance, the degree of spousal dysfunction, and the intensity of the child projection process. When the degree of emotional cutoff remains the same along with the number and intensity of stressors, one can get a better read on the impact of an increase in basic level of differentiation on functioning. And when basic level of differentiation and degree of emotional cutoff remain steady, it is possible to study the impact of a change in the number and intensity of stressors on emotional process in the nuclear family. Each set of variables influences the others.

Every concept of Bowen theory interlocks with every other concept. However, differentiation of self and level of anxiety are the two main variables of the theory and as such influence the way each of the other concepts plays out. Triangles function differently depending on the level of differentiation and the level of anxiety. Triangles are more flexible the lower the level of anxiety and the higher the basic level of differentiation. Triangle patterns are more fixed at lower levels of differentiation and as anxiety increases. Changes in the flexibility and intensity of triangles can be studied when the nuclear family is subjected to greater amounts of stress, or emotional cutoff is reduced, or basic level of differentiation increases. At the same time, when people work on changing their automatic functioning position in triangles by becoming, for example, more emotionally neutral about a problem two others are having with each other, while still actively relating to each without taking sides, anxiety may go up initially but will eventually come down. Triangles are so important that Bowen suggested that people do not increase their basic level of differentiation apart from modifying their functioning position in the important triangles of their nuclear and extended families. So triangles function differently depending on one's level of differentiation and the level of anxiety in the system, but changing one's functioning position in the important triangles of the family can also contribute to an increase in level of differentiation and a reduction of anxiety. In addition, the functioning of triangles influences the degree of emotional cutoff and symptom development in the nuclear family. Such is the nature of emotional systems. Each of the important variables influences the others. Like other concepts in the theory, triangles function on a continuum that parallels the other continua including differentiation of self. A good grasp of the functioning of triangles under varying degrees of stress in a family also provides a clue to the basic and functional levels of differentiation of that family.

A comparison of family functioning across generations provides another means of conducting research on level of differentiation. Gathering facts of functioning over many generations of a family gives an important context to the effort to estimate level of differentiation in the present generation. Educational attainment, health, longevity, successfully rearing children, responsible functioning in one's career, stability of marriage, and leadership in the community are indicators that often accompany better levels of differentiation. The stability and intactness of the extended family can also convey an impression about the average level of differentiation of the larger family. The more stable and intact a person's extended family, the more the extended family is a potential resource to him or her.

The concept of the multigenerational transmission process describes the way in which different levels of differentiation get transmitted from one generation to another. Different children in the same family may emerge with different basic levels of differentiation depending on which children were more affected by the family projection process. If, as according to theory, people marry others at the same basic level of differentiation as themselves, a comparison of the functioning of siblings and the functioning of their nuclear families can yield an impression of the intensity of the family projection process. The more intense the projection process on a child, the more the sibling profile of that child is skewed toward the immature characteristics of the sibling position. The more the mature characteristics of the sibling position stand out, the more that sibling is able to remain outside of an intense positive or negative focus by the parents. The facts and functional facts of sibling position, the family projection process, the multigenerational transmission process, and the stability and intactness of the extended family all occur on continua and interlock with the other concepts, especially level of differentiation and level of anxiety. A challenge for systems research is how to use the multigenerational facts of functioning to sharpen the ability to define level of differentiation more precisely.

Murray Bowen insisted that differentiation of self is more than a psychological phenomenon. When the scale was originally devised, he reserved a 100 for the hypothetical being who was perfect in all levels of emotional, cellular, and physiological functioning (Bowen, p. 474). Years later, he wrote that the "self" is "made up of constitutional, physical, physiological, genetic and cellular reactivity factors as they move in unison with psychological factors" (Bowen and Kerr, p. 342). Basic level of differentiation has to do with how the above factors that are part of the emotional system integrate with the intellectual system. Research on differentiation of self cannot ignore developing knowledge in the life sciences and how it may integrate with family systems variables. Much of the very valuable research on the stress response, for example, centers on the physiology of the individual. Bowen theory, with its focus on the family as an emotional unit, describes how the unit functions to determine which member or members of the family end up carrying more of the physiological response to stressors. From a systems perspective, the intensity and duration of the stress response for each individual is heavily influenced by how family members interact within the triangles of the unit. The cascade of responses that occur physiologically in the stress response for an individual cannot be separated from how emotional process is playing out in the family.

The developing field of epigenetics studies the way in which specific environmental conditions can affect the expression of genes. Given the importance of the family in the development of children, research on differentiation of self can study the intensity of the family projection process as a possible variable influencing the expression of genes in children that is relatively independent of variables like socioeconomic status. The family projection process operates in every family, regardless of income and social status. Children who have been part of an intense family projection process and emerge with a significantly lower level of differentiation than the other members of their family are far more vulnerable to poorer health and educational outcomes than their siblings. The day may come when well-trained family systems therapists collaborate with researchers in the natural sciences to build family variables into longitudinal research.

Bowen described his theory as a natural systems theory. He formulated his "blueprint" of emotional systems on a model derived from nature. He viewed natural systems as sets of counterbalancing forces in constant operation (pp. 358–359). Numerous variables make up each of the forces that constantly interact to enable organisms to adapt in nature. Bowen theory purports to define key variables that govern the operation of the "living system" of the family. Given that the concepts and variables of the theory emerged in large part from clinical research, clinical and own family research may be especially useful in testing, refining, and extending Bowen theory. An important challenge for research on differentiation of self is to document the ways in which each of the other important concepts and variables defined by the theory interlock with differentiation. From a Bowen theory perspective, a researcher must get a broad panoramic view of the total human phenomenon in order to be able to see differentiation. Research based on Bowen theory can exploit the myriad ways in which differentiation plays out to better define the concept and apply it.

NOTES

1 All Bowen references in this chapter refer to the 1978 book, *Family Therapy in Clinical Practice*.
2 This scale, like the one on goal directedness that appears later in the chapter, needs to be tested for inter-rater reliability with people who know Bowen theory well.
3 Rodríguez-González, M., & Martínez Berlanga, M. (2014). La teoría familiar sistémica de Bowen. Avances y aplicación terapéutica. Madrid: McGraw-Hill.
4 This formulation was first presented by Kerr and Bowen in their book, *Family Evaluation: An Approach Based on Bowen Theory*.
5 The author is indebted to Dr. Daniel Papero for this observation.
6 To think through a belief entails becoming more aware of the origin of the belief and the degree to which the formation of the belief has been influenced by others and is or is not grounded in fact. Thinking through a belief for self involves separating out what one is "supposed" to believe from what one actually does believe after a process of careful reasoning.
7 This example was cited by Michael Kerr in a 2013 clinical presentation.
8 The author has developed a set of such operational definitions to describe variation in the use of each of the four mechanisms. See Rodríguez-González and Martínez Berlanga (2014).

REFERENCES

Bowen, M. (1978). *Family therapy in clinical practice*. New York: Jason Aronson.
Bowen-Kerr Interview Series. (1980). "Defining a self in one's own family," Part 2. Videotape. Washington, DC: Bowen Center for the Study of the Family. (Producer).
Henry, J. P. & Stephens, P. M. (1977). *Stress, health and the social environment: A sociobiologic approach to medicine*. New York: Springer-Verlag.
Holmes, T. H. & Rahe, R. H. (1967). The Social Readjustment Rating Scale. *Journal of Psychosomatic Research, 11*(2), 213–218.

Kerr, M. E. & Bowen, M. (1988). *Family evaluation: An approach based on Bowen theory.* New York: W. W. Norton.

Miller, M. A. & Rahe, R. H. (1997). Life changes scaling for the 1990's. *Journal of Psychosomatic Research, 43*(3), 279–292.

Rodríguez-González, M. & Martínez Berlanga, M. (2014). La teoría familiar sistémica de Bowen. Avances y aplicación terapéutica. Madrid: McGraw-Hill.

15

EMOTIONAL REACTIVITY, FUSION, AND DIFFERENTIATION OF SELF IN FAMILY PHYSIOLOGY
Clinical Case Research

Victoria A. Harrison

Bowen Theory and the Study of Physiology in the Family

Medicine and mental health practitioners recognize that stress reactions and anxiety play a part in physical and psychiatric symptoms, but they are often confounded by how to understand differences in the physiology of particular symptoms and situations. Most research that informs treatment focuses on reactions within the individual and may include relationships as environmental triggers without considering the family as a system of emotionally interconnected individuals. Bowen theory introduces a natural systems framework with which to study how degrees of emotional fusion between family members and differentiation of self regulate physiological reactivity for individual family members. This study investigates the ways that different degrees of emotional fusion and differentiation of self between family members regulate physiological reactivity associated with anxiety, symptoms, and health for individual family members.

Emotion includes the automatic biological responses that are present for all life in the allocation of energy toward maintaining stability of relationships and toward survival of the individual organism. Emotional fusion is a term that Bowen developed to capture the extent to which family members are "stuck together" or connected to each other in a symbiotic, interdependent fashion.

Murray Bowen (1978) wrote:

> Emotional reactiveness in a family or other group that lives and works together goes from one family member to another in a chain reaction pattern. The total pattern is similar to electronic circuits in

which each person is "wired" or connected by radio to all the other people with whom he has relationships. Each person then becomes a nodal point or an electronic center through which impulses pass in rapid succession, or even multiple impulses at the same time. . . . This family systems theory postulates that all of the characteristics described under "emotional reactiveness" are all part of that part of man that he shares with lower forms of life.

(pp. 420–422)

The human family evolved a degree of connectedness between kin such that the functioning of each individual is regulated by patterns of relating and reacting within the family. People vary in the degree to which they can recognize and regulate emotional reactions for themselves. The "scale of differentiation" describes a continuum from lower to higher degrees of fusion, or symbiosis, between family members with corresponding differences in the interplay between emotional and intellectual functioning within individuals:

. . . the greater the fusion between emotion and intellect, the more the individual is fused into the emotional fusions of people around him. . . . It is possible for man to discriminate between the emotions and the intellect and to slowly gain more conscious control of emotional functioning.

(Bowen, 1978, p. 305)

Differentiation of self, while difficult to quantify in the abstract, defines differences in reactivity within the individual and between family members that can be observed and studied in behavior, relationship patterns, and physiological reactions. Bowen described intense symbiotic relationships as ones in which there is a *somatic reciprocity* such that how one person reacts becomes a reality for the other. At higher levels of differentiation, individuals are somewhat more separate and can better moderate emotional reactivity and interrupt anxious reactions within themselves. At lower levels of differentiation, individuals are regulated more by reactivity in the system and their reactions to each other. Anxiety transfers between people with less interruption and is higher and more prolonged.

Anxiety, in Bowen theory, is defined as emotional reactiveness to threat, real or imagined. It is reflected in physiological reactions, brain activity, perception, behaviors, relationship patterns, thinking, and feeling, with each influencing the others in a dynamic fashion. (The asterisks below indicate physiological reactions that will be measured in this research project.)

The first physiological reaction to threat is a rise in corticotrophine-releasing factor (CRF) in the central nervous system. If threats persist, CRF then stirs several reactions. The sympathetic nervous system (SNS) and increased adrenalin* begin the shift of oxygen and energy to fuel fight or flight through innervation of hollow vessels throughout the body.* Skeletal muscle tension increases.* Prolactin, oxytocin, and vasopressin may rise, fueling protection reactions. Dopamine may activate the reward system, fueling problem-solving or risk-taking.

When stress and anxiety are sustained, prolonged, or cumulative, a variety of other reactions occur. The hypothalamic pituitary axis (HPA) is activated, producing the hormone cortisol from the cortex of the adrenal gland. Cortisol cycles through the bloodstream, interacting with the immune system, reproductive hormones, neurons, and metabolic chemistry in a variety of ways. Cortisol circulates back to the central nervous system, where it turns off the activating hormones. The homeostatic nature of cortisol itself is disrupted when stress reactions are sustained over a long period of time (Calogero, 1988; McEwen, 2002; Sapolsky, 1994).

Stephen W. Porges, PhD, director of the University of Illinois Brain Body Center, describes the sequence of reactions to threat based upon the evolutionary lineage of the autonomic nervous system. The human autonomic nervous system incorporates three different physiological pathways that operate somewhat in sequence. One is an old vagal visceral pathway* that connects the brain and the gut in regulating digestion and energy metabolism. The second, an SNS pathway,* increases metabolic output and inhibits the visceral vagus to promote "fight-or-flight" responses. The third, the mammalian vagal pathway, connects facial and cranial nerves with the heart to facilitate engagement and detachment from the social environment. Initial reactions to threats activate this third system, built to rely upon facial expression, voices, and information about relationships, as a reference point. If relationships are absent or anxious, SNS activation fuels mobilization to fight or flee, evident in smooth muscle constriction* and increased skeletal muscle activity.* If stress continues or SNS strategies are ineffective, the old vagal visceral system is activated to produce "freeze or sleep or play dead" reactions* (Porges, 2009).

Conventional stress research and the study of anxiety focus on the nature of threats and duration of reactions to understand variation in physiological reactions and their association with symptoms. Bowen theory provides a framework to study ways that individuals adapt to each other and how anxiety reactions are sustained or interrupted through relationships in the family. The following research will explore how physiological reactivity, indicating states that are "anxious, active and at ease, and relaxed," measured with biofeedback and neurofeedback instruments, reflects emotional fusion and differentiation of self in the emotional triangle between mother, father, and child.

Emotional triangles are fundamental to human relationship systems. Reactivity between any two people is related to their relationship with a third person. Anxiety reactions cycle and circulate in triangles, producing patterns of closeness and distance, conflict, alliances, focus on problems in another, over/underfunctioning, and symptoms in an individual. Bowen wrote, "With the involvement of a third person, the anxiety level decreases. It is as if the anxiety is diluted as it shifts from one to another of the three relationships in a triangle" (1978, p. 400). The degree and duration of anxiety and the level of differentiation of self are reflected in the patterns of reacting and relating in emotional triangles between family members.

At lower levels of differentiation, emotional fusion between family members magnifies the anxiety experienced by individuals, with more reactions to, with, and for each other. Health problems, social or behavioral problems, relationship disruption, psychiatric diagnoses, or other symptoms associated with anxiety are predictable. At higher levels of differentiation, circumstances stir anxious reactions, but greater emotional separateness between individuals affords more interruption of anxiety and more ability to operate thoughtfully.

Background of Research Project and Biofeedback

Murray Bowen saw biofeedback instruments as one way to study physiological reactivity, anxiety, and differentiation of self. During videotaped interviews with me for the Bowen Clinical Conference Series in 1985, Bowen commented:

> Differentiation is exemplified by physiological functioning . . . I think physiology is a grand and glorious entrée to differentiation. It is not all of it but it is important . . . There could be something very important about checking physiological states.
>
> (Harrison, 1985)

The Biofeedback Program, established by Dr. Lillian Rosenbaum at the Georgetown Family Center in 1976, provided an opportunity to study physiological reactions and symptoms while learning about biology and the brain from scientists and research at Georgetown University Medical School, National Institutes of Health, and the National Library of Medicine. Adding biofeedback and later neurofeedback instruments to family systems psychotherapy offered a lens to study relationships and physiology associated with various symptoms that influence health and reproduction. Rosenbaum (1989) described early research and clinical work in *Biofeedback Frontiers*.

Biofeedback and neurofeedback instruments measure aspects of anxiety or stress reactions. Skin sweat response, or electrodermal response (EDR), measures the electrical activity that increased adrenalin, an indicator of SNS activity, produces at the palm. Digital skin temperature (DST) measures changes in temperature that occur when SNS activity produces vasoconstriction in the little vessels that carry blood and oxygen through the fingertips. DST also measures the rise in fingertip temperature that accompanies reactivity characteristic of the old vagal reaction—shut down or exhaustion after prolonged stress. Electromyography (EMG) records skeletal muscle activity associated with increased and decreased muscle tension. Neurofeedback, or electroencephalography (EEG), measures electrical activity in the brain using sensors placed upon the scalp.

Early clinical observations with biofeedback instruments strengthened my conviction that physiology in one family member is related to anxiety in another. An eleven-year-old boy was referred by his pediatrician for nausea and migraine headaches. The boy's physiology, measured on biofeedback instruments while talking with him and his mother, exhibited reactions associated with his symptoms as his mother focused on dangers in the world and possible injury or accident for her son at school. When Mother was asked, "Is there any basis in the history of your family for worry about a youngster your son's age?" she talked about her ten-year-old brother, who drowned while she was in charge of her younger siblings. The boy's physiology began to recover while his mother talked about her family history instead of her fears for her son.

The mother continued consultation, working on how she reacted and related to unrealistic responsibilities she had assumed from her mother, aunt, and grandmother. She was able to restrain herself from taking on their responsibilities in day-to-day life. She began to interrupt and reduce her own anxiety. The son became symptom free and his physiological measures indicated stability during follow-up measures (Harrison, 1989, pp. 224–226).

Observations like this inspired long-term plans to use multiple biofeedback instruments to examine the physiological reactions of family members as indicators of emotional fusion, how reactivity and anxiety are managed, and perhaps differentiation of self. Realities of life and work delayed that research until 2005, when I was able to acquire three identical F1000 biofeedback units.

Frank and Mary Deits, an engineer and a therapist, designed the F1000, an instrument that measures physiological reactions and brain waves, presents information on a computer screen in various training modes, and stores the data for statistical analysis using Excel software (Deits, 1994). Priscilla Friesen introduced the F1000 at the Bowen Center in 1994. I began working with one unit in clinical practice in 1998. In 2005 I built an office large enough for three identical F1000 instruments. Frank Deits created software to link them so that those units obtain simultaneous measures. They have been superior for clinical and research purposes.

This chapter describes one such research project, a clinical case study that provides the basis for analysis of physiological measures and investigating how they reflect anxiety, emotional fusion, and differentiation of self in family triangles.

Clinical Research: Physiological Reactivity, Fusion, and Differentiation of Self in One Family

The research participants are five members of the A family: Mother, Father, and three adult children. Initials and names have been assigned to assure confidentiality. The family has granted permission for facts about the family and physiology to be presented and published. Mrs. A and her daughter, Sally, the second child, had been referred for family systems psychotherapy with biofeedback and neurofeedback by Sally's physician when the 20-year-old young woman developed constant vomiting and nausea that did not respond to medical treatment. She had returned home for medical care within weeks of beginning her junior year in college.

As mother and daughter participated in psychotherapy using biofeedback and neurofeedback, each developed some control over anxiety reactions associated with Sally's symptoms. Mrs. A began to see the value of helping her daughter by focusing more broadly on her own anxiety in other areas of the family and life. She could observe ways that distance with her siblings and mother, dissatisfaction in her work life, and cutoff from her extended family contributed to a comfortable but intense closeness with her children. She saw her own anxiety reactions on the biofeedback instruments and considered how her anxiety might impact others. She described tension in her marriage and how she and her husband were closer when they focused on problems in their children.

Mrs. A began to define a career direction for herself. She made contact with her siblings and mother without taking sides in their battles. It became easier for her to disengage her anxious focus on helping her daughter. Sally's nausea improved. Pain lifted. Sally began to focus on how to rebuild her life and regain independence. She still cried easily and felt discouraged, but she continued to focus on being responsible for herself. She found a part-time job and paced herself until she was working full time and could buy a car.

Mrs. A continued therapy after her daughter became busy with her own life. She obtained a job with advancement potential. She began working to understand patterns of relating and reacting in the triangles around her mother. She spent individual time with her mother and initiated contact with her mother's estranged brother.

During this time, Sally met the man she would later marry. They began to live together while Sally completed college out of town. After graduation, the couple moved back to Houston, where both sets of parents lived. Sally and her partner each took a job of convenience. Within a few months, a pregnancy occurred in spite of Sally's polycystic ovarian syndrome diagnosis. They married before the baby was born and moved into their own home in Houston.

Mrs. A had participated in therapy, off and on, for five years when the family agreed to participate in the research project. Though Sally's health and the family's functioning had improved, the family was not symptom free. The A marriage remained strained, and the younger daughter was having a difficult time in the summer prior to college. Everyone agreed a great deal could be learned about physiological reactions and patterns of emotional fusion and anxiety in the family.

The following family diagram (see Figure 15.1) and family history were developed as part of family systems psychotherapy and expanded for the research project. The nuclear family history and extended family history

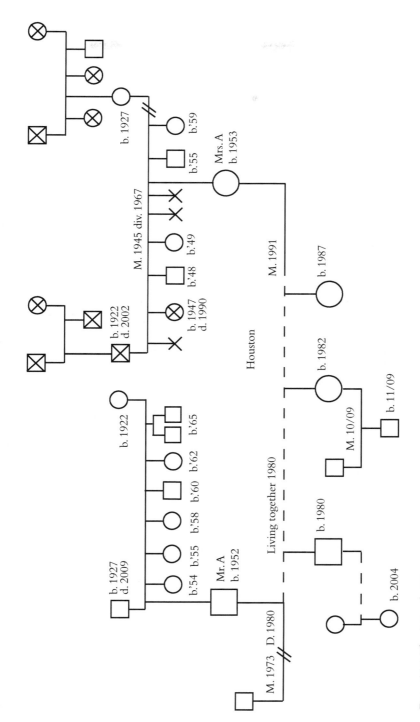

Figure 15.1 The A Family Diagram

include facts and factors that indicate: 1) levels of differentiation of self; 2) intensity of emotional fusion between family members; 3) patterns of reacting in family triangles; and 4) chronic anxiety present.

Nuclear Family History

Mr. and Mrs. A met when she was married to a high school sweetheart she wed immediately after graduation. That marriage ended in affairs for both. Mrs. A explained that she and Mr. A had a passionate and rocky romance. They might have broken up in 1980 had she not conceived their first child, Adam. Instead, they settled into family life without marriage until after their third child, a daughter, Mary, was born. When their son pointed out that none of his friends had unmarried parents, the couple married. Mrs. A described the relationship with her husband as perpetually unsettled. When he was critical of her, she distanced into friendships, where she complained about her marriage. She said, "I poured myself into my children. Being a good mother was the most important thing in my life. I did not complain about their father to the children, but I supported and protected them from his gloomy, dour moods. He was harsh and critical of them."

The young parents focused anxiously on their first child during an incorrect but frightening medical diagnosis. These reactions stirred a ripple effect through the family. Mrs. A said the family focused on her son's timidity and lack of friends until, at nine, he discovered the swim team.

The second pregnancy was uncomplicated and Sally was an easy infant, but anxious focus shifted to her when she developed prolonged vomiting at age four. Mrs. A said that their son "slipped away like a fish from a net" when he no longer was the focus of anxiety. Sally started menstruating at nine, with nausea, pain, and fatigue accompanying her monthly cycles through junior high and high school. She had a busy and successful school life, nonetheless, until her third year of college. Many medical evaluations and treatments preceded the referral to family systems psychotherapy.

The first two children did very well in school, graduated with honors, and left for college. Adam established himself out of town after college and got a job, living alone. He maintained close friendships and fell in love with someone who was unavailable. In 2003, a good friend in a lesbian marriage asked him to father her child. His daughter lives with her mothers, but the A family members are an active extended family.

The third child, Mary, struggled in school and began to drink heavily after both siblings left home. When Sally returned home with symptoms, her younger sister stabilized somewhat. Mary's drinking and behavior indicated heightened anxiety during the summer before college and her parents' increased their worried focus on this child.

Mr. and Mrs. A experienced what some would consider symptoms, but these did not receive much focus. Mrs. A was overweight and managed high blood pressure with medication. She described her husband as depressed and irritable. Both drank as a way of dealing with stress and for the improved mood that came with good wine and good food. The marriage was distant and became uncomfortable when Mr. A became critical of his wife.

Extended Family History

Both husband and wife were distant from their families when Mrs. A began therapy. Mr. A grew up the oldest of eight siblings, with his parents relying on him to take responsibility for the younger ones. He did exceptionally well in school and stayed close to home to finish college. When his younger brothers were 12, he moved away for graduate school and then work. He maintained distant, dutiful contact with his parents and saw his siblings infrequently, with the exception of one younger brother who moved closer to Mr. A when he married and had one child. There were no major symptoms in the siblings but his parents' marriage was conflictual. Mrs. A described her mother-in-law as well intended but intense and intrusive, with a tendency to speak for her husband and for her children. Visits with his parents left Mr. A irritable and critical of them.

Mrs. A described the years before her parents' divorce as idyllic but marred by serious drug and life problems for her oldest sister. Her parents had an affectionate, fun-loving marriage. Her father was financially successful, and her "full-time mother" enjoyed the attentions of her husband and the closeness with her children.

Tensions rose in the twentieth year of marriage and their bitter divorce changed life for everyone. Mrs. A's older siblings, who had left home, took Dad's side. Her mother would become so upset if the younger children had contact with their father that they stopped talking to or about him. Life was chaotic, with frequent moves as her mother tried to work and establish stability and finally settled in Houston. Mrs. A, a junior in high school, focused on moving out as quickly as possible. Early marriage was a way to do so. She moved in with her first husband, maintaining little contact with her family. Her sisters and mother remained in Houston, where Mrs. A found herself embroiled in their problems and the conflicts between the sisters and her mother. She developed ways to maintain emotional distance with calm superficial relationships with her family. This research project occurred after Mrs. A resumed psychotherapy to continue efforts to modify her functioning in her family of origin and better manage the impact of anxiety in the lives of her adult children.

All five family members participated in this clinical research project to investigate whether physiological reactions measured in Mother, Father, and each child demonstrated patterns consistent with 1) levels of emotional fusion, 2) indicators of higher or lower differentiation, 3) chronic anxiety, and 4) patterns of reacting in each triangle. Mrs. A recognized the relevance of these observations to her purposes, as well as the potential for better under-standing and treatment of difficult symptoms in the lives of others.

Research Project Protocol

Physiological measures for all five family members, one triangle at a time, were obtained in the same afternoon. Mother, Father, and one child sat side by side while each was connected to the F1000 equipment. The same interaction protocol was used with each triangle. Everyone sat quietly for one minute. Then two family members were asked to interact for three minutes while the third observed. Mother and Child talked with each other; then Father and Child; then Mother and Father, with a one-minute pause between conversa-tions. Their instructions were "to have a personal conversation about self and the other for three minutes." The audiotaped conversations were superficial for the most part.

Measures of Physiological Reactivity

During these interactions, an F1000 unit measured skeletal muscle activity (EMG), fingertip skin temperature (DST), skin sweat response (EDR), and electrical brain activity (EEG) for each person.

Wires from each computer were connected to electrodes placed at two specific sites (Cz and T3) at the center of the scalp and right temple for EEG and for EMG. Wires also connected the computer to a band with sensors across the palm for EDR. Wires connected one thermal sensor to the inside pad of the right middle finger for DST. The equipment could provide visual and/or auditory feedback for observing and changing reactivity, but this was not done during the research protocol. Each instrument stored, graphed, and statistically analyzed the data over the session. The average and range of each measure were provided for the time frame. The mathematical data were provided via USB port for Excel analysis.

Research data are in mathematical and electronic format that is available for download and analysis in Excel:

- Twelve minutes of 14 Hz EEG measured and stored in .002 increments of a minute = 542 measures/minute (graphed in a manual selection process);
- Twelve minutes of EMG in μV (microvolts = one millionth of a volt) measured and stored in .002 increments of a minute = 542 measures/minute (graphed in a manual selection process);
- Twelve minutes of DST in degrees F in .002/minute increments = about 110 measures/minute;
- Twelve minutes of EDR in $\mu\mho$ (micromhos) of skin conductance in .002/minute increments = about 110 measures/minute.

Data analysis for this chapter is based upon averages of EMG, DST, and EDR (physiological measures of reactivity and anxiety) for each person during the interaction sequence of Mother and Child, Father and Child, and Mother and Father, for each triangle (Figures 15.3–15.5).

Physiological Measures and Anxiety

Criteria for evaluating physiological reactivity measures, established through numerous studies, are compiled in *Standards and Guidelines for Biofeedback Applications in Psychophysiological Self-regulation* (Amar, 1993). Specific physical reactions have been associated with increased anxiety or stress, while others are associated with relaxation and with being active but at ease (Rosenbaum, 1989). Porges' polyvagal theory of nervous system functioning provides additional perspective for interpreting physiological measures associated with chronic anxiety and an old vagal state of collapse (Porges, 2009).

An early signal of increased anxiety to what is perceived as an immediate threat is constriction of small blood vessels in the fingertips and feet (DST). This signals a shift in blood flow and oxygen away from the body's perimeter and toward the muscles or brain, where it can fuel flight, fight, or problem-solving activity. Increased adrenalin, evident in palm sweat response (EDR), is another signal of increased SNS activity. Elevated skeletal muscle activity (EMG) signals mobilizing or bracing the body as a reaction to threat.

Physiological signs of chronic, ongoing, or cumulative anxiety reactions also are evident in fingertip temperature, levels of palm sweat, and muscle activity. Fingertip temperature (DST) above 95°F indicates vagal activity that occurs in the presence of sustained SNS activity without effective action or problem-solving. This reaction is characteristic of what Porges has described as an immobilization or shutdown reaction, reflecting the unmyelinated vagal visceral pathway connecting the brain to the heart and abdomen (Porges, 2009). Adrenalin, with sustained activation over time, becomes flat and exhausted. Skeletal muscle activity may be high, inhibited, or exhausted.

The criteria for evaluating measures of physiological reactions are these:

- Fingertip temperature or digital skin temperature (DST) reflects the constriction of blood vessels in fingertips produced when increased SNS and adrenalin stimulate hollow vessels throughout the body. DST of 93° to 95°F is characteristic of an active but at-ease state, without SNS activity. DST below 93°F indicates vasoconstriction produced by increased SNS activity. DST above 95°F shows activation of the "old vagal reaction," a shutdown or collapsed state following sustained and ineffective SNS and somatic reactions;
- Palm sweat levels, or electrodermal response (EDR), is another indicator of adrenalin level stirred by SNS. A flat EDR at 1–2 μ℧ signals

exhaustion. EDR of 2–4 μ℧ indicates active but at-ease levels of adrenalin. EDR of 4–20 μ℧ shows increased SNS activity;

- Skeletal muscle activity (EMG) of 2–4 μV indicates relaxation. EMG between 4 and 8 μV is characteristic of an active but at-ease state. Between 8 and 50 μV indicates tension.

Physiological Reactivity and Anxiety in Individual Family Members

A simple average of physiological reactions (EMG, DST, and EDR) for each family member indicates that everyone in this family experiences anxiety during the research protocol. There are differences between family members in which physical reactions exhibit the greatest anxiety and in the level of anxiety experienced (see Figure 15.2).

Mother experiences anxious physiology in all three systems measured. Hypertension is often associated with elevated skeletal muscle tension and vasoconstriction. James Lynch, PhD, who directed the University of Maryland Cardiovascular Health Program, observed that avoiding conflict and deferring to others are relationship patterns commonly present with high blood pressure (Lynch, 1985). Mrs. A would describe herself as operating in those ways in her marriage. Mother's physiological reactions are almost opposite those of her husband.

Father consistently expresses anxiety with increased adrenalin (EDR), the highest in the family, along with lower EMG and warmer DST. It is likely that his physiological reactivity indicates chronic levels of anxiety tipping into fatigue or shutdown, which his wife describes as a dour, grumpy, irritable mood. He, too, relies on alcohol and good food for stress reduction. Adrenalin in Father and muscle tension in Mother may reflect the effort each exerts, in different physiological systems, reacting to each other.

The oldest child, Adam, has an average EMG similar to his father. His DST indicates greater SNS vasoconstriction than anyone else, but his EDR level is lower than anyone else's in the family. It is likely that his average

	EMG	DST	EDR
Mother	17.47 μV	91.00°F	10.35 μmhos
Father	8.03 μV	93.10°F	14.09 μmhos
Child #1	8.61 μV	87.50°F	7.59 μmhos
Child #2	20.38 μV	94.55°F	10.15 μmhos
Child #3	10.45 μV	89.99°F	13.00 μmhos

Figure 15.2 Averages of Physiological Measures per Individual

levels of EMG, EDR, and DST reflect the shifts in his anxiety that occur while interacting with each parent and while observing the parents interacting with each other. Those patterns, and their implications for functioning, are described in Figure 15.3.

The second child, Sally, whose symptoms provoked referral, experiences anxious physiology in all three systems: the highest level of EMG, elevated EDR, and an average DST that indicates the vagal state of exhaustion. She and Mrs. A had very similar levels of EMG and EDR. It is unclear whether these measures indicated 1) a high level of fusion with the parents in which she experienced their anxious physiology as her own, tipping her into a vagal state, 2) a reciprocity in which she moved into a vagal state counterbalancing the parents' elevated tension, or 3) delay in her ability to recover. Any of those could contribute toward a more chronic, ongoing level of anxiety reactions consistent with her symptoms.

The youngest child, Mary, also experiences anxious physiology in all three systems measured. Average levels of anxious physiology for her might be predictive of symptom development later in young adult life.

Individual averages suggest that Mother, Sally, and Mary experience more chronic heightened anxiety than do Father and Adam. Individual averages, however, do not provide information about the biological reality of how reactions vary for individuals in relation to each other. The patterns of physiology while interacting and observing the interactions of others provide more information about the impact of anxiety, emotional fusion, and perhaps differentiation of self.

Physiological Reactivity and Anxiety in Relationship Triangles

Each of the next three figures presents the averages of physiological measures (EMG, DST, and EDR) for Mother (circle on the top right), Father (square on the top left), and each adult child (square or circle below) in the three triangles: Mother and Child interacting while Father watches, Father and Child interacting while Mother watches, and Mother and Father interacting while Child watches.

For Mother, Father, and Adam, (see Figure 15.3) anxious physiology, particularly EDR, is higher for everyone while Mother and Son interact. Mother and Son experience similarly anxious physiology during their interaction (increased EMG and lower DST), while Father has less anxious EMG and DST with higher, more anxious EDR. Although increased anxiety may be predictable for the first interaction of the research project, the fact that everyone experiences increased anxious physiology while Mother and Adam interact may also indicate a degree of emotional fusion in which all react in similar fashion.

Father and Son experience decreased anxiety while interacting with each other, somewhat independently from Mother, who sustains her levels of EMG and EDR while watching them talk. Mother's level of anxious physiology

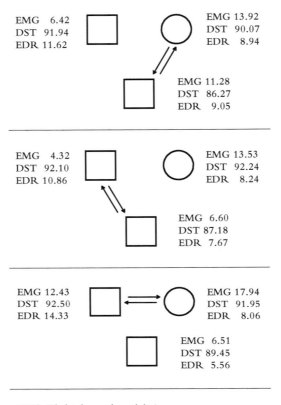

EMG 6.42 DST 91.94 EDR 11.62

EMG 13.92 DST 90.07 EDR 8.94

EMG 11.28 DST 86.27 EDR 9.05

EMG 4.32 DST 92.10 EDR 10.86

EMG 13.53 DST 92.24 EDR 8.24

EMG 6.60 DST 87.18 EDR 7.67

EMG 12.43 DST 92.50 EDR 14.33

EMG 17.94 DST 91.95 EDR 8.06

EMG 6.51 DST 89.45 EDR 5.56

EMG (Skeletal muscle activity)

2 – 4 µV indicates a relaxed state.

4 – 8 µV is characteristic of an active but at ease state.

8 – 50 µV indicates tension.

DST (Fingertip temperature)

Below 93°F indicates increased sympathetic nervous
     system constriction of blood vessels.

93° to 95°F is characteristic of an active but at ease state.

Above 95°F shows activation of a vagal reaction.

EDR (Palm sweat levels)

1 – 2 µmhos signals exhaustion.

2 – 4 µmhos indicates active but at ease levels of adrenalin.

4 – 20 µmhos shows increased adrenalin.

Figure 15.3 Physiological Measures for Triangle One: Mother, Father, and Adam

may be consistent with her perception that Adam requires her protection from a harsh and critical father. She does experience slightly warmer fingertip temperature, indicating decreasing SNS activity during the interaction between Father and Son.

Mother and Father are most anxious interacting with each other. Skeletal muscle tension rises for both. EDR is high, though both experience warmer DST. Anxiety reactions for Adam decline while he watches his parents talk. The pattern of increased anxiety while interacting and decreased anxiety while observing is strikingly consistent with a lifestyle of living at a distance from family and close friends, although it provides Adam an apparent lower overall level of anxious physiology.

Both Mother and Father experience increased anxiety while interacting with Sally (see Figure 15.4).

This child has sustained anxiety during those interactions. Mother and Father exhibit slight decreases in anxiety while observing the others interact. Mother and Father again experience highest anxiety interacting with each other. Sally experiences sustained anxiety observing her parents interact, with only slight decreases in EMG and EDR. Her rise in skin temperature indicates a shift toward vagal activity characteristic of shutting down in the face of chronic anxiety (see Figure 15.5).

In Triangle Three, Mother and Daughter experience anxious physiology interacting with each other. Father has lower EMG and less SNS activity while watching their interaction and becomes less anxious while interacting with Mary. Mother's EMG and EDR decrease slightly and her DST warms while watching Father and Mary.

Mother and Father again are most anxious interacting with each other. EMG and EDR are elevated for both. Mother experiences more SNS activity and cooler DST than her husband. Observing her parents interact, Mary experiences decreased anxiety, lower EMG, warmer DST, and much lower EDR.

Patterns of Emotional Reactivity, Fusion, and Physiology in Family Triangles

The most consistent pattern of reactivity is increased anxious physiology in Mother and Father as they interact with each other in each triangle with a child. This increased anxiety between spouses while interacting with each other is in keeping with the distance and discomfort Mother describes in the marriage and with a process described in family systems theory. Bowen observed that immaturity in the parents and emotional fusion in the marriage play their part in a triangle where focus on a child decreases the anxiety for the parents while contributing toward anxiety in the child in various ways (Bowen, 1978, pp. 97, 434–436).

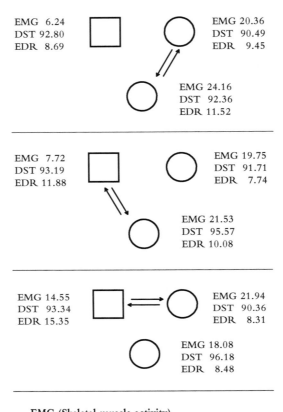

| EMG 6.24
DST 92.80
EDR 8.69 | | EMG 20.36
DST 90.49
EDR 9.45 |

EMG 24.16
DST 92.36
EDR 11.52

EMG 7.72
DST 93.19
EDR 11.88

EMG 19.75
DST 91.71
EDR 7.74

EMG 21.53
DST 95.57
EDR 10.08

EMG 14.55
DST 93.34
EDR 15.35

EMG 21.94
DST 90.36
EDR 8.31

EMG 18.08
DST 96.18
EDR 8.48

EMG (Skeletal muscle activity)

2 – 4 μV indicates a relaxed state.

4 – 8 μV is characteristic of an active but at ease state.

8 – 50 μV indicates tension.

DST (Fingertip temperature)

Below 93°F indicates increased sympathetic nervous
system constriction of blood vessels.

93° to 95°F is characteristic of an active but at ease state.

Above 95°F shows activation of a vagal reaction.

EDR (Palm sweat levels)

1 – 2 μmhos signals exhaustion.

2 – 4 μmhos indicates active but at ease levels of adrenalin.

4 – 20 μmhos shows increased adrenalin.

Figure 15.4 Physiological Measures for Triangle Two: Mother, Father, and Sally

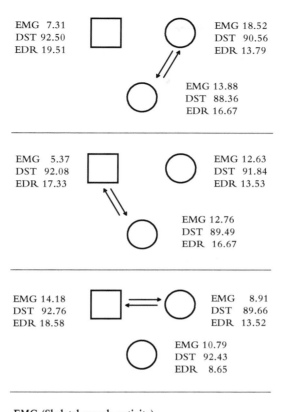

EMG 7.31
DST 92.50
EDR 19.51

EMG 18.52
DST 90.56
EDR 13.79

EMG 13.88
DST 88.36
EDR 16.67

EMG 5.37
DST 92.08
EDR 17.33

EMG 12.63
DST 91.84
EDR 13.53

EMG 12.76
DST 89.49
EDR 16.67

EMG 14.18
DST 92.76
EDR 18.58

EMG 8.91
DST 89.66
EDR 13.52

EMG 10.79
DST 92.43
EDR 8.65

EMG (Skeletal muscle activity)

2 – 4 μV indicates a relaxed state.

4 – 8 μV is characteristic of an active but at ease state.

8 – 50 μV indicates tension.

DST (Fingertip temperature)

Below 93°F indicates increased sympathetic nervous
system constriction of blood vessels.

93° to 95°F is characteristic of an active but at ease state.

Above 95°F shows activation of a vagal reaction.

EDR (Palm sweat levels)

1 – 2 μmhos signals exhaustion.

2 – 4 μmhos indicates active but at ease levels of adrenalin.

4 – 20 μmhos shows increased adrenalin.

Figure 15.5 Physiological Measures for Triangle Three: Mother, Father, and Mary

Father is consistently less anxious observing Mother and each child interact. He experiences a slight decrease in anxiety while interacting with Adam and Mary. Mother experiences anxiety while interacting with each child and slightly less anxiety while watching Father and each child interact. Increased anxiety for the parents while interacting with each other and decreasing anxiety while watching the other parent interact with a child may contribute toward distance in the marriage and encourage involvement of one parent with each child in a way that is calming to the other parent. It is surprising to see anxiety rise for Mother while she interacts with each child, but perhaps that is an indicator of the anxious focus on each child she experiences.

Children grow up with different ways of reacting in the triangle with their parents, with different degrees of emotional fusion and levels of differentiation of self. The three adult children in this study vary in their physiological reactivity to the interaction with a parent and in the triangle with parents.

Adam has lower EMG and EDR than his sisters but experiences more SNS vasoconstriction, particularly while interacting with either parent. He experiences decreased anxious physiology while watching his parents interact. It is not clear whether this interruption in anxiety indicates less emotional fusion between parents and child or is a pattern of physiological reactivity associated with distance as a way of reacting to emotional fusion. Adam lives at a distance from family and maintains contact with good friends and with his biological daughter from afar. He describes his relationship with his family as positive and warm. He misses them and speaks to his sisters and parents frequently. Distance may be a way of managing anxiety activated by proximity in the face of emotional fusion.

The increase in anxiety that Mother and Son experience interacting with each other suggests a resonance to each other associated with emotional fusion. Father and Son decrease anxiety while interacting with each other. Mother's anxiety declines while watching their interaction. One person's decline in anxiety may demonstrate the flexibility in emotional reactivity afforded by the emotional triangle. If, however, a decline in anxiety in one is dependent on distance or on the decline of anxiety in others, it would indicate greater emotional fusion.

Physiological measures in Sally suggest a greater degree of emotional fusion and demonstrate how that magnifies anxious physiology associated with symptoms. Sally, the daughter whose symptoms initiated referral, experiences anxious levels of EMG, EDR, and DST (rising above 95°) throughout each interaction sequence. Mother also experiences anxious physiology throughout the three interactions, in all indicating a level of emotional fusion that operates to reflect and magnify anxiety in each. Father is slightly more at ease while observing Mother and Sally interact and while interacting with his daughter, but it does not appear to interrupt or alter the anxiety present for Mother and Daughter. Sally maintains anxious physiology while watching her parents talk to each other and does not experience an interruption of anxiety but continues to react and adapt to the anxiety in others. Her rising fingertip temperature (exceeding 95°) indicates vagal reactivity characteristic of sustained anxiety and the nausea and fatigue symptoms she has experienced.

Of the children, Mary experiences the highest level of adrenalin (EDR), one similar to her father, with moderate EMG and less SNS than her siblings. She and Mother experience heightened anxiety interacting with each other, a pattern perhaps consistent with greater emotional fusion. Mary experiences decreased anxious physiology while interacting with Father (whose anxiety decreases) and while watching her parents interact. Mother declines slightly in anxious physiology while watching Father and Daughter interact. The greater anxiety in Triangle Three might predict future symptom development, but it is not clear whether the ability of Mary to decrease anxiety in the presence of anxious parents might serve as an indicator of less emotional fusion or of distance as a way of becoming comfortable.

At the time of the research, Mary was living at home the summer before her junior year of high school. Her parents were concerned about her drinking and adjustment to the upcoming move from home. She had begun a relationship with a man with drug, alcohol, and work problems. Her physiological reactions, anxiety, and emotional fusion would predict challenges over the next few years.

The graphs of physiological activity in each triangle show that Adam and Mary experienced a shift toward active but at-ease physiology (decreased adrenalin, SNS, and skeletal muscle tension) when the parents engaged with each other. Bowen observed in his early family research, and ongoing clinical work with families, that the functioning of children improved when parents were more involved with each other and when parents were more involved with their own family of origin and extended family. This does not mean that parents "get along better" but that they engage each other and the anxiety between them in a more active way.

Since this study, Mrs. A and Mr. A have become more involved with their extended families and with each other. Adam has lived closer to his daughter while he worked on a research project in his field and is now living with his parents as he makes decisions about graduate school and career directions. Sally currently lives with her husband and son near her parents. She is in contact with a wide array of relatives and continues to pursue her vocational interests. She experiences only moderate symptoms, which do not interfere with her functioning. Mary dropped out of college to live with her boyfriend, working in daycare to support him. She eventually broke up with him, moved home, and is reorganizing her life. Repeating the research protocol now would allow observation of changes in levels and patterns of emotional reactivity, fusion, and physiology that might be associated with these changes in family functioning.

Conclusion/Discussion

Bowen observed that the emotional involvement between parents and children creates different degrees of emotional fusion and differentiation of self in the next generation. Children leave home with a level of differentiation about the same as their parents, slightly lower or slightly higher, depending upon several factors. Every moment of anxious reactivity is a part of a historical process that is formative and cumulative and sets the stage for variation in levels of differentiation of self in each of the children.

The levels of anxious physiology in parents and children, as well as patterns of emotional reactivity evident in these family triangles, suggest that different degrees of emotional fusion are present with slightly different levels of differentiation of self. Even this simple analysis of physiological measures suggests that:

- Different degrees of emotional fusion between parents and each child are evident in higher and lower levels of anxious physiology and in how children react to their parents and in the family triangles;
- Variations in anxious physiology are associated with distance, closeness, and child focus in the family triangles;
- Physiological reactions of individuals are associated with their symptoms and with their functioning in life;
- Variation in levels of differentiation of self are suggested but require further study.

With more sophisticated analysis, data from this study can reveal more about patterns of emotional reactivity, anxiety, emotional fusion, and levels of differentiation of self. The actual 12 minutes of physiological measures in each family triangle provide a richer picture of reactivity within each individual and between family members in the triangles than averaging allows.

Further work with these data will involve adapting Excel tools to map physiological measures for each person onto those of others in the triangle. Excel formulas will be designed to examine the interaction of reactivity between family members in each triangle, to determine when reactivity in any one physical system is operating in counterbalancing or reciprocal fashion between family members. It will be possible to graph reactivity in each triangle to identify when individuals are reacting "with each other," "opposite to each other," or independently of each other. It will be possible, for example, to examine whether anxiety reactions in one person rise or fall with another or when they move in a more independent pattern. This may better distinguish degrees of emotional fusion and variation in levels of differentiation of self. For example, if the percentage of the time reactivity in each family member is linked to the others in a patterned fashion that would be an indicator of emotional fusion. The percentage of time that reactivity in each family member appears to occur independently of others and that would be an indicator of greater differentiation of self.

Another formula will examine the sequence of reactions to identify when people are triggering each other and what may be a time delay in activation of anxious physiology or in recovery. Higher levels of differentiation may be evident in more independent physiological reactions or more delay in response.

One of the most profound implications of understanding the family as a single organism is that physiological reactions in one family member occur in reaction to others in triangles and reflect the levels of differentiation of self of family members. Excel formulas will make it possible to better observe the interplay between different physiological reactions for all three people in each triangle over the 12 minutes of interaction. For example, is there an association between Father's EDR, Mother's EMG, and the vagal state evident in DST for Sally?

This study suggests that the mechanisms of reacting to emotional fusion identified by Bowen—distance, child focus, conflict, development of symptoms within the individual, and over/underfunctioning—involve physiological reactivity as well as behavior and psychological states. Distance may interrupt anxious reactions, for example, but does distance represent greater independence from reactivity to others? It does not appear to be the case in this study. Does the "outside position" in family triangles allow someone to develop more self over time? This study raises such questions but cannot address them. Variation of reactivity in each sibling and his/her triangle with the parents raises questions about how to distinguish physiological changes associated with those patterns of reacting or with birth order from physiological reactions associated with emotional fusion and differentiation of self.

Further work is necessary to establish a template for studying physiological reactivity on a wider basis with families who exhibit distinctly higher and lower levels of differentiation of self and those who employ different ways of managing the intensity of reactivity to each other. Such a design might include:

- Asking each family member to complete the Skowron Differentiation of Self inventory to consider whether different patterns of physiological reactivity correspond to differences identified in the inventory (Skowron, 1998);
- Asking family members to each complete a brief questionnaire about what they were thinking while observing the interaction of others and what they were doing 24 hours prior to the study;
- Videotaping research interactions to capture eye contact and content of conversations;
- Asking participants to each complete a checklist of patterns of reacting (distance, symptoms experienced, conflict, over/underfunctioning, and focus on a child) they observe in their family; and

351

- Expanding the interaction instructions to include asking the parents to talk about the child in order to better observe the difference that makes in the parents' physiology.

Such an expanded protocol could be used to address several questions, including what differences in physiological reactivity and anxiety for a family are associated with changes in their functioning over time. Mrs. A described the clinical implications for this research when, after seeing the biology of her own anxiety and considering its impact on others in her family, she said, "I realized that I could not fake it. I really had to do something about my anxiety level in order to benefit my children." What difference does it make in the functioning of all family members when one family member can recognize and modify her anxiety reactions? Does that bring about changes in physiological reactions associated with anxiety, symptoms, and health? Further investigation of how emotional fusion between family members and differentiation of self regulate physiological reactivity can increase knowledge about the family system as a fundamental influence over sickness and health. Perhaps such research can be part of the contribution Bowen theory makes toward understanding variation in human adaptation.

Acknowledgments

Several people, in addition to those referenced, have been particularly helpful in the work on this research and in writing this chapter. They warrant mention. Thank you to Michael Kerr for connecting the dots between reactivity in the family and many physiological reactions associated with cancer and other symptoms; to Kathleen Kerr for early inspiration to study physiological states in one person as a reflection of reactivity in another family member; to Daniel Papero for careful and challenging thinking about emotional process in the family; to Adrian Ryan Guzman and Robert Knetsch for computer engineering; to Katie Long for editorial expertise; to Sara Mason, who read this chapter with the eye of a graduate student; to Ann Jones and Linda MacKay for careful reading and recommendations for clarity; to Raoul LeBlanc and David Mason for formatting Excel for future analysis; and to Elizabeth Utschig for graphic artistry.

REFERENCES

Amar, P. (1993). *Standards and guidelines for biofeedback applications in psychophysiological self-regulation*. Wheat Ridge, CO: Association for Applied Psychophysiology and Biofeedback.

Bowen, M. (1978). *Family therapy in clinical practice*. New York: Jason Aronson.

Calogero A., Gallucci W. T., Gold P. W. & Chrousos, G. P. (1988). Multiple regulatory feedback loops on hypothalamic corticotropin releasing hormone secretion. *Journal of Clinical Investigation, 82,* 767–774.

Deits, F. (1994). *F1000 Instrumentation System.* Ridgecrest, CA: Focused Technology.

Harrison, V. (1985). "Interview with Dr. Murray Bowen." Videotape. Clinical Conference Series, Tape 3. Georgetown Family Center. Washington, DC.

Lynch, J. (1985). *The language of the heart: The body's response to human dialogue.* New York: Basic Books.

McEwen, B. & Lasley, E. N. (2002). *The end of stress as we know it.* New York: Dana Press.

Porges, S. (2009). The polyvagal theory: New insights into adaptive reactions of the autonomic nervous system. *Cleveland Clinic Journal of Medicine, 76,* 86–90.

Rosenbaum, L. (1989). *Biofeedback frontiers.* New York: AMS Press.

Sapolsky, R. (1994). *Why zebras don't get ulcers.* New York: W. H. Freeman.

Skowron, E. & Friedlander, M. L. (1998). The Differentiation of Self Inventory: Development and initial validation. *Journal of Counseling Psychology, 45,* 235–246.

16

TOWARD A GREATER UNDERSTANDING OF DIFFERENTIATION OF SELF IN BOWEN FAMILY SYSTEMS THEORY

Empirical Developments and Future Directions

Elizabeth A. Skowron, John J. Van Epps, and Elizabeth A. Cipriano-Essel

Bowen family systems theory is arguably considered the most comprehensive theory of human functioning from a systems perspective. Grounded in natural systems theory, Bowen family systems theory is a theory of multigenerational emotional functioning, and the concepts of "differentiation of self" and the "emotional system" characterize essential elements of Bowen theory. About 15 years ago, the first author initiated a program of research designed to operationalize the concept of differentiation of self and examine the central tenets in Murray Bowen's family systems theory. The original focus of the work was to develop a psychometrically sound tool to assess the role of therapist and client differentiation of self in 1) psychotherapy outcome, and 2) the process of effective psychotherapy. The Differentiation of Self Inventory (DSI) was first developed in 1991, and since that time, the measure has undergone two revisions to refine items and subscale definitions, minimize social desirability bias, and enhance the DSI's construct validity (e.g., Skowron and Friedlander, 1998; Skowron and Schmitt, 2003). Further, the first two authors have engaged in postgraduate training at the Bowen Center for the Study of the Family in Washington, DC, under the direction of Michael E. Kerr, MD, and the first author remains a member of Daniel Papero's research group at the Bowen Center, where she continues to consult and engage with Bowen scholars in the conceptualization and design of research informed by Bowen theory. This constellation of experiences with the Bowen Center has greatly assisted the authors in clarifying their thinking about Bowen theory and provided invaluable access to developments in thinking within the theory that have evolved since publication of Bowen's *Family Therapy in Clinical Practice* (1978) and Kerr's *Family Evaluation* (Kerr and Bowen, 1988).

Nonetheless, we acknowledge that the ideas in this chapter emerge out of our individual viewpoints through which we each have studied and thought about Bowen theory.

In this chapter, we review published research on differentiation of self that is grounded in Bowen family systems theory and uses the DSI, and we summarize what is known and not yet known about the role of differentiation of self in health and relationship functioning, including psychotherapy. We then highlight two of Bowen's concepts—family emotional process and the multigenerational transmission process—that have received little empirical attention to date, and elaborate on a conceptual model that we are exploring that posits a set of mechanisms through which differentiation of self may be transmitted across generations of a family. Our current research is focused on mapping the patterned regularities and disruptions over time in parent-child behavioral streams that account for variation in children's developing capacity for differentiation of self, as evidenced in behavior and autonomic physiology. Examination of such a complex question requires good working knowledge of family systems theory and research designs that employ intensive observation of moment-to-moment interactions in family relationships. We conclude with a brief review of several important theoretical notions that remain untested and some suggestions for next step research that is informed by Bowen family systems theory.

Defining Differentiation of Self

In our program of research on Bowen theory, we define differentiation of self as the capacity of a family system and its members to manage emotional reactivity, act thoughtfully under stress, and allow for both intimacy and autonomy in relationships. Differentiation of self is thought to operate on both intrapersonal and interpersonal/relational levels. On an intrapersonal level, differentiation of self involves the capacity to distinguish the thinking and feeling systems, to engage in thoughtful examination of situations, and maintain an awareness of one's emotions. More differentiated adults are thought to be more capable of reflecting on, experiencing, and modulating their emotions, as well as being better able to cope with uncertainty and ambiguity while remaining calm within their relationships. Thus, as one's basic level of differentiation increases, so does the capacity to distinguish between thinking and feeling processes, regulate strong emotion, and think clearly under stress. In contrast, less differentiated persons are thought to be more emotionally reactive, and have difficulty thinking clearly under stress and maintaining a solid sense of self in close relationships (Bowen, 1978; Kerr and Bowen, 1988).

On an interpersonal level, differentiation of self reflects an ability to develop mature emotional connections with others *and* to preserve autonomy within those significant relationships (Bowen, 1976, 1978). More differentiated individuals are thought to establish greater autonomy in their relationships without experiencing debilitating fears of abandonment, and to achieve emotional intimacy in those relationships without experiencing fears of feeling smothered or incorporated (Bowen, 1978; Kerr and Bowen, 1988). More differentiated persons are thought to be capable of supporting the best interests of others at times, without feeling a loss of self-direction or selfhood in the process (Schnarch, 1997), of maintaining connections in the midst of conflict with those who hold different opinions, and of resisting the use of emotional cutoff or relational control to maintain calm (Schnarch, 1997; Skowron and Friedlander, 1998). More differentiated parents are better able to provide support and nurture their children's age-appropriate autonomy and developing capacities for self-regulation. In sum, differentiation of self is a fundamental property of a family relationship system, and thus level of differentiation is thought to be roughly consistent throughout a family system, while allowing for sibling variation within and across generations of a family. At its core, differentiation of self as it is expressed in individual family members involves the capacity to self-regulate emotion and behavior within important relationships, which in turn enables the relational capacities for authentic, mature intimacy and an ability to define a clear sense of self-in-relation with important others.

The Differentiation of Self Inventory

The Differentiation of Self Inventory (DSI; Skowron and Friedlander, 1998) was developed to operationalize these intrapersonal and relational dimensions of Bowen's concept of differentiation of self. Using a construct approach to test construction (e.g., Jackson, 1970; Loevinger, 1957; Nunnally, 1978), Skowron and Friedlander conducted a series of three studies grounded in Bowen theory to develop the DSI and assess its content and construct-related validity. Drawing from the writings of Drs. Murray Bowen, Michael Kerr, Daniel Papero, and others, a pool of items was created and subjected to a principal components analysis of responses from a national sample of $N = 313$ adults. This resulted in identification of four subscales that were labeled Emotional Reactivity, (difficulty taking an) I-Position, Emotional Cutoff, and Fusion with Others. Next, DSI items was further revised and subjected to content analyses by experts in Bowen theory (e.g., Dr. Robert Noone and others), followed by statistical item analyses including assessment of social desirability bias. Internal consistency reliabilities for the DSI full scale and each of the four subscales were good (DSI = .88, Emotional Reactivity = .84; I-Position = .83, Emotional Cutoff = .82; Fusion with Others = .74). An examination of the DSI's factor structure using confirmatory factor analyses yielded support for the four-factor structure, representing the four DSI subscales as factors, with differentiation of self identified as a single higher-order latent factor: $\chi^2(50, N = 137) = 94.6$, $p < .0001$, $GFI = .91$, adjusted GFI = .86, and χ^2/df = 1.89 (Skowron and Friedlander, 1998). Tests of the DSI's initial construct-related validity demonstrated theoretically predicted relations between lower DSI scores and higher chronic anxiety, greater symptomatic distress, and lower marital satisfaction (Skowron and Friedlander, 1998).

A revision was published in 2003 that focused on strengthening the psychometric rigor of the DSI Fusion with Others scale through conceptual revisions, new item generation, and content validity analyses conducted by a panel of Bowen theory experts, followed by statistical item analyses and an assessment of the FO scale's construct-related validity. Results indicated that greater fusion with others as assessed by the DSI Fusion with Others scale predicted higher scores on two dimensions of attachment insecurity: Fear of Abandonment and Desire to Merge with Partners (i.e., Experiences in Close Relationships scale; Brennan, Clark, and Shaver, 1998), and greater Spousal Fusion on the Personal Authority in the Family System scale (PAFS; Bray, Williamson, and Malone, 1984).

Since the DSI-Fusion with Others subscale was revised, only a small handful of the total 35 studies reported here have used the revised DSI-FO scale. Of those, about half reported theoretically consistent findings for the scale, including the validation study reported previously. However, fusion scores were not associated with effortful control in an adult sample (Skowron and Dendy, 2004) or with variations in Jewish-Russian immigrants' acculturation process (Roytburd and Friedlander, 2008). Thus further research is needed to evaluate the DSI-FO scale's construct-related validity and to use the FO subscale to examine specific theoretical predictions.

The current version of the DSI consists of a 46-item self-report measure of differentiation of self in adults, their significant relationships, and current relations with family of origin. The DSI contains four subscales: an 11-item Emotional Reactivity (ER) scale, an 11-item I-Position (IP) scale, a 12-item Emotional Cutoff (EC) scale, and a 12-item revised-Fusion with Others (FO) scale. The ER scale assesses one's tendency to respond to environmental stimuli on the basis of autonomic emotional responses, emotional flooding, or lability. The IP scale assesses the extent of one's clearly defined sense of self and ability to thoughtfully adhere to one's convictions even when pressured to do otherwise. The EC scale consists of items reflecting emotional and behavioral distancing and fears of intimacy or engulfment in relationships. The FO scale contains items that tap emotional overinvolvement with others, overreliance on others to confirm one's beliefs, decisions, and convictions, and a tendency to hold few clearly defined beliefs or convictions of one's own. Participants rate items using a six-point, Likert-type scale, ranging from 1 (not at all true of me) to 6 (very true of me). Scores on select items are reversed and summed across scales, so that higher scores on each subscale and the full scale all reflect greater differentiation of self (i.e., less emotional reactivity, greater ability to take an I-position in relationships, less emotional cutoff, or less fusion with others). However, though we developed and refined the DSI to assess differentiation of self in adulthood, to our knowledge, no measure of differentiation of self in childhood exists to date.

In both Bowen (1978) and Kerr's (Kerr and Bowen, 1988) writings, differentiation of self is conceptualized as the opposite of fusion. In developing the DSI, we elected to use Bowen's concept of "emotional reactivity" to describe the blurring of boundaries between thinking and feeling processes that serves as the underlying fuel leading one to either emotionally cut off or fuse with others under stress. We elected to use the phrase "fusion with others" to signify behavioral manifestations of low differentiation of self in relationships that are driven by greater emotional reactivity and lie on one end of a continuum ranging from fusion to emotional cutoff.

What Do We Know About Differentiation of Self?

In research using the DSI to operationalize differentiation of self, support for basic aspects of Bowen theory has been accumulating as studies show that differentiation of self is linked to lower chronic anxiety, greater psychological adjustment (Skowron and Friedlander, 1998), physical health (Peleg-Popko, 2002), marital satisfaction (Skowron, 2000), self-regulatory skills (Skowron and Dendy, 2004), lower relationship violence (Skowron and Platt, 2005), and substance abuse (Thorberg and Lyvers, 2006). Some support for the cross-cultural validity of the DSI has emerged in recent years, with greater differentiation of self among persons of color linked to better psychological adjustment (Knauth and Skowron, 2004; Tuason and Friedlander, 2000), problem-solving, and positive feelings toward one's ethnic group (Skowron, 2004). Greater differentiation of self among low-income mothers is associated with greater academic achievement and fewer behavior problems in their children (Skowron, 2005). However, the few studies conducted to date (e.g., Skowron, 2000; Spencer and Brown, 2007) have failed to support Bowen's similarity hypothesis, which asserts that married couples tend to have similar levels of differentiation.

While the intrapersonal thinking and feeling process is inextricably intertwined with the relational manifestations of differentiation of self, several studies have deconstructed and examined these two dimensions separately. For example, the intrapersonal dimension of differentiation is reflected in one's ability to balance thinking and feeling systems as outlined in Bowen theory and involves the extent to which emotional reactivity is managed and I-positions can be taken in important relationships. At its core, differentiation of self on an intrapersonal level consists of a capacity to self-regulate emotion and behavior, to self-soothe when anxious, and to think clearly in the midst of strong emotion. Some evidence has emerged to support the notion of an intrapersonal dimension of differentiation, in that the DSI Emotional Reactivity and I-Position subscales together have been shown to form a single "self-regulation" factor that reflects the extent of one's comfort with emotion, capacity to reflect on or think about emotion, and capacity to maintain a clear sense of self (Skowron, Holmes, and Sabatelli, 2003). Another study observed that adults who were less emotionally reactive and better able to take I-positions in their relationships were also better able to engage in conscious, effortful control of their behavior even after controlling for variance associated with adult attachment security (Skowron and Dendy, 2004). Wei and her colleagues (Wei, Vogel, Ku, and Zakalik, 2005) conceptualized the DSI Emotional Reactivity and Emotional Cutoff scores as indicators of affect regulation and examined the extent to which they mediated relations between attachment security, negative mood, and interpersonal problems. Results of structural equation modeling demonstrated support for their model: Relations between attachment anxiety and 1) negative mood and 2) interpersonal problems were 1) fully and 2) partially accounted for, respectively, by individuals' DSI-Emotional Reactivity scores. Similarly, relations between attachment avoidance and 1) negative mood and 2) interpersonal problems were also 1) fully mediated and 2) partially mediated, respectively, by DSI-Emotional Cutoff scores (Wei et al., 2005). These few studies lend initial support for the notion that differentiation of self is reflected in greater ability to manage emotional reactivity in one's relationships and is associated with mature relationship functioning. As Bowen stated, "At higher levels of differentiation, the functioning of emotional and intellectual systems are more clearly distinguishable" (1978, p. 363). In the sections that follow, we present a summary of empirically derived inferences about the theoretical propositions regarding differentiation of self.

Differentiation of Self, Psychological, and Health Functioning

Kerr and Bowen (1988) asserted that less differentiated individuals experience greater chronic anxiety, become dysfunctional under stress more easily, and thus suffer more psychological and physical symptoms than do more differentiated persons. Further, family systems are seen as interdependent emotional units, and as such, symptoms are viewed as disorders of the family emotional system. Thus, when allostatic load is high and level of differentiation of self is low, Kerr (2008b) argues that anxiety gets bound into physical, psychological, or social symptoms. In more differentiated relationships, Kerr states that people can put more energy into what Henry and Wang (1989) call attachment—affiliative behaviors *or* autonomous behaviors—and can adapt to stressors without a buildup of anxiety that can impair functioning

(Kerr, 2008b). In other words, individuals at higher levels of differentiation of self

> . . . have enough confidence in their ability to deal with relationships, even emotionally intense ones, so that they neither avoid them nor become highly anxious in encountering them.
>
> (Kerr and Bowen, 1988, p. 118)

Generally, empirical research conducted using the DSI has supported these propositions. For example, Skowron and Friedlander (1998) found that lower DSI scores, particularly greater emotional reactivity and emotional cutoff, highly correlated with greater global distress and trait (i.e., chronic) anxiety scores. Aldea and Rice (2006) investigated the difference between two different domains of perfectionism, 1) adaptive perfectionism or high personal standards and 2) maladaptive perfectionism with a high self-critical aspect. These authors found that emotion dysregulation, as measured by DSI Emotional Reactivity scores and scores on the Splitting Index (i.e., emotional lability and relationship instability; Gould, Prentice, and Ainsle, 1996) fully accounted for relationships between both adaptive and maladaptive perfectionism and psychological distress. Specifically, adaptive perfectionists reported lower emotional reactivity or higher levels of emotion regulation, which in turn predicted lower distress levels. In contrast, maladaptive perfectionists reported greater emotional reactivity and lability, or lower emotion regulation, which then predicted higher distress. In general, the findings from these studies demonstrate that greater emotional reactivity and emotional cutoff as measured by the DSI are associated with greater levels of anxiety and distress in individuals.

Research has investigated the impact of differentiation of self on health-related behaviors. For example, lower levels of differentiation predicted greater somatic complaints and social anxiety in a sample of young Israeli adults (Peleg-Popko, 2002). Among study participants and their partners who were identified as needing genetic screening because of inherited cancer risk, Bartle-Haring and Gregory (2003) found that those with higher levels of differentiation experienced less avoidant and intrusive thoughts about inheriting cancer and experienced fewer psychological symptoms over time. Further, they found that differentiation of self mediated the relationship between the stress of genetic cancer testing and partner distress, such that higher levels of partner differentiation predicted lower partner distress while engaged in genetic counseling. In a sample of individuals with fibromyalgia, recall of negative life stressors in the year previous to symptom onset and differentiation of self levels predicted reports of physical symptom severity (Murray, Murray, and Daniels, 2007). Differentiation of self also appears to play a role in physical health functioning, providing some initial support for Bowen theory assertions that physical symptoms are one manifestation of lower differentiation of self levels (1978; Kerr and Bowen, 1988).

Because more differentiated individuals are thought to have more mature, emotionally supportive social networks, environmental stressors are expected to affect them less than may be the case among those who are less differentiated. However, it is not clear from Bowen's writings whether differentiation of self is thought to be a moderator or mediator of relationships between stress/anxiety and functioning. Two published studies to date have focused on this question and conclusions are mixed. In a sample of college students, Murdock and Gore (2004) conducted a study investigating the relationships between stress, coping, and differentiation of self and the extent to which these contributed to psychological functioning. They found that differentiation of self was positively related to reflective coping, which is a more adaptive and thoughtful coping style. Likewise, differentiation of self was negatively related to avoidant and reactive coping, less adaptive coping styles. Further, they found an interaction between DSI scores and perceived stress in predicting psychological distress. In particular, when experiencing high levels of stress, differences in psychological distress were more pronounced between participants with higher and lower levels of differentiation. This study provides evidence for a moderation model because stress intensified the relationship between undifferentiation and psychological distress.

Skowron, Wester, and Azen (2004) tested both a mediating and moderating model of differentiation, stress, and functioning. A mediating model attempts to identify an intermediate process that explains the relationship between a predictor and outcome variable. Moderation models focus on factors that strengthen or influence the direction between a predictor and outcome variable. Only support for the mediating model was observed. Differentiation of self partially mediated relations between college-related stress (academic, financial, and social stressors) and adjustment, suggesting that young adults' ability to maintain connections with their families of origin while also maintaining a sense of healthy autonomy impacted their ability to cope with common stressors in college.

These two studies highlight the complex role that differentiation of self likely plays in affecting the relationship between stress and functioning. These studies demonstrate that differentiation may serve to strengthen and act as an intermediate process in describing the relationship between stress and psychological functioning. Therefore, differentiation of self may be an important variable to consider in psychotherapy because of its associations to an individual's feelings of stress and overall functioning. However, more studies are needed to further clarify the role that differentiation of self plays in this interaction.

Research on Adolescents and Older Adults

A number of studies have also investigated differentiation of self in adolescent and emerging adult populations, particularly as it relates to their psychosocial functioning, cognitive performance, and identity development. Knauth and Skowron (2004) found that adolescent reports of higher differentiation of self were associated with reports of lower anxiety and overall symptomatology. Additionally, they found that higher levels of differentiation mediated the relationship between anxiety and symptomatology, with higher levels of differentiation predicting fewer adolescent reports of symptoms over and above their anxiety. Another study demonstrated that adolescents' anxiety mediated the relationship between differentiation of self and problem-solving, suggesting that adolescents who were more differentiated were better at managing their anxiety, and this in turn allowed them to engage in more effective problem-solving (Knauth, Skowron, and Escobar, 2006).

Peleg-Popko (2004) investigated the relationship between adolescent differentiation, family differentiation, and adolescent test and trait anxiety. Results showed that adolescents who reported greater self and family differentiation also reported lower test and trait anxiety. Additionally, adolescents who perceived their mothers as more differentiated posted better cognitive performance on an IQ test. Another study conducted by Johnson, Buboltz, and Seeman (2003) explored the role of differentiation in young adult identity development. Interesting relationships were revealed between DSI subscales and stages of identity. Young adults who reported relatively greater ability to take I-positions in their relationships in turn showed the highest levels of identity achievement (i.e., reflecting a clear commitment to personal and ideological issues after a sustained period of personal exploration of alternatives). In contrast, young adults who reported greater fusion with others were more likely to report identity foreclosure (i.e., an ideological commitment characterized by incorporating one's parents' views and little or no personal exploration), whereas those who were more emotionally cut off scored highest on identity diffusion (i.e., reflecting a lack of exploration and lack of commitment; Johnson et al., 2003).

As can be seen by empirical research with adolescents, levels of differentiation have been associated with anxiety and symptomatology, cognitive performance, and identity development. However, reports indicate that the DSI, which was developed for use with adult populations, may post lower internal consistency reliabilities when used with young adolescent samples (e.g., Knauth and Skowron, 2004). Therefore, some adaptations may be needed to use the DSI as a measure for adolescents in order for it to continue to be a reliable and valid construct in this population. Further, no studies have assessed the longitudinal development of adolescents' DSI into adulthood, particularly over the course of the launching phase of the family life cycle. As with other research testing Bowen family systems theory, the majority of published studies conducted using the DSI in adolescent populations have been fairly homogeneous in terms of ethnicity and socioeconomic status (SES). However, as reflected by the contributions of authors in this edited volume, research with diverse populations is expanding and continuing to clarify the role of differentiation of self in adolescent functioning.

We could find only a few studies that have been conducted examining differentiation of self and psychological distress among older adults. Results revealed that greater emotional reactivity and emotional cutoff and less I-position predicted greater report of distressing symptomatology by adults older than 62 years (Kim-Appel, Appel, Newman, and Parr, 2007). More research is needed that will investigate use of the DSI in older adults. Similar to research with adolescents, the psychometric properties need to be assessed with this population in order to determine whether the current DSI is a reliable and valid measure for this population.

Cross-Cultural Research on Differentiation of Self

A growing body of research is focusing on elucidating the relationship between differentiation of self and cultural worldview. The continuum of individualism and collectivism is considered one of the most important dimensions along which cultures vary (Kagitçibasi, 1996). Some have argued that Bowen's concept of differentiation of self places an overemphasis on Western values of independence (e.g., Essandoh, 1995; Rothbaum, Weisz, Pott, Miyake, and Morelli, 2000; Tamura and Lau, 1992) while failing to acknowledge the role of interconnection observed in collectivist cultures. Others have disagreed and maintain that Bowen theory is one of the few theories of human functioning that adequately elevates the role of healthy connections with others to one of central importance to healthy development and maturity (e.g., Boyd-Franklin, 1989; Carter and McGoldrick, 1999; Guisinger and Blatt, 1994; Gushue and Sicalides, 1997). As such, some controversy exists as to whether the concept of differentiation of self is relevant for persons of color from non-Western cultures that hold differing worldviews.

Research studies to date indicate that differentiation of self is consistently associated with less chronic anxiety and symptomatology in cross-cultural studies with U.S. and international samples. Tuason and Friedlander (2000) found that differentiation of self in a Filipino sample of adult children and their parents was related to symptomatology and trait anxiety in ways that were consistent with results found in a North American sample. Skowron (2004) found that higher levels of differentiation of self—that is, less emotional reactivity, better ability to take I-positions in relationships, less emotional cutoff or fusion with others—predicted lower psychological symptom scores and better problem-solving abilities in a U.S. sample of young adults of color. Interestingly, the DSI scores of the Persons of Color sample were not significantly different from a sample of European Americans matched on key demographic variables. Finally, individuals of color who were less emotionally cut off reported stronger feelings of ethnic group belonging, lending some support to the DSI's cross-cultural validity.

In addition to the work presented in this edited volume, research with international samples has observed links between higher differentiation of self scores and global well-being. For example, in a study of Israeli university students, Peleg-Popko (2002) found that higher levels of differentiation were associated with less social anxiety and fewer physiological symptoms among participants. In another study, of Russian Jews, I-position uniquely predicted former Soviet Union Jews' acculturative trends. Greater I-position was associated with more American acculturation, whereas greater difficulty taking I-positions in relationships and experience of discrimination were associated with staying closer to Russian culture (Roytburd and Friedlander, 2008).

These results lend some support to the notion that Bowen's concept of differentiation may have universal aspects; however, future research is needed to better understand relations between culture, worldview, differentiation of self, and mental health. More research on specific groups within the United States also is needed to better understand how culture and differentiation manifest themselves in relationships and life functioning within and across cultures. We have strived to remove cultural bias in the DSI through a rigorous, construct approach to test construction and a program of research informed by multicultural theory and research. However, cross-cultural interpretation of the differentiation construct requires careful attention, and the DSI may require adaptations for use in different ethnic groups and international populations, to enable it to be more sensitively attuned to important cultural differences in human experience. Careful attention also should be paid to how cultural worldviews affect research designs, hypotheses investigated, and the inference drawn from study findings. In closing, how differentiation of self manifests is likely dependent on the cultural context within which a relationship system is embedded, although underlying patterns may be similar across cultures.

Differentiation of Self, Marital Satisfaction, and Adult Attachment

One line of empirical research has explored how the concept of differentiation of self is associated with marital quality, relationship satisfaction, and quality of attachment. Bowen (1976, 1978) proposed that more differentiated individuals would be more likely to remain in good contact with their families of origin, to work out person-to-person relationships with members of their extended family, and to establish more mature, satisfying marriages. Researchers (e.g., Kosek, 1998; Skowron, 2000; Skowron and Friedlander, 1998; Spencer and Brown, 2007) have explored whether couples' level of differentiation of self was related to their overall marital satisfaction, and consistently observed that higher DSI scores predicted greater marital satisfaction among heterosexual and same-sex couples. Further, lower marital satisfaction in both husbands and wives was most predicted by greater emotional cutoff in husbands (Skowron, 2000). Similarly among lesbian couples, greater emotional cutoff resulted in the highest levels of relationship dissatisfaction (Spencer and Brown, 2007). Research has also demonstrated that greater couple complementarity in emotional reactivity and emotional cutoff predicted high levels of marital discord (Skowron, 2000). Parsons, Nalbone, Killmer, and Wetchler (2007) found further support for the DSI's ability to predict satisfaction in marriages. Among spouses whose partners were of a different religious faith, greater differentiation of self—that is, better ability to balance thinking and feeling while remaining in emotional contact—predicted greater marital satisfaction, perhaps because they were better able to cope with the tension, ambiguity, or differences of opinion that may emerge in an interfaith marriage. However, after controlling for the effect of intimacy and spousal support, another study failed to find a significant association between differentiation of self and marital satisfaction (Patrick, Sells, Giordano, and Tollerud, 2007).

A central tenet to Bowen theory is that married couples are similar in their level of differentiation. Recent studies tested this assertion by comparing DSI difference scores among married heterosexual (Skowron, 2000) and lesbian (Spencer and Brown, 2007) couples and randomly matched pseudo-couples and found no differences in level of similarity across actual and randomly matched couples' DSI difference scores. More definitive tests of the similarity hypothesis are needed to empirically test this central assertion in Bowen theory. Perhaps comparing intact couples with separated and divorced couples would provide a definitive test of the similarity hypothesis given that Bowen theory asserts that people partner at similar levels of differentiation of self. Thus with the existing research designs, there may be insufficient variance in DSI difference scores to observe an effect if it is present in the population. In sum, these findings suggest that while strong relationships exist between couple differentiation and marital quality, the role of similarity in levels of differentiation may be more complex to empirically discern and requires further investigation.

Other studies have looked at the relationship between differentiation of self and attachment anxiety and avoidance, as measured by the Experiences in Close Relationship scale—short form (ECR; Brennan, Clark, and Shaver, 1998). Several studies have consistently observed strong correlations between DSI-Emotional Cutoff scores and ECR Attachment Avoidance scores, and between higher scores on the ECR Attachment Anxiety scale and lower DSI-Emotional Reactivity scores, indicating greater emotional reactivity (Skowron and Dendy, 2004; Thorberg and Lyvers, 2006; Wei, Russell, Mallinkrodt, and Vogel, 2008). In a sample of clients being treated for drug abuse, those who reported greater attachment insecurity also reported lower DSI sores, compared with non-drug-abusing individuals (Thorberg and Lyvers, 2006). Further, in a sample of young adults who were not yet parents, Skowron and Platt (2005) found substantial correlations between lower differentiation of self scores—namely greater emotional reactivity and emotional cutoff—and higher risk for child abuse.

Williamson, Sandage, and Lee (2007) conducted a study to test the relationship between feelings of social connectedness and guilt and shame and whether this relationship was mediated by individuals' DSI and feelings of hope. Results revealed that the DSI mediated the relations between social connectedness and feelings of shame. In particular, individuals who had greater social connectedness reported higher DSI and thus had fewer feelings of shame.

Research has also revealed some gender differences in terms of males' and females' DSI subscale scores suggesting that males tend to score higher on emotional cutoff and females higher on emotional reactivity (e.g., Johnson, Thorngrin, and Smith, 2001; Kim-Appel et al., 2007; Peleg-Popko, 2004; Skowron, 2000; Skowron and Friedlander, 1998). Do gender differences exist in levels of differentiation? Or is differentiation of self invariant across gender? It is possible that that these findings may be more related to cultural values and social display rules than actual sex inequities in felt emotions and expressivity. For example, Barrett, Robin, Pietromonaco, and Eyssell (1998) found that sex differences in emotional feeling and expressivity were only elicited in opposite-sex dyads and global self ratings but not in observed interactions or in same-sex dyads. This supports the notion that culture shapes how emotions are expressed and dealt with across sexes rather than reflecting innate biological or psychological processes.

Despite empirical support for the contribution of differentiation to marital quality, attachment, potential relationship violence, and other outcomes, it must be noted that most of these studies relied primarily on self-report measures. In order to reduce potential biases found with self-reports, future research must begin to employ designs that rely on multiple informants or observational measures to clarify the role of differentiation in marriage and other significant relationships. Additionally, most of the studies were conducted in homogeneous samples in terms of age, ethnicity, and SES. Therefore, research needs to be conducted in more diverse populations and should consider the culture in which the sample is embedded because differentiation of self may have different meanings to people of different cultures.

Further, Bowen theory asserts that children take on the level of differentiation of self in their family system, and that these levels are largely stable throughout one's life. However, to empirically test this tenet, it is necessary to conduct longitudinal research investigating the relationships between differentiation, relationship status, and functioning, in order to determine whether an individual's differentiation level is stable. Additionally, research is needed to better understand variations in functional levels of differentiation across time and within and across different relationship systems (i.e., with spouses, parents, friends, and children and in work systems).

Parental Differentiation of Self and Its Influence on Child Outcomes

According to Bowen theory (Bowen, 1978; Kerr and Bowen, 1988) levels of differentiation of self are transmitted across generations of a family, with parent level of differentiation roughly constraining the level of differentiation the children can achieve. According to Murray Bowen:

> All things being equal, you emerge with about the same basic level of differentiation your parents had. This is determined by the process before your birth and the situation during infancy and early childhood. . . .
>
> (1978, p. 409)

Bowen (1978) proposed a revolutionary idea that family emotional process (e.g., via triangling and child focus) yields different levels of functioning among children in the same family, and Kerr (2008a) more recently delineated a set of hypothesized processes through which these variations in sibling functioning unfold over time. In our studies to date, we have focused our efforts on testing the more basic aspects of 1) whether levels of differentiation of self among parents and their children roughly converge, and 2) modeling the interpersonal processes through which children come to acquire levels of differentiation of self roughly similar to those of their parents.

Several studies have focused on families with young children and investigated how parental level of differentiation influences aspects of children's development. Skowron (2005) investigated how parental DSI predicted children's cognitive functioning, self-esteem, and pro-social behavior in a low-income urban sample. After accounting for neighborhood violence and family life stress, results revealed that mother's differentiation of self significantly contributed to children's vocabulary and math skills, even after controlling for parent education levels. Parents who reported higher DSI scores had children who showed better vocabulary and math skills. Further, both family stressors and parental differentiation significantly predicted children's aggression such that greater report of family stress and lower parental differentiation of self was associated with more aggression in children.

Peleg, Halaby, and Whaby (2006) conducted a study investigating how parental DSI scores related to Israeli-Druze children's separation anxiety and adjustment to kindergarten. Results revealed that greater parental differentiation of self in general, and lower emotional cutoff in particular, were associated with lower levels of children's observed separation anxiety. Further, greater anxiety in children, as reported by teachers, was related to lower levels of parental differentiation of self. However, children of parents who reported greater fusion with others displayed less separation anxiety than children of less fused parents. It would be interesting to learn whether these results would replicate if the revised DSI Fusion with Others subscale were used instead.

These studies both reveal that parental differentiation is associated with children's developmental outcomes in a low-income and Israeli-Druze population. However, Skowron's study was a cross-sectional design, and Peleg and colleagues conducted their study when children were in kindergarten. Thus, it is not known how parental differentiation of self influences children's development from infancy into childhood, and therefore, longitudinal work needs to be conducted.

Studies focused on the role of differentiation of self in relationships between adult children and their parents have relied heavily on retrospective reporting and to date have yielded mixed results. For example, Schwartz, Thigpen, and Montgomery (2006) found that college students' retrospective reports of family of origin emotion-related parenting were associated with students' current levels of differentiation. Specifically they found that for young men, parental disapproval of negative emotions was associated with difficulty taking an I-position in relationships, while for young women, parent dismissal and mother-specific disapproval predicted greater Fusion with Others scores. Johnson et al. (2001) investigated retrospective reports of family functioning as it related to 813 undergraduate students' differentiation of self scores. Students from intact families reported higher levels of differentiation than students from divorced families. Reports of family of origin conflict were positively linked and family health competence negatively linked with lower DSI scores, namely greater emotional reactivity, more difficulty taking I-positions in relationships, greater cutoff, and fusion with others. Gender differences in DSI scores were observed, with men reporting more emotional cutoff, less emotional reactivity, and less fusion than their female counterparts. While cohesion in the family of origin was related to less emotional reactivity, surprisingly, family of origin expressivity was related to more fusion and reactivity and less cutoff.

Yet studies directly examining levels of DSI across generations have failed to find support for the emotion transmission process directly. For example, in a study examining extent of correspondence between adult children and their parents' levels of differentiation in a Filipino sample, Tuason and Friedlander (2000) found no significant associations between parents' and their adult children's DSI scores. However, future research on the transmission would benefit from use of multiple informants and experimental, multilevel methods to assess differentiation of self levels in parents and their children.

Current Research Focus

Our current research is focused on unpacking the patterned regularities and disruptions over time in parent-child autonomic physiology and interpersonal transactions that account for the extent to which children's developing levels of differentiation of self are roughly on par with or match those of their parents. Examination of such complex questions require good working knowledge of family systems theory and research designs that employ intensive observation of moment-to-moment interactions in family relationships.

Differentiation of Self and Self-regulation of Physiology, Emotion, and Behavior

We theorize that differentiation of self is manifested in early childhood in a child's developing capacity for self-regulation of emotion and behavior. Self-regulation development is critical to children's overall functioning, as it affects children's ability to behave in healthy, adaptive ways (e.g., Denham et al., 2003; Eisenberg and Morris, 2002; Kopp, 1982; 1989; Thompson, 1994). The capacity for self-regulation of emotions and behavior begins in infancy and continues to develop throughout childhood (Kopp, 1982, 1989; Thompson, 1994). Research indicates that early in life children rely on parents and other external sources to help them regulate their emotions and behavior, and then by preschool, children increasingly develop strategies to internally control, or self-regulate, behavior and emotions (Thompson, 1991; Winsler, Diaz, Atencio, McCarthy, and Chabay, 2000). Failure to develop these abilities sets children on a course leading to problematic developmental outcomes that can continue into adulthood.

Effortful control is an important aspect of self-regulation essential to children's development because of its influence in multiple domains. Effortful control is a behavioral measure of temperament reflecting an ability to actively modulate arousal engage in nondominant responding, and allows children greater conscious control of attention, enabling regulation of behavioral impulses, and more mindful selection of behavioral strategies (Rothbart, Ahadi, and Evans, 2000; Rothbart and Bates, 2006). With the maturation of early attentional networks, effortful control is believed to emerge by 12 months and continues to develop rapidly, with individual differences in this ability becoming more detectable throughout the toddler and preschool years (Kochanska, Murray, and Harlan, 2000; Kopp, 1982; Rothbart, Derryberry, and Posner, 1994; Rothbart and Posner, 2000). Further, we have observed in previous research that differentiation of self uniquely predicts greater effortful control among adults (Skowron and Dendy, 2004).

Developing the ability to self-regulate emotions is another critical skill children must master. Emotion regulation is defined as the internal and external processes involved in initiating, maintaining, and modulating the occurrence and intensity of emotional expressions and being able to adapt to stressful demands and emotional experiences (Cole, Michel, and Teti, 1994; Thompson, 1994). In infancy, children rely heavily on caregivers to help them regulate their emotional arousal. However, infants possess early rudimentary forms of emotion regulation strategies, such as using gaze aversion and disengaging attention from an arousing stimulus in order to decrease negative affect (e.g., Johnson, Posner, and Rothbart, 1991; Rothbart, Ziaie, and O'Boyle, 1992). Children's behavioral repertoires of self-regulation strategies continue to expand in toddlerhood when they begin to assert their autonomy, develop a sense of self awareness, and experience maturation of cognitive skills (Kopp, 1982, 1989). These behaviors include more planful use of attentional strategies and self-comforting behaviors to regulate emotional arousal (e.g., Grolnick, Bridges, and Connell, 1996). By the time children reach preschool, they are increasingly capable of self-regulating their emotions and require less input from external sources of regulation. The development of language abilities leads children to rely more on verbal regulation of emotion (Cole et al., 1994; Kopp, 1989), and children begin to internally regulate their representations of what is causing them to become emotionally aroused (Rothbart and Sheese, 2007). Emotion regulation development is critical for children because poor regulation of emotion has been associated with greater social, emotional, and behavioral problems (e.g., Cole et al., 1994; Eisenberg, Fabes, Nyman, Bernzweig, and Pinuelas, 1994).

We theorize that children's self-regulation of emotion and behavior is at the core of a developing capacity to differentiate a self in family relationships. From a family systems perspective, differentiation of self facilitates the development of healthy self-regulation in early childhood. Parents' capacities for regulating emotion, thinking clearly under stress, and promoting both intimacy and autonomy in family relationships in turn provide optimal support for a child's developing capacities to self-regulate emotion and behavior. As the developmental needs of the child shift over time from infancy to toddlerhood and into the preschool years, we expect that in more differentiated families, parents and children are transitioning smoothly from co-regulation of the child's physical states, emotions, and behavior to the child's increasing self-regulation of his or her own emotions and behavior. More differentiated parents are thought to be better able to support and encourage their preschool child's budding autonomy strivings and engage in supportive, comforting behaviors that are adaptive when their child experiences stress. In contrast, less differentiated parents are more dependent on their relationships to manage stress, stabilize, and calm self (Kerr, 2008b). Behavioral exchanges between parent and child take on anxious automaticity (Kerr, 2008b), and parents struggle more with the challenges of simultaneously providing support for child autonomy and child's needs for comfort and connection.

In short, level of differentiation of self in the family system is thought to be transmitted across generations of the family through an emotional process that is rooted in evolutionary forces, which becomes self-sustaining and bi-directionally maintained. In less differentiated systems, people are more dependent on relationships to stabilize and calm themselves and manage their stress response (Kerr, 2008b). Bowen provides an example of these emotional processes that underlie differentiation transmission, in which the relational transfer of anxiety between mother and child unfolds through a series of interchanges. He explained:

> . . . the process begins with anxiety in the mother. The child responds anxiously to mother, which she misperceives as a problem in the child. The anxious parental effort goes into sympathetic, solicitous, overprotective energy, which is directed more by the mother's anxiety than the reality needs of the child. It establishes a pattern of infantilizing the child, who gradually becomes more impaired and more demanding. Once the process has started, it can be motivated either by anxiety in the mother, or anxiety in the child.
>
> (1978, pp. 380–381)

In this example, the child becomes attuned to the mother's anxiety and acts in a way that the mother is "pulling for," which reduces the mother's upset, and in response, the child feels less anxious in relating to a less anxious parent. The child relies on the parent for signals indicating how to behave in ways that maintain relationship calm, and thus continues to rely on other-directed regulation of his/her emotions and behavior. In short, mother and child learn to calm self, not by focusing on self, but rather by adjusting their own behavior in order to regulate the other. At lower levels of differentiation, more borrowing and trading of "self" is thought to occur and there is more "emotional pressure" to respond to the other in a complementary, fused way. The scenario is repeated countless times and explains the development of the pseudo-self and an overreliance on an orientation to looking outward toward the other to regulate self.

Self-regulation of emotion and behavior has been shown to operate on a physiological level as well. Bowen (1978) theorized that one's level of differentiation of self is manifest not only in one's overt behavior, but also on an autonomic/physiological level. In fact, research with both children and adults (Wilson and Gottman, 2002) has documented the importance that the parasympathetic branch may play in an individual's ability to self-regulate emotions and behavior, a central component of differentiation. While the sympathetic branch of the autonomic nervous system (ANS) functions to maintain homeostasis by regulating sympathetic *excitation* of heart and respiratory rates, the parasympathetic branch of the ANS functions to maintain homeostasis through flexible *inhibition* of heart and respiratory rates. Respiratory sinus arrhythmia (RSA) is a measure of the change in oscillatory dynamics of the heart across the respiration cycle and is considered to be a measure of the parasympathetic nervous system's influence on cardiac function (Berntson et al., 1997; Porges, 1995). Cardiac vagal tone—defined as individual variability in heart rate due to respiration changes controlled by the brain—is believed to be indicative of physiological capacity to regulate emotions and behavior and flexibly respond to moderate environmental challenge (Porges, 2001). Vagal tone is measured by isolating the variability in heart rate due to respiration, i.e., RSA. Under baseline conditions, parasympathetic influence is high, exerting a slowing on cardiac activity that is reflected in greater levels of RSA. Higher levels of baseline RSA (i.e., higher vagal tone) reflect the extent of an individual's regulatory capacity, or the degree to which arousal can be increased through parasympathetic withdrawal before sympathetic activation is needed (Porges, 2001). During engagement with the environment, parasympathetic withdrawal releases this dampening effect on the heart, resulting in an immediate increase in arousal, as reflected in lower levels of RSA. Though findings of better psychological function have been associated with RSA suppression during challenge (e.g., Calkins, 1997; Calkins, Smith, Gill, and Johnson, 1998; Porges, Doussard-Roosevelt, Portales, and Greenspan, 1996), recent studies suggest that the implications of RSA response to challenge may be highly context specific (i.e., individual vs. family/relational contexts; Bazhenova, Plonskaia, and Porges, 2001; Butler, Wilhelm, and Gross, 2006; Obradović et al., 2010; Skowron et al., 2011).

Understanding physiological regulation is critical because it is associated with children's social engagement (Fox and Field, 1989), social competence (Eisenberg et al., 2005), and influences on one's ability to regulate emotions (Porges, 1991). Research suggests that historical and current family of origin experiences may impact abilities to effectively regulate emotions and can be influential in the manifestation of psychological and physiological symptoms in children (Calkins et al., 1998; Diener, Mangelsdorf, McHale, and Frosch, 2002; Gottman and Katz, 2002; Jahromi, Putnam, and Stifter, 2004; Lunkenheimer, Shields, and Cortina, 2007; Maughan and Cicchetti, 2002; see Rogosch, Cicchetti, and Aber, 1995, for a review).

Research has shown that more negative and controlling behaviors by parents during a positive task (Calkins et al., 1998) are related to poor vagal regulation in lower-risk children. Likewise, among preschool children exposed to abuse and neglect, those who received more maternal support for autonomy and less strict, hostile control parenting during a challenge task displayed higher vagal tone during interactions with their mothers (Skowron et al., 2011). Gottman and Katz (2002) found that children who showed better physiological regulation at ages four and five predicted better emotion regulation at age eight, and this relationship was partially mediated by children's ability to maintain a low heart rate during stressful interactions with their parents. Lunkenheimer et al. (2007) found that parents' use of more emotion-dismissing behaviors with their children was related to poorer emotion regulation and behavior problems. Further, Bornstein and Suess (2000) observed that vagal regulation in mother and young children becomes more highly correlated over time from birth, and in light of the low correlations observed between mother and child baseline vagal tone, they concluded that their pattern of findings signified that the children's relationship experiences with mother over time likely play an important role in shaping a child's developing capacity for physiological regulation.

Studies conducted in our lab provide some support for the notion that a parent's level of differentiation predicts their child's capacity for self-regulation of emotion, physiology, and behavior. For example, Skowron et al. (2011) observed that mothers' greater use of warm autonomy-support was linked to higher vagal tone in their preschool children while completing joint puzzle tasks together. While this preliminary evidence supports the assertion that differentiation of self assessed in parents will predict their young children's self-regulation of emotion, the interpersonal mechanisms through which differentiation of self is transmitted across generations must be clarified so that they may be subjected to empirical examination. Are levels of differentiation transmitted across generations of a family? If so, how do children come to acquire levels of differentiation roughly similar to those of their parents?

Multigenerational Transmission of Differentiation via Complementarity

We have recently completed a five-year, NIMH-funded project informed by Bowen family systems theory designed to clarify the ways in which survey, behavioral, and physiological indices of differentiation of self in parents converge and diverge, and shed light on the degree of correspondence between parent differentiation of self and developing self and emotion regulation in their preschool-aged children. Our procedures consist of observing moment-to-moment transactions that unfold over time in a sample of at-risk families, considering the bi-directional influence of parent on child and vice versa, and simultaneously tracking parent and child underlying physiological reactivity and regulation during these interchanges. We use the DSI to assess differentiation of self in parents, the Structural Analysis of Social Behavior (SASB; Benjamin, 1996), an observational coding system to assess interpersonal transactions, and engaged in synchronized monitoring of parent and child heart rate variability (i.e., vagal tone; Porges, 2001) using ambulatory ECG equipment. The project is designed to map important components of Bowen's multigenerational transmission process. Future work will expand our investigations to include a focus on triadic dimensions of family emotional process. For example, relationship triangles play a central role in the emotional process in family systems, and subsequent work is being designed to model and test the role of triangular processes in the multigenerational transmission process.

Important constitutional factors such as child temperament may also contribute, which, when considered together with the family's level of differentiation, may help to predict the level of functioning. For example, more temperamentally reserved children may respond to a parent's anxious overprotection in a submissive manner, resulting in a form of "positive" fusion that serves to calm the parent's anxiety and thus calm the child. Alternately, children who are temperamentally more exuberant and less fearful may respond to parent complaints/criticism or inconsistent responding with oppositional behavior (i.e., sulking, defiance). In both examples, parent and child together establish patterns of relating that serve to alleviate relationship anxiety and promote homeostasis. In sum, we posit that there are important components of physiological reactivity and regulation that underlie anxious family patterns, and our program of research is focused on clarifying the ways in which differentiation of self as evidenced in developing self-regulation of attention, emotion, and behavior, including autonomic physiological processes, together shape the level of functioning in nuclear and multigenerational family systems.

Summary

In this chapter, we presented an overview of our program of research on differentiation of self that has been guided by Bowen theory. We began by defining differentiation of self and describing the development of the Differentiation of Self Inventory (DSI). The DSI (Skowron and Friedlander, 1998; Skowron and Schmitt, 2003) is a 46-item self-report measure of differentiation of self in adults, their significant relationships, and current relations with family of origin, containing four subscales: Emotional Reactivity (ER), I-Position (IP), Emotional Cutoff (EC), and Fusion with Others (FO). Respondents rate items using a six-point, Likert-type scale, ranging from 1 (not at all true of me) to 6 (very true of me), and scores on select items are reversed and summed across scales, so that higher scores on each subscale and the full scale all reflect greater differentiation of self (i.e., less emotional reactivity, greater ability to take an I-position in relationships, less emotional cutoff, or less fusion with others).

The existing research on differentiation of self was reviewed, with particular attention to newer work examining the relationship between differentiation of self and self-regulation of emotion, physiology, and behavior. Consistent with Bowen theory, greater differentiation of self has been linked with lower chronic anxiety, fewer psychological and physical health problems, greater self-regulation of attention and behavior, lower attachment anxiety and avoidance, and less marital distress, conflict, and family violence. Further, higher parent levels of differentiation predict attachment security, fewer child behavioral problems, and better performance on cognitive tests. Within both U.S. ethnic minority and international populations, studies conducted to date have linked higher levels of differentiation of self with greater well-being, lower chronic anxiety, greater ethnic identity and feelings of ethnic group belonging, and the acculturation process. More international research like that reflected in this volume is needed to better understand relations between culture, worldview, differentiation of self, and indices of health and well-being. With a few recent exceptions, research on Bowen theory in general and differentiation of self in particular has relied heavily on use of self-report indices and cross-sectional designs.

Our current NIMH-funded research has focused on clarifying: 1) the ways in which survey, behavioral, and physiological indices of differentiation of self in parents converge and diverge; 2) the degree of correspondence between parent differentiation of self and developing self and emotion regulation in young children; and 3) a model of intergenerational transmission of differentiation of self.

According to Bowen theory, an individual comes to acquire the level of differentiation of self in one's family system, and that level, give or take a few points, is transmitted across generations of the family. However, there are no longitudinal studies that have empirically tested this assumption. In order to do so, it is necessary to understand how differentiation of self begins to develop in infancy and early childhood and to develop sound measures to assess this construct at these ages. Perhaps an adapted version of the DSI for adults can be developed into an observer rating measure for children, in order to capture children's differentiation of self levels and the development of differentiation over time. Additionally, it is necessary to observe parent-child interactions—using reliable and valid measures—in order to understand the timing and course of differentiation transmission over time in a family, and model the reciprocal nature and contingent emotional responding of parent to child and vice versa. We are confident that the keys to understanding multigenerational transmission lie in unlocking the patterned regularities and emotional undertones of dyadic and triadic interactions between parents and children.

REFERENCES

Aldea, M. A. & Rice, K. G. (2006). The role of emotional dysregulation in perfectionism and psychological distress. *Journal of Counseling Psychology, 53,* 498–510.

Barrett, L. F., Robin, L., Pietromonaco, P. R. & Eyssell, K. M. (1998). Are women the "more emotional" sex? Evidence from emotional experiences in social context. *Cognition and Emotion, 12,* 555–578.

Bartle-Haring, S. & Gregory, P. (2003). Relationship between differentiation of self and the stress and distress associated with predictive cancer genetic counseling and testing: Preliminary evidence. *Families, Systems, & Health, 21,* 357–381.

Bazhenova, O. V., Plonskaia, O. & Porges, S. W. (2001). Vagal reactivity and affective adjustment in infants during interaction challenges. *Child Development, 72,* 1314–1326.

Benjamin, L. S. (1996). Introduction to the special section on structural analysis of social behavior. *Journal of Consulting and Clinical Psychology, 64,* 1203–1212.

Berntson, G. G., Bigger, J. T., Eckberg, D. L., Grossman, P., Kaufmann, P. G., Malik, M. & van der Molen, M. W. (1997). Committee report: Heart rate variability: Origins, methods, and interpretive caveats. *Psychophysiology, 34,* 623–648.

Bornstein, M. H. & Suess, P. E. (2000). Child and mother cardiac vagal tone: Continuity, stability, and concordance across the first 5 years. *Developmental Psychology, 36,* 54–65.

Bowen, M. (1976). Theory in the practice of psychotherapy. In P. J. Guerin, Jr. (Ed.), *Family therapy: Theory and practice* (pp. 42–90). New York: Garner Press

Bowen, M. (1978). *Family therapy in clinical practice*: New York: Jason Aronson.

Boyd-Franklin, N. (1989). *Black families in therapy: A multisystems approach*. New York: Guilford Press.

Bray, J. H., Williamson, D. S. & Malone, P. E. (1984). Personal authority in the family system: Development of a questionnaire to measure personal authority in intergenerational family processes. *Journal of Marital and Family Therapy, 10,* 167–178.

Brennan, K. A., Clark, C. L. & Shaver, P. R. (1998). Self-report measurement of adult attachment: An integrative overview. In J. A. Simpson and W. S. Rholes (Eds.), *Attachment theory and close relationships* (pp. 46–76). New York: Guilford Press.

Butler, E. A., Wilhelm, F. H. & Gross, J. J. (2006). Respiratory sinus arrhythmia, emotion, and emotion regulation during social interaction. *Psychophysiology, 43,* 612–622.

Calkins, S. D. (1997). Cardiac vagal tone indices of temperamental reactivity and behavioral regulation in young children. *Developmental Psychobiology, 31,* 125–135.

Calkins, S. D., Smith, C. L., Gill, K. L. & Johnson, M. C. (1998). Maternal interactive style across contexts: Relations to emotional, behavioral and physiological regulation during toddlerhood. *Social Development, 7,* 350–369.

Carter, E., & McGoldrick, M. (1999). *The expanded family life cycle: Individual, family, and social perspectives* (3rd ed.). Boston: Allyn & Bacon.

Cole, P. M., Michel, M. K. & Teti, L. O. (1994). The development of emotion regulation and dysregulation: A clinical perspective. In N. A. Fox (Ed.), *The development of emotion regulation: Biological and behavioral considerations*. Monographs of the Society for Research in Child Development, *59*(2–3, Serial No. 240), 73–100.

Denham, S. A., Blair, K. A., DeMulder, E., Levitas, J., Sawyer, K., Auerbach-Major, S. & Queenen, P. (2003). Preschool emotional competence: Pathway to social competence. *Child Development, 74,* 238–256.

Diener, M. L., Mangelsdorf, S. C., McHale, J. L. & Frosch, C. A. (2002). Infants' behavioral strategies for emotion regulation with fathers and mothers: Associations with emotional expressions and attachment quality. *Infancy, 3,* 153–174.

Eisenberg, N. A., Fabes, R. A., Nyman, M., Bernzweig, J. & Pinuelas, A. (1994). The relations of emotionality and regulation to children's anger-related reactions. *Child Development, 65,* 109–128.

Eisenberg, N. & Morris, A. (2002). Children's emotion-related regulation. In R. V. Kail (Ed.), *Advances in child development and behavior* (Vol. 3, pp. 189–229). San Diego, CA: Academic Press.

Eisenberg, N., Sadovsky, A., Spinrad, T. L., Fabes, R. A., Losoya, S. H., Valiente, C., Reiser, M., Cumberland, A. & Shepard, S. A. (2005). The relations of problem behavior status to children's negative emotionality, effortful control, and impulsivity: Concurrent relations and prediction of change. *Developmental Psychology, 41,* 193–211.

Essandoh, P. K. (1995). Counseling issues with African college students in U.S. colleges and universities. *Counseling Psychologist, 23,* 348–360.

Fox, N. A. & Field, T. M. (1989). Individual differences in preschool entry behavior. *Journal of Applied Developmental Psychology, 10,* 527–540.

Gottman, J. M. & Katz, L. F. (2002). Children's emotional reactions to stressful parent-child interactions: The link between emotion regulation and vagal tone. *Marriage & Family Review, 34,* 265–283.

Gould, J. R., Prentice, N. M. & Ainslie, R. C. (1996). The Splitting Index: Construction of a scale measuring the defense mechanism of splitting. *Journal of Personality Assessment, 66,* 414–430.

Grolnick, W. S., Bridges, L. J. & Connell, J. P. (1996). Emotion regulation in two-year olds: Strategies and emotional expression in four contexts. *Child Development, 67,* 928–941.

Guisinger, S. & Blatt, S. J. (1994). Individuality and relatedness: Evolution of a fundamental dialectic. *American Psychologist, 49,* 104–111.

Gushue, G. V. & Sicalides, E. I. (1997). Helms's racial identity theory and Bowen's family systems model: A case study. In C. E. Thompson and R. T. Carter (Eds.), *Racial identity theory* (pp. 127–145). Mahwah, NJ: Erlbaum.

Henry, J. P. & Wang, S. (1989). Effects of early stress on adult affiliative behavior. *Psychoneuroendocrinology, 23,* 863–875.

Jackson, D. N. (1970). A sequential system for personality scale development. In C. D. Spielberger (Ed.), *Current topics in clinical and community psychology* (Vol. 2, pp. 61–96). New York: Academic Press.

Jahromi, L. B., Putnam, S. P. & Stifter, C. A. (2004). Maternal regulation of infant reactivity from 2 to 6 months. *Developmental Psychology, 40,* 477–487.

Johnson, M. H., Posner, M. I. & Rothbart, M. K. (1991). Components of visual orienting in early infancy: Contingency learning, anticipatory looking, and disengaging. *Journal of Cognitive Neuroscience, 3,* 335–344.

Johnson, P., Buboltz, W. C. & Seeman E. (2003). Ego identity status: A step in differentiation process. *Journal of Counseling and Development, 81,* 191–195.

Johnson, P., Thorngren, J. M. & Smith, A. J. (2001). Parental divorce and family functioning: Effects on differentiation levels of young adults. *The Family Journal, 9,* 265–272.

Kagitçibasi, C. (1996). *Family and human development across cultures: A view from the other side.* Mahwah, NJ: Erlbaum.

Kerr, M. E. (2008a). Why do siblings often turn out very differently? In A. Fogel, B. J. King, and S. G. Shanker (Eds.), *Human development in the twenty first century* (pp. 206–215). London: Cambridge University Press.

Kerr, M. E. (2008b). "From individual homeostasis to family homeostasis." Lecture presented to the Special Postgraduate Program, Bowen Center for the Study of the Family, Washington, DC, March 2008.

Kerr, M. E. & Bowen, M. (1988). *Family evaluation: An approach based on Bowen theory.* New York: Norton & Co.

Kim-Appel, D., Appel, J., Newman, I. & Parr, P. (2007). Testing the effectiveness of Bowen's concept of differentiation in predicting psychological distress in individuals age 62 years or older. *The Family Journal, 15,* 224–233.

Knauth, D. G. & Skowron, E. A. (2004). Psychometric evaluation of the differentiation of self inventory for adolescents. *Nursing Research, 53,* 163–171.

Knauth, D. G., Skowron, E. A. & Escobar, M. (2006). Effect of differentiation of self on adolescent risk behavior: Test of the theoretical model. *Nursing Research, 55,* 336–345.

Kochanska, G., Murray, K. & Harlan, E. (2000). Effortful control in early childhood: Continuity and change, antecedents, and implications for social development. *Developmental Psychology, 36,* 220–232.

Kopp, C. B. (1982). Antecedents of self-regulation: A developmental perspective. *Developmental Psychology, 18,* 199–214.

Kopp, C. B. (1989). Regulation of distress and negative emotions: A developmental view. *Developmental Psychology, 25,* 343–354.

Kosek, R. B. (1998). Self-differentiation within couples. *Psychological Reports, 83,* 275–279.

Loevinger, J. (1957). Objective tests as instruments of psychological theory. *Psychological Reports, 3,* 635–694.

Lunkenheimer, E. S., Shields, A. M. & Cortina, K. S. (2007). Parental emotion coaching and dismissing in family interaction. *Social Development, 16,* 232–248.

Maughan, A. & Cicchetti, D. (2002). Impact of child maltreatment and interadult violence on children's emotion regulation abilities and socioemotional adjustment. *Child Development, 73,* 1525–1542.

Murdock, N. L. & Gore, P. A. (2004). Stress, coping, and differentiation of self: A test of Bowen theory. *Contemporary Family Therapy, 26,* 319–335.

Murray, T. L., Murray, C. E. & Daniels, M. H. (2007). Stress and family relationship functioning as indicators of the severity of fibromyalgia symptoms: A regression analysis. *Stress and Health, 23,* 3–8.

Nunnally, J. C. (1978). *Psychometric theory.* New York: McGraw-Hill.

Obradović, J., Bush, N. R., Stamperdahl, J., Adler, N. E. & Boyce, W. T. (2010). Biological sensitivity to context: The interactive effects of stress reactivity and family adversity on socioemotional behavior and school readiness. *Child Development, 81,* 270–289.

Parsons, R. N., Nalbone, D. P., Killmer, J. M. & Wetchler, J. L. (2007). Identity development, differentiation, personal authority, and degree of religiosity as predictors of interfaith marital satisfaction. *American Journal of Family Therapy, 35,* 343–361.

Patrick, S., Sells, J. N., Giordano, F. G. & Tollerud, T. R. (2007). Intimacy, differentiation, and personality variables as predictors of marital satisfaction. *The Family Journal, 15,* 359–367.

Peleg, O., Halaby, E. & Whaby, E. (2006). The relationship between maternal separation anxiety and differentiation of self to children's separation anxiety and adjustment to kindergarten: A study in Druze families. *Anxiety Disorders, 20,* 973–995.

Peleg-Popko, O. (2002). Bowen Theory: A study of differentiation of self, social anxiety, and physiological symptoms. *Contemporary Family Therapy: An International Journal, 24,* 355–369.

Peleg-Popko, O. (2004). Differentiation and test anxiety in adolescents. *Journal of Adolescence, 27,* 645–662.

Porges, S. W. (1991). Autonomic regulation of attention. In B. Campbell, H. Hayne, and R. Richardson (Eds.), *Attention and information processing in infants and adults.* Hillsdale, NJ: Erlbaum.

Porges, S. W. (1995). Orienting in a defensive world: Mammalian modifications of our evolutionary heritage: A polyvagal theory. *Psychophysiology, 32,* 301–318.

Porges, S. W. (2001). The polyvagal theory: Phylogenetic substrates of a social nervous system. *International Journal of Psychophysiology, 42,* 123–146.

Porges, S. W., Doussard-Roosevelt, J., Portales, A. & Greenspan, S. (1996). Infant regulation of the vagal "brake" predicts child behavior problems: A psychobiological model of social behavior. *Developmental Psychobiology, 29,* 697–712.

Rogosch, F. A., Cicchetti, D. & Aber, J. L. (1995). The role of child maltreatment in early deviations in cognitive and affective processing abilities and later peer relationship problems. *Development and Psychopathology, 7,* 591–609.

Rothbart, M. K., Ahadi, S. A. & Evans, D. E. (2000). Temperament and personality: Origins and outcomes. *Journal of Personality and Social Psychology, 78,* 122–135.

Rothbart, M. K. & Bates J. E. (2006). Temperament. In W. Damon and R. Lerner (Series Eds.) and N. Eisenberg (Vol. Ed.), *Handbook of child psychology: Vol. 3, social, emotional and personality development* (6th ed., pp. 99–166). New York: Wiley.

Rothbart, M. K., Derryberry, D. & Posner, M. (1994). A psychobiological approach to the development of temperament. In J. E. Bates and T. D. Wachs (Eds.), *Temperament: Individual differences in biology and behavior* (pp. 83–116). Washington, DC: American Psychological Association.

Rothbart, M. K. & Posner, M. (2000). Developing mechanisms of self-regulation. *Development and self-regulation, 12,* 427–441.

Rothbart, M. K. & Sheese, B. E. (2007). Temperament and emotion regulation. In J. J. Gross (Ed.), *Handbook of emotion regulation* (pp. 331–350). New York: Guilford Press.

Rothbart, M. K., Ziaie, H. & O'Boyle, C. G. (1992). Self-regulation and emotion in infancy. In N. Eisenberg and R. A. Fabes (Eds.), *Emotion and its regulation in early development* (pp. 7–23). San Francisco: Jossey-Bass.

Rothbaum, F., Weisz, J., Pott, M., Miyake, K. & Morelli, G. (2000). Attachment and culture: Security in the United States and Japan. *American Psychologist, 55,* 1093–1104.

Roytburd, L. & Friedlander, M. L. (2008). Predictors of Soviet Jewish refugees' acculturation: Differentiation of self and acculturative stress. *Cultural Diversity and Ethnic Minority Psychology, 14,* 67–74.

Schnarch, D. (1997). *Passionate marriage.* New York: W. W. Norton.

Schwartz, J. P., Thigpen, S. E. & Montgomery, J. K. (2006). Examination of parenting styles of processing emotions and differentiation of self. *The Family Journal, 14,* 41–48.

Skowron, E. A. (2000). The role of differentiation of self in marital adjustment. *Journal of Counseling Psychology, 47,* 229–237.

Skowron, E. A. (2004). Differentiation of self, personal adjustment, problem solving, and ethnic group belonging among persons of color. *Journal of Counseling & Development, 82,* 447–456.

Skowron, E. A. (2005). Parent differentiation of self and child competence in low-income urban families. *Journal of Counseling Psychology, 52,* 337.

Skowron, E. A. & Dendy, A. K. (2004). Differentiation of self and attachment in adulthood: Relational correlates of effortful control. *Contemporary Family Therapy: An International Journal, 26,* 337–357.

Skowron, E. A. & Friedlander, M. L. (1998). The Differentiation of Self Inventory: Development and initial validation. *Journal of Counseling Psychology, 45,* 235–246.

Skowron, E. A., Holmes, S. E. & Sabatelli, R. M. (2003). Deconstructing differentiation: Self regulation, interdependent relating, and well-being in adulthood. *Contemporary Family Therapy: An International Journal, 25*(1), 111–129.

Skowron, E. A., Loken, E., Gatzke-Kopp, L. M., Cipriano, E. A., Woehrle, P. L., Van Epps, J. J., . . . & Ammerman, R. T. (2011). Mapping cardiac physiology and parenting processes in maltreating mother–child dyads. *Journal of Family Psychology, 25,* 663–674. NIHMSID 436913.

Skowron, E. A. & Platt, L. F. (2005). Differentiation of self and child abuse potential in young adulthood. *The Family Journal, 13,* 281–290.

Skowron, E. A. & Schmitt, T. A. (2003). Assessing interpersonal fusion: Reliability and validity of a new DSI Fusion with Others subscale. *Journal of Marital and Family Therapy, 29,* 209–222.

Skowron, E. A., Wester, S. R. & Azen, R. (2004). Differentiation of self mediates college stress and adjustment. *Journal of Counseling & Development, 82,* 69–78.

Spencer, B. & Brown, J. (2007). Fusion or internalized homophobia? A pilot study of Bowen's differentiation of self hypothesis with lesbian couples. *Family Process, 46,* 257–268.

Tamura, T. & Lau, A. (1992). Connectedness versus separateness: Applicability of family therapy to Japanese families. *Family Process, 31,* 319–340.

Thompson, R. A. (1991). Emotional regulation and emotional development. *Educational Psychology Review, 3,* 269–307.

Thompson, R. A. (1994). Emotion regulation: A theme in search of definition. In N. A. Fox (Ed.), *The development of emotion regulation: Biological and behavioral considerations.* Monographs of the Society for Research in Child Development, *59*(2–3, Serial No. 240), 25–53.

Thorberg, F. A. & Lyvers, M. (2006). Attachment, fear of intimacy and differentiation of self among clients in substance disorder treatment facilities. *Addictive Behaviors, 31,* 732–737.

Tuason, M. T. & Friedlander, M. L. (2000). Do parents' differentiation levels predict those of their adult children? And other tests of Bowen theory in a Philippine sample. *Journal of Counseling Psychology, 47,* 27–35.

Wei, M., Russell, D. W., Mallinkrodt, B. & Vogel, D. L. (2008). The experiences of close relationship scale (ECR)-short form: Reliability, validity, and factor structure. *Journal of Personality Assessment, 88,* 187–204.

Wei, M., Vogel, D. L., Ku, T.-Y. & Zakalik, R. A. (2005). Adult attachment, affect regulation, negative mood, and interpersonal problems: The mediating roles of emotional reactivity and emotional cutoff. *Journal of Counseling Psychology, 52,* 14–24.

Williamson, I., Sandage, S. J. & Lee, R. M. (2007). How social connectedness affects guilt and shame: Mediation by hope and differentiation of self. *Personality and individual differences, 43,* 2159–2170.

Wilson, B. J. & Gottman, J. M. (2002). Marital conflict, repair, and parenting. In M. H. Bornstein (Ed.), *Handbook of parenting: Social conditions and applied parenting* (2nd ed., Vol. 4, pp. 227–258). Mahwah, NJ: Lawrence Erlbaum.

Winsler, A., Diaz, R. M., Atencio, D. J., McCarthy, E. M. & Chabay, L. A. (2000). Verbal self-regulation over time in preschool children at risk for attention and behavioral problems. *Journal of Child Psychology and Psychiatry, 41,* 874–886.

Appendix I

A KEY FOR THE FAMILY DIAGRAM

Males are drawn as squares, females as circles: Male= □   Female= ○

Date of birth and death are written next to the person's symbol. Age may be shown within the square or circle. Death is indicated by an X through the symbol.

⊠ b. 1953   Birth Date
   d. 1988   Death Date

Couples are shown by a line connecting their symbols as follows, with the relevant dates written on the line:

M. 1990   Marriage

M. 1990 / S. 1993   Separation

D. 1994   Divorce

1984   Intimate relationship but unmarried

Children are shown left to right, oldest to youngest

Parents

Oldest → ○ □ □ ← Youngest

Children

Here is an example of some of the family characteristics you can show:

Father   Mother

Age → | 13 | 12 | 9 | 9 | 8 | 7 | ⊠ | ● | X | △

Oldest   Second Son   Twins   Adopted Daughter   Foster Son   Stillbirth   Miscarriage   Abortion   Pregnancy

Emotional relationships between people can be indicated by a second set of lines:

emotional connection: □——○

emotional fusion: □═══○

conflict: □∿∿∿○

emotional distance: □—|—○

emotional cutoff: □—>←—○

383

Appendix II

EDUCATIONAL AND TRAINING PROGRAMS IN BOWEN FAMILY SYSTEMS THEORY AND THERAPY

Bowen Center for the Study of the Family

Anne S. McKnight, Director
4400 MacArthur Blvd NW Suite 103
Washington, DC 20007-2521
Phone: 800-432-6882 or 202-965-4400
E-mail: info@thebowencenter.org
www.thebowencenter.org

Bowen Family Systems Clinical Seminars of Kansas City

Margaret Donley
Prairie Village, KS
www.bfsclinicalseminars.com

Bowen Theory Academy

Michael E. Kerr, President
1523 Pripet Woods Lane
Islesboro, ME 04848
207-542-6082
www.bowentheoryacademy.org

Center for Family Consultation

Sydney Reed, Director of Training
820 Davis Street Suite 504
Evanston, IL 60201
Phone: 224-567-2888
E-mail: info@centerforfamilyconsultation.net
www.centerforfamilyconsultation.net

Center for Family, Organizational, and Natural Systems Education

Charles M. White, Founder and Principal Associate
Ellen Rogan, Principal Associate
PO Box 875
Westfield, NJ 07091
Phone: 908-451-5818
E-mail: charleswhitejr@cfonse.org ellenrogan@cfonse.org

The Center for Family Process

Myrna Carpenter, Partner and Faculty
Mickie M. Crimone, Partner and Faculty
10601 Willowbrook Drive
Potomac, MD 20854
Phone: 410-799-7774 or 301-299-7475
E-mail: contactus@centerforfamilyprocess.com
www.centerforfamilyprocess.com

The Center for the Study of Human Systems

Roberta M. Gilbert, MD, Director
P.O. Box 693
Stephens City, VA 22693
Phone: 540-868-0866
Email: rgoffice136@gmail.com
www.hsystems.org

Center for the Study of Natural Systems and the Family

Victoria Harrison, Director
PO Box 701187
Houston, TX 77007
Phone: 713-790-0226
E-mail: vaharrison@sbcglobal.net
www.csnsf.org

Center for the Study of Natural Systems and the Family

Programs at the Border (El Paso, TX, and Ciudad Juárez, Mexico)
Louise Rauseo, Director
PO Box 1387
El Paso TX 79948
Phone: 443-623-4021

E-mail: louise@rauseos.net or rauseo1@verizon.net
www.csnsf.org/borderprograms

The Family Systems Institute

Jenny Brown, Director
Grosvenor Cottage
30 Grosvenor Street, Neutral Bay
Sydney, NSW, 2089 Australia
Phone: 02 9904 5600
E-mail: info@thefsi.com.au
www.thefsi.com.au

The Florida Family Research Network, Inc./ Bowen Theory Postgraduate Training Program of South Florida

Eileen Gottlieb, Education Director
232 SW 28th Avenue
Delray Beach, FL 33445
Phone: 561-279-0861
E-mail: ebgfamilycenter@comcast.net
www.ffrnbowentheory.org

ISS Wofoo Family Institute

International Social Service Hong Kong Branch
Peggy Chan
Yaumatei, Kowloon, Hong Kong
www.isshk.org

Kansas City Center for Family and Organizational Systems

Margaret Otto, Director
3100 NE 83 Street, Suite 2350
Kansas City, MO 64119
Phone: 816-436-1721
E-mail: motto@kcfamilysystems.com
www.kcfamilysystems.com

Leadership Coaching, Inc.

John Engels, President
63 Klink Road
Rochester, NY 14625
Phone: 585-381-9040

E-mail: heidi@leadershipcoaching.com
www.leadershipcoachinginc.com

Leadership in Ministry

Robert Dibble, Coordinator
www.leadershipinministry.org

The Learning Space

Priscilla J. Friesen, Founder
4545 42nd Street NW, Suite 201
Washington, DC 20016
Phone: 202-966-1145
Priscilla@thelearningspacedc.com
www.thelearningspacedc.com

Living Systems

Randall Frost, Director of Training and Research
Lois Walker, Faculty
209–1500 Marine Drive
North Vancouver, BC V7P1T7
Phone: 604-926-5496
E-mail: info@livingsystems.ca
www.livingsystems.ca

New England Seminar on Bowen Theory

Ann V. Nicholson, Chair
25 Medway Street
Dorchester, MA 02124
Phone: 617-296-4614
E-mail: annvnicholson@gmail.com
www.bowentheoryne.com

Northampton Seminar on Bowen Theory and Its Applications

Peter Titelman, Faculty
53 Center Street
Northampton, MA 01060
Phone: 413-584-7733
www.familytherapyandconsulting.com

Princeton Family Center for Education, Inc.

Joan McElroy, Director
PO Box 331
Pennington, NJ 08534
Phone: 609-924-0514
E-mail: joanmcelroy@princetonfamilycenter.org
www.princetonfamilycenter.org

Programs in Bowen Theory

Laura Havstad, Executive Director
120 Pleasant Hill Avenue N #370
Sebastopol, CA 95472
Phone: 707-823-1848
E-mail: info@programsinbowentheory.org
www.programsinbowentheory.org

Southern California Education and Training in Bowen Family Systems Theory

Carolyn Jacobs, Director
625 Third Avenue
Chula Vista, CA 91910
Phone: 619-525-7747
E-mail: info@socalbowentheory.com
www.socalbowentheory.com

Vermont Center for Family Studies

Erik Thompson, Executive Director
PO Box 5124
Essex Junction, VT 05453–5124
Phone: 802-872-1818
E-mail: info@vermontcenterforfamilystudies.org
www.vermontcenterforfamilystudies.org

Western Pennsylvania Family Center

James B. Smith, Director
733 North Highland Avenue
Pittsburgh, PA 15206
Phone: 412-362-2295
E-mail: info@wpfc.net
www.wpfc.net

INDEX

Note: Page numbers with *f* indicate figures.

Printed by PGSTL